CITY | LAW TUTOR

PGDL STUDY GUIDE

Postgraduate Diploma in Law

PGDL Notes 2024

Thank you for downloading our Postgraduate Diploma in Law (PGDL) workbook 2024. The PGDL is a law conversion course that teaches you to think like a lawyer and prepare for the realities of life in legal practice.

These 2024 PGDL notes have been written by one of our PGDL Law tutors who has covered the compulsory modules of the PGDL in this workbook. Designed to be as relevant to as many law schools as possible and provides the foundation for the pathway into practice for non-law graduates who want to progress onto the SQE1.

If you need PGDL tutoring and support for the PGDL our PGDL tutor (that got a Post Graduate Diploma in Law: Distinction) who achieved a distinction in all 8 modules, averaging 79 overall. Including Constitutional Law (81), Criminal Law (77), Equity and Trusts (84), Land Law (82) and Tort Law (84).

Workbook Contents

This Postgraduate Diploma in Law (PGDL) workbook 2024 contains:

Tort Law
Contract Law
Criminal Law
English Legal Systems
Equity & Trusts
Land Law
Law of Organisations
Human Right and Administrative Law

Contents

Contract Law

Agreement and Contractual Intention

A contract is formed when there is an **agreement, contractual intention and consideration.** In order for parties to reach an agreement, one party must make an offer which is then accepted by the other party

- Lord Justice Goff in ***Allied Marine Transport Ltd. v Vale do Rio Doce Navegaçao SA; The Leonidas D. [1985] 1 W.L.R. 925:*** 'If the offeror so acts that his conduct, objectively considered, constitutes an offer, and the offeree, believing that the conduct of the offeror represents his actual intention, accepts the offer, then a contract will come into existence'.

Intention to Create Legal Relations

- The assessment of a parties' intention is objective (***Smith v Hughes***)
- For the courts to treat an agreement as binding, the parties themselves must have intended it to be legally enforceable
- Contract do not have to be formal (e.g. for the contract to be in writing) → oral agreements are enforceable

Domestic and Social Agreements

For **domestic and social agreements** (i.e between family members), the **presumption** is that there is ***no*** intention to create legal relations

Case Law Example:

- ***Balfour v Balfour [1919]***: a husband working overseas agreed to send maintenance payments to his wife. The relationship later soured and the husband stopped making the payments
  - Court held that this was a purely social and domestic agreement and therefore it was *presumed that the parties did not intend to be legally bound*

Rebuttal of the Presumption

In order to rebut this presumption, the court will take into account:

The consideration involved → either the benefit conferred to the other party or the detriment suffered by the claimant

The greater the value of the consideration, the likelier the parties intended legal relations

The parties to the agreement are not on good times (e.g. if a couple is separated) → bargaining at arm's length

If it is a formal agreement in writing

Case Law Example:

- ***Merritt v Merritt [1970]***: separated marriage. Husband signed a written agreement stating that he would pay his wife £40 a month & in consideration of her repaying the mortgage on their joint-owned home, he would transfer it to her as sole ownership
  - Example of a presumption being rebutted as the agreement was *intended* to be legally binding

Commercial Agreements

There is a strong presumption that the parties *intended* the agreement to be legally binding (***Edwards v Skyways [1964]***)

An easy way to rebut this presumption, is to explicitly state it in the contract:

Rose and Frank Co v Crompton Bros [1925]: an agreement between two parties included an 'Honourable Pledge Clause' which stated that it was not entered into as a 'formal or legal agreement'

Offers

Defining an Offer

Definition:

Professor Treitel: 'an offer is an **expression of willingness to contract on certain terms**, made with the intention that it **shall become binding** as soon as it is accepted by the person to whom it is addressed'

- Confirmed in Allied Marine Transport ***v Vale do Rio Doce Navegacao SA (Leonidas)***

An Invitation to Treat?

An invitation to treat is a **statement inviting negotiation** (e.g. 'I am thinking of selling my car, would you buy it for £7000) → there is **NO** intention to be bound

- **Goods on display** in a supermarket are regarded as an invitation to treat. If they were to be held as an offer, then the customer would be regarded as accepting the offer as soon as they took the goods off the shelf

  Case Law Example:

- *Pharmaceutical Society of Great Britain v Boots Cash Chemists [1953]*: The offer to buy and the acceptance takes place *at the payment point* → it is only at that point that a binding contract is concluded

- **Advertisements** are usually regarded as invitations to treat

  Case Law Example:
  - *Partridge v Crittenden [1968]:* defendant was charged with 'offering for sale' a live wild bird, contrary to the Protection of Birds Act 1954, after publishing the sale in an advertisement

    Court held the defendant not guilty as the advertisement was only an invitation to treat

- BUT: **an advertisement of a reward** (e.g. cash reward in exchange for information) is considered an offer → there is an intention to be bound as soon as the information is given

  Case Law Example:
  - *Carlill v Carbolic Smoke Ball Co [1893]*: A manufacturer released an advertisement for a Carbolic Smoke Ball stating that a reward of £100 would be paid to anyone who contracted the flu after using the ball 3 times a day for 2 weeks. Carlill sued after getting the flu despite using the appliance
    - Court found the advertisement had been sincere, that it did not matter that it was addressed to the world (comparable to an offer of reward) and that the wording of the advertisement waived the need to communicate acceptance

Unilateral Contracts

Unilateral Contract = a promise in return for an act

- This commitment is one-sided → if you do something I promise to ....

- The promisor is only bound to perform if the person to whom the promise is made performs the specified act (typically an offer for reward)
- The general view is that unilateral contracts carry no obligations until the specified act is completed → acceptance only occurs when performance is complete
- BUT: some judicial authorities suggest that *partial performance* of a unilateral contract *is sufficient to prevent revocation* by the offeror

Case Law Example:
- *Harvard Law Review (McGovney, 27 Harvard Law Review 644*: in addition to the express offer, with unilateral contracts there is also an implied promise not to revoke if the specified act is started within a reasonable time
  - Here, the acceptance and consideration for the implied promise is the commencement of the act

- *Errington v Errington and Woods [1952]*: A father bought a house and allowed his son and daughter in law to live in it, promising that if they paid the mortgage instalments he would transfer the house to them. When the father died, his widow sought possession of the house
  - Example of a unilateral contract as the couple did not promise to repay the mortgage, *they simply did so*
  - Court held that the father's promise was irrevocable, as long as the couple continued to pay the instalments

Bilateral Contracts

Bilateral Contract = where one party makes a promise, in return for a promise from the other party

E.g. 'I promise to sell you my car for £7000 if you agree to buy it for £7000

Auctions:	Tenders:
The **auctioneer** asking for **bids** is an **invitation to treat**. The **bids** are the **offers**. • The auctioneer offers a unilateral contract with the bidder to *promise* to accept the highest bid • According to the ***Sale of Goods Act***, a sale by auction is complete on the fall of the auctioneer's hammer → acceptance • If the auctioneer accepts a bid, a contract (bilateral) of sale is formed between the bidder and the owner of the goods *Reserve Price:* • The lowest price that the auctioneer would accept for the lot (can be 'without reserve') → auctioneer must accept the highest price → example of a unilateral contract as there is a promise to accept the highest bid ○ ***Barry v Davies t/a Heathcote Ball & Co) [2000]*** → Barry was informed that the auction would be without reserve. Auctioneer refused to accept his bid and withdrew the goods from sale (despite Barry's bid being the highest). Barry sued the auctioneer for breach of contract	If a company is **outsourcing functions** (from outside contractors), often will invite a number of contractors to submit written tenders for the job • General rule is that invitations to tender are invitations to treat (***Spencer v Harding***). The tenders are then the offers ***Blackpool and Fylde Aero Club v Blackpool Borough Council [1990]:*** **exception** to the rule. The council had impliedly offered to consider all tenders which were submitted on time and in the correct form → the Club had accepted this offer by submitting a tender - An invitation to tender can imply a unilateral contract to consider all timely bids

Acceptance

Acceptance = the complete and unqualified acceptance of all of the terms of the offer, without qualification or addition

- The offeree must know of the offer in order to accept it
    - ***Australian case of R v Clarke (1927)***: 'There cannot be assent without knowledge of the offer; and ignorance of the offer is the same thing whether it is due to never hearing of it or forgetting it after hearing.'

Communication of Acceptance

- The general rule is that acceptance must be communicated (either by the offeree or its authorised agent) → ***Entores Ltd v Miles Far East Corp [1955]***
- An offeror can waive the need for communication of acceptance in certain situations
    - E.g. in a unilateral contract, the performance of the act can amount to acceptance
    - ***Carlill v Carbolic Smoke Ball Co [1893]***: using the smoke ball in the prescribed manner was the act of acceptance → company had waived the need for communication

Silence?

An offeror *cannot* take an offeree's **silence** as acceptance

- Exists to protect an unwilling offeree

Case Law Example:

- ***Felthouse v Bindley (1862)***: an uncle offered to buy his nephew's horse. Provided an offer for £30.15s and stated that if he did not hear from him, he would consider the horse his.
    - The nephew did not respond so the court held that there was no contract between the uncle and nephew

The Postal Rule

Subject to certain limitations, a **letter of acceptance,** which is **posted,** is **complete when posted** and the contract will be formed at that point

Case Law Examples:

Adams v Lindsell (1818): Adams sent a letter to Lindsell accepting the terms of a contract. After the letter was posted, but before it had arrived, Lindsell sold the good to a third party

- Court found that Lindsell had entered a binding contract with Adams as soon as Adams' letter had been sent

- In **_Household Fire and Carriage Accident Insurance Co (Ltd) v Grant (1879)_**: a letter of acceptance was posted, but never arrived
    - The court found that the postal rule applied and that acceptance was valid on posting

Limitations:

1. Only applies to **acceptances** (e.g. would not apply to revocations)
2. Only applies where it is **reasonable** for the acceptance to be sent by post
3. The letter must be **properly** stamped, addressed and posted
4. The rule can be **excluded** by the offeror (either expressly or by implication)

Case Law Example:

- **_Holwell Securities Ltd v Hughes [1974]:_** The defendant granted the claimant an option to buy a house, expressed as being 'exercisable by notice in writing to [the defendant]'
    - The claimant wrote to the defendant accepting but the letter never arrived
    - The offeror stated 'notice in writing to [the defendant] → the court held that by using the word notice, the offeror had impliedly excluded the postal rule

Electronic Communication:

- A telexed acceptance is effective when it would be reasonable to expect the recipient to have read it, even if it is not read until a later time

Continuing Negotiations

- Most people will make it clear that they don't intend to be held to anything unless and until they enter into a formal legal agreement
- Occasionally, when people don't seek legal counsel, parties see themselves as gradually building up their contract
- If issues arise, the parties may disagree about whether they reached a deal at all and if they did, when it was struck or what its terms were

Case Law Example:

- ○ ***Hussey v Horne-Payne (1878)***: the parties in correspondence had agreed the terms of a deal for the sale of a property. Two letters, when looked at in isolation, seemingly demonstrated a contract. BUT no mention of payment by instalments
  - Was apparent that at the time when the letters were written, both parties saw the issue of payments by instalments as part of the deal still to be negotiated
  - The Lord Chancellor, Earl Cairns found that a contract must be found by taking into consideration the whole of the correspondence

Battle of Forms:

A **battle of the forms** is where **2 businesses** who are in **negotiation** purport to **contract on their own standard terms** (Ts & Cs), which are **likely to be different**

- Often the job of the court to then find the least unsatisfactory solution
- The 'last shot' will often win 'the battle', although there are some exceptions:

Case Law Examples:

- ○ ***TRW Ltd v Panasonic Industry Europe GmbH and another company [2021]*** → Contract between English based (TRW Ltd) and German Panasonic. Both companies supplied their own T&Cs during negotiation, each stipulating that their national courts would have jurisdiction. TRW included their T&C's in the purchase order, making it the 'last shot'
  - BUT TRW had previously signed Panasonic's 'customer file' acknowledging that German law would apply to the contract
  - Court sided with Panasonic → signing the customer file *overruled* the last shot

  Butler Machine Tool Co Ltd v Ex-Cell-O Corporation (England) Ltd [1979]. Claimant offered to sell machinery for a price of £75,000. The form said that the claimant's terms were to prevail over any terms of the defendant's standard form. Claimant's terms included a price variation clause (allowing an increase in price in line with inflation)
  - The defendant sent back a form purporting to accept the claimant's offer, but that the price must be fixed. The form of acceptance included a tear-off slip which provided the terms of the defendant should prevail
  - The claimant signed and returned the slip but then tried to invoke the price variation clause
  - COURT found a contract on the defendant's terms

- ○ ***Lidl UK Gmbh v Hertford Foods Ltd & Anos [2001]:*** Court found a contract on neither party's terms → neither party got the benefit of their own terms and conditions into the contract, but neither party was burdened with the other side's terms and conditions
  - Generally, when this happens, the purchaser of the goods and services will be in the more comfortable position

Terminating an Offer

→ **An offer may be terminated in the following ways**

Rejection / Counter-Offer

An offeree may reject an offer, either expressly or impliedly

- A counter-offer implies rejection → acceptance must match exactly the terms of the offer
- A request for further information *does not* destroy the offer (***Stevenson Jacques and Co v McLean (1880)***

Case Law Example:

- ***Hyde V Wrench (1840)***: the claimant made a counter offer to the original asking price of a farm but 2 days later agreed to pay the original asking price. The defendant refused to complete the sale → held that there was no contract, since the counter-offer was an implied rejection

Revocation

Revocation = withdrawal of the offer by the offeror

- An offer can generally be revoked at *any time before acceptance*
- Notice of withdrawal must be given and communicated to the offeree for it to be effective (***Byrne & Co v Van Tienhoven & Co (1880)***

Exceptions:

1. A revocation sent to a business is effective on receipt, where it is reasonable to expect a member of staff to be available to read the notice (***The Brimnes [1975]***)
2. An offer made to the public at large (e.g. an advertisement) may be revoked through the same channel as it was made (***Shuey v US* N.B. US law)**
3. Can be communicated by a reliable third party (not necessarily from the offeror)
    - ***Dickinson v Dodds (1876)*** → the third party need not have been authorised by the offeror & must be objectively perceived as being reliable.
4. If it is a unilateral contract, revocation is not possible once the act of acceptance has begun (***Errington v Errington & Woods***)

Lapse of Time
An offer may become incapable of acceptance through **lapse of time** • Any offer that contains an express condition of lapse after a specific time does not result in a contract, if acceptance takes place outside of this time period • In all other cases, an offer will lapse after a reasonable time

Consideration, Contractual Intention and Agency

Consideration

Defining Consideration

In order to hold the other party to a deal, there must be **something in return** → this something in return is **referred to as consideration**

- *Sir Frederick Pollock*: consideration is '**an act of forbearance of one party**, or the promise thereof, is the **price for which the promise of the other is bought'**

Often quoted definition of consideration in ***Currie v Misa (1875)***:

> 'A valuable consideration may consist either in some right, interest, profit or benefit accruing to the party or some forbearance, detriment, loss or responsibility, given, suffered or undertaken by another'

- What is provided by way of consideration should either be a **benefit to the person receiving it**, or a **detriment to the person giving it** (usually both)
    - When you buy a good → the seller gains money (the benefit) whilst the buyer loses money (the detriment) ***AND*** the buyer gets a good (the benefit) whilst the seller loses a good (the detriment)

Can also be seen as the **price one party pays for the other party's promise** (a promise to do something may be consideration)

→ <u>*'Consideration need not be adequate, but must be sufficient'*</u>

Adequacy:	Sufficiency

'Need not be adequate' = consideration does not need to adequately reflect the value of the promise in return for which it is given - Because contracts are voluntarily entered into → people are free to strike own deals	**'Must be sufficient'** = consideration must have some value Value was generally inferred as relating to the need for 'economic value' Less strict now: Lord Somervell in ***Chappell & Co Ltd v Nestlé Co Ltd [1960]:*** 'a contracting party can stipulate for what consideration he chooses' *Case Law Example:* ○ ***White v Bluett (1853)***: A father promised not to enforce a debt against his son, on condition that the son stopped moaning about the distribution of his father's property → court found that the son had not provided consideration for the father's promise Public policy reasoning → allowing such a promise to amount to consideration would open the floodgates to litigation Also held that it was a domestic relationship, not commercial

Past Consideration:

- **Past consideration is no consideration** → e.g. if something is promised at a later date (after the act has already taken place, it does not count as consideration)

  Case Law Example:

  Roscorla v Thomas [1842]: Roscorla bought a horse from the defendant. After the purchase was made, defendant assured Roscorla that the horse was 'sound and free from vice' → proved to be untrue → Roscorla sued for breach of contract
  - Not enforceable → Roscorla had not given any consideration for the defendant's promise (already bought the horse)

Exceptions:

1) The act must have been done at the **promisor's request** ***and***
   - ***Lampleigh v Brathwait (1615)***: defendant asked the claimant to seek a royal pardon for the defendant → claimant made considerable efforts and the defendant later promised £100 to the claimant for doing it

- Promise was held to be enforceable

2) The parties must have **understood from the outset** that the act was to be rewarded in some way ***and***
   - ***Re Casey's Patents, Stewart v Casey [1892]:*** defendant had asked the claimant to manage certain patents for them → defendant later promised Casey a one-third share of the patents for the work
     - Court held that it must always have been assumed that Casey's work would be paid for in some way → the defendant's promise simply crystallised that reasonable expectation

3) The payment, or conferment of other payment, must have been **legally enforceable** had it been promised in advance.

Performance of Existing Duties

1) Existing Duty Imposed by Law

As a general rule, the performance of an **existing duty imposed by law** is **not sufficient consideration** in exchange for a promise of payment

Case Law Example:

- ***Collins v Godefroy (1831)*** → defendant could not promise the claimant money in exchange for testifying in court → was *already legally bound* to attend as a witness
  - Policy reasoning → against public interest to allow it

Exceptions - Exceeding the Existing Public Duty:

Ward v Byham [1956]: the father of an illegitimate child promised to pay the mother an allowance if the child was 'well looked after and happy' → mother already had a duty imposed by law to support the child
- Court of Appeal had to decide if the mother had given any consideration in exchange for the father's promise
- Found that the mother had exceeded her legal duty by promising to keep the child well looked after and happy → consideration was found

- ○ ***Glasbrook Bros Ltd v Glamorgan County Council [1925]***: owners of a mine, during a coal strike, sought assistance from the police to protect the workers who were continuing to maintain the mine. Offered to pay the council in order to have them at the mine's location
  - Later, owner denied any legal obligation to pay on the basis that the police had been carrying out their legal obligations
  - HoL found that the Police had provided protection over and above the necessary provision → exceeded their public duty and this was the consideration for the agreed sum

2) Existing Contractual Duty Owed to a Third Party

- If a person is **already bound to perform a particular act under a contract**, the performance of this act ***can*** amount to sufficient consideration for a **separate contract with someone else**
  - The performance of an existing contractual duty owed to a third party *will* amount to consideration

<u>*Case Law Example:*</u>

- ○ ***Scotson v Pegg (1861)***: a promise to deliver a cargo of coal to the defendant was held to be consideration, even though the claimant was already contractually bound to a third party to make such a delivery

Variation of the Contract

Existing Contractual Duty Owed to the Other Party

- 'Other Party' generally refers to the **established person in the contract**
- If a contract is already established, a promise of additional payment for continued performance of the existing contract ***does not* equal consideration**
  - The promiser gets no extra benefit (contract remains the same) and the other party has no additional detriment (no other tasks required)

<u>*Case Law Example:*</u>

- ○ ***Stilk v Myrick (1809)***: Established the basic rule that simply performing an existing contractual duty owed to the other party will not be sufficient consideration in exchange for a promise by the other party to pay more money

- Return voyage from London to Baltic → 2 of the crew deserted halfway. The captain promised to split the wages of the deserters equally among the rest of the crew if they would work the ship home
- Did so but then the captain refused to pay → court held that the captain's promise was unenforceable for want of consideration (promise of extra money for an already established contract)

Exceptions - Exceeding the Existing Contract:

In ***Hartley v Ponsonby (1857)***: facts were similar to Stilk v Myrick but instead of 2 deserters, was half the crew → meant the return journey was much more dangerous for remaining crew

- Court held that remaining crew had exceeded the original contractual obligation and so there was sufficient consideration for the promise of extra payment

Exceptions - Gaining Practical Benefits:

Williams v Roffey Boys [1991]: contract to refurbish a block of flats. Defendant was the main contractors, subcontracted the carpentry work to the claimants for £20,000 → halfway, claimants realised they had underestimated the cost → defendant promised to pay the claimants extra money in order for the work to be completed on time

- Sued when not paid the extra money
- Court of Appeal found that the defendants had gained practical benefits (i.e. avoiding liability from not finishing construction and expense of finding new sub-contractors) → was the consideration for the extra payment
- Performance of an existing duty owed to the other party will be consideration, provided the other party receives a practical or commercial benefit (and there is no duress)

→ Allows contracts to be modified when unexpected difficulties arise

Take into account economic duress:

- No consideration where there has been economic duress

Part Payment of an Undisputed Debt

- **Part payment** of a debt is *not usually* consideration for a promise by the creditor to **forgo the balance due**

- The debtor is already bound to pay the full amount → by paying less they will not be providing consideration in return for the creditor's promise to accept part payment and forgo the balance (***Foakes v Beer (1884)***
- ***Re Selectmove***: the part payment of a debt could did not count as a practical benefit for the purpose of satisfying the principles laid down in ***Williams v Roffey (***only work done / goods supplied could be a practical benefit)
    - Would directly override ***Foakes v Beer*** which was a House of Lords case

Exception (rare and very old)

Pinnel's Case (1602):

- Exception to the rule is where the debtor can show that they **gave something different for the creditor's agreement to accept the lesser sum** (something that isn't money)
- Paying a smaller amount before the due date (as consideration does not have to be adequate)

Promissory Estoppel

It is a legal principle designed to **stop a party going back on a promise** that they have made to another party (which has then been *relied* and *acted on* to their *detriment*)

Intended to *stop* a promisor from arguing that an underlying promise should not be legally upheld or enforced

Helps injured parties recover on promises made that have led to economic loss when not met

- The principle rests on **equity rather than law** → it is considered inequitable not to uphold a promise made to someone who had then acted to their detriment
- Seen as an **alternative** to the doctrine of consideration

    Prevents a defendant from denying the existence of a contract if there was no consideration but a promise was made

Key Case:

Central London Property Trust Ltd v High Trees House Ltd [1947]:

- High Tree leased a block of flats from CLP (landlord) → falling occupancy rates during WWII → CLP agreed to reduce the rent by half
- Defendants continued to pay the rent at this new rate → once flats were back at full occupancy, CLP sued for the original (higher) rate to be paid. No consideration was provided by High Trees for the variation
- Judge found that the promise to reduce the rent was intended to apply only as a temporary measure during the war. Determined that in the future, High Tree must pay the full amount of rent (original price)
- BUT: were not required to repay the full amount from the war years (right had been extinguished)

'A promise intended to be binding, intended to be acted on and in fact acted on, is binding so far as its terms properly apply.'

Requirements for Promissory Estoppel:

1) No Legal Rights:

The promisor must be clear that they **do not intend to enforce their legal rights** (no ambiguity)

- e.g. to reduce rent

2) An Action

The promisee must have acted on that promise (either to their detriment or altering their course of action)

- The promisee does not need to suffer detriment (***WJ Alan & Co v El Nasr [1972]***)

3) It is used as a defence

The doctrine of Promissory Estoppel can **only be used as a defence**

Case Law Example:

- ***Combe v Combe [1951]***: husband and wife getting divorced, husband promised to pay wife £100 as permanent maintenance → when he did not pay, wife sued based on his promise
  - Court of Appeal stated that the doctrine could only be used as a defence, not a cause of action

4) Inequitable / Unjust to go back

It must be **inequitable/unjust for the promisor to go back on their promise** and insist on their full legal rights

Case Law Example:

- ***D&C Builders v Rees [1966]***: defendant owed the claimants £482 → claimant was in financial difficulties so defendants offered £300 in full settlement (indicted that if they did not accept, would not get payment at all) → claimants accepted but then sued for balance
  - Court found that the defendants could not rely on promissory estoppel → it was not inequitable for the claimants to go back on their promise since it had been freely given

5) Legal Relationship

There must be an existing legal relationship (***Harvey v Dunbar Assets***)

The effects of Promissory Estoppel:

- If all 4 categories are met, the doctrine will either **suspend** legal rights (what usually happens) or **extinguish them completely**
  - This depends on what would be equitable and / or possible on the particular facts

Continuing Obligations

→ Usually results in **suspended ongoing payments**, whilst the **right to past payments is usually extinguished**

- Generally requires a notice of changed circumstances if no time limits are put in place → in High Trees case, CLP had to give reasonable notice of the increase back to full rent in the future
  - What amounts to reasonable notice will be a question of fact and equity in each case
  - You don't always need notice: ***Tool Metal Manufacturing Co v Tungsten Electric Co Ltd [1955]***: → 'there are some cases where the period of suspension clearly terminates on the happening of a certain event or the cessation of a previously existing state of affairs .... In such cases no intimation or notice of any kind may be necessary'

- If the promisee cannot be returned to their original position, the promisor's rights may be extinguished completely
  - Lord Hodson in ***Emanual Ajayi v RT Briscoe (Nigeria) Ltd [1964]:*** 'The promise only becomes final and irrevocable if the promisee cannot resume his position'

One-Off Debts:

- Remains unclear → all the cases where promissory estoppel has been applied concerns continuing obligations
- Position may depend on what would be fair on the particular facts

Contents of a Contract

Classification of Terms

All terms which impose contractual obligations on a party (express or implied) will be either **conditions, warranties or innominate terms** (up to the court to determine)

Condition or Warranty

Traditionally, a court would classify a term as either a condition or a warranty:

Condition = a major term / a term going to the root of the contract

Warranty = a minor, less important term

Objective Test:

An *objective test* is applied to determine if a term is a condition or warranty

→ What would a *reasonable* person think the parties *intended* the term to be

Will consider:

a) The circumstances surrounding the making of the contract
b) The contract as a whole
c) Any descriptions

Case Law Example:

- ***Schuler v Wickman Machine Tool Sales Ltd [1974]***: the parties had described a particular term as a condition, but the HoL decided that the parties had not intended to use the word in its strict legal sense → presumption was rebutted

- If it is a **condition**, and the contract has not been fully performed:
  a) The innocent party will usually have the option of **terminating** the future performance of the contract **and**
  b) Obtaining **damages** for any additional loss suffered

- If a **warranty**, the innocent party:
  a) ***Cannot* terminate** the contract but
  b) Can **sue for damages** for loss suffered

→ This can be unfair as a party may use a breach of condition as an excuse to end the contract, even where the breach is fairly minor (and vice-versa)

Innominate Terms

Instead of classifying all terms of the contract as conditions or warranties, a second approach is to say that **a term is innominate** (also referred to as intermediate terms).

- The right to terminate depends on the *nature* of the breach, rather than just the fact of the breach

Hong Kong Fir Shipping Co Ltd v Kawasaki Kisen Kaisha Ltd [1962]:

- Diplock LJ suggested that the test which should be used to determine whether the innocent party could terminate the contract was **whether the event which had occurred** (i.e. the breach of contract) had deprived the innocent party of **substantially the whole benefit of the contract**
    - This test would not need to be used in cases where the parties might expressly agree when the innocent party could terminate
    - Could still class terms as conditions or warranties if very simple

Express Terms

Express terms = terms in a contract **specifically agreed to by the parties**

- This can be in writing or oral
- In general, parties are free to agree to any terms they choose

Implied Terms

Implied terms = not expressly created by the parties but are implied into the contract

Can occur if the parties share a common background and so make certain assumptions which they don't explicitly state in the contract (seem obvious)

If parties have had previous consistent dealings, may assume that their latest contract will contain the same provisions

A term may be implied in order to protect one of the parties (usually implied by statute)

Hartley v Hymans → delivery is of the essence in commercial transactions

Terms Implied by the Court:

- If there is a disagreement about the provisions of a contract, a court may imply a term based on local custom or trade usage (***Hutton v Warren (1836)***)
    - It is not possible to imply a custom into a contract if the contract contains a provision which contradicts this custom

Where a contract is of a kind which frequently occurs, the court may identify provisions that are typical of that kind of contract and say that these provisions will be implied terms unless the parties make contrary provision (e.g. tenancy agreements and employment contracts)

There are 2 tests which the court will use to imply terms into a contract, based on the presumed intentions of the parties:

1) Business Efficacy Test

Established in ***The Moorcock (1889):*** the court should consider whether a term is necessary to make a contract work commercially (whether it is necessary to give business efficacy to the contract)

2) Officious Bystander Test

Established in ***Shirlaw v Southern Foundries Ltd [1939]***: a term can only be implied if the point was so obvious that it went without saying that it was what the parties intended

Case Law Example:

- ***Liverpool City Council v Irwin and Another [1977]***: tenants withheld rent in protest of quality of flats owned by local authority. The agreement did not contain any provision about repair and maintenance of the contentious areas
  - HoL had to decide whether there was any implied duty on the landlords to repair and maintain these common parts
  - Did not imply an absolute obligation to repair as it would go beyond what was necessary in the circumstances
  - Implied a term that the landlord should take reasonable care to keep the common parts in reasonable repair

Terms Implied by Statute:

The Sale of Goods Act (SGA) 1979:

This statute **implies terms into contracts for the sale of goods** (with exceptions)

- Only applies to contracts for the sale of goods which are made ***business* to *business***, ***consumer to consumer*** or ***consumer to business***
  - In relation to consumers, only when they are acting in the course of business (e.g. a private individual selling a second hand car)
- *Doesn't* apply for contracts for the sale of goods made between a trader and a consumer

The Main Terms:

Section 8:

→ **Ascertainment of Price**

- ***s 8(2)***: where the price is not fixed in the contract or ascertainable in one of the ways stated in ***s 8(1)***, the buyer must pay a reasonable price
- ***s 8(3)***: what is a reasonable price is a question of fact, dependent on the circumstances of each case

Section 13:

→ **Sale of Goods by Description:**

- Where there is a contract for the sale of goods by description, there is an implied condition that the goods will correspond to that description
    - ***Harlingdon & Leinster Enterprises Ltd v Christopher Hull Fine Art Ltd [1991]***: in order for ***s 13*** to apply, the buyer must rely on the description
- These terms will be implied in business and individual cases (unlike ***s 14***)
- There can also be a sale by description, even where the buyer has seen the goods and examined them (***Beale v Taylor [1967]***)
- Liability for breach of ***s 13*** is strict → the buyer does not have to prove that the seller is at fault (CONDITION)

Section 14:

→ **Satisfactory Quality and Reasonable Fitness for Purpose:**

- The implied terms of satisfactory quality (***s 14(2)*** and reasonable fitness for the buyer's purpose (***s 14(3)*** apply **only** if the seller sells in the course of a *business*
    - ***s 14(2a):*** goods are of a satisfactory quality if they meet the standard that a reasonable person would regard as satisfactory
    - ***s 14(2b):*** quality of a good includes: fitness for its typical purpose, appearance, freedom from minor defects, safety & durability
    - ***Section 14(3)***: if you intend to use goods just for their normal purpose, you do not have to tell the seller what this is (made known by implication)
        - If you have a special/unusual purpose in mind, then to get the benefit of ***s 14(3)*** you should tell the seller what this is

Liability for breach of ***s 14(2)*** and ***14(3)*** is **strict** → the buyer does not have to prove that the seller is at fault (CONDITION)

- Seller not able to say that they were unaware of a defective good

Available Remedies

The SGA 1979 provides some *basic* rights and remedies which apply if there is a breach of one of the terms implied by the Act:

- Even if the breach is minor, the buyer is able to **terminate** the contract and **reject** the goods:
    a. Will not have to perform any further obligations under the contract
    b. Can recover money paid (but must give the goods back)

c. Buyer can sue for damages if there is further loss

The buyer can also affirm the contract, keep the goods and sue for damages for any loss suffered

Exceptions - acceptance of goods:

The right to reject the goods is lost where the buyer has accepted the goods (***s 11 (4) and s 35***)

S 11(4) → the buyer cannot reject the goods if the buyer has accepted them
S 35 → Outlines the situations where the buyer will be deemed to have accepted a good (e.g. if they retain the goods beyond a reasonable time without intimating rejection → matter of fact per case)

Exceptions - minor breach:

The right to reject will be lost if the breach is so slight that it would be unreasonable for the buyer to reject them (***s 15A of the SGA 1979***)

For example, if the goods are usable but very slightly defective
Cannot reject, restricted to damages
Up to the seller to show that the breach is so slight

The Supply of Goods and Services Act (SGSA) 1982:

The SGSA 1982 implies terms into contracts for **services**, and contracts for **work and materials** that are ***not*** **made between a trader and consumer**

- Work and material contracts (**s 3 /4**) = predominantly for work, but which necessarily involve the supply of goods (e.g. building of an office block)
- Service contract (**s 13/14/15**) = where the supplier is contracting to provide a service

The Main Terms (supply of goods):

Section 3:
→ **Implied terms where transfer is by description**

- Under a relevant contract for the transfer of goods, implies a term that the goods will correspond with the description

Section 4:

→ **Implied terms about quality or fitness:**

- ***s 4(2)***: where the transferor transfers the property in goods in the course of a business, there is an implied condition that the goods will be of satisfactory quality
- ***s 4(5)***: implies a term that the goods are reasonably fit for any particular purpose which the transferee makes known
- ***s 6(5)***: does not apply where the transferee does not rely on the skills or judgement of the transferor

The Main Terms (supply of services):

Section 13:

→ **Implied term about care and skill**

- Implies a term that where the supplier of a service is acting in the course of a business, the supplier will carry out the service with reasonable care and skill
- Innominate term

Section 14:

→ **Implied term about time for performance:**

- ***s 14(1)***: Where the supplier of a service is acting in the course of a business and the time for the service to be carried out is not fixed by the contract or determined by a course of dealing between the parties, there is an implied term that the service will be carried out within a reasonable time
- ***s 14(2)***: what is a reasonable time is a question of *fact*

Section 15

→ **Implied term about consideration**

- ***s 15(1)***: Where the consideration for the service is not determined by the contract or by a course of dealing between the parties, there is an implied term that a reasonable charge will be paid
- ***s 15(2)***: what is a reasonable charge is a question of *fact*
- Innominate term

The Consumer Rights Act (CRA) 2015:

The ***CRA 2015*** applies only to contracts made between a **trader and consumer**

- Trader = a person acting for purposes relating to that person's trade, business craft or profession (can be an individual / entity / business → wider definition in practice)
- Consumer = an individual acting for purposes that are wholly or mainly outside that individual's trade, business craft or profession (where they are acting purely for personal use)

The Main Terms (Sales Contracts):

The implied terms largely reflect those implied by ***ss 13-14 of the SGA 1979*** and ***ss 3 and 4 of the SGSA 1982***

- ***S 9***: goods must be of satisfactory quality
- ***S 10***: goods will be reasonably fit for their particular purpose
- ***S 11***: goods will be as described

Available Remedies:

Section 19: if the goods do not conform to the contract because of a breach of ***ss 9-11***, the consumers rights are:

- ***Sections 20 and 22***: the short term right (up to 30 days) to reject and get a full refund
- ***Sections 23:*** the right to repair or replacement (if appropriate)
- ***Sections 20 and 24:*** The right to a price reduction or the final right to reject and get a partial refund to reflect the consumer's use of the goods

The Main Terms (Service Contracts):

The terms implied by ***ss 49, 51*** and ***52*** are similar to ***ss 13-15 of the SGSA 1982***

- ***S 49***: service/work will be carried out with reasonable care and skill
- ***S 51***: where no price has been fixed, a reasonable price will be paid for the service/work
- ***S 52***: where no time for performance has been fixed, service/work will be performed within a reasonable time

Available Remedies:

Section 54: where a service/work does not conform to the contract, because of either breach or an express term relating to the performance of the service/work or breach of the implied term to exercise reasonable care and skill (***s 49***), the consumer has the right to require repeat performance (where reasonable) or to a price reduction

In relation to a breach of the implied term as to performance within a reasonable time (***s 52***), the consumer has the right to an appropriate price reduction

→ Apart from ***ss 13 and 15 of the SGSA (***services), (innominate), all above implied terms are conditions

Exemption Clauses

Exemption Clause = seeks to **exclude liability completely**, or to **limit liability** if a breach of contract occurs or a tort is committed

- A clause which attempts to restrict or limit a party's remedies for breach of contract is also an exemption clause

For an exemption clause to be relevant, there must be a breach of contract or tort

Incorporation

There are 3 main ways in which a provision may be incorporated:

1) By signature
2) By giving reasonable notice
3) By consistent course of dealings between parties

By signature:

- General rule: if you sign a contractual document then the clauses in that document will normally be incorporated as part of the contract
  - ***L'Estrange v Graucob Ltd [1934]***: exemption clause was in 'regrettably small' print but was legible so was incorporated
- Only the claimant needs to have signed (not the party relying on the clause)
- The document must be a contractual document

Exemption - illegible

Exemption - inaccurate description

An exemption clause will not be incorporated if the effect of the clause has been described inaccurately and the innocent party has reasonably relied on the inaccurate description when entering the contract

Case Law Example:

- *Curtis v Chemical Cleaning & Dyeing Co [1951]*: claimant took a wedding dress to defendant's shop for cleaning → asked to sign a receipt exempting defendant from liability for damage to beads and sequins
    - Receipt was actually also for damage to dress altogether → when stained tried to claim not liable (court held defendant could not rely on the clause as had been misrepresented)

Exemption - unusual or onerous

An exemption clause will not be incorporated if the clause is unusual and onerous and is not fairly and reasonably drawn to the attention of the other party

Case Law Example:

- ***Blu-Sky Solutions Ltd v Be Caring Ltd [2021]***
- ***Thornton v Shoe Lane Parking Ltd [1971]***
- ***Interfoto Picture Library Ltd v Stiletto Visual Programmes Ltd [1989]:*** claimant delivered 47 transparencies with a delivery note containing conditions that they had to be returned by March 19 otherwise there would be a fine of £5 per transparency per day
    - Defendant did not notice → returned 14 days late → claimants claimed £3,783
    - Clause regarded as onerous as it imposed a very high charge for failing to return the transparencies
    - Reasonable steps had not been taken → no attention drawn

By notice:

Where terms are **contained in notices** at the point of sale or transaction or on the **back of tickets**, the defendant must show that they've given reasonable notice of the terms at or before the time of the contract

- There must be **actual notice** - on the facts did the claimant know of the exemption clause and **constructive notice** (were clear steps taken)
    - The innocent party must either know of the clause, or the party relying on the clause must have taken reasonable steps to bring it to the other's notice before the contract is finalised (***Parker v South Eastern Railway (1877)***

- The document containing the clause must be contractual in nature
    - *Chapelton v Barry Urban District Council [1940]*: court decided that a deck chair ticket was not contractual in nature as a reasonable person would regard it as a receipt (not a doc with terms about the hiring arrangement)

Reasonable Steps

The court will take into account:

- The position of the clause on the document (e.g. if it is on the back, should draw attention to this)
- The prominence of the clause on the doc
- The type and nature of the clause (e.g. unusual or onerous)
    - ***Spurling Ltd v Bradshaw [1956]***: in order to give sufficient notice of an onerous or unusual clause, it would be necessary for the clause to be 'printed in red ink with a red hand pointing to it or something equally startling'
- Where an exemption clause is expected, simply handing over the doc will amount to reasonable steps
- The timing of reasonable steps → generally, before the contract is finalised
    - ***Olley v Marlborough Court Ltd [1949]***
    - ***Thornton v Shoe Lane Parking Ltd [1971]***

Consistent Course of Dealings:

In order for a clause to be incorporated on this basis, the dealings must be both consistent and amount to a 'course' of dealings (a sufficient amount of regular dealings) (***Spurling Ltd v Bradshaw)***

Case Law Example:

- ***Kendall (Henry) & Sons v Lillico & Sons Ltd [1969]***: 2 businesses had dealt with each other 3 /4 times a year for 3 years. After each contract, a 'sold note' would be sent to the buyer containing exemption clauses
  Court decided that the clauses were incorporated in the latest contract because of the previous consistent course of dealings
- ***Hollier v Rambler Motors [1972]***: claimant had had a car serviced by the defendant's garage only 3/ 4 times over 5 years → did not amount to a course of dealings
- ***McCutcheon v David MacBrayne Ltd [1964]***: although parties had dealt with each other many times, inconsistency in when the doc containing exemption clause would be signed → HoL: dealings not consistent.

Construction

The construction of the exemption clause **must actually exempt the liability in question**

- Even if an exemption clause is incorporated into a contract, the party in breach will not be able to rely on it unless, as a matter of construction, the clause covers the breach of contract and loss of damage which has occurred

Construe the exemption clause in light of the:

Words used

The other terms of the contract

Any relevant commercial background to the contract

The Contra Proferentem Rule

If a party tries to rely on a clause which is ambiguous or unclear, the **court will interpret the clause against the defaulting party** (person not relying on the clause)

- This relates to any clause which is unclear or ambiguous (not just exemption)

    <u>*Case Law Example:*</u>

    - ***Houghton v Trafalgar Insurance [1954]***: a 5 seater car involved in an accident whilst carrying 6 people. Insurance company tried to exempt itself from liability through cause carrying an 'excessive load'
        - Court decided the clause did not cover a situation where the car was carrying too many people
        - Clause was ambiguous to the word 'load' → usually applied to goods, not people

Negligence Cases

If an exemption clause is intended to cover liability for the tort of negligence or a negligent breach of contract, clause must be carefully worded

Canada Steamship Lines v The King [1952] guidelines:

If the clause expressly exempts a party from liability for negligence (i.e. the word negligence or a synonym is used) then it will be effective

If there is no express reference to negligence, the court must decide whether the words are wide enough to exclude liability for negligence

The court must then ask if the clause could cover liability other than negligence (e.g. strict liability) where the proof of fault is not required → if yes, the court may decide that it covers this other liability and not negligence

- The court should look at the facts and realities of the situation at the time of the contract and ask what the potential liability the parties had in mind (***Monarch Airlines Ltd v London Luton Airport Ltd [1997]***)
- Courts are reluctant to allow one party to exclude their liability, or make a claim, where their liability or claim arises as a result of their own negligence, unless that's clearly what the parties intended

Serious Breaches of Contract

- ***Photo Productions Ltd v Securicor Transport Ltd [1980]***: where there has been a very serious or deliberate breach of contract, it is a matter of construction whether the exemption clause covers the breach
    - If the clause is clearly worded, it may cover the breach which has occurred even if that breach is very serious or deliberate

The Unfair Contract Terms Act 1977

The ***UCTA*** was passed to try and **control the use of exemption clauses**

- Lays down further tests to decide whether an exemption clause can be relied on
- Seeks to either render the exemption clause **void** or subject it to a **reasonableness test**

  (UCTA 1977 does not cover exemption clauses in contracts between trader to consumer (governed by the ***CRA 2015***)

- The ***UCTA*** leaves the common law rules in place → the tests it imposes are *in addition* to the tests
- Must first assess incorporation and construction of the exemption clause before using the ***UCTA***

The Main Terms - Goods:

These sections apply to clauses which exempt liability for breaches of the terms implied by the ***SGA 1979*** and ***SGSA 1982*** in relation to goods

Section 6:

→ **Deals with s 13 and s 14 of the SGA 1979**

- Deals with clauses which attempt to exempt liability for breach of the terms implied by ***s 13*** and ***s 14*** of the ***SGA 1979*** (goods must fit their description, be of satisfactory quality and reasonably fit for purpose)

↳ ***S 6 of UCTA 1977***: a seller can exclude or restrict liability for breach of these terms provided the exemption clause satisfies the reasonableness test

Section 7:

→ **Deals with s 3 and s 4 of the SGSA 1982**

- Deals with attempts by a business to exempt liability for breach of terms implied by ***ss 3 and 4*** of the ***SGSA 1982*** (goods transferred fit their description and are of satisfactory quality and purpose)

↳ ***S 7 of UCTA 1977***: a seller can exclude or restrict liability for breach of these terms provided the exemption clause satisfies the reasonableness test

The Main Terms - Negligence:

Section 2 applies to clauses which exempt liability for **negligence or a negligent breach of contract**

E.g. breach of an implied term in a contract that services/work carried out in the course of a business shall be done with reasonable care and skill

Section 2(1):

- ***S 2(1)***: a business cannot exclude or restrict its liability for negligence, where it causes death or personal injury

Section 2(2):

- ***S 2(2)***: in relation to other loss or damage caused by negligence, a business can exclude or restrict its liability provided the exemption clause satisfies the reasonableness test

The Main Terms - Express Terms:

Section 3 applies to clauses in standard form contracts which exempt liability for breaches of **express terms**

Only tends to be used where there has been a breach of an express term of the contract

Only applies where one party deals on the other party's written standard terms of business

↳ Where ***s 3*** does apply, a business can exclude or restrict its liability for breach only if the terms satisfies the reasonableness test

⇓

The Reasonableness Test

Section 11 of UCTA 1977 sets out the reasonableness test

S 11(1): 'the exemption clause must have been a fair & reasonable one to include, having regard to the circumstances which were (or ought reasonably to have been) known to the parties or within the contemplation of the parties when the contract was made'

S 11(5): the burden of proof is on the party seeking to rely on the exemption clause to show that it is reasonable

Take a cautious approach:

- When drafting exemption clauses, encouraged to be on the side of caution (as it is unclear whether the entire exemption clause must be reasonable, or just the part that the defendant is relying on)

  Case Law:
  - ***Stewart Gill Ltd v Horatio Myer & Co Ltd [1992]***: Court of Appeal held that the court should consider the clause as a whole, not just the part relied on
    - Lord Donaldson MR: 'the issue is whether the term [the whole term and nothing but the term] shall have been a fair and reasonable one to be included'
  - ***Watford Electronics Ltd v Sanderson CFL Ltd [2001] EWCA Civ 317***: Court of Appeal decided that an exemption clause could be split into 2 parts, serving 2 distinct purposes → the reasonableness of each part could be decided separately
  - ***Goodlife Foods Ltd v Hall Fire Protection Ltd [2018] EWCA Civ 1371***: defendant sought to rely on a clause which excluded all liability for loss caused to 'property, goods, persons or the like, directly or indirectly resulting from our negligence..'

    Court of Appeal held the clause to be reasonable and valid

The Sch 2 Guidelines for Reasonableness:

The court will take into account:

a. Bargaining Positions:

- The relative strength of the bargaining positions of the parties (equal bargaining position makes exemption clause more reasonable)

Watford Electronics Ltd v Sanderson CFL Ltd: Chadwick LJ's judgement: 'Where experienced businessmen representing substantial companies of equal bargaining power negotiate an agreement, they may be taken to have had regard to the matters known to them. They should, in my view, be taken to be the best judge of the commercial fairness of the agreement which they have made.'

b. Any inducement?

- Did the customer receive an inducement to agree to the exemption clause, or in accepting it did the customer have an opportunity to enter into a similar contract with someone else (without having to accept one)
- If they were offered a lower price for accepting a contract with an exemption clause and higher price for one without → would make the clause reasonable

- If the customer had the opportunity to go elsewhere and avoid an exemption clause, makes clause more reasonable

c. **Knowledge of the Clause:**
   - Whether the customer knew, or ought to reasonably have known, of the existence and extent of the clause (taking into account any trade customs or previous dealings between parties)

d. **Practical to Comply?**
   - Whether it was reasonable at the time of the contract to expect that compliance with the condition applying exemption was practicable
   - E.g. if there is a time limit on when exemption applies

e. **Special Order Goods?**
   - Whether the goods were manufactured, processed or adapted to the special order of the customer

Smith Additional Guidelines

Set out in ***Smith v Eric Bush [1990] 1 AC 831 HL,*** Lord Griffiths' judgement added additional guidelines which the court may take into account when deciding if an exemption clause is reasonable:

a. **Difficulty of Task:**
   - The difficulty of the task being undertaken for which liability is being excluded
   - When a very difficult or dangerous undertaking is involved, there may be a high risk of failure (makes it more reasonable to exclude liability)

b. **Practical consequences**
   - The practical consequences of the decision on the question of reasonableness
   - E.g. the sum of money potentially at stake and the ability of the parties to bear the loss involved

Limitation clauses:

- ***s 11(4)*** **adds guidelines which apply to limitation clauses:**
  The resources which the defendant could expect to be available for the purpose of meeting the liability should it arise
  How far it was open to the defendant to cover itself by insurance

Consumer Rights Act 2015

The CRA 2015 consolidated consumer rights, protection and remedies in contracts made with **traders**

For Sales Contracts:
Section 31(1) of the CRA 2015: there is **no exclusion or restriction** for: ***S 9***: goods to be of satisfactory quality ***S 10***: goods to be reasonably fit for purpose ***S 11***: goods to be as described ***Section 31(2)***: a term in a sales contract is not binding on the consumer to the extent it would: a) Exclude or restrict a right or remedy in respect of breach of ***ss 9-11*** b) Make such a right or remedy or its enforcement subject to a restrictive or onerous condition c) Allow a trader to put a person at a disadvantage as a result of pursuing such a right or remedy d) Exclude or restrict rules of evidence or procedure

For Service Contracts:
Section 57(1): a trader cannot *exclude or limit* liability for breach of ***s 49*** (the implied term to perform a service with reasonable care and skill) ***Section 57(3)***: a trader *cannot* restrict liability for breach of ***s 49, s 51 and s 52*** if it would prevent the consumer in an appropriate case *from getting a refund* ***Section 57(4)***: a trader cannot: a) *Exclude or restrict* a right or remedy in respect of liability for breaches of ***ss 49-52*** b) Make such a right or remedy or its enforcement subject to a restrictive or onerous condition c) Put a person at a disadvantage as a result of pursuing such a right or remedy, or exclude or restrict rules of evidence or procedure

Unfair Terms:

- A term is unfair if, contrary to the requirements of good faith, it causes a significant imbalance in the parties' rights and obligations under the contract to the detriment of the consumer
- An unfair term in a contract between a trader and consumer will not be binding on the consumer
- Determining if a term is fair takes into account the subject matter of the contract and all the circumstances at the time of the contract

Exemption Clauses and Third Parties:

- General rule: an exemption clause in a contract cannot protect a third party, as the privity rule provides that only a party can rely on a clause in a contract (***Adler v Dickson [1955]***)
- Exception contained in the ***Contracts (Rights of Third Parties) Act 1999***. A third party can acquire rights if:
    - ***s 1(1)(a):*** The contract expressly provides that he may acquire a benefit (the third party does not have to be named, provided he is identified by class or description)

s 1(1)(b): The term purports to confer a benefit on him

- *s 1(2)*: does not apply if on a true construction of the contract, it was not intended that the term be enforceable by a third party

Remedies (Damages)

Establishing Damages

Defining damages:

A breach of any term of a contract gives the innocent party the right to claim damages

- Aim is to compensate the claimant for their loss, not to punish the defendant.

Loss includes any harm to the person or property of the claimant and any injury to the claimant's economic position.

Is it a Specified Damage Clause / a Penalty Clause?

The parties may choose to include a provision in the contract which states the amount of compensation to be paid if the contract is broken

Specified Damages Clause / Liquidated Damages Clause = attempts to pre-estimate the loss which is likely to be caused by the breach

The sum specified is the amount that will be paid, *regardless* of the *actual* loss which the claimant has suffered

- **Penalty** = attempts to put pressure on a party to perform a contract (unenforceable)
  - Court is free to assess damages in the usual way (damages, remoteness, mitigation etc)

→ Although parties may specifically use the word penalty / specified damages in a contract, the wording is not conclusive and the court may choose

- The *innocent* party may want to argue that the clause *is a penalty* if the claimant's actual loss is *greater* than the amount stated in the clause
- The *party in breach* may want to argue that the clause *is a penalty* and not binding, where the *amount* stated in the clause is *greater* than the *actual loss* of the innocent party

Dunlop Guidelines

Guidelines set out in ***Dunlop Pneumatic Tyre Co Ltd v New Garage & Motor Co Ltd [1915]*** to determine whether a clause is a specified damages clause or a penalty:

a) **Penalty** if the sum stated in the clause is extravagant & unconscionable in amount, in comparison with the greatest loss that could conceivably be proved to have followed from the breach
   - Not compared to the loss actually suffered, but with the loss that might have followed from the breach (usually greater than what acc occurred)

b) **Penalty** if the breach consists only in not paying a sum of money and the sum stated in the clause is greater than the amount which ought to have been paid

c) **Penalty** (presumed) if a single lump sum is payable, even if there are several events, varying in severity

d) **Specified Damages Clause** if it is difficult or impossible to pre-estimate precisely the loss which might be caused by the breach

- ***Philips Hong Kong Ltd v Attorney-General of Hong Kong (1993)***: looking at subsequent events and what actually happened could be valuable evidence as to what could reasonably be expected to be the loss at the time the contract was made

Cavendish Guidelines

Cavendish Square Holding BV v Makdessi; ParkingEye Ltd v Beavis [2015]: reformulated the test for a penalty:
Whether the clause is a genuine pre-estimate of loss does not necessarily determine whether it is a penalty

↳

1) What legitimate business interest of the innocent party is served and protected by the clause (does not have to be just financial)
2) Whether the remedy provided for the breach is exorbitant or unconscionable in the context of that interest (i.e. is the clause penal in nature)
   - Did the clause impose a detriment on the contract-breaker which was out of proportion to any legitimate interest of the innocent party in the enforcement of the contract

Where *compensation* for the breach is the *only* legitimate interest, can use the guidelines in ***Dunlop*** to determine if the clause is penal

- In a commercial context, where compensation might not be the only legitimate interest of the innocent party and the contract was negotiated between properly advised parties of comparable negotiating power, the presumption is that the parties themselves were the best judges of their interests

Remoteness

A party **will not be awarded damages for loss which is too remote** a consequence of the breach

- Takes into account what was in the reasonable contemplation of the parties, at the time the contract was made

Hadley v Baxendale

The test for remoteness was established in ***Hadley v Baxendale (1854):***

> 'The damages which the other party ought to receive in respect of breach of contract should be such as may fairly and reasonably be considered either arising naturally from the breach of contract … or may reasonably be supposed to have been in the contemplation of both parties at the time they made the contract'

Referred to as the 2 limb test:

1. **Limb One**: loss which arises naturally from the breach will normally be within the parties' reasonable contemplation
2. **Limb Two**: unusual loss will be within the parties' reasonable contemplation, only if the special circumstances which give rise to the loss are known to both parties at the time the contract is made

Case Law Interpretation:

Balfour Beatty Construction v Scottish Power

Balfour Beatty Construction (Scotland) Ltd v Scottish Power plc 1994:

Established that there is *no general rule* that contracting parties are presumed to have knowledge of all techniques in each other's business practices. Although this may be different if the project was deemed to be simple.

Victoria Laundry v Newman Industries

Victoria Laundry (Windsor) Ltd v Newman Industries Ltd [1949]

The defendant was liable for the loss of ordinary business profit as it was a reasonably foreseeable result of the late delivery (the defendant knew the nature of the claimant's business and that they intended to put the boiler to immediate use)

- The defendant was *not liable* for the loss of profit on the highly lucrative contracts with the Ministry of Supply → went beyond ordinary profit (defendant did not know of these special circumstances so loss was too remote)

Koufos v C Czarnikow

Koufos v C Czarnikow Ltd, The Heron II [1969]

HoL disapproved of the phrase 'reasonably foreseeable' used in ***Victoria Laundry.***

Reinstated use of 'within the reasonable contemplation of the parties' to compensate for the fact that in contractual agreements, you are normally aware of the other party and can therefore take steps to ensure you recover for unusual losses (not the case in tort)

- The question to ask is whether the loss is 'of a kind which the defendant, when he made the contract, ought to have realised was not unlikely to result from [the] breach'
    - Imputed knowledge = what the defendant could be taken to know (i.e. what is reasonable for them to know in the ordinary course of things)
    - Actual knowledge = what a defendant actually knows

→ The decision in Victoria Laundry is *still held*, it is just now in relation to what was in the reasonable contemplation

Parsons v Uttley

Parsons (Livestock) Ltd v Uttley Ingham Ltd [1978]

If the defendant can contemplate the type of loss as a serious possibility, then all loss of that type is recoverable, even if the extent of the loss could not have been contemplated (e.g. property damage)

- The defendants were liable for the death of the claimant's pigs as some harm to the pigs was within the reasonable contemplation of the parties, as a result of the defective installation of the hopper

Brown v KMR Services

Brown v KMR Services Ltd [1995]

Losses were of the same type as ones that were contemplated and so were not too remote

- Held that loss of ordinary business profits is different in kind from loss of a particular contract which gives rise to very high profits (as established in *Victoria Laundry*)

Measuring Damages

The normal aim of the court in assessing damages was stated in the judgement of Parke B in ***Robinson v Harman (1848)***:

> 'The rule at common law is that where a party sustains loss by reason of a breach of contract, he is so far as money can do it, to be placed in the **same situation** with respect to damages **as if the contract had been performed'**

It will generally be for the claimant to decide whether to seek damages on an **expectation** or a **reliance loss basis**

Expectation Loss?

The claimant will generally be able to recover for loss of the benefit which they would have obtained **had the contract been performed properly** → expectation loss basis

- The court will take into account the costs the claimant would have incurred in order to obtain the benefit

Goods / Services

→ **Defective Goods:**

- If goods are defective, the basic rule is that the amount of damages awarded will be the difference in value or **the cost of cure**
- Usually, damages will be the difference between the actual value of the goods and the value the goods would have had if they had not been defective

→ **Services Contracts:**

- With contracts for services, the basic rule is that the amount of damages awarded will be the cost of putting the work right (i.e. the cost of cure)
- Can also award the difference in value for defective services if reasonable

Damages for Lost Opportunity:

Case Law Examples:

- ***Chaplin v Hicks [1911]***: Daily Express ran a talent contest → top 50 contestants had to attend an audition where 12 winners would be selected → organisers didn't tell the claimant where the audition was taking place
  - Claimant entitled to damages to compensate for the loss of the chance of being one of the 12 winners
- ***Blackpool and Fylde Aero Club v Blackpool Borough Council [1990]***: Council had a duty to consider all properly submitted tenders (did not look at the claimant's tender, despite it being submitted)

Where there is no quantitative loss:

Addis v Gramophone Co Ltd: general rule is that the claimant cannot recover damages for injured feelings, except for when the object of the contract is to afford pleasure.

- The sole object of the contract does not need to be to provide pleasure, enjoyment or peace of mind → sufficient if it is an important object of the contract (***Farley v Skinner [2001]***)

Case Law Example:

- ***Ruxley Electronics and Construction v Forsyth [1996]:*** Ruxley broke contract by building a swimming pool at Forsyth's home at the wrong measurements
  - Ruxley argued that the pool was still safe for diving and the cost of re-building was unreasonable and disproportionate to the actual loss suffered (the cost of cure was £21,560). Whilst Forsyth argued that as Ruxley had failed to perform his specific obligations, he should be entitled to damages which would place him back in the original position
    - Court held that as the wrong measurements did not decrease the value of the pool, the difference in value was *nil* → damages are designed to compensate for an established loss, not to provide a gratuitous benefit
    - The cost of cure (reinstatement) was also wholly disproportionate to the non-monetary loss suffered (through a test of reasonableness)
  - Decided Forsyth could recover £2,500 for loss of amenity (nominal award).
    - Seemed to be compensation for Forsyth's disappointed expectations
  - ***Jarvis v Swans Tours [1973]***: defendants were a travel agent, claimant booked a holiday through them which was not as advertised.
    - The trial judge initially took the difference in value between the holiday the claimant paid for and the holiday he received
    - Court of Appeal held that damages for distress and disappointment could be recovered where there is a contract to provide entertainment and enjoyment

Reliance Loss?

Sometimes, the claimant may ask for damages to cover the **expenses incurred in reliance on the contract** → worked out on a reliance loss basis

- Covers expenditure wasted as a result of breach of contract (***Anglia Television v Reed [1972]***)
- The claimant must prove that they suffered loss due to the defendant's breach:
    - ***Omak Maritime Ltd v Mamola Challenger Shipping Co (The Mamola Challenger) [2010]***: the claimants had mitigated their loss from the breach of contract and so were not able to recover damages for wasted expenditure (there was no loss to remedy)

Mitigating Damages

Has the defendant mitigated their loss?

There is a requirement for the claimant to mitigate their loss → they should take reasonable steps to ensure their loss is kept to a minimum

(***British Westinghouse Electric & Manufacturing Co Ltd v Underground Electric Railway Company of London Ltd [1912]***)

- The claimant *cannot* recover damages for losses which they could have avoided by taking reasonable steps
- As long as they can prove they have taken steps to mitigate, they *can claim* any expenses incurred even if the attempt is *unsuccessful*
- The onus of proof is on the party in breach to show that the claimant could have mitigated

Time for Assessment of Damages:

- Damages are assessed by reference to the time of the breach (e.g. if breach of contract for sale of goods, would be awarded damages based on the price of goods at the time the contract was formulated)
- Where a seller refuses to deliver goods, the buyer should act quickly and buy replacement goods, rather than delaying and risking a rise in prices

Contributory Negligence:

- If the only cause of action for breach of contract is a negligent breach (breach of the term implied by ***s 13*** of the ***Supply of Goods and Services Act 1982***), contributory negligence would apply (claimant's damages may be reduced)

Other Remedies

Action for an Agreed Sum

If the contract provides that one party shall pay a definite sum of money to the other, then if the duty to pay has arisen but the payer refuses to pay, the payee can bring a **claim for the agreed sum**

- Involves suing for an amount of money due (normally the price of goods or services supplied under a contract)
- Seen as a more direct remedy than a claim for damages → the claimant is not asking to be compensated for not getting money, they are simply suing for the money
- Can only sue once the duty to pay has arisen
- Do not have to prove loss or remoteness

Termination of a Contract

The innocent party **may be able to terminate the future performance of the contract if**:

a) A condition is broken; or
b) An innominate term is broken and the effects of the breach are major

- **Repudiatory Breach** → where a breach does entitle a party to terminate, the breach is often said to be repudiatory
- **Right of Election of the Innocent Party**: where a contract has been fully performed by both parties, it is not usually possible to terminate
    - If the innocent party has the right to terminate the future performance of the contract, can either choose to affirm it or terminate

Terminating	Affirming
If the innocent party terminates, the contract is at an end and future obligations will be discharged • The innocent party can sue for damages for any loss suffered	If the innocent party affirms the contract, then the contract is not over and both parties should continue to perform their obligations • The innocent party can still claim damages for loss suffered • May not always be possible → e.g. if the continuation of the contract is dependent on the co-operation of the other party who is refusing to perform

Sale of Goods Contracts:

- Special rules apply to sale of goods contracts
- If the seller breaches ***ss 9 - 11*** of the ***Consumer Rights Act 2015*** or ***s 13 or 14*** of the ***Sale of Goods Act 1979***, the buyer may be entitled to reject the goods (even though the contract has been fully performed → i.e. the buyer has received the goods and paid for them)

Anticipatory Breach

Where a party gives **advance warning that it is not going to perform its contractual obligations** → requires an advanced indication that the contract will not be properly performed

If this occurs, the other party can:

- Terminate the contract and sue for damages immediately, or
- Treat the contract as continuing and wait until the time fixed for performance in the hope that the party in breach will change its mind and perform the contract

Specific Performance

Specific Performance is an order of the court which **requires a party to perform its contractual obligations** → failure to comply is considered contempt of court

- For example, in the purchase of a house, if the seller backs out, damages may not be an equitable remedy - the buyer wanted that house not just a house

- It is an equitable remedy and therefore discretionary
- Can be combined with a claim for damages

There are certain **principles** which govern the award of specific performance:

Will not be awarded where damages are adequate
Traditionally, specific performance has not been granted **where an award of damages is an adequate remedy** If a seller refuses to deliver goods, the buyer is unlikely to get specific performance where substitute goods can be purchased (unless substitute goods are not available)

Will not be awarded for contracts requiring supervision by the court
Specific performance may not be granted where the court would have to **supervise the parties over a period of time** because of the difficulty of continuous supervision

Will not be awarded for service contracts
Service contracts usually depend on a certain amount of trust and confidence → if the relationship between the parties has broken down, it would not be advisable to force them to work together

Only when it is just and equitable to do so
As it is an equitable remedy, it will be awarded only when it is **just and equitable to do so**, at the discretion of the court (not granted by right) Will consider if the order would cause disproportionate hardship to the defendant

Injunctions

An **injunction** can either be prohibitory (forbidding a person doing a particular act) or mandatory (requiring a person to put right a breach of contract)

An injunction is an **equitable remedy** so available at the discretion of the court

- Will not be granted if the effect would be to compel the defendant to do acts which the defendant could not have been ordered to do by specific performance
    - E.g the court will not grant an injunction to force an employee to work for a particular employer
    - It is unlikely to be granted if the injunction will have the effect of seriously affecting the party's career

Case Law Examples:

- ***Warner Brothers Pictures Incorporated v Nelson [1937]***: Nelson entered into a contract with Warner Brothers → a clause stipulated that 'she will not, during the term of the contract, render any services for or in any motion picture production or productions of any other persons'
    - Court was prepared to grant an injunction as the defendant was not being forced to act for the claimants and could seek employment elsewhere (just not in acting)
    - The injunction sought would not force the defendant to perform her contract or remain idle

- ***Page One Records v Britton [1968]***: claimant was a pop group manager. Clause in the contract stipulated that they would 'not engage any other person, film or corporation to act as managers or agents or to act themselves in such capacity'
    - The claimant applied for an injunction to prevent the group from employing another person as manager after he was fired
    - Distinguished from ***Warner Bros*** → held it would not be fair to force the group to employ the claimant as their manager, when there was lost confidence

→ Reinforced that the court **should not enforce negative promises in a contract of personal services** if the injunction would mean that the defendant either had to remain idle or perform the positive covenants in the contract

Restitution

Restitution aims to prevent one party being **unjustly enriched at the expense of the other**

A claim may arise when:

a) Money has been paid by one party to another under a contract and there has been a complete failure of the consideration (i.e. no work completed)
b) One party has done work for the other, or supplied goods to the other, and wants to be compensated for the work done or goods delivered

a) Recovering Money

A payer can bring an action in restitution to recover the money if the payee is in breach as there has been a total failure of the consideration

- For example, where the payee has not done any part of what the payee was supposed to do under the contract or what has been done is completely useless
- If the payer ends up having to pay more than the initial consideration elsewhere, they would also have to bring a damages action (as well as or instead of restitution)

b) Compensation for service / goods

If one party has supplied goods or done work for the other and the other party is in breach of contract, the party supplying the goods/doing the work may be able to bring a claim in restitution for a reasonable sum for work done or goods supplied as an alternative to a claim for damages

- They would receive a '***quantum meruit***' → a reasonable sum for work done
- Also takes place where a party has done work for another, before a contract has been formed (but was expecting that a contract will come into existence)

<u>*Case Law Example:*</u>

- ***British Steel Corp v Cleveland Bridge and Engineering Co Ltd [1984]***:
  Whilst no contract had been formed (parties were still in negotiation), the claimants were entitled to recover a reasonable sum for the work they had done

Restitutionary Damages

The traditional purpose of an award of damages is to compensate the claimant for the loss they have suffered as a result of the defendant's breach

Restitutionary damages considers an award of remedies based instead on the gains made by the defendant, at the expense of the claimant

→ The aim is to prevent the unjust enrichment of one party, at the expense of the other.

If the other party has done anything at all in performance of the contract, the advance payment will not be recoverable in restitution (although may be recoverable as part of a damages claim)

An account of profits

An award of profits is a remedy only for exceptional circumstances (realistically, very rarely introduced)

<u>*Case Law Example:*</u>

- ***Attorney-General v Blake [2001]***: Blake was a traitor (worked in secret service for 17 years and then became an agent for the Soviet Union). Sentenced to 42 years' imprisonment but escaped → wrote an autobiography (awarded £150,000 in royalties)

  Even though the Crown had suffered no financial loss as a result of the publication of the book, it should receive the benefit of the profits from its publication

  → Considered an account of profits (crown was awarded the profits Blake made from the breach of contract)

Negotiating Damages

Falls in between compensation for financial loss and an account of profits

Negotiating damages are available where the only loss to the innocent party is loss of opportunity to negotiate a fee for releasing the other party from a contractual restriction

- Negotiating damages are assessed on the basis of a hypothetical negotiation between two willing parties who acted reasonably
- Should not be awarded as an alternative to conventional damages (***Morris-Garner v One Step (Support) Ltd [2018]***)

<u>*Case Law Example:*</u>

Wrotham Park Estate Co Ltd v Parkside Homes Ltd [1974]: established principle of negotiating damages - where the only loss is the opportunity to negotiate a release fee. Awarded a sum of 5% of the developer's profit.

- The damages in Wrotham were to compensate the claimant for the notional loss of the opportunity to bargain → 'the wrongdoer cannot be better off because he did not ask permission'

Guarantees and Indemnities

Guarantees

A contract of guarantee is a contract under which one person (the guarantor), guarantees that if another person (the debtor) does not pay back money owed, then the guarantor will pay the money instead

It is a *secondary obligation to pay*, if the debtor does not pay the money owed

Contracts of guarantee must be 'evidenced in writing' → whilst the contract itself does not need to be written, there must be some written evidence of the transaction.

- This evidence must exist before the creditor seeks to enforce the contract and must be signed by the guarantor

Indemnities

An indemnity creates a *primary obligation* → one party promises to reimburse pound-for-pound the other party, in respect of a particular loss arising under the contract

Does not have to be evidenced in writing

Performance and Discharge of a Contract

Order of Performance:

- The parties may state in their contract when each party must perform their contractual obligations (e.g at which point payment would be due)
- If the parties do not make the order of performance clear in their contract, there are statutory provisions which can assist (e.g. Sale of Goods Act 1979)

The Doctrine of Complete Performance:

The Doctrine of Complete Performance

The doctrine of complete performance → where the contract states that one party has to perform their obligations, *only when* the other party has performed their part of the contract (***Cutter v Powell (1795)***)

E.g. a contractor is only entitled to the price (agreed sum) for work if performance is complete and precise

If an **exception** applies, then some payment can be recovered even though the contractual obligations have not been performed precisely and exactly:

1) Wrongful prevention of performance by the other party

If one party changes their mind in the middle of the contractual obligations → the innocent party should not be prejudiced for the other party changing their mind (***Planche v Colburn***)

The innocent party would be able to recover lost profit, subject to a duty to mitigate loss by taking reasonable steps to look for alternative work

Could also claim a *quantum meruit* for the reasonable amount of work done (although damages is typically better as allows a larger sum to be recovered)

2) Voluntary Acceptance of Partial Performance by the Other Party

For there to be voluntary acceptance of partial performance of the work, the defendant must have an option to take or not to take the benefit of the work done

It would not apply if the party had no option but to accept partial performance

Case Law Example:

- ***Sumpter v Hedges [1898]***: claimant agreed to build 2 houses for the defendant (with an agreed fee payable on completion). The claimant ran out of money and was unable to complete the building works (had performed just over half). The defendant completed the rest of the work himself
    - Claimant sought to recover payment for half the work completed → argued that in completing the work himself, the defendant have voluntarily accepted partial performance
    - Court held that the defendant had no choice but to accept partial performance as he was left with a half completed house on his land.

Where there is voluntary acceptance of partial performance, the person who has done the work can claim a *quantum meruit* from the other party

S 25(1) of the Consumer Rights Act 2015 also states that where a trader delivers to a consumer a quantity of goods, less than the trader contracted to supply, if the consumer decided to accept them, they must pay at the contract rate

3) Substantial Performance

A party who substantially performs their obligations may be able to claim some money for the work → the work must be finished, but considered slightly defective (***H Dakin & Co Ltd v Lee [1916]*** or ***Hoenig v Isaacs [1952]***)

May be useful to compare the contract price with the amount needed to rectify the defects

Case Law Example:

- ***Hoenig v Isaacs***: the cost of remedying the defects was £55 compared to a contract price of £750 (whilst borderline, held as substantial performance as only 1/14th of total price)
- ***Bolton v Mahadeva [1972] 1 WLR 1009, CA***: substantial performance not fulfilled → contract price was £560 and it would cost £174 to remedy (1/3rd of the contract price

Can claim the contract price minus the cost of defect

4) Divisible Obligations:

Where the **obligations are divisible** (e.g. if the parties have agreed payments for a distinct part or stage of the work, **each part or stage is treated like a separate contract**)

Once the distinct part of the contract has been completed, then the party is entitled to be paid for that part

Discharge by Frustration

Frustration

Context

A contract may be frustrated if an **unforeseen event** occurs **after the contract has been formed**, which was **not the fault** of either party and which makes the contract **impossible to perform**, or which makes performance of the contract **radically different.**

- If a contract is frustrated, there is no breach of contract in relation to the frustrated event

- The contract will come to an end automatically *at the time of the frustrating event* and the parties do not have to perform their future obligations
- Matter of law if all the criteria are met (not down to judge discretion)

The Original Common Law Rule

Originally at common law, if a party assumed an absolute obligation in a contract, then if circumstances made performance of the obligation impossible, the *party would still be liable*

- Was considered the responsibility of the party concerned to protect itself by including a suitable provision in the contract (***Paradine v Jane (1647)***

Modifications:

The modern law of frustration is said to date from ***Taylor v Caldwell (1863) 3 B & S 826***:

- Music hall which had been rented set on fire. Neither party to the contract was at fault
- Contract was discharged by frustration: judge thought there was an implied condition in the contract that the parties would be excused if performance became impossible because without the fault of the parties, the music hall perished
- This can also be applied to the continued existence or availability of a person

Construction Theory:

The idea of frustration resting on a term implied between the parties was dismissed in ***Davis Contractors Ltd v Fareham Urban District Council [1956]***:

- 'The meaning of the contract must be taken to be, not what the parties did intend, but that which the parties, as fair, and reasonable men, would presumably have agreed upon if, having such possibility in view, they had made express provision as to their several rights and liabilities in the event of its occurrence'

When does Frustration Occur

1) Unavailability of a specific thing or person vital to the contract

There are 3 factors which determine whether a person not being available leads to frustration:

1) Length of the contract

2) Length of period of absence
3) Does the contract have to be performed by that particular individual or can a substitute do the work?

<u>Case Law Examples:</u>

- ***Morgan v Manser [1948]:*** music artist unable to perform as called up for military service
- ***Condor v Barron Knights [1966]:*** contract frustrated as a drummer suffered a mental breakdown and was told by his doctor that he could not perform.
- ***Taylor v Caldwell (****see above****):*** for case law on unavailability of a specific thing (not a person)

2) Non-occurrence of a Fundamental Event

Where a particular event taking place is essential to the contract and the event is cancelled, this may frustrate the contract

<u>Case Law Examples:</u>

- ***Krell v Henry [1903]***: Defendant rented the claimant's flat for 2 days, as the window's had a view of the coronation procession of Edward VII. The contract contained no express reference to the procession or any other purpose for which the flat was taken. Coronation was cancelled, defendant refused to pay rent
    - Judge thought that the coronation procession and the relative position of the rooms was regarded as both parties as the basis of the contract
    - The rooms had a special qualification which led to their selection

- ***Herne Bay Steamboat Co v Hutton [1903]***: defendant agreed to hire a ship for 2 days to take out a party 'for the purpose of viewing the Naval Review and for a day's cruise round the fleet'. Naval Review was cancelled
    - Held that the cancellation did not discharge the defendant from his obligations as the happening of the royal review was not the foundation of the contract (also the day's cruise relevant)

3) Government Intervention

<u>Case Law Examples:</u>

- ***Metropolitan Water Board v Dick Kerr and Company [1918]***: Kerr entered into a contract with the Metropolitan Water Board to build a reservoir → govt ordered Kerr to stop work so that the men and equipment could be used in the war effort
    - Contract was frustrated by the government intervention → the whole character of the contract could be revolutionised by indefinite delay
    - Such an interruption couldn't have been in the contemplation of the parties at the time the contract was made

4) Delay

Not every case of delay frustrates a contract (usually breach). Factors which are relevant are:

a) Whether the contract provides for what should be the consequences of the delay
b) The likely length of the delay
c) Any time set in the contract for the obligations to be performed
d) If the contract is resumed after the delay, weather it is radically different from the contracts the parties had originally made

<u>*Case Law Examples:*</u>

- ***Tsakiroglou & Co Ltd v Noblee Thorl [1962]***: sellers agreed to ship groundnuts from Port Sudan to Hamburg (assumed via the Suez Canal, but not specified). → closure of the Canal meant that the goods had to be shipped via the Cape of Good Hope
  HoL found that the contract was not frustrated → whilst the contract had become more difficult and expensive for the sellers, it could still be performed and was not radically different
- ***Davis Contractors Ltd v Fareham Urban District Council [1956]***: agreed to build 78 houses within a period of 8 months but experienced shortages of labour and materials → contract took 22 months to complete.
  - HoL found the contract was not frustrated
  - 'It is not hardship or inconvenience or material loss itself which calls the principle of frustration into play. There must also be such a change in the significance of the obligation that the thing undertaken would, if performed, be a different thing from that contracted for'

5) Illegality

The performance of a contract **can become legally impossible** → e.g. as a result of a change in law or outbreak of war (cannot trade with the enemy)

<u>*Case Law Examples:*</u>

- ***Fibrosa Spolka Akcyjna v Fairbairn Lawson Combe Barbour Ltd [1943]***: the respondent country (English) agreed to manufacture machinery for a Polish company → Germany invaded. HoL held that the contract was frustrated

Restrictions on the Doctrine of Frustration

If a restriction applies, the contract will not be frustrated

1) Can't be foreseen

a) Where the parties have made express provision in the contract covering the event which has occurred and explained how any loss caused by the event will be borne by the parties

b) Or, where the court feels that the parties foresaw or should have foreseen the event (although no express provision)

Express Provision (force majeure):

A **'force majeure'** clause may be inserted to cover events outside the control of the parties (except in the event of the contract becoming illegal).

Must be worded carefully to cover all the events the parties intended

Metropolitan Water Board v Dick Kerr: the court decided that the delay clause in the contract did not actually cover the event which had occurred

If related to a business-to-business interaction, must be subject to ***s 3 of the UCTA*** and the reasonableness test

No Express Provision (but foreseen):

There is a conflict of opinion as to whether there can still be frustration if the event is foreseen

Davis Contractors v Fareham UDC: if the event was foreseen the contract would not be frustrated

The Eugenia [1964]: obiter comment that the contract could still be frustrated even if the contract was foreseen (the only essential thing was that the parties should not have made provision for the event in the contract)

Event beyond the control of the parties

The event which makes the contract impossible or radically different must be **beyond the control of the parties**

- A party whose own act or election has given rise to the frustrating event *cannot* rely on the doctrine of frustration → frustration is 'self-induced'
    - ***Maritime Fish Ltd v Ocean Trawlers Ltd [1935]***
    - ***J Lauritzen AC v Wijsmuller BV, The Super Servant Two [1990] 1 Lloyd's Rep 1, CA:*** any act by a party which contributes to the event will prevent the contract from being frustrated
- The burden of proving fault is on the party alleging it (***Joseph Constantine Steamship Line Ltd v Imperial Smelting Corporation Ltd [1942]***

Lease of Land

Previously it was thought that frustration could not apply to a lease of land, as the lease created an interest in the land and this interest would endure, even if you couldn't use the land for the intended purpose, (separate to a licence to occupy the premises)

An interest in land was not a perishable commodity like goods

National Carriers Ltd v Panalpina (Northern) Ltd [1981]: appellants leased a warehouse from the respondents for a term of 10 years → local council closed the street which had access to the warehouse (envisaged to be opened 2 years later) → could not use the warehouse

- Lease was not frustrated as was not a sufficiently grave circumstance → still had another further 3 years of the lease remaining after access was re-established
    - HoL said that the doctrine of frustration was **capable of applying to a lease of land if a frustrating event occurred during the currency of the term**
    - Will take into account the length of the lease and how long the party will be deprived of the use of the property

Effect of Frustration at Common Law

1. If a contract is frustrated, it **comes to an end automatically** at the time of the frustrating event
2. Both parties are **released from all future obligations**
3. Neither party will be in breach of contract in respect to the frustrating event

Under the original common law, if one party had paid money to the other before the frustrating event, it could not be recovered. If any money was due and payable before the event, it still had to be paid

- ***Krell v Henry***: cancelled coronation → could not recover the £25 deposit but did not have to pay the outstanding £50 (obligation to pay after the frustrating event)
- ***Chandler v Webster [1904]***

→ This position produced unfair outcomes as the parties had to pay money but received nothing in return (severely prejudiced by an event outside their control)

↓

Fibrosa Spolka Akcyjna v Fairbairn Lawson Combe Barbour Ltd [1943]

- Only if there had been a **total failure of consideration**, then the money already paid could be recovered and money due and payable before the event didn't have to be paid
    - BUT: did not address the problem of a party who had incurred expenses carrying out their contractual obligations before frustration occurred

The Law Reform (Frustrated Contracts) Acts 1943

The act dealt with:

a) Money paid and or payable by a party before a frustrating event

b) Expenses incurred by the payee
c) Valuable benefits obtained by either party

Overrides decision in *Fibrosa* → **there does not have to be a total failure of consideration**

Section 1(2):

Money ***already*** paid before the frustrating event can be ***recovered***

Money ***payable*** before the frustrating event ***ceases*** to be payable

The court may allow the payee to ***retain or recover expenses*** incurred in performing the contract before frustration → only ***up to*** the amount of money which was paid **and or** payable to them ***before*** the frustrating event (if the court considers it just to do so)

- The upper limit will either be the sum of expenses spent, or the total of what was paid and or payable before the frustrating event (whatever is lower)
    - E.g. if expenses were £70, and the amount paid and or payable was £100, total amount to be recovered would be £70
    - If expenses were £100 and total amount paid and or payable was £70, total amount to be recovered would be £70
- Burden of proof is on the payee to show that it is just in all the circumstances to allow them to retain or recover money for the expenses they have incurred
- As it is discretionary, not entirely certain for the parties

Case Law Example:

Gamerco SA v ICM/Fair Warning (Agency) Ltd [1995]

- The defendant payee had incurred expenses of $50,000 in performing the contract before the frustrating event.
- The judge did not make an award for expenses under ***s 1(2)*** as the payer's expenses were considerably higher than the payee's

The Common Law rule still governs the amount that was meant to be paid after the frustrating event, not Law Reform

Section 1(3):

- If one party has received a ***valuable benefit*** before the frustrating event because of something done by the other party in performance of the contract, then the court may order the recipient to pay such sum as the court considers just, but not exceeding the amount of the benefit
    a) All the circumstances must be taken into account (including any expenses the party who received the benefit may have incurred)
    b) The court is *not limited* to the amount paid or payable before the frustrating event

Case Law Example:

BP Exploration Co (Libya) Ltd v Hunt [1979]

Two stages for an award under ***s 1(3):***

a) The benefit has to be identified and valued → forms the upper limit of the award
    - Any expenses incurred by the party obtaining the benefit must be deducted from the value of the benefit

b) The court has to assess the just sum (won't exceed the value of the benefit)
  - May take into account the consideration in the contract as evidence of the appropriate level of remuneration

- The benefit under ***s 1(3)*** is the end product of what the claimant has provided, not the value of the work that has been done

Will not include any value gained *as a result* of work done by the payer

E.g. claimants hire a machine to recover artefacts, machine is then broken by a hurricane so the project could not be finished, but some of the artefacts were recovered. Only the use of the machine for a few days is the valuable benefit (the artefacts are not)

Section 1(5):
- The court will not take into account insurance payments unless there was an express term of the contract imposing an obligation to insure

Section 2:

Allows the parties to put a clause in the contract excluding the Act and making their own provisions about the effects of frustration on the contract

Weakness of the Legislation

Section 1(2):
- The amount recoverable in expenses is limited to the total of the sums paid and payable before the event → if no money was paid, no remuneration or if the expense was large
- Inconsistencies in how the act is exercised as no real guidance

Section 1(3):

Produces undesirable results where the work carried out is completely destroyed by the frustrating event → 0 remuneration

False Preliminary Statements and Mistake

False Preliminary Statements

A statement made during contractual negotiations may be:

Mere puff → claims which are extravagant in an obvious way / an advertising gimmick. No right of action.

An express term → a term part of the contract.

A representation → a statement made by one party to the contract, which may have induced the other party to enter into the contract but does not form part of it.

In most commercial contracts, there will be a clause purporting to **exclude liability for false preliminary statements**

- Aims to stop a sales representative binding the seller to any preliminary statement which they might make in trying to promote a sale
- Will have to consider whether the clause is reasonable and valid

Where there is no exclusion clause, the focus is on the classification of the false preliminary statements to determine the remedies available to the innocent party

Terms vs Representations

Must recognise whether a false preliminary statement is a **term** or only a **representation**

- Will first look at the common intention of the parties when they entered the contract
  → *Did they intend the particular statement to be a contractual term, or just a representation*

Where their intentions are not clear, the court will use the below guidelines:

- The court applies an objective test to decide whether a statement is a term of the contract → looks at what an *intelligent bystander* would reasonably infer

Knowledge of the parties

Likely to be considered a term, where the party states a fact which *is or should be* within their own knowledge and of which the other party is ignorant (typical where one party has greater knowledge / skill on the topic)

- Or where a party makes a statement about something which is or should be under their own control (***Birch v Paramount Estates Ltd (1956)***)

<u>*Case Law Example:*</u>

- ***Oscar Chess Ltd v Williams [1957]***: defendant sold a second-hand car to the claimant (a motor dealer) for £290 (higher price as first registered in 1948)
  - Claimant then discovered from the manufacturer that the car was a 1939 model (would have only had to pay £175)
  - Action failed → defendant had made an innocent misrepresentation
    - The claimant knew that the defendant had no personal knowledge of when the car was manufactured
- ***Dick Bentley v Harold Smith Motors***: car dealer sold a car to a private individual → had told the claimant that the car had only done £20,000 miles (false)
  - Statement held to be a term of the contract as it had been made by a car dealer (who was *in a position to know* or find out the information)

Oral → Written

More likely to be a term, where a preliminary oral statement is repeated in a written doc

- Although not a 100% rule → in ***Birch v Paramount Estates Ltd*** the seller's oral promise was not repeated in the written contract but was still considered a term

Statement is important

More likely to be a term, where the recipient of the statement makes it clear that the statement is of vital importance

- ***Bannerman v White (1861)***: the buyer of hops asked the seller if the plants had been treated with sulphur (would not be prepared to buy if they had) → assurance was held to be a term of the contract

Verification

More likely to be a representation, if the maker asks the other party to verify it

Where the seller tells the buyer not to bother with a survey, points to the statement about the quality of goods being a term (***Schawel v Reade [1913]***)

Case Law Example:

- ***Ecay v Godfrey (1947)***: seller of a boat asked the buyer if they were going to have it surveyed. This question indicated that the seller did not intend his previous statement about the condition of the boat to be a term

Lapse of Time:

Where there is a lapse of time between the statement and the contract, the longer the lapse, the more likely it is that the statement is just a representation (***Routledge v McKay***)

- The court will consider all relevant factors. If one factor points to the statement being a term of the contract and another factor points to it being only a representation, the court will have to decide how much weight to attach to each.

Remedies?

→ Where a false preliminary statement is considered an **express term** of the contract, will then consider **remedies for breach**

→ Where a false preliminary statement is a misdescription of goods, it may amount to breach of the statutory implied condition that goods sold by description should match that description (then must consider damages / rejection / or remedies)

→ If the representation amounts to a **misrepresentation**, you would then look at the **remedies** available for a misrepresentation

Misrepresentation

Defining a Misrepresentation

Misrepresentation = a false statement of fact, made by one contracting party to the other, before the contract was made, and which was one of the factors which induced the other party to enter into the contract

The party who alleges that a misrepresentation has occurred bears the burden of proving misrepresentation

1) False statement

There must be a false statement (can be oral, in writing or by conduct)

<u>*Case Law Example:*</u>

Spice Girls v Aprilia World Service BV [2000]: court held that by participating in the filming of a TV commercial, the group represented that they did not know or have reasonable ground to believe that any members intended to leave (which was untrue)

- Participation amounted to a misrepresentation by conduct

Smith v Land and House Property Corporation (1884): claimant wanted to buy a house with a tenant living in part of it. The seller (defendant) told the claimant that the tenant is a 'most desirable' tenant. After buying the property, the claimant found that the tenant had been in arrears with rent and the seller was aware of this

'A statement of opinion by a person who is in the best position to know the true position would often be a statement of fact because there is an implicit assertion that the statement maker knows of facts that justify the statement'

Silence is not a misrepresentation:

Silence does not normally constitute a misrepresentation (***Hamilton and Others v Allied Domecq plc [2007]***

Except where there is an obligation to disclose facts:

Where there is a fiduciary relationship between the parties

Where the contract is one of the utmost good faith

Where there has been a half truth → misrepresentation by what is left unsaid (***Curtis v Chemical Cleaning and Dyeing [1951]***)

Where a statement of fact is true when the contract was formed. But a change in circumstances (before the contract was finalised) makes the statement untrue. Failure to disclose the change in circumstances may amount to a misrepresentation (***With v O'Flanagan [1936]***)

2) Which is a fact (not opinion or intention)

To amount to a misrepresentation, the statement **must be one of fact and not opinion**

- Where an opinion is not genuine, or there are no reasonable grounds for the maker to believe it is true, there may be an implied false statement of fact which may amount to a misrepresentation if other elements are satisfied
  - Also the case if the statement is made by a person who is in the best position to know the true facts

  <u>*Case Law Example:*</u>

  Bisset v Wilkinson [1927]: seller of a farm was asked about the number of sheep the farm could sustain. Farm had never had sheep so seller used their personal judgement (held as an opinion, not a fact as both parties aware of the seller's lack of knowledge)

A statement of intention will not amount to a misrepresentation, *unless* it can be shown that the intention was never held

<u>*Case Law Example:*</u>

Edgington v Fitzmaurice (1885): director of a company said the purpose of borrowing money was to expand the company's business (was actually to pay their debts) → had made a misrepresentation as never intended to use money in that way

- Had made a false statement about the state of their minds

3) Made between parties to a contract

If the maker of the statement is not the other contracting party, there *cannot* be a claim for misrepresentation

4) The statement induced the party to enter the contract

The statement does not have to be the only reason why a party enters a contract, just that it did encourage them to do so (***Edgington v Fitzmaurice)***

Can partly rely on an expert and the seller (seller still considered to induce)

<u>*Case Law Example:*</u>

- ***Attwood v Small (1938)***: claimant wants to buy a cottage, asks the seller if they think there is anything wrong with the drains → seller says they think there isn't, but can't say for certain
    - Claimant then gets an expert to inspect the drains (also say there are no problems)
    - Claimant then buys the property but discovers drains are defective
    - The seller did not misrepresent the facts as the claimant did not rely on the seller's statement, but the experts

Don't need to verify facts

A person does not lose the right to claim that a misrepresentation had been made, just because they are given the opportunity to discover the truth but fail to do so (e.g through looking at a company's accounts) (***Redgrave v Hurd (1881)***.

Except where the true position was set out in the contract signed by the claimant

- ***Peekay Intermark Ltd v Australia and New Zealand Banking Group Ltd [2006] 2 Lloyd's Rep 511***: an experienced businessperson had an investment described by a bank in general terms. Later sent a contract which set out the full terms and conditions.
    - Claimant only looked at the contract briefly before signing, assuming the terms were in line with what he had been told previously (not the case)
    - Court held the bank had not misrepresented the written contract → claimant was an experienced businessperson

Types of Misrepresentation

Fraudulent Misrepresentation:

Misrep is fraudulent if it is made:

a) With knowledge that it is false; or
b) Without belief in its truth; or
c) Recklessly, not caring whether it is true or false

→ Need proof of fraud

Damages for Fraudulent Misrep:

If the innocent party can prove that **misrepresentation was made fraudulently**, can sue for **damages in tort of deceit**

- **Fraudulent misrepresentation** = where a false representation was made knowingly or without belief in its truth, or recklessly, careless whether it be true or false (***Derry v Peek (1889)***
- Onus on the party wishing to allege fraud to prove it → can be hard to prove when one person's word against another
- Damages aim to put the innocent party in the position they would have been in if the misrepresentation had not been made
    - I.e. the position of the claimant if they had never heard that misrepresentation → with goods, if the claimant had not been misrepresented about the state of a good, may not have bought it (so damages likely to be price paid - value now)
    - The usual tort rule of reasonable foreseeability does not apply (claimant can recover for all loss directly resulting from the defendant's misrepresentation)

→ Don't need to prove remoteness

<u>*Case Law Example:*</u>

East v Maurer [1991]: defendant was an experienced hairdresser who ran 2 salons in neighbouring areas → claimant bought one of them after defendant falsely represented that he did not intend to work at the other salon

- Action brought for damages in the tort of deceit
- Court of Appeal held that damages must be calculated so as to compensate the claimant for the profit they might have made had the misrepresentation not been made
    - Calculated according to what profit the claimant might have made if they had bought another hairdressing business for a similar sum
- If it was assessed instead on contract principles, aim would be to put the claimant in the position they would have been if the statements were true (i.e. the profits made if the defendant had not worked at another salon)

Negligent Misrepresentation:

Negligent Misrepresentation = statements that were made carelessly

- Where the belief in the truth of the statement was honestly held, but not on reasonable grounds
- Reversal of normal burden of proof → requires the statement maker to prove that the statement was honest and reasonable

Damages for Negligent Misrep:

Seeking damages under ***s2(1) of the Misrepresentation Act*** just requires the claimant to show that there was a misrepresentation that caused loss

- Awarded in accordance with tort principles → put the innocent party in the position they would have been if the misrepresentation had not been made
- Damages under ***s2(1)*** should be awarded in the same way as damages for fraudulent misrepresentation in the tort of deceit (***Royscot Trust Ltd v Rogerson [1991]***

- Can only be used by a party to a contract against the other contracting party
- Burden of proof is on the party making the misrepresentation
    - Once the claimant establishes that a misrepresentation has been made, the defendant will be liable to pay damages *unless the defendant* proves that they had reasonable grounds to believe and honestly did believe that the facts were true
        - → An honest belief that the statement is true is not sufficient to avoid liability under **s 2(1)** → belief must also be *reasonable*

<u>*Case Law Example:*</u>

- ○ ***Howard Marine & Dredging v Ogden [1978]***: owner of a barge (defendant), told a potential charterer that its capacity was around 1,600 tonnes (based on their recollection of the entry in the Lloyd's Register)
    - Capacity was much less → charterers sought damages under ***s2(1)***
    - Defendant had failed to prove that it had had reasonable grounds to believe in the truth of the statement (hadn't looked at the ship's documents which stated the correct capacity). Looking at Lloyd's Register was not enough to give reasonable grounds for believing it to be true

Innocent Misrepresentation:

- Where the statement maker can establish that they had reasonable grounds to believe that the statement was true
- No damages available (although may still be able to rescind)

Remedy - Rescission

A misrepresentation makes the contract voidable → the contract is valid until the innocent party rescinds it (set aside / avoided)

- The innocent party could choose to affirm the contract
- Available for both fraudulent and non-fraudulent misrepresentation

How to rescind a contract

In order to rescind the contract, the innocent party must notify the other party so that they are aware

- Where a party has disappeared, could report the matter to the police or governing association (***Car and Universal Finance Co Ltd v Caldwell [1964]***)
- A claimant can also apply to court for a formal order of recission

Bars to rescission

Rescission is an equitable remedy and the right to rescind will be lost in certain situations (a bar to rescission):

1) If an innocent purchaser acquires an interest in the property before the contract is rescinded

An **innocent purchaser** who acquires an interest in the property before the contract is rescinded is a bar to rescission

- In the case of ***Car and Universal Finance Co Ltd v Caldwell [1964],*** had the facts been different and the car was sold to an innocent third party before the contract was rescinded, there would have been a bar to rescission

2) Affirmation

On discovery of misrepresentation, if the innocent party **elects to affirm** the contract, they cannot then change their mind

- Affirmation can be express or implied (where the innocent party behaves in such a way as to lead the other party to believe that they are continuing with the contract)

3) Undue Delay

A **significant lapse of time** can act as a bar on rescission:

- The court does not necessarily look at when the misrepresentation was actually discovered, but at when it should have been discovered

  Except for cases of fraudulent misrepresentation → time runs from when the misrepresentation was discovered)

Leaf v International Galleries [1950]

- Claimant bought a painting which had been described as an original John Constable. 5 years later, discovered it was not. Tried to rescind the contract but failed due to lapse of time
- Court found that the claimant had the chance to examine the picture within a few days of purchase to discover the misrepresentation

4) Where it is impossible for a party substantially to restore goods of property to the other

Where **restoration** of property is impossible, the rescission would be barred

Erlanger v New Sombrero Phosphate Co (1878):

- A contract for the purchase of a mine was rescinded, even though the mine had been worked and so not in the same state as when it was purchased.
  - Court ordered the purchaser to give an allowance to the seller for the profit they had made using it and for its deterioration

A contract for the sale of a business is rarely rescinded:

Crystal Palace FC (2000) Ltd v Iain Dowie [2007]

- Claimant entered into a compromise agreement with Dowie (former manager), releasing him from his employment contact with the club.
  - Defendant had been required to pay the club £1m compensation if he left prematurely to work for another club (released from this obligation)
  - Shortly after entering this agreement, the defendant was appointed manager of another club
  - Court held that whilst Dowie had deceived Crystal Palace into entering the compromise agreement, barred from rescission
- If the compromise agreement had been rescinded, would have revived the defendant's employment contract with the claimant → can't be employed by 2 different clubs

The effects of rescission

The aim of rescission is to **restore** both parties as far as possible to their **pre-contract positions**

- When a contract is rescinded, each party should return to the other money or property transferred under the contract
- Neither party needs to perform future obligations

Rescission → indemnity

An indemnity creates a primary obligation → one party promises to reimburse pound-for-pound the other party, in respect of a particular loss arising under the contract

If a contract is rescinded, the *innocent party* can claim an indemnity for expenses necessarily incurred as a result of entering into the contract

An indemnity is ***only likely*** **to be claimed** in a situation **where the claimant has no right to damages** (previously, damages could only be claimed for fraudulent misrepresentations)

<u>*Case Law Example:*</u>

Whittington v Seale-Hayne (1900): claimant took a lease of premises belonging to the defendant which included a clause that the tenant would do certain repairs and pay rent and rates. Claimant planned to use the premises to breed chickens. Defendant had told the claimant that the premises were in a good sanitary condition (not the case) → chickens died.

- Claimant wanted to rescind the contract and ask for an indemnity
- Court decided that the claimant could receive an indemnity for the rent, for the repairs and for the rates paid
- Could not receive an indemnity for the cost of the chickens, the loss of profit on the chickens, the vets bill or medical expenses (the lease did not say the farm had to be used to breed chickens)

Damages in lieu of rescission

The court can award damages instead of rescission, only if the misrepresentation is innocent (***S 2(2) of the Misrepresentation Act 1967)***

This is at the *discretion of the court* (takes into account the nature of the misrepresentation, the loss that would be caused if the contract was upheld and the loss that the rescission would cause to the other party)

Will *not apply* if one of the bars to rescission applies

Usually only where the false statement was about a *minor matter* (would be unjust to allow the other party to rescind the contract)

Mistake

The **doctrine of mistake** operates only in exceptional circumstances where one party (or both), can establish that the contract was entered into under a mistake which was *so fundamental*, as to effectively negate agreement and therefore the existence of a contract

- The mistake must have preceded the contract and have induced it

There are three types of mistakes:

a) **Common mistake** → where both parties have made the same fundamental mistake
b) **Cross-purpose mistake** → where the parties are at cross-purposes about a crucial aspect of the contract
c) **Unilateral mistake** → where only one party is mistaken

⟶ Damages are not available for mistaken identity, the only remedy is that the contract can be voided

Common Mistake

Where both parties have made the same fundamental mistake

Also known as 'identical mistake' or 'shared mistake'

There are strict limitations on the operation of common mistake (difficult to establish):

a) It will not operate if one party is at fault

b) The contract must not make express provision on the matter
c) The mistake must be fundamental (render the performance of the contract impossible / radically different from anticipation)

Case Law Example:

- ***Bell v Lever Bros [1932]***: B and A (defendants) entered into contracts with Lever Bros (claimants) to terminate their service contracts, in return for substantial compensation. Then discovered that they had breached their service contracts and so would have been dismissed without compensation (they had honestly forgotten this fact so not a false representation)
    - Lever Bros argued settlement agreements were void for mistake as both parties had wrongly thought the service contracts were valid
    - HoL held that the mistake was not fundamental enough to render the settlement agreements void (did not make performance radically different)

Cross-purpose Mistake

Where it is impossible to resolve the ambiguity over what was agreed in a contract

- The only possible conclusion is that there was no contract

Case Law Example:

Raffles v Wickelhaus (1864): contract to sell cotton from the ship, Peerless, sailing from Bombay. There were 2 ships (sailing in Oct and Dec). Mistaken ambiguity about which ship the cotton was meant to be delivered on → no way to resolve this ambiguity

Unilateral Mistake

Often relied on where there has been a mistake as to the identity of the other contracting party

- Only a genuine mistake of this nature - where the identity of the other party is of vital importance - will render the contract void.
- Mistaken identity rarely succeeds where the deal was struck in a face-to-face situation

Case Law Example:

Cundy v Lindsay (1878): where a bona fide purchaser has already acquired the goods, there are 2 innocent parties (mistaken party and the innocent purchaser) → only one is entitled to the goods, other must sue the rogue for damages

Lewis v Averay [1972]: plaintiff advertised their car for sale. Sold to a man claiming to be a well-known actor (signed cheque with his name and produced an identity form).

The man then sold the car to an innocent purchaser, despite his cheque then being dishonoured

Plaintiff had to try establish mistake (as rescission for misrepresentation was barred). BUT court, held that the plaintiff was more concerned about the man's creditworthiness, compared to his identity (mistake to an attribute)

Mistake v Misrepresentation

Following guidelines for establishing if the contract is voidable (misrepresentation) or void (mistake)

a) If the parties are dealing face-to-face (unlikely to be a mistake)

b) Where dealings are conducted exclusively in writing, the written agreement must be construed to determine with whom the innocent party intended to contract (void for mistake if it was someone other than the rogue)

c) The nature of the transaction may indicate that it is vital for the rogue to possess a particular attribute (e.g. a contract for a portrait) → void

d) If the person / entity who the rogue is pretending to be actually exists and is known to the mistaken party → void

Illegal Contracts

Another argument for saying a contract is void is that it is illegal (either at the time of formation or the way they have been performed)

A contract is illegal where its formation, purpose or performance involves the commission of a legal wrong

- Where the illegal act is purely incidental to performance of the contract, unlikely to affect its validity (e.g. a driver delivering goods is caught speeding) (***St John Shipping Corp v Joseph Rank Ltd [1957]***)

The contract is void → cannot recover benefits conferred in its performance

Where a contract is performed illegally, and both parties were aware that performance was illegal, neither party can enforce the contract (***Ashmore, Benson, Pease & Co Ltd v AV Dawson Ltd [1973]***)

- Where one party didn't know of the illegal performance of the contract by the other party, the innocent party may be able to enforce it

Contracts Illegal at Common Law

The court will refuse to enforce some contracts at common law on the basis that they are contrary to **public policy or morality**

- Common form clauses which are prima facie void as being contrary to public policy are covenants in restraint to trade → individuals and businesses should be able to work and operate to generate income for themselves
- Restraints of trade may be enforceable if:

  There is a legitimate business interest to protect and,

  The restraint is reasonable in terms of geographical area, duration and scope of the prohibited activities

Duress and Undue Influence

A party who has been forced into a contract by threats or undue pressure should not necessarily be bound by it

The essence of agreement is that the parties freely consent to the agreed terms

Duress

Duress may take the form of **violence or illegitimate threats or pressure which coerce** a party into **entering or varying a contract**

The burden of proving duress is on the party who alleges it

Definition

Physical threats

Duress does not need to be the only reason why a person entered into a contract

Barton v Armstrong [1975]

- Armstrong threatened to kill Barton if Bardon did not buy his shares in the company
- Barton agreed (but not solely because of the threats) → evidence that he thought it was a satisfactory business arrangement
- *Still* did not have to be bound by the agreement

Economic Duress

To amount to economic duress, the threat must be an improper or illegitimate threat

- Legitimate commercial pressure (e.g. a threat to take business elsewhere or sell to a competitor) does not count as economic duress

Case Law Example:

Atlas Express v Kafco [1989]: Atlas (claimants) were delivery drivers. Kafco (defendants) were manufacturers. Atlas agreed to deliver Kafco's cartoons to Woolworth stores for £1.10 per carton. Atlas thought Kafco would provide more cartoons for them to deliver (200 instead of the 400 which they thought (although hadn't been specified in the contract))

- Atlas refused to make any more deliveries unless Kafco agreed to pay more money

- Kafco were a small business → hard to find another company to deliver the goods (risked breaching contract with Woolworths) → agreed to pay extra amount but later refused (sued by Atlas)
- Court found that there was economic duress → Kafco only agreed to pay extra money as a result of illegitimate pressure (*had no practical choice but to concede*)
- Also no consideration for the promise of extra money (still delivering same amount of goods) → performing an existing contractual duty and had been obtained by duress so the principle in ***Williams v Roffey*** does not hold

Defining Economic Duress:

Carillion Construction Ltd v Felix (UK) Ltd [2001]:

The ingredients of actionable duress are that there must be:

Pressure

Whose practical effect is that there is compulsion on, or a lack of practical choice, for the victim (no alternatives)

Which is illegitimate, and

Which is a significant cause inducing the claimant to enter into the contract

Factors taken into account for illegitimate pressure:

Carillion Construction Ltd v Felix (UK) Ltd [2001]:

Factors taken into account:

- Whether there has been an actual or a threatened breach of contract
- Whether the person allegedly exerting the pressure has acted in good or bad faith
- Whether the victim had any realistic practical alternative but to submit to the pressure
- Whether the victim protested at the time
- Whether the victim affirmed and sought to rely on the contract

Illegitimate Pressure

Illegitimate pressure includes unlawful threats or a threat to break a contract

Effects and Remedy

Duress makes an original or renegotiated contract voidable

- The ***only*** remedy for duress is rescission
- If the contract is to be rescinded, *normal* rules and bars apply
- Where there was an original good contract and a variation in it was by duress, only the later variation will be rescinded (not the whole contract)

Case Law Example:

North Ocean Shipping v Hyundai Construction Co (The Atlantic Baron) [1979]

Shipbuilders demanded more money for construction of a ship and threatened to stop work unless it was paid. Claimants agreed and paid (had a future contract which required ship to be built)

8 months later the claimants asked for repayment of extra money due to duress

Whilst court accepted there was economic duress, refused to rescind the variation → effectively barred due to affirmation and delay

Payment amounted to affirmation (when it was paid, no longer under threat / pressure)

Delay → leaving it for 8 months

Adam Opel GmbH v Mitras Automotive Ltd:

- Mitras was the sole supplier of a particular type of van bumper mounts for Opel
- Opel no longer needed the van bumper → notice to terminate contract in 6 months
- Mitras then asked for an increased price to be paid during notice period (threatened to suspend supplies if not agreed)
- Opel paid but then sought repayment → argued it was unenforceable due to duress and no consideration
- Contract was voidable

  Conflicting interpretation on whether the contract is void or voidable

  In Williams v Roffey, was held that where one of the five conditions are not met (including duress), the contract is void

  In this case, held that duress only makes the contract *voidable*

Where a business makes the payment *whilst still under duress*, payment won't amount to an affirmation

Undue Influence

Undue influence = influence which goes beyond what is regarded as acceptable (not threats or violence)

- Undue influence also makes a contract voidable
  - Only remedy is rescission
- Often look at relationships that are unequal and then to consider whether the transaction resulted from the **dominant person abusing that relationship**
- Will be presumed where there is a fiduciary relationship between the parties and a transaction which calls for explanation

  Helps innocent parties as can otherwise be difficult to prove (what goes on behind closed doors)
- Only remedy is rescission → unable to obtain damages

Actual Undue Influence

The claimant must prove that the defendant used undue influence

- ***Daniel v Drew [2005]***: Drew was an elderly lady who hated confrontation → afraid of her nephew and the prospect of going to court
  - Felt unable to refuse signing a contract as otherwise would face court action

Presumed Undue Influence

There must be (*Royal Bank of Scotland v Etridge (No 2) [2001]*):

a) A relationship of trust and confidence; and
b) The transaction must be one that calls for an explanation

Relationship of Trust and Confidence

Certain relationships, it is **irrebuttably presumed that one party places trust and confidence in the other**, e.g:

- Solicitor and client
- Doctor and patient
- Parent and child (under 18)
- Religious advisers and followers

Where it is **not presumed, innocent party must prove it** (e.g. husband and wife)

<u>*Case Law Example:*</u>

Tate v Williamson (1866): defendant was a financial adviser to an undergraduate, who was pressed by creditors. Recommended the sale of the estate and offered to buy it for £7,000 (didn't disclose that worth double)

Held that the defendant had wrongfully exploited the commanding position in which the defendant stood

O'Sullivan v Management Agency Ltd [1985]: between a young unknown singer and his manager

Transaction needs an explanation

The transaction must call for an explanation

I.e it is *not* readily explicable by the relationship between the parties

Position of Third Parties

The original view was that a commercial lender would *not* be affected by the undue influence of a third party debtor *unless* the debtor had been acting as agent for the lender in obtaining security for the loan

***Barclays Bank v O'Brien [1994]* → introduced the idea of notice**

If the creditor had **actual or constructive notice** of the **debtor's impropriety**, it would be tainted with it, and any security contract obtained *as a result* would be **voidable**

Proving Constructive Notice:

Constructive notice = where the creditor ought to have been put on inquiry of the risk of undue influence by the debtor and it did not take reasonable steps to ensure that the surety was aware of the implications of what they were signing

Is the lender on enquiry?

The bank should be regarded as put on inquiry in every case where:

- The relationship between a surety and debtor is non-commercial and
- The loan is not for their joint benefit
  - If money is advanced to a husband and wife jointly, the bank is not put on inquiry, *unless* the bank is aware the loan is being made for the husband's purposes alone (***Royal Bank of Scotland v Etridge)***

Reasonable Steps

Where a bank if on enquiry, they must **take reasonable steps to satisfy itself that the practical implications of the transaction had been brought to the innocent party:**

Reasonable steps include (*Royal Bank of Scotland v Etridge (No 2) [2001]*:

a) Insisting that the wife attend a private meeting with a representative of the bank and:
   i) Told the extent of liability as surety
   ii) Warned of the risk the wife is running
   iii) Urged to take independent legal advice

Where the contract is so disadvantageous (not a familial relationship), must insist that the surety take independent legal advice (can't accept proposed security otherwise) (***Credit Lyonnais Bank Nederland NV v Burch)***

Case Law Examples:

CIBC Mortgages plc v Pitt [1993]:

- Wife able to prove actual undue influence by the husband
- Husband wanted to raise a second mortgage on their home in order to finance share dealings → wife worn down by husband's persistence and signed the mortgage application
- Nothing to alert to the lender about the risk of impropriety → no actual or constructive notice → can't set the transaction aside
- Distinguished a joint advance from a situation where a wife stands as a surety for the husband's debts
    - Standing as a surety there is increased risk of undue influence

Royal Bank of Scotland v Etridge (No 2) [2001]:

- Wife argued that the bank had constructive notice of the husband's undue influence and so shouldn't get possession of the house
- Failed as the wife's solicitor had advised about the content and effect of the charge → bank was entitled to rely on the solicitor's confirmation (reasonable to not take further steps)
- If a wife acts as surety for the husband's debts, then the bank is put on inquiry
- If money is advanced to a husband and wife jointly, the bank is not put on inquiry, *unless* the bank is aware the loan is being made for the husband's purposes alone
- Where a bank is put on inquiry, it should take reasonable steps to satisfy itself that the innocent party has been informed, in a meaningful way, of the practical implications of the proposed transaction. **Reasonable steps include:**

b) Insisting that the wife attend a private meeting with a representative of the bank and:
   i) Told the extent of liability as surety
   ii) Warned of the risk the wife is running
   iii) Urged to take independent legal advice

Credit Lyonnais Bank Nederland NV v Burch [1997]:

- Involved a relationship between an employer (owner of the business) and a junior employee
- The employee remortgaged their flat to secure the unlimited liabilities of the employer's business (although had no financial interest)
- Employee told by the bank of the effects of the agreement → confirmed that she was aware of this
- Pleaded undue influence when the business failed and the bank tried to enforce the agreement against the employee
- Court made a presumption of undue influence → the bank had not done enough to satisfy itself that the employee's consent was freely given (contract was so disadvantageous required significant advice)
    - Had to insist that the surety take independent legal advice and if they didn't, not accept the proposed security
    - Relates more to the relationship between the surety and the debtor → here was so obviously disadvantageous as a employee to employer (where it is a familial relationship, may be less so unless the security is extortionate)

Doctrine of Privity of Contract:

- Basis of the doctrine is that only parties to the contract can acquire rights and be subject to liabilities under it
- ***Contracts (Rights of Third Parties) Act 1999*** came into force → allows a third party to enforce a contract term if:
    1) The contract expressly provides that they may, or
    2) The term purports to confer a benefit on them (unless it appears that the parties did not intend the term to be enforceable by the third party) → e.g. if A paid B to fix C's car (C would have a direct contractual claim as the contract was expressly entered into for her benefit)

Capacity

- Capacity = the legal power to make a contract
- Minors and people with a mental incapacity have limited capacity to enter into contracts

Minors

- The basic common law principle is that minors are not bound by contracts they have entered into. The other party is bound and can be sued, but not the minor

Except:

Contract for Necessaries

- A contract for 'necessaries' binds minors
- Necessaries = goods 'suitable to the condition in life of the minor and to his actual requirements at the time of sale and delivery'
- What is necessary for a particular minor will depend to an extent on their social status and their actual requirements at the time of purchase

Contract of Services (beneficial)

A contract of service, which are *on the whole* beneficial to the minor, tends to bind them

- E.g. contracts of employment under which a minor gains training and experience (e.g. an apprenticeship) as long as, on balance, the contract is more favourable than not to the minor

  <u>*Case Law Example:*</u>

- *Proform Sports Management Ltd v Proactive Sports Management [2006] (aka the 'Wayne Rooney case'):* Rooney, aged 15, played for Everton FC. He then entered into a 2 year contract with Proform (agent). Terminated his contract before the 2 year mark
  - Court held that he was entitled to do so as the contract with Proform was not a contract for necessaries

Mental Incapacity:

- Either those suffering from mental impairment or those who are drunk when the contract is made
- Contracts with either person is generally valid unless, at the time that the contract was made, the person was incapable of understanding the nature of the transaction and the other party knew that to be the case
- Results in the contract being **'voidable'** → it remains binding unless the person suffering from the mental impairment / inebriation rescinds it

Corporations:

Corporation = 2 or more people forming an association for the purpose of some concerted enterprise
- An association becomes a corporation when it has been incorporated by law

- A corporation is treated by the law as having a separate legal identity from the person, or persons, who constitute it

Three main types:

Registered companies
- Most corporations are registered under the Companies Act 2006
- An act undertaken by the company with an outsider cannot be challenged if it is beyond the powers granted in the company's constitution
  - Both the company and the other party to the transaction are bound by the act
  - A registered company can be bound by a contract outside its stated range of activities provided the other party acted in good faith.

Statutory corporations

These corporations are created by statute (e.g. local authorities)

The statute creating each corporation will set out the purpose for which the corporation may enter contracts

Limited liability partnerships
- Created by the Limited Liability Partnerships Act 2000 and benefit from unlimited capacity

An unincorporated association is not a separate legal entity with capacity to enter a contract.

Agency

Agency = the relationship which arises when one person (the agent) acts on behalf of another (the principle) and has power to affect the principal's legal position with regard to a third party

- E.g. if company directors (the principle) delegate power to management (the agent) to enter into contracts on behalf of the company
- Agents all have the power to change the legal relations of the person they're an agent for
- Agents can include travel agents, ticket agents, football agents, shop assistants, auctioneers, lawyers etc…

Generally a contract is formed between a principal and agent outlining what they can and can't do in the principal's name

On top of this, there are also some equitable duties in place (principal may expect that the agent would act in good faith), e.g.:

a) Act with reasonable care and skill
b) Not act outside of their authority (if only implied)
c) Not make secret profit (e.g. from bribes or spreading of confidential info)
d) Not let their own interests conflict with those of their principal
e) Account for money and property received

The Agents Authority

Actual Authority

Actual Authority = when the principle gives the required authority to the agent to contract on its behalf → i.e. agency will arise by express appointment

- Can be granted expressly or implied
- The law regards an agent as having implied actual authority to do such things as are incidental to the exercise of what they've been expressly authorised to do
- ***Freeman & Lockyer v Buckhurst Park Properties (Mangal) Ltd [1964]***: Lord Justice Diplock: 'actual authority is a legal relationship between principal and agent created by consensual agreement to which they alone are the parties'

Apparent Authority

Apparent Authority = when the principle has given the distinct but false impression that the agent has the authority to enter into a particular contract (***Freeman & Lockyer v Buckhurst Park Properties (Mangal) Ltd [1964]***)

- Agents are not able to unduly claim that they have authority when they don't. The agent cannot cloak themselves with authority (i.e. make out as if they do when they don't)

Three Conditions:

a. At some stage the principal must have represented that the agent had authority
b. The third party must rely on this representation believing that the agent had authority
c. The third party must then alter their position (e.g. entering a contract)

Warranty of Authority

Warranty of Authority = when the agent enters into a contract with a third party but with **no authority** (actual or apparent)

- The law regards agents as warranting their authority to act → if they act with no established agency, they are in breach of warranty of authority and liable to be sued (by the third party)

Undisclosed Principal

Undisclosed Principal = Where the fact that there is an agent acting is undisclosed to the third party

- An undisclosed principal can only sue if the agent had actual authority to enter the transaction at the time it was formed (i.e. not if there's ratification)
- The principle can only intervene where they can do so without ratification
- Where the contract is consistent with the agent acting as agent, rather than as principal

The Effects

In cases where the principal refuses to fulfil a contract established by the agent and the third party, the agent is not liable → the contract is between the principal and the third party

Cases of Apparent Authority

Ratification:	**Estoppel:**

When the principle accepts an act carried out by an agent who was acting without 'actual authority' Ratification validates the unauthorised acts of the agent, and back-dates the authority Allowing the principal to ratify the contract puts the third party back in the position they were expected to be in anyway

In cases of apparent authority, contract is formed ● Because the principal cannot deny the authority that the third party perceived as existing (based on the principal's representation or lack of clarity of the agent's position) ● When the third party does not attempt to enforce the contract, the principle has no right to sue the third party

Cases of Warranty of Authority

- The third party cannot sue the principal (and vice-versa)
- The third party can sue the agent in deceit (for breach of implied warranty of authority) BUT NOT for breach of contract (there was never a contract between the agent and third party)

Ending an Agent Relationship

- Agency can usually be brought to an end by agreement or the withdrawal of consent
- Termination of an agency will normally be effective, even where the principal acts in breach of contract when terminating the agency
- Some circumstances where the principal can't terminate the agency → e.g. agency given to protect a security interest

Contractual Certainty

The contract will be enforceable unless the contract is either unworkable or too uncertain without the term in question being added in

- Where the purported contract has been performed, only an omission or uncertainty which renders the contract completely unworkable, and which can't be remedied by any implied term, is likely to force the conclusion that the contract is void for uncertainty

Where contracts are vague, will first try to find a meaning for the words used which are:

1. **Sufficiently certain** to allow the court to work out whether the contract has been complied with
2. Also reflect the **intentions of the parties**

Courts will use **customs**, **trade usage** and **previous dealings** of parties to help resolve uncertainties

- A term will be implied by custom if the custom is notorious, certain and reasonable and generally regarded as binding
    - ***Hillas v Arcos***: the parties had previously dealt on the basis of supplies being of 'fair specification' and the court considered that they meant this arrangement to apply to their current contract

- The courts will generally not require parties to go to arbitration to sort out disputes
- The courts will generally *not use* each party's subjective intentions to resolve difficulties of meaning. Instead aim to workout what a **reasonable person** would have taken the parties to have meant

Can use the factual background to the contract (the matrix of fact) to work out what the parties meant

- When using the reasonable standard, it is assumed that they have the background knowledge reasonably available to the parties

Where something 'key' or 'legally essential' is omitted, the agreement cannot be enforced

- What's essential to any particular deal will depend on the individual facts
- Generally up to the parties to determine what is essential (***Pagnan v Feed Products***)

A term will be implied in fact **if it is necessary to give the contract business efficacy**

- If the parties have left something out, without which the contract would be unworkable, helps to fill in the gaps

A term will be implied in law, if it's what **the nature of the contract itself implicitly requires**

Certain situations where the parties may reach some sort of agreement, even though there are outstanding issues to be resolved:

- The parties can agree the main terms of the contract, but make it clear that they don't wish to be bound until they have settled the remaining terms
- Parties can reach interim agreements which are legally binding, but not complete (it will only be void if a failure to reach agreement on further terms renders the whole contract unworkable)

Criminal Law

Actus Reus and Mens Rea

In order to secure a conviction, the prosecution must establish:

1) Guilty conduct by the defendant (***actus reus***)
2) Guilty state of mind by the defendant (***mens rea***)
3) Absence of any valid defence

Actus Reus

A defendant will not be liable for a criminal offence unless the *actus reus* of the offence is proved (***Deller [1952]***)

- Criminal liability usually requires a positive act by the defendant → must have done something

The *actus reus* consists of one or more of:

a) An act (or sometimes failure to act) by the defendant
b) The existence of certain circumstances or 'state of affairs' at the time of the defendant's conduct
c) Certain circumstances flowing from the defendant's conduct

Factual Causation

Factual causation = the 'but for' test

⟶ *But for* the defendant's actions, the result *would not* have occurred

<u>*Case Law Examples:*</u>

- ***R v White [1910]:*** defendant laced his mother's drink with potassium cyanide, intending to kill her. She drank some of it and was found dead the next morning. BUT → medically had died from heart attack
    - Defendant acquitted of murder as it *could not be shown* that he was the factual cause of his mothers death

- ***Mitchell [1983]***: while in a queue, defendant pushed the person in front of him who fell into an 89 year old women → she fell, broke her hip and developed a blood clot and died
    - Defendant was guilty → factual causation was established

Legal Causation

Legal causation = the 'chain of causation'

⟶ prosecution must prove that there was no *novus actus interveniens* (new intervening act) which *broke* the chain of causation

1) The consequence (e.g. death) must be due to a culpable act, including a failure to act where the defendant is under a duty (***R v Dalloway***)

2) The culpable act must be more than a minimal cause of the consequence (***R v Pagett***)
    - 'In law, the defendant's act need not be the sole cause, or even the main cause, of the victim's death, it being enough that his act (or omission) contributed significantly to that result' (***R v Pagett (1983)***)
    - Usually if his conduct was the 'operating and substantial cause' of that result ⟶ i.e. more than minimal ***(Smith [1959] and Malcherek; Steel [1981])***

3) But does not need to be the sole cause (***R v Benge***)

4) The chain of causation must not be broken:

Intervening Acts:

The link between the defendant's act and the end result can't be broken by an intervening act (a *novus actus interveniens*)

The argument will not succeed if:

a) Despite there being an intervening event, the injuries inflicted by the defendant were still an operating and substantial cause of death
b) If there was an intervening act, this was foreseen or foreseeable

The 'thin skull rule'

A victim's particular susceptibility to an injury due to a pre-existing condition does not break the chain of causation

Case Law Example:

- ***Blaue [1975]***: defendant stabbed a women, piercing her lung. Taken to hospital where she was told to get a blood transfusion ⟶ refused due to her religious beliefs
    - Died from blood loss & defendant convicted

- Thin skull rule also applies to religious beliefs → extends to the 'whole man'

Escapes

For an escape to break the chain of causation, it must be:

1) Unforeseen and voluntary
2) A foreseeable consequence of the unlawful act (must be proportionate to the threat posed)

Case Law Example:

- ***Roberts (1971):*** defendant made sexual advances to a women in a car. Told her he had previously beaten women who refused him. She jumped out of the moving car and was injured
    - Defendant found guilty → caused her escape

Victim's self-neglect

Self-neglect by the victim does not release the defendant from liability:

- Can include refusing medical treatment / committing suicide
- As long as the defendant's act was a cause of the victim's death, it does not matter that it was not the sole cause (***Dear [1996]***)

Case Law Example:

- ***R v Wallace [2018]***: defendant threw a glass of sulphuric acid into victim's face → permanent and life-changing injuries.
    - 15 months later, went to Belgium to request voluntary euthanasia
    - Defendant charged with murder → initially, acquitted on the basis that the act of euthanasia was voluntary and broke the chain of causation
    - Court of Appeal found that the request for euthanasia was a 'direct response to the inflicted injuries and to the circumstances created by them for which the defendant was responsible'

Third Party:

An act by a third party might break the chain of causation if that act is a voluntary one which contributes to the result

Case Law Example:

- ***Pagett (1983)***: defendant used his pregnant girlfriend as a shield whilst shooting at the police. Police shot back and killed the girlfriend
    - Defendant convicted of manslaughter of his girlfriend
    - The police shooting was an involuntary act, caused by the conduct of the defendant and did not release the defendant from liability

Negligent Medical Treatment:

Generally, the conduct of a doctor, even if negligent, does not release the defendant from liability (***Smith [1959]***)

<u>*Case Law Example:*</u>

- ***Cheshire (1991)***: defendant shot victim in leg & stomach → treated in hospital but died of blocked windpipe 2 months later
  - Whilst medical staff were negligent, original attacker was convicted
  - 'Unless the negligent treatment was so independent of his act, and it itself so potent in causing death, that they regard the contribution made by his acts as insignificant' - Beldam LJ

Natural Events:

A natural event which was not reasonably foreseeable will break the chain of causation

- The foreseeability of the subsequent event is the determining factor for liability

Must be a voluntary act

The conduct of the defendant must be voluntary

- In order for the defence of automatism to be successful, the defendant must suffer a total loss of voluntary control (***Broome v Perkins (1987)***)
  - Where a defendant has some voluntary control over his actions, defence will fail (***Attorney General's Reference (No. 2 of 1992) [1994]***)

<u>*Case Law Example:*</u>

- ***Bratty v Attorney General for Northern Ireland [1963]***: automatism is an act which is done by the muscles without any control by the mind; or an act done by a person who is not conscious of what he is doing
- ***Hill v Baxter [1958]***: court gave example of a person being attacked by bees whilst driving → couldn't commit the *actus reus* of the offence of careless driving as actions were not voluntary

Omissions?

In most cases, a defendant would have taken positive steps in relation to a particular crime (have actually done something)

Whilst the general principle is that there can be no criminal liability for failing to act, **exceptions**:

Special Relationship

Where there is a special relationship between the defendant and victim (e.g. family / duty) the defendant could incur criminal liability for failing to act

- A special relationship is formed if one assumes a duty to care for the victim

<u>*Case Law Example:*</u>

- ***R v Gibbins and Proctor (1918)***: the defendants were convicted of murdering a 7 year old child who died of starvation → first defendant was the father, second his partner
    - As a parent, had a duty of care for his child

- ***R v Stone and Dobinson [1977]*** the 2 defendants took in Stone's sister, Fanny to live with them → she suffered with anorexia and was bed-ridden
    - Defendants did not properly assist her → she died of blood poisoning
    - Charged with a duty of care (sister & had taken limited steps to care)

- ***R v Ruffell [2003]***: a defendant assumed a duty of trying to revive a friend who had taken drugs → convicted of manslaughter when he failed to care for him properly (left him outside the house and he died of hypothermia)

Terminally ill:

Duty also remains if you follow the wishes of a terminally ill family member (and they are deemed unable to have made rational decisions at the time)

- ***R v Smith [1979]***: defendant was charged with manslaughter of his wife who died after still-birth → wife had instructed not to seek medical attention

BUT: duty can be released in some medical situations:

- ***Airedale NHS Trust v Bland [1993]***: Bland was a victim of the Hillsborough disaster → left in a persistent vegetative state
    - Doctors applied to the courts for permission to discontinue medical treatment (must first seek permission)

Contractual Duty to Act:

If a contract of employment specifies certain obligations to act, a failure to comply can lead to criminal liability (e.g. doctors, emergency services, lifeguards)

Case Law Example:

- ***R v Pittwood (1902)***: was a railway crossing gate-keeper → failed to close the gate and a person was killed by a train
  - Liable in criminal court for the consequences of his failure to act

Public Duty to Act:

A defendant may be under a public duty to act if they hold a position of public authority or responsibility

Case Law Example:

- ***Dytham [1979]***: police officer, while on duty, saw a man being beaten to death by a club bouncer. Did not intervene → convicted

Statutory Duty to Act:

Where a legislative provision has imposed a duty on individuals to act in a certain way, given a set of circumstances

- E.g. car drivers stopping at traffic lights
- Usually results in prosecution for the omission itself (e.g. failing to stop at a red light), rather than for the consequences of that omission (e.g. if you crashed and someone died)
- Penalties usually result in a fine

Defendant who creates a dangerous situation:

Can be criminal liability if you fail to take action to remove a danger you created

- The duty is established on the *subjective realisation of the danger created* → when they ought to have realised the danger
- Necessary to invoke the Miller principle only in the case of a *result crime*
  - ***R v Miller [1983]***: a squatter lit a cigarette and fell asleep. Cigarette fell on the mattress causing it to smoulder.
    - Instead of taking steps to stop the smouldering he moved rooms
    - Charged with causing criminal damage to the property after it caught fire

Mens Rea

In most criminal offences, the defendant must have **a guilty mind at the time of their guilty conduct**

- In most offences, the defendant must have shown either to have intended something to happen or to have been reckless as to whether certain circumstances would exist

Intention:

Direct Indirect?

In most cases, if the defendant intended something to happen (it was their aim, purpose, goal or desire) → **they have direct intent**

If not:

→ Indirect / Oblique Intent?

Where the defendant argues that the outcome was **not their main aim**, but an **unfortunate by-product of what they set out to achieve,** jury are asked to consider the virtual certainty test

Guidance was established by the Court of Appeal in ***R v Nedrick [1986]:***

a) Was the consequence *virtually* certain to occur as a consequence of the defendant's actions?
b) If so, did the defendant foresee this consequence as a *virtual certainty*? → subjective

→ If the Jury answers yet to both, **indirect intention can be inferred**

Also: ulterior intent?

Ulterior Intent = The prosecution must prove an 'extra' element of *mens rea* against the defendant, before they can secure a conviction

- Must prove that the defendant intended to produce some consequences which went beyond the *actus reus* of the crime

Recklessness:

Recklessness = foreseeing a consequence as possible or probable yet going ahead and taking that risk, where the risk was unjustifiable or unreasonable (***R v G [2004]***)

Was the risk unjustified?

Courts will consider the social utility or benefit involved in taking the risk when deciding whether it was justified

- Assessed according to the s**tandards of a reasonable person**
- The jury must ask themselves whether they would have considered there to be any merit in taking the risk if they had been in the defendant's position

Was the risk foreseeable?

Typically, courts take the view that a defendant was reckless if *they* foresaw a risk that something might happen (***R v Cunningham [1957]***) → subjective test

- Defendant must have foresaw a risk (subjective) and went on to take it, and the risk is unjustified (objective) (***R v G [2004]***)

Did they go on to take that risk?

Always need *mens rea*?

Transferred Malice:

Cases where the wrong party is injured (contrary to the defendant's initial intent)

- **Transferred Malice** = the *mens rea* the defendant had in relation to their original victim is transferred to the *actus reus* they commit against another, unintended victim
- Means a defendant cannot be absolved of criminal liability, simply because their plan did not succeed
    - ***R v Latimer (1886)***: accidentally assaulted a third party

→ Only applies if the *actus reus* committed is the same type of crime as the defendant originally had in mind

- ***R v Pembliton (1874)***: defendant threw a stone at someone, missed and broke a window. Successfully appealed his conviction of an offence of 'unlawfully and maliciously' causing damage to property

Negligence

In some cases, an offence can be committed without proof of intention or recklessness → may be punished for failing to meet the standards of a reasonable person

- Liability cannot be attached to a careless individual, unless there is a specific crime created to cover that type of negligent behaviour
- E.g. under s 3 of the Road Traffic Act 1988, intention or recklessness do not have to be established to secure a conviction
    - One of the few offences where someone can incur criminal liability for falling below the standards of the reasonable person

Strict Liability Offences:

Another occasion where a defendant may be convicted of a crime without having *mens rea*

E.g drunk driving → a person who drives drunk is guilty, even if they did not know or foresee the risk that the amount of alcohol they had consumed would exceed the prescribed limit (or if they were unaware that they had been drinking (spiked))

Usually created by statute to try and regulate behaviour

When the statute is unclear, rules set out in ***Sweet v Parsley [1970]***:

Where there is no indication, there is a presumption that the courts should 'read in words appropriate to require *mens rea*' in order to give effect to the will of Parliament

- Typically, the higher the social stigma and greater the penalty, the more likely *mens rea* is required

This presumption can be overturned if 'some reason can be found for holding that *mens rea* is not necessary'

Where a statute is silent on *mens rea*, the court will need to go outside the wording of the Act to establish Parliamentary intention

Misunderstandings?

- There is no requirement for the defendant to appreciate that what they are doing is criminal
- Ignorance of the criminal law is never a defence, even where it was impossible for the defendant to have known the law

Mistake of fact?

- Mistake of fact where the defendant believes their conduct is innocent
- Generally, the more unreasonable the defendant's mistake, the less likely the court is to believe that it was an honest one

Coincidence of *Actus Reus* and *Mens Rea*:

As a general rule, the *actus rea* and *mens rea* should coincide in time (occur at the same time)

If a victim dies later than intended by the defendant (i.e. their initial *mens rea* has passed), must still be found guilty (***Thabo-Meli v R [1954]***)

- Seen as a series of acts in order to achieve an original plan

<u>*Case Law Example:*</u>

R v Le Brun [1991]: defendant assaulted his wife, when he tried to move her she slipped and died → defendant charged with manslaughter

- Tried to argue that he had the *mens rea* of assault, but did not mean for her to die
- Court found that the final act causing her death was part of the same sequence of events

Assaults

Simple Assault

Simple Assault = any act which intentionally or recklessly causes another person to apprehend immediate and unlawful personal force (***Fagan v Metropolitan Police Commissioner [1969]***)

- Has a maximum sentence of 6 months' imprisonment
- Charged under ***s. 39 of the Criminal Justice Act 1988***

Actus Reus:

***Actus reus* of simple assault** = causing another person to **apprehend immediate** and **unlawful** personal force

Must apprehend the force:

The victim must believe they are about to be unlawfully touched

- If the victim does not apprehend immediate personal violence, there is no assault
- It is a subjectively assessed

<u>*Case Law Example:*</u>

- *Lamb [1967]*: victim thought the defendant was pointing a revolver at him as part of a game (did not apprehend immediate personal violence)

Words can amount to an assault:

- Words or silence could amount to an assault, without any other gesture (***R v Ireland [1997]***)
- Also confirmed that silent telephone calls could amount to assault, depending on the facts (the impact of the caller's potentially menacing call or calls on the victim') → usually requires a pattern of silent calls

Threat must be of immediate force:

The threat must be of **immediate** unlawful personal force → not just that it may occur, victim must anticipate that the fore will occur immediately

- Sufficient to fear that it *could* occur immediately

Case Law Example:

- ***R v Burstow [1997]***: defendant had stalked victim over a number of years (photographs / letters / phone calls / visiting home) → the victim feared that the defendant could strike at any time

Can be a conditional threat

A conditional threat also satisfies the immediate force requirement (***Read v Coker (1853)***)

- E.g. 'if you don't shut up, I will slap you'
- Law takes into account that such an imposition on the victim and the unjustified restriction on their personal liberty is unwarranted and so liable for assault

Mens Rea:

The defendant must (*R v Venna [1976]*):

a) **Intend** to cause the victim to apprehend immediate unlawful personal force, **or**
b) Be **reckless** as to whether such apprehension be caused

The test for recklessness is subjective → the defendant must foresee the risk that the victim will apprehend immediate unlawful personal force and go on to take that risk (***R v Spratt [1991]***)

Physical Assault

Physical assault = the infliction of unlawful personal force (battery)

- You can have a physical assault without a simple assault (if the victim does not see the defendant before the assault takes place)
- Charged under ***s 39 of the Criminal Justice Act 1988***

Actus Reus:

The *actus reus* of physical assault is the infliction of unlawful personal force on the victim

- No injury is required (***Faulkner v Talbot [1981]***)
- The application of force can be indirect (e.g placing an obstacle behind a door so you trip) (***DPP v K [1990]***)
- Only touching which goes beyond generally acceptable standards of conduct is subject to punishment
    - ***Collins v Wilcock (1984):*** consent is a defence to battery → most of the physical contacts of ordinary life are not actionable as they are impliedly consented

Mens Rea:

The defendant must:

a) **Intend** to inflict unlawful force on another person, **or**
b) Be **reckless** as to whether such unlawful force would occur

The defendant must have intended or foreseen the actual infliction of force (not just the victim's apprehension)

Assault Occasioning Actual Bodily Harm (s 47)

It is an **aggravated form of assault or battery**

- Assault occasioning actual bodily harm (ABH) is an either way offence, carrying up to 5 years' imprisonment (***S 47 of the Offences Against the Person Act 1861 (OAPA 1861)***)

Actus Reus:

The *actus reus* consists of 3 elements:

An assault;
Which occasions (causes);
Actual bodily harm

Defining ABH:

Actual bodily harm = any hurt or injury calculated to interfere with the health or comfort of the victim (***R v Miller [1954]***)

- The CPS use a Charging Standard Code to decide what offence to charge:
  - 'Serious injuries include damaged teeth or bones, extensive and severe bruising, cuts requiring suturing and those that result in lost consciousness'
  - Academic side may be different to practical implications
  - Medical treatment or medical assessment may indicate serious injury
- Can include psychiatric injury (but must be a recognisable clinical condition) (***R v Ireland [1997]***)
  - Any physical or psychiatric injury doesn't need to be permanent, but 'should not be so trivial as to be wholly insignificant' (***Chan-Fook [1994]***)

Mens Rea:

The defendant must (*R v Savage; R v Parmenter [1991]*):

Intend to *cause* ***assault or battery***, or
Be **reckless** as to whether an assault or battery would occur

The prosecution does not need to prove that the defendant intended or was reckless to any harm caused (just the assault) → same *mens rea* as physical assault
ABH is only relevant to the *actus reus* of the offence and not the *mens rea*

Wounding or Inflicting Grievous Bodily Harm (s 20)

S 20 of the Offence Against the Person Act 1861 = 'whoever shall unlawfully and maliciously wound or inflict any grievous bodily harm upon any other person, shall be liable to imprisonment for a term not exceeding 5 years'

Actus Reus:

The *actus reus* of s 20 is to **unlawfully wound** *or* **inflict grievous bodily harm** on another person

1) Unlawfully

Unlawfully = not done with any lawful jurisdiction (i.e. not in self-defence or in defence of another) (***R v Horwood [2012]***)

2) Wound, or

Wound = both layers of the skin must be broken (***Moriarty v Brookes (1834)***)

- Bruising or internal bleeding aren't wounds as skin has not been broken (***JJC (a Minor) v Eisenhower [1984]***)

3) Inflict GBH

Grievous bodily harm = 'really serious harm' (***DPP v Smith [1961]***)

- Case law provides no further guidance, so jury must decide what amounts to really serious (e.g. fractured skull, severe internal injuries and broken limbs)
- ***R v Burstow [1997***: psychiatric problems could amount to grievous bodily harm if severe enough
- In deciding whether to charge a defendant with ABH or GBH, the prosecutor should consider the effect of the harm on the particular complainant, taking into account their age, health and other factors

Mens Rea:

The defendant must (*R v Savage; R v Parmenter [1991]*):

Intend to *cause actual bodily harm*

Be reckless as to whether actual bodily harm would occur

It does not need to be proven that the defendant foresaw really serious harm, or the exact nature of the harm that occurred, just ABH

Wounding or Causing Grievous Bodily Harm with Intent (s 18)

Offences Against the Person Act 1861, s 18: 'Whosoever shall unlawfully and maliciously by any means whatsoever wound or cause any grievous harm to any person … with intent … to do some … grievous bodily harm to any person, or with intent to resist or prevent the lawful apprehension or detainer of any person, shall be guilty of an offence, … [and shall be liable] to imprisonment for life'

- Section 18 is the most serious non-fatal offence against the person → receives a maximum of life imprisonment (indictable offence)
- The offence is more serious as the *mens rea* requires intention

Ordinary Victim

Actus Reus:

There are 2 ways to commit the *actus reus* of an offence (against an ordinary person):

a) To wound; or
b) To cause grievous bodily harm to a person

Mens Rea

The defendant must (against an ordinary person):

a) Intend to cause GBH

- Recklessness is not enough
- Intending to wound is not enough for *mens rea* of ***s 18***

Police Officer

Actus Reus:

There are 2 ways to commit the *actus reus* of an offence (against a police officer):

a) To wound; or
b) To cause grievous bodily harm

Mens Rea

Against a police officer, the defendant must:

Intend to resist or prevent the lawful apprehension or detainer of any person, ***and***
Intend / be reckless as to causing *actual bodily harm* (ABH)

Consent

General rule is that consent is only a defence to assault and battery (not to ABH)

The law doesn't specify a specific age or degree of mental disability which precludes someone giving a valid consent → question of fact per case

- Take into account victims capacity to consent (mental disorders, intoxicated, youth or immaturity etc)

→ You give valid consent only if you know the identity of the defendant and the nature and quality of the act

Originally led to controversial results →

R v Richardson [1999]: dentist suspended by the General Dental Council → whilst suspended, carried out dentistry → court held consent given was valid

Adapted in ***R v Tabassum [2000]:***

- Defendant claimed he was medically qualified and carrying out a study on breast cancer (not true)
- Distinguished from earlier cases → court held that the victims must know the nature and quality of the act if their consent was to be valid
- Victims believed they were consenting to an examination by a medically qualified professional for medical purposes → did not know the quality of act

Sexual Assault:

R v Clarence (1888): defendant had sexual intercourse with his wife, knowing he was suffering from a STD (wife unaware)

Charged under s 20 but court held he had not assaulted his wife as she had consented (knowing the identity and nature of the act)

Clarence overturned:

R v Dica [2004]: defendant infected sexual partner with HIV

- Defendant had the relevant *mens rea* because he was reckless as to whether the victim might become infected (foresaw a risk of causing some harm)
- Would not have consented, had they known the defendant's position
- The defendant inflicted grievous bodily harm upon the victim (*actus reus*) and was reckless as to whether she might become infected (*mens rea*)

R v Konzani [2005]: defendant had sex with 3 complainants after being informed he had HIV → all 3 contracted the virus

Convicted of a s 20 assault

Consent as a Defence?

Three questions to ask about consent:

1) Was there implied or express consent
2) Did the victim give effective consent to the act
3) Was the conduct performed in a context in which the law accepts that consent be validly given

☑ A consent can be a defence to simple or physical assault, provided no harm was caused or intended

✕ Cannot be a defence to an assault causing harm unless it falls under one of the recognised exceptions (***Attorney-General's Reference (No 6 of 1980) [1981]***):

a) Surgical operations
b) Dangerous exhibitions (e.g. circus acts)
c) Properly conducted sport (e.g. boxing and rugby)
    - ***R v Barnes [2005]***: level of criminality in sport cases would be assessed objectively (by the jury) and would be determined by the type of sport, the level at which it was played, the nature of the act, the degree of force used, the extent of risk of injury and the state of mind of the defendant
d) Cases of 'lawful activities' such as ritual circumcision, tattooing and ear-piercing, where they are in the public interest, or is there was a 'good reason' for the harm to be risked/caused (***R v Brown [1994]***)

✕ The law does not permit a person to consent to serious harm being caused to them for the purpose of sexual gratification

Case Law Example:

R v Brown [1994]: appellants belonged to a group of sado-masochistic homosexual men who willingly participated in the commission of acts of violence against each other (consented)
- Charged under ss 47 and s 20 of the OAPA 1861 → general rule that a victim cannot consent to the harm

○ ***R v Wilson [1996]***: defendant (at the instigation of wife) used a hot knife to brand his initials on her → charged and convicted of an offence under s 47 of the OAPA 1861
- Acquitted on the basis that the activity was too close to tattooing (capable of consent) & it would not be in the public interest to criminalise

R v Emmett [1999]: sado-masochistic acts between two consenting heterosexual adults → court held that the issue of consent was immaterial where there was a realistic risk of harm 'beyond a merely transient or trivial injury'

○ ***R v BM [2018]***: defendant (tattooist by trade) was charged with a s 18 offence after removing part of the victim's ear, a nipple and splitting their tongue to resemble a lizard
- A person cannot consent to such serious, irreversible injuries
- Constituted medical procedures performed for no medical reason and with none of the protections provided to patients by medical practitioners

- ○ ***R v Dica [2004]***: debate over consent to sexual intercourse with a person whom the victim knew was infected
  - Part of the *obiter* statement, the Court of Appeal held that the defence of consent would not be available where there was a deliberate infliction of grievous bodily harm (unless activity was lawful)

Reasonable Force Defences

Self-Defence

Common law recognises that an individual may justifiably use force to act in self-defence in certain circumstances

- ***s 75 and 76 of the Criminal Justice and Immigration Act 2008*** codified some of the principles around self-defence

The **defence has the evidential burden to prove self-defence** and the **prosecution must then disprove it** beyond all reasonable doubt

Reasonable Force

Where a defendant claims to have acted in self-defence / prevention of crime, they will be able to rely on the defence **only if they used reasonable force:**

a) The defendant must argue that they used (objectively) reasonable force
b) In the circumstances (subjectively) as they believed them to be

The defendant does not need to retreat first or wait for the assailant to hit them first (***R v Bird***)

- 'To ward off or prevent an attack which he honestly anticipated' → must be imminent (***Devlin v Armstrong)***

Will take into account that the defendant may have had to make rash decisions in extreme situations (***Palmer v R [1971]***).

Relevant Factors:

Whether reasonable force was used is a question of fact for the jury, will take into account:

- The degree of force or seriousness of the original offence
- The degree of force used in defence
- Whether the claimant could have reasonably prevented the wrong by doing something else
- Mistakes made (e.g. if they were wrong about the potential for attack)
- Was the self-defence just retaliation/revenge

- Was the perceived attack imminent

Mistaken Belief?

Will take into account whether the defendant was mistaken in deciding that force was necessary or about what the other party was going to do

- The defendant is judged on the facts as they believe them to be (even if that honestly held belief is unreasonable) (***R v Williams (Gladstone) (1984)***)
- A defendant can't rely on facts that they were unaware of when they committed the offence (***R v Dadson (1850)***)

Case Law Example:

- ***R v Martin (Anthony) [2002]***: Martin was convicted of murder when he shot and killed a burglar after discovering him in his house
  - He suffered from a paranoid personality disorder and so perceived a greater danger to his physical safety than the average person → court held inadmissible

Unless Intoxicated:

R v O'Grady [1987] QB 995 and R v Hatton [2005]: a mistaken belief in the need of force is no defence if that mistake is based on voluntary intoxication

Householder Cases

Cases where a defendant used force on someone they found in their dwelling

- The accused does not need to be a homeowner, *just not a trespasser*
- 'In a householder case, the degree of force used by D is not to be regarded as having been reasonable in the circumstances as D believed them to be if it was grossly disproportionate in those circumstances' (***5A of the Criminal Justice and Immigration Act***)
  - Opposed to just disproportionate in regular cases
- Concerns proportional force → may be able to use more than proportional force, as long as it is not grossly disproportionate

Case Law Example:

- ***R (Collins) v Secretary of State for Justice [2016]***: Collins was restrained by a householder by means of a headlock → suffered personal injuries (unrecoverable)
  - CPS decided not to prosecute householder (reasonable use of force)

Preventing Crime / Arrest

S 3 of the Criminal Law Act 1967: 'a person may use such force as is reasonable in the circumstances in the prevention of crime, or in effecting or assisting in the lawful arrest of offenders or suspected offenders'

Reasonable Force?

European Court emphasises that cannot use lethal force to stop a person suspected of a non-violent offence who does not pose an immediate risk of harm to anyone

Where someone is acting in defence of their own property, can argue was acting in prevention of crime (but can rarely, if ever, be reasonable to use deadly force)

Immediate apprehension

R (DPP) v Stratford Magistrates' Court: emphasised that in order to plead the s 3 defence, there must be a link between the use of force and an imminently apprehended crime

- Reiterated that citizens are normally expected to call the police, not take the law into their own hands

Reasonable Chastisement:

R v Hopley (1860): parents can use force to discipline their children, as long as it amounts to no more than moderate and reasonable chastisement

Case Law Example:

- ***A v UK (1998)***: 9 year old was beaten by his step-father with a garden cane (bruised) → charged with s 47 but raised defence of reasonable chastisement (acquitted)
    - ECHR found that the UK was in breach of its obligation as it had failed to provide adequate protection to children against treatment or punishment which could constitute 'inhumane or degrading treatment'

- ***Children Act 2004, 2 58***: although mild smacking is allowed under a defence of reasonable chastisement against common assault, any punishment that causes visible bruising, grazes, scratches, minor swelling or cuts could lead to prosecution

Murder and Manslaughter

Homicide

Actus Reus

To prove the *actus reus* of homicide, the defendant must **cause the death of a human being**

Death = 'the irreversible death of the brain stem, which controls the basic functions of the body such as breathing. (***R v Malcherek and Steel [1981]***)

Not in the womb:

It is not homicide to kill a child in the womb → abortion not considered murder

The child must be wholly expelled from the mother's body to be alive & must have an existence independent of the mother (***R v Poulton (1832)***)

Case Law Example:

- ***Re A (Children) (conjoined twins: surgical separation) [2000]***: whether to allow the separation of conjoined twist which would result in the death of the weaker twin (Mary) → had been argued that as she had an underdeveloped heart, lungs and brain and depended on the stronger twin for survival, she was not a separate person so it would not be murder
    - Court of Appeal held that as Mary had been born (existence independent of her mother) - was an alive and separate child

Attorney-General's Reference (No 3 of 1994) [1997]: murder could not be committed where unlawful injury had been deliberately inflicted to a mother carrying a child, where the child was subsequently born alive and then died as a result of the injuries inflicted

- In this case, defendant stabbed his girlfriend who was pregnant → *mens rea* that the defendant had in relation to the mother couldn't be transferred to the unborn foetus
- Defendant could be liable for unlawful act manslaughter

Factual Causation:

Did the defendant, as a matter of fact, cause the victim's death

'But for the defendant's conduct, would the victim's death have occurred in the way that it did' (***R v White)***

Where the defendant's conduct accelerated death, the acceleration must be significant (more than negligible) (***R v Cheshire [1991]***)

Legal Causation:

→ Prosecution must prove that there was **no *novus actus interveniens*** (new intervening act) which *broke* the chain of causation

1) The death must be due to a culpable act, including a failure to act where the defendant is under a duty (***R v Dalloway***)
2) The culpable act must be more than a minimal cause of the death (***R v Pagett***)
3) But does not need to be the sole cause (***R v Benge***)
4) The chain of causation must not be broken (intervening act)

SEE ACTUS REUS SECTION FROM UNIT 1

Murder

Murder:

The defendant unlawfully causes the death of a person

With an intention to:

Kill, or

Cause GBH

Mens Rea:

Defined in ***R v Moloney [1985]*** as either an intention to kill or an intention to cause GBH

- Recklessness does not suffice
- *It is a subjective test* → did the individual defendant intend to kill or cause grievous bodily harm

Case Law Example:

- ***Vickers [1957]***: defendant broke into a house intending to steal → confronted by the owner of the house → struck the elderly women, killing her
  - Argued that he did not have the *mens rea* for murder
  - Court held that as the defendant intended to cause GBH, he had sufficient *mens rea* for murder

Direct Intent:

The defendant desired something to happen, or it was their aim, purpose or goal (***R v Moloney)***

Indirect Intent?
Where the defendant's primary aim or desire was not the forbidden consequence, but where they foresaw the consequence as virtually certain (***Nedrick [1986] 1 WLR 1025*** and ***Woollin [1999]***) • VIRTUAL CERTAINTY test from unit 1 • Only applies to murder → can't be used where there is a reckless element in the *mens rea*

Voluntary Manslaughter

Where a defendant has **both the *actus reus* and *mens rea* for murder**, BUT, also one of **3 special partial defences** are available, will be liable for **voluntary manslaughter**

The 3 special partial defences are:

a) Diminished responsibility
b) Loss of control
c) Suicide pact

Diminished Responsibility

Set out in ***s 52 of the Coroners and Justice Act 2009*** and incorporated into ***s 2(1) of the Homicide Act 1957:***

A defendant who kills or is party to the killing of another *is not to be convicted* of murder if they were suffering from **an abnormality of mental functioning which**:

Arose from a recognised medical condition, and

Substantially impaired their ability to:

Understand the nature of their conduct
To form a rational judgement or
To exercise self-control, and

Provides an explanation for their acts and omissions in doing or being a party to the killing

It is for the **defendant to prove this defence on a 'balance of probabilities'**

I.e. must prove that it was more likely than not that they were suffering from diminished responsibility

1) Abnormality of Mental Functioning

- Jury will make the decision having heard expert medical evidence
- Must be a recognised medical condition
    - Medical experts who give evidence may refer to the WHO's international classification of diseases
    - May use a recognised medical specialist to give evidence about conditions (if not mentioned on the list)
    - CPS in its *Legal Guidance on Homicide*: 'Examples of recognised medical conditions within these classificatory lists are schizophrenia, phobic anxiety disorders, bipolar affective disorder, depression and battered person syndrome'

Case Law Example:

- ***R v Dietschmann [2003]***: defendant was a heavy drinker and had been prescribed antidepressants and sleeping tablets by his doctor. Was drinking with friends when he was involved in a fight where he killed the victim
    - Defendant raised the defence of diminished responsibility → psychiatrists both agreed that at the time of the killing, the defendant was suffering from an abnormality of mind
    - Defence of diminished responsibility would stand if the jury found that, even if he had not been drinking, the defendant would have killed & been under diminished responsibility
    - HoL: the abnormality of mind did not need to be the sole cause of the defendant's acts → despite the drinking, the abnormality of mind also impaired the defendant's mental responsibility

- ***R v Wood [2008]***: in deciding whether the defendant's mental responsibility was substantially impaired as a result of his alcoholism, the jury should focus exclusively on the effect of the alcohol consumed as a result of the defendant's illness (ignoring the effect of any alcohol consumed voluntarily)
    - Self-induced intoxication cannot produce an abnormality of mind
- ***R v Dowds [2012]***: voluntary acute intoxication, uncomplicated by an alcoholism or dependence cannot be relied on for diminished responsibility

2) Which substantially impairs defendant's ability

'Substantially impaired their ability to understand the nature of their conduct and/or, to form a rational judgement and/or to exercise self-control'

- Whether there has been a substantial impairment is a question of fact for the jury
- For the impairment to be substantial, it must be 'more than trivial or minimal' (***R v Lloyd [1967]***
- Supreme court concluded that 'substantial' meant 'important or weighty' (***R v Golds [2016]***)

3) Provides an explanation for the killing

There must be some casual connection between the abnormality of mental functioning and the killing in order for the partial defence to succeed

- ***S 52 of the Coroners and Justice Act 2009***: for the partial defence to succeed, any such abnormality of mental functioning must have been at least a significant contributory factor in causing the defendant to act as he did
- Does not need to be the only, the main or the most important, but it must be more than merely trivial
- Defence must show that the homicide would not have occurred if the mental abnormality had not been present

Loss of Control

The law is accepting that sometimes people reach a breaking point and lose their self-control → this person is less morally culpable → liable for voluntary manslaughter

- Situations commonly pleaded would be a reaction to racial taunts, ridiculing physical disabilities, insults to family members or cheating
- ***S 54(6)***: the trial judge will decide whether there is enough evidence to raise the defence as an issue → must be 'sufficient' evidence
  - The burden is then on the prosecution to disprove the defence beyond all reasonable doubt
  - If the prosecution can prove that *just one* of the 3 elements is missing, the defence will fail

Ss 54 and 55 of the Coroners and Justice Act 2009:

a) The defendant's acts and omissions in doing or being a party to the killing resulted from their loss of self-control; and

b) The loss of control had a qualifying trigger; and

c) A person of the defendant's sex and age, with a normal degree of tolerance and self-restraint and in the same circumstances, might have reacted in the same or similar way to the defendant

☑ **The defendant does not have to 'suddenly snap'** (*s 54(2)*)

- Lord Judge CJ in ***Dawes***: 'provided there was a loss of control, it doesn't matter whether the loss was sudden or not. A reaction to circumstances of extreme gravity may be delayed… the loss of control may follow from the cumulative impact of earlier events'

✕ **Can't be for revenge**

- Law Commission: 'a defendant who acts in a considered desire for revenge is to be distinguished from a defendant who acts on impulse or in fear or both'

There must be a qualifying trigger

S (55) of the Coroners and Justice Act 2009: sets out the meaning of 'qualified trigger':

a) If the defendant's loss of self-control was attributable to the defendant's **fear** of **serious violence** against themself or another identified person

b) If the loss of self-control was attributable to an act which constituted circumstances of an extremely **grave character** and caused the defendant to have a **justifiable sense of being seriously wronged**

Fear of serious violence:

If the defendant's loss of self-control was attributable to the defendant's **fear** of **serious violence against themself or another identified person**

- ***S 55(3)***: No objective element → jury must consider whether the defendant would have been in fear of serious violence at the time of the killing
- ***S 56(6)(a)***: A fear of serious violence will be disregarded if it was caused by an act which the defendant incited to be done or said for the purpose of providing an excuse to then use violence

Grave character & justifiably wronged

If the loss of self-control was attributable to an act which constituted circumstances of an extremely **grave character** and caused the defendant to have a **justifiable sense of being seriously wronged**

- ***S 55(4)***: a parent witnessing their child being raped may apply
- ***S 55(6)***: sexual infidelity does not count as a relevant act

→ Whether the defendant's sense of being seriously wronged was 'justifiable' is **objectively assessed**

Case Law Example:

R v Clinton, Parker and Evans [2012]: where the sexual infidelity is part of the context of other possible relevant triggers, evidence relating to that sexual infidelity may be relevant when assessing the other possible qualifying trigger

The Objective Test:

S 54 (1)(c) of the Coroners and Justice Act 2009: a person of the defendant's sex and age, with a normal degree of tolerance and self-restraint, and in the circumstances of the defendant, might have reacted in the same or in a similar way

- Confirmed that the reasonable person is the same sex and age as the defendant in ***DPP v Camplin [1978]***
- If a defendant was intoxicated, they would be assessed against a sober person in the defendant's circumstances
- The Jury should not take into account any personality disorders if its only relevance is that it may impact a person's capacity for tolerance and self-restraint ***(Wilcocks [2016] EWCA Crim 2043, [40])*** & ***(Rejmanski [2017])***
    - A mental disorder can be relevant, where it affects something other than the defendant's general capacity for tolerance and self-restraint
        - E.g. may be relevant to the gravity of the qualifying trigger
        - Would still be able to plead diminished responsibility if their mental disorder renders him unable to exercise the degree of self-control of a 'normal' person

Involuntary Manslaughter and Intoxication

Unlawful Act Manslaughter

→ Also referred to as 'constructive manslaughter'

The **commission of an unlawful act which inadvertently causes death** (the defended does not need to intend to kill or foresee the death)

There must be no available defences (***Webster v Crown Prosecution Service)***
- 'If the application of force is committed in lawful self-defence, it does not constitute an assault and it is not unlawful. There will be no conviction for manslaughter'

Actus Reus

For unlawful act manslaughter, the defendant must:

a) Do an unlawful act;
b) Which is dangerous; and
c) Which causes the victim's death ***(Larkin (1944))***

Do an unlawful act:
The defendant must have **committed a crime requiring proof of intention of recklessness** (***R v Lamb***)

- The unlawful act will usually be an assault but doesn't have to be
- A failure to act *cannot* give rise to a charge of unlawful act manslaughter

Case Law Example:

- ***DPP v Newbury and Jones***: defendant's pushed a paving stone over a bridge into the path of a train, smashed through the windsor and killed the guard
  - The defendant did not need to intend or foresee the risk of frightening or harming anyone
  - The unlawful act could be criminal damage, burglary or theft (didn't need to be assault)

R v Lowe: defendant was convicted of awful act manslaughter of a child after neglecting it, causing its death → Court of Appeal quashed conviction as no unlawful act had been committed

Which is dangerous

A dangerous act is an act which is **likely to injure** another person (***Larkin (1944)***)

- The act must carry the risk of some harm to some person, albeit not serious harm ***(R v Church*** and ***DPP v Newbury)***
  - Burglary could amount to an unlawful and dangerous act if the burglary in question was objectively dangerous (***R v Bristow)***
  - An act creating shock may amount to a dangerous act (***R v Dawson)***

The test is **entirely objective** → whether a reasonable and sober person would think the act was dangerous

- This person does not need to recognise the precise form or 'sort' of harm which occurred
- Assumed to have the knowledge of someone present at the scene of the crime and watched the act being performed (***R v Dawson)***
- Where the risk of harm becomes obvious to the reasonable person present at the scene of the crime, the defendant's unlawful act becomes dangerous ***(R v Watson)***

Drugs:

- Where the defendant injects the victim with drugs, the unlawful act may be the malicious administration of a poison or noxious thing as to endanger life or inflict grievous bodily harm (***Cato [1976]***)
  - A consent by the victim to the injection is *no defence* to manslaughter
- Where the defendant supplies the drugs, the courts have struggled to justify convictions for unlawful act manslaughter
  - A supplier of drugs is not guilty of unlawful act manslaughter → the free and voluntary act of self-administration breaks the chain of causation(***Kennedy (No. 2))***

Mens Rea

Intention to do the unlawful act

Manslaughter by Gross Negligence

Where the defendant has caused the death of a human, but **without a guilty state of mind**

There was no intention / recklessness to cause death or grievous bodily harm

Occurs through a breach of duty of care owed to that victim

- A reasonable person would have foreseen that the defendant's breach exposed the deceased to an obvious and serious risk of death ***(R v Zaman)***

You don't need to prove that the defendant was aware of the risk that his conduct might fall below the standard of the reasonable person, merely that it did ***(Attorney General's Reference (No. 2 of 1999)***

The test (*R v Adomako*)

Test for establishing manslaughter by gross negligence (*R v Adomako*):

a) There is a duty of care owed by the defendant to the victim
   - Question of law for the jury (***Evans [2009]***)
b) There must be a breach of that duty of care
c) It was reasonably foreseeable that the breach of duty gave rise to a serious and obvious *risk of death* (not serious injury) (***R v Singh)***
d) Evidence that the breach of duty did cause the death of the victim
e) The circumstances of the breach were truly exceptionally bad and so reprehensible as to justify the conclusion that it amounted to gross negligence and required criminal sanction (crime against the state)

→ **Ordinary principles of negligence apply (except for defence of illegality)**

Dangerous driving:

- A very high degree of negligence is required to be proved before the felony is established' (***Andrews v DPP [1937]***)

Omissions?

Gross Negligence Manslaughter can occur as a result of a failure to act, where there is a duty to do so (***R v Adomako)*** **and** (***R v Khan)***

A person will become liable where he realises the danger that he has created and then fails to take reasonable steps to avert the danger

Case Law Example:

- ***R v Evans [2009]***: defendant supplied heroin to the victim (half-sister) → victim overdosed and defendant chose not to seek medical assistance → convicted of gross negligence manslaughter
  - There does not need to be a special relationship

> - 'When a person has created or contributed to the creation of a state of affairs which he knows, or ought reasonably to know, has become life threatening, a consequent duty on him to act by taking reasonable steps to save the other's life will normally arise'

Intoxication

Intoxication is generally not a defence, unless it caused the defendant to lack the relevant *mens rea* for that offence

If the defendant did not have the necessary *mens rea*, two further questions will be asked:

a) Was the intoxication voluntary or involuntary
b) Is the crime one of basic or specific intent

Voluntary Intoxication:

Intoxication is *only involuntary* if either the defendant had no knowledge that they were taking any alcohol or drug (spiking) or there is an unusual side effect of a medically prescribed drug (taken in accordance with the instructions)

A defendant is still voluntarily intoxicated if they were drinking, but merely *underestimated* the amount or the effect it was having on them (***R v Allen [1988]***)

→ Even if the defence is successful, will generally still be guilty of another (lesser) offence

Crime of Specific Intent:

Voluntary intoxication will only provide a defence to crimes of specific intent (***DPP v Majewski [1976]***)

- Crimes of specific intent are those where the *mens rea* of the offence requires intention and nothing less (e.g. murder)
- Crimes of basic intent are ones where the *mens rea* can be established by something other than intention (e.g. proof of recklessness)
- Voluntary intoxication will not provide a defence to any sexual offences (***R v Heard [2007]***)

Dutch Courage:

A defendant could not rely on voluntary intoxication if they had the *mens rea* for the crime before they started to drink

- ***Attorney-General for Northern Ireland v Gallagher [1963]***: defendant decided to kill his wife and drank most a bottle of whiskey to give himself 'dutch courage'

Involuntary Intoxication:

A defendant who is **involuntarily intoxicated**, may have a **defence to any crime (either basic or specific intent)**, if they did not have the *mens rea* for it

<u>*Case Law Example:*</u>

- ***R v Hardie [1984]***: defendant took valium and later started a fire (charged with arson) → claimed he did not know what he was doing because of the effect of the drug
    - Held that his intoxication was involuntary → whilst he had voluntarily taken the drug, there was no evidence that he knew, or ought to have known, that the valium would render him aggressive and incapable of appreciating risks

- ***R v Kingston [1994]***: defendant was given coffee which was spiked with drugs → then assaulted a young boy → prosecution were able to prove that the defendant had committed the offence with the necessary *mens rea* (the man had known paedophile tendencies)

Drunken Mistakes:

If a defendant mistakenly thought he was being attacked, and that belief was due to his intoxication, then the defence of self-defence must fail (***R v O'Grady [1987]***)

- Affirmed in ***R v Hatton [2006] 1 Cr App R 16*** that it doesn't matter if it was basic or specific intent

Loss of Control:

Loss of control due to intoxication is unlikely to hold up as no adequate qualifying trigger (mistaken fear of violence or mistaken belief of being seriously wronged)

Criticisms:

Seems contrary to logic and common sense that:

An accused who was drunk and therefore did not have the intention to kill or cause grievous bodily harm is not guilty of murder, whereas

An accused who because they were drunk thought they were about to be viciously attacked and so defends themselves is guilty

Theft and Fraud

Theft

Theft is defined in ***s 1(1) of the Theft Act 1968 (TA 1968)***:

- 'A person is guilty of theft if he dishonestly appropriates property belonging to another, with the intention of permanently depriving the other of it'

All 5 elements must be present at the same time

Actus Reus of Theft

Appropriation

Appropriation = the physical act required by a defendant in order to establish the *actus reus*

- ***Section 3(1)***: 'any assumption by a person of the rights of an owner amounts to an appropriation, and this includes, where he has come by the property (innocently or not) without stealing it, any later assumption of a right to it by keeping or dealing with it as an owner'

<u>*Case Law definition:*</u>

- In ***R v Morris [1984]*** the judges decided that an appropriation was:
    a) An act which adversely interferes with or usurps 'any right of an owner' (it is an act which is unauthorised)
    b) An assumption of any *one* right of an owner (to appropriate, the defendant had to usurp only one of the many rights of an owner, not all of them)

Decided in ***Lawrence v Metropolitan Police Commissioner [1972]*** and confirmed in ***DPP v Gomez [1993]*** that authorisation of the owner was irrelevant

- Confirmed that an appropriation occurred, even if the property passed with the consent or authorisation of the owner
- Means virtually anything a person does to property that is not theirs is an appropriation

Appropriation and Gifts

R v Hinks [2000]: it was decided that an indefeasible title to property could amount to an appropriation

- There can still be an appropriation, even when there was a valid gift of property to the defendant according to civil law

Appropriation - Later Assumption of the Rights of an Owner

S 3(1): an appropriation includes 'where he has come by the property without stealing it', but there is a 'later assumption of a right to it by keeping or dealing with it as an owner'

- This would cover someone who comes into possession of property legitimately, but later does something which assumes the right of an owner

Appropriation occurs once

Once the defendant has stolen the property (and appropriated with full *mens rea*), **a later assumption of rights by them will *not* amount to another theft of the property**

It is up to the jury, as a question of fact, to decide whether the appropriation was continuous or complete

Case Law Example:

R v Atakpu [1994]: defendants arrested at Dover, driving cars which had been hired abroad using false documents to then sell in England. Convicted of conspiracy to steal but quashed as Court of Appeal found that the elements of theft had been made out when the cars were first hired

- Any later dealing with the cars could not found a charge of theft or of conspiracy to steal as there was no appropriation (had already stolen the cars when they hired them)

Innocent third party

In situations where a **third party is sold a stolen item**, they will **not have deemed to have stolen it**

- ***S 3(2) of the TA 1968***: a person is not liable for theft if, when they acquired the goods:
    a) The transfer was 'for value' and so payment was made → (money or exchange of goods)
    b) The purchaser acted 'in good faith', with no doubts or concerns about the transaction and its legality

Not the case if you are gifted a stolen item → would be considered appropriation if you came by it innocently (as a gift), but later assumed the rights of an owner by keeping it

Limitations on Appropriation:

R v Briggs [2004]: the defendant's aunt and uncle (the Reid's) were selling their home. Briggs sent the conveyancers (who were dealing with the transaction) a letter of authority signed by the Reid's to authorise them to send money to solicitors acting for the vendors of the Reid's new house

- Title of the new house was vested in Briggs
- Reid's argued that their consent to the transaction had been induced by fraud as they believed that the title would be transferred to them
- Court held that as Briggs had caused her relatives to perform an act in relation to their own bank account, did not render her dishonest and deceptive conduct an appropriation (it would have been an appropriation if she had performed it herself)

Property

There must be an appropriation of 'property' to meet the *actus reus* of theft

- *S 4(1) of the 1968 Act*: 'property includes money and all other property, real or personal, including things in action and other intangible property'

Includes:

Money = any currency

Real Property = land and things attached or fixed to it

Personal Property = any tangible object that is not real property. List is virtually endless (***R v Smith, Plummer and Haines [2011]***)

Things in Action = property which cannot be touched or felt, but is something that can be enforced by a legal action, e.g. a bank account or copyright)

Other intangible property = e.g. a patent (not considered things in action even though cannot be touched)

Case Law Examples:

- ***Chan Man-sin v R [1988]***: defendant was a company accountant who forged company cheques
  - By drawing, presenting and negotiating cheques he had assumed the right of an owner (appropriation). The account was a thing in action and so amount to property

- In ***R v Navvabi [1986]***: the defendant knew his bank account was overdrawn but continued to use his bank card to support cheques
  - Charged with theft from the bank → but held he was not guilty as he had dealt only with his own account, so had not assumed the rights of an owner over someone else's thing in action

Oxford v Moss [1979]: confidential information was not property

Low v Blease [1975]: electricity cannot be stolen as it was not property

Land:

There are only very limited circumstances where land can be stolen

- *S 4(2) of the TA*: only in the following cases can a person steal land:

  When he is a trustee or personal representative, or is otherwise authorised to sell or dispose of land belonging to another, and appropriates the land by dealing with it in breach of the confidence reposed in him (e.g. when someone sells land which they owned jointly)

  When he is not in possession of the land and appropriates anything forming part of the land by severing it (e.g. chopping down a tree / removing something which has been severed)

When, being in possession of the land under a tenancy, he appropriates the whole or part of any fixture or structure let to be used with the land (basically taking something fixed to the land which they are not supposed to, e.g. a tenant removing a shelving unit from their rental)

Wild Flowers and Plants:

S 4(3): 'a person who picks mushrooms growing wild on any land, or who picks flowers, fruit or foliage from a plant growing wild on any land, does not steal what he picks, unless he does it for reward or for sale or other commercial purposes

Wild Creatures:

S 4(4): 'wild creatures, tamed or untamed, shall be regarded as property; but a person cannot steal a wild creature not tamed nor ordinarily kept in captivity, unless it has been reduced into possession by or on behalf of another person and possession of it has not since been lost or abandoned, or another person is in course of reducing it into possession'

Wild creatures shall be regarded as property and can be stolen when they are tamed and or kept in captivity and or in the possession of another

Belonging to Another

Property that is appropriated must 'belong to another'

- ***S 5(1):*** 'property shall be regarded as belonging to any person having possession or control of it, or having in it any proprietary right or interest'
  - So can include people other than the actual legal owner:
  - If property is loaned to someone, if it was then stolen, would have taken property from both the owner and the loaner
  - If someone holds property on trust, they are also included

Companies

If a company director took some of the company assets, they would have stolen property 'belonging to another' (as the property belonged to the company)

- Includes sole shareholders in a company as it is still considered a separate legal entity

Your own property

If you loaned your property to someone else and then took it back early → you would be appropriating property 'belonging to another'

- Joint ownership of a property → if the other person sells it without acceptance they would have the actus reus of theft as the other person has a 'proprietary right or interest'

Case Law Example:

- ***R v Turner (No 2) [1971]***: Turner took his car to a garage to be repaired and then left without paying → held that the garage had a 'lien' over the car and so were able to retain possession of the car until payment → the property belonged to another

Abandoned Property

If property has been abandoned, it does not belong to anyone and so cannot be stolen

Case Law Example:

- ***Williams v Phillips (1957)***: rubbish left outside a house for a local authority to collect was the householder's property up until the collection point (when it then became the property of the local authority as was abandoned by the householder)
- ***R (Ricketts) v Basildon Magistrates' Court [2011]***: defendant caught taking clothes left outside a charity shop → held that the property had not been abandoned (was either the original owners still or now the charity's)

Obligation to deal with property in a particular way

Section 5(3) was introduced to cover a situation where the owner parts with their property to another party, with the understanding that they would deal with the property in a particular way

- 'Where a person receives property from or on account of another, and is under an obligation to the other to retain and deal with that property or its proceeds in a particular way, the property or proceeds shall be regarded as [still] belonging to the other'

Contrary to the normal rule that ownership of cash passes when it is handed over

- The accused must be under a legal obligation (not just a moral one)

Case Law Example:

- ***DPP v Huskinson [1988]***: defendant applied for a Housing Benefit → received £479 but paid only £200 to his landlord (spent the rest on himself) → not guilty of theft
  - No legal obligation to deal with the money in a particular way (did not have to spend the Housing Benefit on rent)
- ***R v Hall [1973]***: a travel agent received money from clients to pay for flights → defendant did not pay for the flights, nor refund the money

- Although the defendant was under a contractual duty to buy his clients their tickets, he was not required to use that specific money → was not under an obligation to deal with the property or its proceeds in a particular way

- ***R v Wain [1995]***: defendant misappropriated money which he had raised for charity and collected in a special bank account
    - He transferred the money into his own account and when he cashed the cheque to the charity, there were insufficient funds
    - Was charged with theft as he was under an obligation to retain the proceeds which he had credited into a separate account

At the Time of the Dishonest Appropriation

The property must belong to another at the time of the dishonest appropriation as all 5 elements of the offence must be established at the same time

- If ownership, possession and control of the property had already passed to the defendant at the time of their dishonest appropriation, they are *not* guilty of theft

Case Law Example:

- ***Edwards v Ddin [1976]***: the defendant enters a garage and fills up his car with petrol. Then decided not to pay and drives off. At the time the defendant was dishonest (i.e. when he decided not to pay), the property had already passed to him
    - The *actus reus* element of belonging to another did not coexist with the *mens rea* elements of theft
    - If the defendant had always intended to leave without paying, the dishonest appropriation starts when he first dispenses the petrol and so would be liable for dishonestly appropriating property belonging to another

Mens Rea of Theft

There are two elements which must be proved:

a) The defendant was dishonest
b) They had an intention permanently to deprive the owner of the property

The Defendant was Dishonest

***S 2(1)* provides 3 situations where, if applicable, the defendant is *not* dishonest:**

It is a subjective test → whether the defendant believed the circumstances existed

1) If he appropriates the property in the belief that **he has in law the right to deprive the other of it,** on behalf of himself or a third party
   - E.g. where the defendant thought the property the victim had was theirs and that they had the legal right to take it back

2) If he appropriates the property in the belief that **he would have the other's consent** if the other knew of the appropriation and the circumstances of it
   - The defendant must believe that the other would have consented (not just ought or might)

3) If he appropriates the property in the belief that the person to whom the property belongs **cannot be discovered by taking reasonable steps** (except where the property comes to him as a trustee or personal representative)
   - E.g. picking up lost property where the owner cannot be found
   - If the defendant subsequently realises the owner can be found, they could now be guilt of theft (appropriating the property by keeping it)

S 2(2): 'a person's appropriation of property belonging to another may be dishonest **notwithstanding that he is willing to pay for the property'**
   - A willingness to pay is not an automatic defence to a charge of theft - question of fact for the jury

The Ivey Test

The test for dishonesty, where ***s 2(1) of the TA*** is *not* applicable, is laid out in ***Ivey v Genting Casinos [2017]***:

1) **Subjective**: what was the defendant's knowledge or belief as to the facts
2) **Objective**: was what the defendant did dishonest, according to the standards of reasonable and honest people

Intention Permanently to Deprive

S 1(1) of the TA 1968: they must also have the **intent permanently to deprive** the other of the property that they have appropriated

It is possible to intend permanently to deprive someone who had only a limited interest in the property

Case Law Example:

- ○ ***R v Velumyl [1989]***: if a person takes money from someone, intending to repay it, there is an intention permanently to deprive → they intended to deprive the owner of the particular notes and coins they took

S 6(1): a person is ***not*** liable for theft if they intend only to borrow something

- Except where the intention was to treat the property as their own to dispose of, regardless of the other's rights
- This includes where a defendant takes items and then offers them back to the owner in exchange for payment (***R v Raphael [2008]***)

<u>*Case Law Example:*</u>

R v Marshall [1998]: defendant was charged with theft, after implementing a scheme which involved acquiring used but unexpired tickets from tube passengers (to sell on)

Whilst defendant argued that he had no intention permanently to deprive the tube of the tickets as they would be returned via the second wave of passengers

Court held that by acquiring and re-selling the tickets, the defendant had intended to treat them as his own to dispose of, regardless of the rights of the Tube company

R v Lloyd [1985]: defendant worked at a cinema → used to remove films to make 'pirate' copies and then return the films to the cinema

- Court ruled that as there was still a practical value to the films, the borrowing was not equivalent to an outright taking or disposal

S 6(2): 'where a person parts with the property (belonging to another), under a condition as to its return which he may not be able to perform, this amounts to treating the property as his own to dispose of regardless of the other's rights

- E.g. pawning → requires departing from property with a condition as to its return which may not be performed

Fraud

The Offences Under the Fraud Act 2006 was designed to implement recommendations made by the Law Commission to overhaul the law in relation to situations where the defendant deceives someone

- ***S 1(2)* sets out the methods by which fraud may be committed:**
    - By *making* a false representation
    - By *failing* to disclose information
    - By *abuse* of position

There is no requirement for the prosecution to prove the defendant actually obtained anything by their actions, just that they **intended to do so**

Fraud by False Representation

***S 2 (1):* of the Act provides that a person is in breach if he:**

a) Dishonestly makes a false representation ***and***
b) Intends, by making the representation to
    i) Make a gain for himself or another, ***or***
    ii) Cause loss to another or to expose another to a risk of loss

Actus Reus of False Representation Fraud

The *actus reus* of fraud is **making a representation** (conduct) and that **representation is false** (circumstance)

Making a representation

Under s 2(3) a representation is:
Any representation as to fact or law, including a representation as to the state of mind of -

a) The person making the representation, or
b) Any other person

- ***S 2(4):*** This can be express or implied
    - If a defendant says (or implies) that they will do an act in the future, or that some event will occur in the future, it usually implies a representation
    - 'Can be stated in words or communicated by conduct, there is no limitation on the way in which the words must be expressed'

That is a false representation

Under *s 2(2)*: a representation is *false* if:

a) It is untrue or misleading ***and***
b) The person making it knows that it is (or might be), untrue or misleading

- Can also situations where nothing is said, but the individual's behaviour creates a false impression (e.g. using a stolen credit card)
- If a defendant says something they believe to be false but is actually true, the *actus reus* will not be established
- Down to the courts to determine what is untrue or misleading

Can be done to a machine, not just a person:

- ***S 2(5) of the Fraud Act 2006***: 'a representation may be regarded as made if it (or anything implying it) is submitted in any form to any system or device designed to receive, convey or respond to communications (with or without human intervention)

<u>*Case Law Example:*</u>

- ***Idrees v DPP [2011]***: defendant got someone to impersonate him to sit his driving test → the false representation was made by the defendant when he booked the test online
- ***R v O'Leary [2013]***: defendant visited home of two elderly victims with dementia and demanded payment for repair work on their roof (hadn't done this)
- ***DPP v Ray [1974]***: friends went out for dinner, after eating they decided not to pay, but waited until the waiter had left the room before leaving
    - The defendant had impliedly represented that he had the means and intention of paying. That representation by his conduct became false when he decided not to pay
- ***R v Lambie [1981]***: the defendant exceeded the limit on their credit card but continued to use it → HoL held that she had falsely represented that she had authority to use the card by continuing to use it once she had exceeded her credit limit

Mens Rea of False Representation Fraud

Under *s(2)* the *mens rea* of fraud by false representation is:

a) To be dishonest; and
b) Intend, by making the representation, to make a gain for themselves or another, or to cause loss to another or to expose another to a risk of loss; ***and***
c) Know the representation is untrue or misleading, or know that it might be so

To be dishonest

There is no definition of dishonesty in the Act - left to the court to assess

- Further guidance indicates that the common law test (the ***Ivey Test***) can be used → whether the defendant's behaviour would be regarded as dishonest by the ordinary standards of reasonable and honest people

Intent to make a gain / cause loss

The defendant must dishonestly make the false representation with the intention, by making the representation, of **making a gain for themselves or another, or of causing loss to another or exposing another to a risk of loss.**

- There must be an intended causal link; the defendant must intend the gain or loss to be as a result of the false representation

S 5: gain and loss extend only to gain or loss in money or other property (real or personal) and includes any such gain or loss *whether temporary or permanent*

When is the offence committed:

- Occurs as soon **as the false representation is made** - there is no need for any consequence to follow from the representation
- The full offence is complete, as soon as the false representation is made, provided the defendant has the requisite *mens rea*

Fraud by Failing to Disclose Information

Under the Fraud Act 2006, a person is guilty of fraud under *s 3* if they:

a) *AR*: dishonestly fail to disclose to another person information which they are under a legal duty to disclose ***and***
b) *MR*: intend, by failing to disclose the information, to make a gain for themselves or another, or to cause loss to another or to expose another to a risk of loss

It only becomes a criminal offence if the defendant fails to disclose information when they are **under a legal duty to do** so:

- This includes 'duties under oral contracts as well as written contracts' (statute, good faith contracts, express or implied terms of a contract, custom of a trade or the existence of a fiduciary relationship)

Fraud by Abuse of Position

Covers defendants who are in some form of privileged position in relation to the victim

- The offence is complete once the defendant carries out the act that is the abuse of their power → immaterial whether they succeed and whether any loss or gain is actually made

***S 4:* a person is in breach of this section if they:**

a) *AR*: Occupy a position in which they are expected to safeguard, or not to act against, the financial interests of another person;
b) *AR*: Dishonestly abuse that position ***and***
c) *MR*: Intend, by means of the abuse of that position, to make a gain for themselves or another, or to cause loss to another or to expose another to a risk of loss

Actus Reus of Fraud by Abuse of Position

Occupation of relevant position

There must be an existence of a position of financial trust between the dependent and victim

- One in which the defendant is expected to safeguard or not to act against the financial interest of another person
- Quite a wide interpretation

Case Law Example:

R v Valujevs [2014]: unlicensed gang-masters abused their position by exploiting migrant workers, making lawful deductions from their wages and charging excessive rent payment

Abuse of position

The abuse can be committed either by a positive act or by an omission

Case Law Example:

R v Rouse [2014]: defendant was the deputy manager of a care home with access to residents' bank and credit cards & account details.

- Abused his position when he withdrew money out of the cards for personal use

Mens Rea of Fraud by Abuse of Position

Dishonesty and an intention to make a gain for themself or another, or to cause loss to another, or to expose another to risk of loss

Offence of Making Off Without Payment:

S 3 of the Theft Act (TA) 1978:

'A person who, knowing that payment on the spot for any goods supplied or services done is required or expected from him, dishonestly makes off without having paid as required or expected and with intent to avoid payment of the amount due shall be guilty of an offence'

- Helpful for situations where the defendant has committed the *actus reus*, but only later forms the appropriate *mens rea* (can't be guilty of theft as the *actus reus* and *mens rea* do not coincide in time)

Actus Reus

1. Goods must be supplied or services done
2. The defendant must make off from the spot where payment is required
3. Without paying as required or expected (can't be a worthless cheque)

Exception:

- ***S 3(3) of the TA 1978:*** does not apply 'where the supply of goods or the doing of the service is contrary to law, or where the service done is such that payment is not legally enforceable'

Mens Rea

1) Dishonestly
2) Knowledge that payment on the sport was required or expected
3) Intent to avoid payment

Defences:

- ***R v Vincent (Christopher James) [2001]***: where the defendant has obtained the agreement of the 'victim' that payment can be made in the future
- ***R v Allen [1985]***: someone who makes off, intending to return at a future date and pay, cannot be liable for this offence

Burglary and Robbery

Robbery

Robbery is an indictable only offence, with a maximum sentence of life imprisonment (***s 8(2) of the Theft Act 1968***).

There are 4 elements that must be established in order to convict a defendant of robbery (*s 8(1)*):

1) That the defendant stole (i.e. committed an offence of theft); ***and***
2) That the defendant either:
   a) Used force on any person, ***or***
   b) Put or sought to put any person in fear of being then and there (immediately) subjected to force; ***and***
3) That the force or threat of force was immediately before or at the time of the theft; ***and***
4) That the force or threat of force was used *in order to steal*

1) Theft

Must first establish that a theft has occurred (all 5 elements must be present → appropriation of property belonging to another, dishonesty and with an intention permanently to deprive)

- Must prove both the ***actus reus* and *mens rea* of theft first**
   - ***R v Vinall [2011]***: the defendants' convictions for robbery were quashed as could not prove that they had an intention to permanently deprive the victim of his property at the point when force was used on the victim

2) Force

Determining if force has been used is left to the jury to determine on a case-by-case basis (***R v Dawson (1976)***)
In the ***Dawson*** case, the victim's bag was grabbed by one of the defendants → as found guilty, implies that the amount of force used does not need to be significant

Where only slight touching is used, (e.g. pickpocketing), *not sufficient* to charge robbery (***P v DPP [2013]***)

a) Force against a person

The use or threat of force does not have to be against the person to whom the property belongs to

- ***S 8(1)***: the force or threat of force can be in relation to 'any person'
- There should *not* be a distinction between applying force to the person or their property (***R v Clouden [1987]***)
- In cases where force is threatened (but not used), the intended victim of the force must be aware of the threat

b) Force immediately before or at the time of theft

The use or threat of force must be broadly simultaneous with the theft in order to establish robbery

- ***S 8(1)***: the threat or use of force must be 'immediately before or at the time' of the theft
- Any force used or threatened after the theft will not give rise to a charge of robbery
- The question of whether the appropriation was continuing at the time the force was used is a question to be determined by the jury (***R v Hale (1978)***)

c) Force in order to steal

The threat or use of force must be made in order to steal (*S 8(1)*)

- Forms part of the *mens rea* of the offence

d) Recklessness

Undecided, but has been suggested that an intention on the part of the defendant to use or threaten force need not be established

- Recklessness to the use or threat of force is suffice (*mens rea* of assault or battery)

Burglary

Burglary is an either-way offence, with maximum imprisonment of 14 years for domestic premises & 10 years for commercial premises

Burglary must occur within a property belonging to someone other than the defendant

***S 9(1)*: a person is guilty of burglary if:**

At the time of their entry into a building (or part of a building) as a trespasser, they *intended* to:

- Steal anything in the building or part of a building in question (theft)
- Inflict on any person grievous bodily harm
- Do unlawful damage (criminal damage) to the building

Or, having entered any building or part of a building as a trespasser, they

- Actually steal or *attempts* to steal anything in the building or that part of it
- Or, inflicts or *attempts* to inflict grievous bodily harm on any person

1) Effective Entry

The actus reus of both ***S 9(1)(a)*** and ***S 9(1)(b)*** requires **an effective entry**

This is a question of fact for the jury (***R v Brown [1985]***)

Entry of some part of the defendant's body into the premises *could* amount to an effective entry (***R v Ryan [1996]***)

- Does not need to be the whole body (***R v Brown)*** → whilst only the upper body entered, was *still* classed as an effective entry

Under the old law, the insertion of an instrument into a building was an entry by the defendant if it was used to commit an offence (regarded as an extension of the defendant's body)

- It would *not* be an entry if the instrument was used simply to enable the defendant to get into the property

2) Into a building or part of a building

a) A Building

The provisions of ***s 9*** **do not give a full definition** of structures that fall within **the definition of a building,** but ***s 9(4)*** states **it does include:**

- Inhabited vehicles and vessels, whether or not the inhabitant is there at the time of the burglary
- Case law suggests that a building must have some degree of permanence about it
- The only time you have to consider if a property is inhabited in order to determine whether it is defined as a building, is where the property is a vehicle or vessel
  - E.g. a campervan is a building if it is a permanent home to someone or is being used as a holiday home at the time of the burglary

b) Part of a Building

Trespassing can be committed either by entry into a building or into part of a building

- It is generally accepted that moving to a different apartment or to a separate room of a building *without permission* can be regarded as moving to a separate part of the building
- Whether the defendant entered a part of a building is a question of fact for the jury

Case Law Example:

R v Walkington [1979]: defendant was convicted of burglary when he went around a three-sided counter in a shop to get to a till

- As the till was a separate part of the building (with a physical demarcation excluding public from this section), defendant entered as a trespasser

As a trespasser

There must be proof that the defendant entered without consent or permission and that they knew or were reckless as to the fact they had no consent or permission to enter

a) Actus Reus

If it cannot be established that the defendant entered as a trespasser, there can never be a conviction of burglary

There must be proof that the defendant entered without consent or permission

Under the old law, permission to enter which was obtained by fraud was not a true permission (***R v Boyle [1954] 2 QB 292***)

A defendant could be a trespasser where they had permission to enter for lawful purposes but *instead* entered for an unlawful purpose, and they knew or were reckless that they were exceeding the terms of the permission given (***R v Jones and Smith [1976] 1 WLR 672***)

- Here, defendant stole from his parents home (had permission to enter the home), but not to enter the home to steal
- Must have exceeded the terms of the consent given, *at the time of entry* (not after entering the property)

b) Mens Rea

In order to establish the trespass element for burglary, prosecution must also prove **guilty state of mind**

- At the time of entry into the building, the defendant must either know they were entering as a trespasser or be reckless as to whether they were a trespasser (***R v Collins [1973] 1 QB 100***)
    - Recklessness: defendant must foresee the risk that they don't have permission to enter and go on, without justification, to take the risk

Is it a s 9(1)(a) or a s 9(1)(b)

ATTEMPT AND INTENT are distinguished

Intend to commit:

For S 9(1)(a):

- If the *actus reus* and *mens rea* of entering a building (or part of a building) as a trespasser is met. Convicted of burglary (***s 9(1)a***) if they also have the following *mens rea*:

They have *intent* to commit theft, GBH or criminal damage (at the time of entry)

- No need for the defendant to *actually* commit any of those offences, just that they intended to do so
- Intent to commit one of the offences must be present **at the time the defendant enters the building as a trespasser**

Actually Commit

For S 9(1)(b):

- If the *actus reus* and *mens rea* of entering a building (or part of a building) as a trespasser is met. Convicted of burglary (***s 9(1)b***) if they also have the following additional *actus reus* & *mens rea*:

They have *actually attempted or committed* theft or GBH

Actus Reus = they commit the actus reus of theft, attempted theft, GBG or attempted GBH

NOT CRIMINAL DAMAGE

Mens rea: they have the *mens rea* for theft, attempted theft, GBH or attempted GBH

The defendant *can* form the mens rea for the offence of theft or causing GBH *after* they have entered

Conditional Intent:

Attorney-General's Reference (Nos 1 and 2 of 1979) [1980] QB 180:

- Where the defendant had entered properties looking for money to steal, a conditional intent to steal was sufficient

- No defence for the defendants to argue that their intent to steal was conditional on there being anything worth stealing in the property

Aggravated Burglary

Criminals who are armed when they commit an offence of burglary can face liability for an aggravated offence of burglary under ***s 10:***

- 'A person is guilty of aggravated burglary if he commits any burglary and *at the time* has with him any firearm or imitation firearm, any weapon of offence, or any explosive'

At the time of the offence

The defendant **must have the weapon with them 'at the time' of committing the burglary**

- For ***s 9(1)(a)*** this is at the time of entry
- For ***s 9(1)(b)*** the relevant time is when the ulterior offence is committed

Case Law Example:

R v Francis [1982]: defendants entered a house armed with sticks but discarded them before committing theft → not guilty of aggravated burglary as could not prove that they had the sticks with them at the moment they intended to steal

R v O'Leary (1986): defendant picked up a knife once inside the property before confronting the occupants → whilst he did not have the knife at the time of entry, was guilty of aggravated burglary under ***s 9(1)(b)*** as he had the weapon with him at the time he committed the theft

They must have an applicable weapon

Weapons include:

- Firearms (including air guns, air pistols and imitation firearms, whether capable of being discharged or not)
- A weapon of offence (meaning any article made or adapted for use for causing injury or incapacitating a person, or intended for such use). This could include:
  a) A machete as it has been made for use in causing injury
  b) A broken bottle adopted for use in causing injury
  c) A hammer intended for such use
  d) A length of rope as this could be used to incapacitate a person
  e) Handcuffs as these are intended for such use
- Explosives

Knowledge of the weapon

The defendant must know they have the item with them, but there is *no need* to prove that they intended to use the weapon during the burglary (***R v Stones [1989] 1 WLR 156***)

R v Kelly (1993) 97 Cr App R 245: the fact that the defendant used a screwdriver in the heat of the moment was not a defence to aggravated burglary as the defendant had the intent to use it, should the need arise

Criminal Damage

There are 4 offences under the Criminal Damage Act 1971:

a) ***S 1(1):*** simple criminal damage
b) ***S 1(2):*** aggravated criminal damage
c) ***S 1(3):*** and s 1(1): simple arson → (criminal damage + fire)
d) ***S 1(3):*** and s 1(2): aggravated arson (aggravated criminal damage (by fire))

Simple Criminal Damage

Simple criminal damage (***s 1(1)***) = 'a person who without lawful excuse destroys or damages any property belonging to another intending to destroy or damage any such property or being reckless as to whether any such property would be destroyed or damaged shall be guilty of an offence'

- Maximum sentence of 10 years (either-way offence)

Actus Reus

There are 3 elements which make up the *actus reus* of the offence:

a) Damage or destruction;
b) Of property;
c) Belonging to another

a) Damage or Destruction

The first requirement is to 'destroy or damage'

- There *does not* have to be extensive or permanent damage (but must be more than merely trivial)
- The issue of whether damage had been caused was a matter of fact and degree to be determined in a common sense way (***Roe v Kingerlee [1986]***)
    - Typically, if expense is involved in restoring the property to its previous condition, the court is likely to find that damage is established

Case Law Example:

- ***Hardman v Chief Constable of Avon and Somerset Constabulary [1986]***: drawings on a pavement using soluble chalks amounted to criminal damage as the local authority incurred expense in cleaning it up
- ***Gayford v Chouler* [1898]:** the defendant trespassed onto a field of deep grass → caused damage to the value of 6d → actual damage had been done to the grass

- *A (a juvenile) v R [1978]*: conviction quashed → appellant spat on a police officer's raincoat, leaving a faint mark (not sufficient damage as the spit could be wiped away)
- *Cox v Riley (1986)*: erasing or altering computer programs or data on computer discs can also constitute damage → held as tangible property
    - Although would now be prosecuted under ***Computer Misuse Act*** instead

b) Property

Wide definition of property (*s 10(1)*)

- Covers property of a tangible nature (real or personal), including money and the property referred to in ***s 10(1)(a)*** and ***(b)***
- Can include certain animals (e.g. pets) and plants (e.g. those growing in a garden)
    - *Does not* include mushrooms growing wild on any land or flowers, fruit or plants growing wild

c) Belonging to Another

S 10(2): property shall be treated as belonging to any person

a) Having the custody or control of it
b) Having in it any proprietary right or interest (so can include a landlord, co-owner or lending institution for a mortgage)
c) Having a charge on it

Mens Rea

The defendant must:

a) Intend to damage or destroy property or be reckless as to such damage or destruction; **and**
b) Know that the property belongs to another or be reckless as to whether the property belongs to another

- It is a **subjective test** → the defendant must have recognised the risk and gone on to take it
    - ***R v Smith [1974]***: defendant (a tenant), damaged fixtures at the property, wrongly believing that those fixtures belonged to him. Conviction quashed as court held that if a person honestly believed property was their own, they lacked the *mens rea*
        - Does not matter whether the belief was reasonably held, as long as it was an honest belief

Defence - Lawful Excuse

S 5(2)(a):

Under ***s5(2)(a)***, a defendant will have lawful excuse (a defence) if they argue that either:

a) They believed they had the **consent** of the person who ***was*** entitled to give permission to the damage to be caused
b) They believed they had the **consent** of the person who ***they thought*** was entitled to give permission for the damage to be caused
c) They believed they ***would have had*** the **consent** of the person entitled to give permission, if that person had known of the damage and the circumstances
d) They believed they ***would have had*** the **consent** of the person who they ***thought was*** entitled to give permission if that person had known of the damage and the circumstances

→ Whether the defendant believed the property was in immediate need of protection and whether the defendant believed the means of protection adopted were reasonable in all the circumstances is judged **subjectively**

Case Law Example:

- ***Denton [1982]:*** defendant was an employee who set fire to his work premises in the belief that his employer had asked him to burn the property down in order to make a fraudulent insurance claim (successful appeal, lawful excuse)
- ***Jaggard v Dickinson [1981]***: an honest mistake is sufficient for the defence of lawful excuse, even if that mistake was not justified or was made due to voluntary intoxication

S 5(2)(b):

Under ***s 5(2)(b)***, the defendant will have lawful excuse if they can argue that:

a) They believed property was in immediate need of **protection**; **and**
b) They believed that the means of protection they adopted (which led to the criminal damage) were reasonable having regard to all the circumstances

→ Under ***s 5(2)(B)***, whether a particular act of destruction or damage was done in order to protect property belonging to another is an **objective test**

- ***R v Hunt (1978)***: defendant set fire to a guest room in an old people's home (claimed he did it in order to draw attention to the defective fire alarm system)
  - Court of Appeal applied an objective test to 'in order to protect property' → the act in itself did not protect or was capable of protecting the property
- ***R v Hill; R v Hall (1989)***: Hill was in possession of a hacksaw blade, intending to use it to cut the fence at a US military base in order to protest against nuclear weapons. Argued they were acting to protect the property of neighbours, whose houses would be destroyed in the event of an attack
  - **Subjective**: did the defendant honestly believe they were protecting property
    - Doesn't matter if this belief is unreasonable
  - **Objective**: on the facts (as the defendant believed them to be), could the act amount to something done to protect property
    - Usually in relation to the immediacy of the threat

Aggravated Criminal Damage

***S 1(2) of the Criminal Damage Act 1971* → the defendant must:**

a) Destroy or damage property (*actus reus*)
    - Can belong to another person or the defendant

b) Intend to destroy or damage any property or be reckless as to whether any property is damaged or destroyed (*mens rea*)

c) Intend **by the destruction or damage to endanger the life** of another or be **reckless** as to whether another's life might be endangered (*mens rea*)

- It must be proved that 'by the damage or destruction', the defendant intended to endanger life or was reckless (***R v Steer [1987]***)
- Doesn't matter if no-one's life was actually put in danger

    R v Dudley [1989]: the defendant set fire to a house (fire bomb). The fire was quickly extinguished but the *mens rea* had to be considered at the time the defendant did the act which caused the damage

    Asquith, Webster and Seamans; Warwick (1995): two cases tried together.

    1) ***Asquith, Webster and Seamans;*** defendants pushed a heavy stone from a railway bridge onto a train passing below. Landed on the roof of a carriage. Passengers hit by debris from the roof but were not physically injured as stone did not go through.
    2) ***Warwick:*** defendant was chased by police in a car. Threw bricks at the police → smashing the window of the police car, glass hit one of the officers

    Held that *s 1(2)(b)* relates to damage envisaged by the defendant → convicted if he intended or was reckless about endangering the life of another by the damage that he envisaged he would cause

    Wenton [2010]: defendant smashed a window of a house and then threw a canister of petrol through the window (did not ignite and occupants unharmed)

    - Not convicted of aggravated criminal damage as the act of smashing the window and of throwing in the canister were considered two unrelated acts
    - Defendant had not foreseen or was reckless to damage to life from the broken window

→ The defence of lawful excuse is *not* valid for aggravated criminal damage

- Only self-defence or prevention of crime can hold up as valid excuses (as long as the force used was reasonable)

Threats to destroy or damage property

Under ***s 2 of the Criminal Damage Act 1971***, it is an offence to threat to commit an offence under ***s 1*** of the Act

- There must be a threat to destroy or damage property belonging to another (can be written, verbal or by conduct)
- **Objective test** → there must be words or actions which, objectively, constitute a threat, and must be a threat which, objectively, amounts to a threat to damage any property ***(Cakmak [2002] 2 Cr App R 158)***

- Doesn't matter if the actual listener perceived the words or actions to be a threat, if it would not objectively be considered one

Secondary Participation and Attempts

Attempt

S 1(1) of the Criminal Attempts Act 1981:

'If, with intent to commit an offence to which this section applies, a person does an act which is more than merely preparatory to the commission of the offence, he is guilty of attempting to commit the offence

There are 2 scenarios where a person could be liable for an attempt / inchoate offence:

a) **An incomplete attempt** → where the defendant has *not done all the acts* necessary to bring about the offence
b) **Complete attempt** → where the defendant has done all the acts necessary to commit the offence, *but the desired result has not followed*

Actus Reus:

The defendant does an act which is **more than merely preparatory to the commission of the offence**

- When the merely preparatory acts have come to an end and the defendant embarks upon the crime proper (***R v Gullefer***)
    - Significant steps need to be taken towards the commission of the full offence
    - BUT it's not necessary to establish that the defendant has done all they intended to do
- *Question of fact* for the jury in each case, after the judge has decided there is some evidence that the defendant has 'embarked upon the crime'

Case Law Example:

- ***R v Jones***: in the following stages of a murder attempt:
    1) Buys a shotgun and ammunition → prep
    2) Shortens the barrel of the shotgun and loads it → prep
    3) Waits for the victim, knowing they will be shortly arriving → prep
    4) Jumps into the victim's car → prep
    5) Points the loaded gun at the victim → on the job
    6) Releases the safety catch on the gun and puts his finger on the trigger → on the job

Omission to Act?
Will not be liable for an omission to act • The *actus reus* of an attempt requires an act → no reference to omission in the definition

Mens Rea:

The defendant must intend to commit the full offence

- Where it is a result crime, the defendant *must intend* the prohibited result (even if a 'lesser' *mens rea* would satisfy the full offence)
  - Recklessness does not suffice, must have intent (***R v Millard and Vernon***) and (***R v Whybrow***)
  - E.g. for attempted murder, intention to cause GBH is not enough
- For attempted aggravated criminal damage, the defendant must intend to damage property but can be reckless as to whether life is endangered (the ulterior *mens rea* will suffice for an attempt charge)
- Conditional intent is adequate

An impossible offence?

Impossibility as to ends and means are no defence to a charge of attempting to commit an offence

- ***S 1(3) of the Criminal Attempts Act 1981***: impossibility will not prevent the establishment of the *actus reus* of attempt (e.g attempting to pickpocket, but the victim's pocket is empty)

Mens Rea:

- The defendant will be deemed to have the intent to commit a crime if, on the facts which they believed to be true, they would have had such an intent
  - Impossibility does not prevent the establishment of *mens rea* of attempt

Case Law Example:

- ***R v Shivpuri***: defendant had the actus reus and mens rea of attempt to harbour drugs, despite the package containing talcum powder (they believed it had heroin or cannabis)

Secondary Participation

Secondary Participation / Accomplice Liability = those who do not commit a crime, but simply encourage or assist (***s 8 of the Accessories and Abettors Act 1861***)

- **Principal offender** = the person who commits the *actus reus* elements of the criminal offence
- **Co-principals** = where two or more people commit an offence together
- **Accomplices** = those who assist in the commission of an offence in some way, whilst not committing the *actus reus* of the offence themselves

Actus Reus:

The *actus reus* of accomplice liability requires the defendant to 'aid, abet, counsel or procure' the commission of the offence

Aid = give assistance

Abet = give encouragement *at the time* of the offence
Counsel = give encouragement *earlier*, so before the crime is committed
Procure = bring about the offence

A person will satisfy the *actus reus* requirements if:

a) They **help to bring about the crime** by acting, advising, assisting or encouraging *before* the crime occurs
b) They are **present *at the scene*** of the crime ***in order to*** assist or encourage
c) They are **present *at the scene*** of the crime ***and do* assist** or encourage

❌ Can't take place after the offence (e.g. helping someone dispose of a dead body can't result in accomplice liability for murder)

❌ Mere presence at the scene *will not* amount to the *actus reus* (must either have pre-arranged with the principal, or encouraged or assisted them once at the scene)

- BUT: paying to attend an illegal event could amount to encouragement of the crime (***Wilcox v Jeffrey***)

☑ Remaining silent, or failing to intervene at the scene of a crime, where there is a right or a duty to act to control the actions of the principal offender, *can* amount to encouragement of the offence (***Du Cros v Lambourne***)

- ***Tuck v Robson***: licensee of a public house (who allowed customers to drink after hours) was held as an accomplice → inactivity = encouragement, as had a duty to do so
- ***R v Russell and Russell***: failure of one parent to intervene to protect their child from ill-treatment by the other parent was encouragement (under a duty to act)

Mental Link

Where the accomplice had **abetted** or **counselled** the principal in the commission of the offence, will usually be a **mental link between principal and accomplice**

- 'Almost inevitably' involved contact (***Attorney-General's Reference (No 1 of 1975) [1975] QB 773***)
- The principal is aware of the encouragement or advice

Where the accomplice **'aided' → no need for a mental link**

- Principal may not even know of the assistance

Where the accomplice had **procured** the commission of the offence, **no need for a mental link**

- Only requires a causal link (e.g. through their behaviour, rather than discussions)

Where there is a meeting of minds as to the harm that parties *might do to one another*, but an *innocent party is harmed*, can still be liable:

R v Gnango: B pulled out a gun and started firing at D (then returned fire). A passer-by was hit by a bullet from B's gun

- D was still charged with murder → engaged in a joint enterprise with B to engage in unlawful violence specifically designed to cause death / serious injury, from which death resulted

Principal not acquitted?

A person cannot be convicted as an accomplice, **unless the *actus reus* of the principal offence is committed** (***R v Dias***)

- BUT: where the principal has the *actus reus* but also a valid defence, an accomplice can still be convicted

Innocent Agent:

Where an individual has used an innocent agent to commit the *actus reus* of a crime, the law will usually charge the instigator as the principal offender

- **Innocent Agent** = someone who commits the *actus reus* of a crime, but who is not guilty of the offence, either because they lack *mens rea* or have a specific defence available

Does not apply to rape → requires personal action on the part of the perpetrator

- Would be charged as an accomplice, having procured the commission of the offence, rather than a charge of being a principal offender acting through an innocent agent

Mens Rea:

Intention to do the act:

Proof that the defendant intentionally (or deliberately):

Did the act that assisted, encouraged or procured the commission of the offence, ***or***

Intentionally spoke the words that advised, procured or encouraged the crime

→ *Mens Rea* is made out, even if the defendant didn't wish the crime to be committed (***National Coal Board v Gamble***)

→ A defendant should refuse to comply with their contractual obligations, if they know that in doing so, they would be assisting a crime

Knowledge of the Circumstances

The defendant must 'know the essential matters which constitute that offence'

Had, within their knowledge, all the circumstances of the principal offence (***Johnson v Youden)***

- They must have known that certain things were going to happen, or contemplated that those things might happen which *in fact* constitute an offence

Don't need to know that an actual crime has been committed

Where it is a strict liability offence, an accomplice must still establish *mens rea* **(*Callow v Tillstone)***

Specific knowledge?

Accomplice must know a 'crime of the type in question was intended' (***R v Bainbridge***) → e.g. knew a theft would occur

Extended to a range of offences within their contemplation → liable for whichever of those offences the principal chose to commit (***Maxwell v DPP for Northern Ireland***)

Same Offence

The accomplice can only be liable for the *actus reus* which is *actually* committed

Once the *actus reus* is committed, if the accomplice had a higher *mens rea* than the principal, they can face a more serious charge (***R v Howe***)

- E.g. if they intended GBH/murder (or in contemplation), but principal only guilty of manslaughter

If the accomplice had a lower *mens rea*, will also face a smaller charge (***R v Gilmour***)

Acts beyond the plan

Where 2 or more people set out to commit an offence, and in the course of the venture, the principal offender commits another offence: (***R v Jogee; Ruddock v The Queen***)

- If, in the course of committing the first offence, the accomplice foresaw the possibility of the principal committing the second offence

  May conclude that the accomplice had the necessary intent that the second offence would be committed if the occasion arose

- It was within the scope of the plan to which the accomplice consented and gave support

Change of Heart?

For the accomplice to have withdrawn from the plan, so as to avoid liability, depends on the 'circumstances of each case'

There must be **timely communication of the intention to abandon the common purpose** (***R v Becerra***)

- Usually where practicable and reasonable
    - The more the accused has done to set up the crime, the more they are expected to do to withdraw from it
    - Seems that simply urging the principal to leave the scene is insufficient (may also need physical intervention)
    - Words will suffice where the withdrawal takes place *before* the crime occurs (***R v Grundy***)
- Whether there was an effective withdrawal is a question of fact

English Legal Systems (Constitutional)

Statutory Interpretation

- Statute is the primary source of law in England and Wales
- Although Parliament makes legislation, it is up to the courts to apply it
- When a statute is unclear, it is the job of the courts to discover how Parliament intended the law to apply and put it into practice

The Rules of Construction

In a legal context, construction means the same as interpretation

⟶ There are 4 rules which Courts follow when interpreting statutes (***the rules of construction***)

- Rules of construction = a method used by lawyers and academics to assist in the interpretation, understanding and administration of legislation
- How a judge arrives at the use of a particular rule of construction is a matter of choice
- These rules are not binding

The Literal Rule

- Where courts apply the language of a statute, using the **ordinary and natural meaning of the words** → if the words are clear, they must be applied
- Based on the principle that the best way to interpret the will of Parliament is to follow the literal meaning of the words they used
    - Helps ensure parliamentary sovereignty → based on the assumption that the words have been carefully chosen in order to carry out the intention of Parliament

Problems with the Literal Rule:
It can result in an absurd or obviously unjust conclusion, going against the initial intention of Parliament <u>*Case Law Example:*</u> ○ ***Whiteley v Chappell (1868):*** A statute aimed at preventing electoral malpractice made it an offence to impersonate 'any person entitled to vote' at an election. The accused was acquitted because he impersonated a dead person and a dead person is not entitled to vote ○ ***London & North Eastern Railway Co v Berriman [1946]*** a railway worker's widow was denied compensation because her husband was killed when oiling points and this was considered 'maintaining' the line and not 're-laying or repairing it' as required by the statute

The Golden Rule

The Golden Rule is an **adaption of the literal rule**

Where there are two meanings to a word or words, they should be **given their ordinary meaning as far as possible**, but only to the extent they **do not produce an absurd or totally obnoxious result** (***Grey v Pearson (1857)***)

- Grammatical and ordinary sense of the words can be modified to avoid absurdity and inconsistency
- It is usually applied in a *narrow sense*, where there is some ambiguity or absurdity in the words themselves
    - ***Maddox v Storer (1963)***: Under the Road Traffic Act 1960, it was an offence to drive at more than 30mph in a vehicle 'adapted to carry more than seven passengers'. The vehicle in the case was a minibus made to carry 11 passengers, rather than altered to do so. The court held that 'adapted to' could be taken to mean 'suitable for'
- It can also be used in a wider sense, to avoid a result which is obnoxious to the principles of public policy (even where words have only one meaning) (***Re Sigsworth [1935] Ch 89)***

The Mischief Rule

Allows judges to interpret a statute so that it effectively tackles the problem that Parliament wanted to deal with → **requires the interpreter of the statute to ascertain the legislator's intention**

- Helps avoid absurdity and injustice and promotes flexibility

4 stage test:

1) What was the law *before* the statute was passed
2) What was the 'mischief and defect' which was *not remedied by the existing law*
3) What *remedy* did Parliament *propose* to put it right
4) What is the *true reason* for the remedy

Case Law Example:

- ***Corkery v Carpenter [1951]:*** under the Licensing Act 1872, a person found drunk in charge of a 'carriage' on the highway is guilty of an offence → the court took the view that a 'carriage' could include a bicycle
    - Act was aimed at preventing drunk people from being in charge of some form of transportation
    - The mischief that the statute intended to remedy was injury to the public, from drunk drivers

Smith v Hughes (1960): The Street Offences Act 1959 made it a criminal offence for a prostitute to solicit potential customers in a street or public place. In the case, the prostitute was soliciting from her window. Judge decided that the aim of the Act was to enable people to walk along the street without being solicited

The Purposive Approach

The European approach to statutory interpretation focuses on **giving effect to the purpose of the legislation**

- Judges look at the reasons why the statute was passed and its purpose, even if it means distorting the ordinary meaning of the words

Used when interpreting retained EU law

The mischief approach is used to look backwards at the root of the problem. The purposive approach is used to look forward at the aims of the legislation.

Aids to Interpretation

→ Judges have a range of materials which can help them to interpret statutes

Internal Aids

The statute & explanatory notes:

Look at the entire Act, not just the provision, at the title, the subheadings, preamble, punctuation and headings

- Explanatory notes published at the same time as the Act

Rules of Language:

Technical tools to help **use the language in a statute to resolve any ambiguity** (usually involving a list)

Eiusdem Generis - 'of the same type':

If a general word follows two or more specific words, that general word will only apply to items of the same type as the specific words

- E.g. if an Act used the phrase 'dogs, cats and *other* animals', the phrase 'and other animals' would probably include other domestic animals, but not wild ones

Steps for using Eiusdem Generis:

1) Are there general words following a list of specific words?
   → **'other** offensive weapon' would count as general words, following a list of specifics

2) What are those specific words?
   → the specific words included are all of a similar type (items designed to be used as weapons)
3) What is the interpretation of the general words
   → does it follow the same type as the specific words)?

Case Law Example:

- ***Wood v Commissioner of Police of the Metropolis [1986]***: defendant was charged for committing an offence under the Vagrancy Act 1824 after using a piece of broken glass
  - Act made it illegal to be armed with 'any gun, pistol, hanger, cutlass, bludgeon or other offensive weapon' with intent to commit a serious offence
  - The court used *eiusdem generis* to decide if the piece of broken glass was an 'other offensive weapon'
  - Decided that broken glass was *not the same type* as it was not made or adapted for causing injury

Expressio unius est exclusio alterius - 'expressing one thing excludes another'

Any mention of one of more specific things may be taken to exclude others of the same type

- E.g. if an Act specifically mentioned 'Persian cats', the term would not include other breeds of cat

Case Law Example:

- In ***R v Inhabitants of Sedgley (1831)***, the court was deciding whether the poor rate levied on occupiers of 'lands, houses and coal mines' (in the Poor Relief Act 1601) could then be levied on owners of other types of mines
  - Using *Expressio*, found that because it specifically mentioned coal mines and not just mines, other types were not admissible

Noscitur a sociis - 'known by the company it keeps'

A word derives meaning from surrounding words

Case Law Example:

- Helped assist in the interpretation of the Factories Act 1961 which required all 'floors, steps, stairs, passageways and gangways' to be kept free from obstruction.
  - In a following court case, '**Pengelly v Bell Punch Co. Ltd [1964]**, had to decide whether a floor used for storage came under the Act
  - The court held that as all the other words were used to indicate passage, a floor used exclusively for storage did not fall within the Act

External Aids

Examples:

- Historical setting
- Dictionaries → referred when a word has no specific legal meaning (particularly useful when judges use the literal approach)
- Reports
- Treaties
- Previous statutes
- Hansard → helps identify the 'mischief' which an Act was intended to remedy
  Can only be used if the statute is ambiguous and the material consists of clear statements by a minister or promoter *of the Bill*
- Interpretation Acts → gives definitions of words commonly found in legislation
- Law Commission
- Academic knowhow
- International conventions

Presumptions:

The courts assumes that certain points are inherently implied in most legislation, including (rebuttable):

1. Statutes *do not* change the common law
   - (Unless a statute expressly states an intention to alter the common law, the interpretation which does not alter the existing law is preferred)
2. The legislature does not intend to remove any matters from the jurisdiction of the courts
3. Existing rights are not to be interfered with
4. Laws which create crimes should be interpreted in favour of the citizen where there is ambiguity
5. Legislation does not operate retrospectively: its provisions operate from the day it comes into force
6. Statutes do not affect the Monarch
7. Against criminal liability without guilty intention → (lack of knowledge in the situation)

Case Law

The Doctrine of Precedent

England and Wales follow a common law jurisdiction → judges do not make law, they instead decide cases in accordance with existing rules (the doctrine of precedent)

Once the decision has been made on how the law applies to a particular set of facts, **similar facts in later cases should be treated in the same way** (*stare decisis*)

- If the facts of a case are sufficiently similar, a judge must follow the precedent set by the earlier case

A case is binding when:

There is a proposition of law

That proposition is part of the *ratio decidendi* of a case

The proposition is decided in a court whose decisions are binding on the present court

There are no relevant distinctions between the two cases (the facts are sufficiently different to allow the judge to arrive at an alternative conclusion)

Proposition of Law:

Proposition of Law = a judicial statement confirming a legal principle, derived typically from statute or case law (can also be from custom or academic commentary)

Separate to a statement of fact (a statement which depends on the evidence per case)

Ratio Decidendi

Ratio Decidendi = it is the central legal reasoning of a case, capable of creating precedent

- Sir Rupert Cross: 'the *ratio decidendi* of a case is any rule of law expressly or impliedly treated by the judge as a necessary step in reaching his conclusions'
- When there are multiple judges, each individual judge will state a *ratio*, and there will also be a *ratio* of the court as a whole

The ratio:

a) Must be a necessary step to the conclusion
b) Must be directly related to the issue
c) Must come from disputes of law
d) Can come in multiple forms:
   i. Common law rules
   ii. Interpretation of statute
   iii. Interpretation of the common law rules

Narrow v Wide ratios:

Judges never state what the *ratio decidendi* of a case is → judges in future cases can argue which bits of the judgement actually form the ratio

- Judgements who do not want to follow precedent can argue that the parts of the judgement which seemingly apply to their case are not part of the *ratio*, but are part of the *obiter dicta* (which they don't have to follow)
- The greater the number of material facts, the wider the *ratio* will be

Obiter Dictum:

Obiter Dicta = 'other things said' → legal reasoning that isn't included in the *ratio*

- These are not binding on future courts, although they may be persuasive
- The easiest type of *obiter dictum* to identify occurs when a judge speculates about the decision they would have made if the facts of the case had been different
- Judgement = ratio + obiter

Hierarchy of the Courts

There are certain courts which bind themselves, and certain courts which bind others

- **General principle**: all courts are bound by superior courts and some are bound by previous decisions of their own courts
- A superior court is able to reverse the decision of a lower court on appeal

1) Supreme Court

The Supreme Court binds all courts below it but it is *not bound by itself* (it can change and develop its thinking) (***Practice Statement (Judicial Precedent) [1966]***)

- Departure from a previous precedent by the Supreme Court is unusual
- Hesitant to depart from its previous decisions where it would disturb existing contracts, property rights and tax arrangements

2) Court of Appeal

Civil Division:

Bound by decisions of the Court of Justice and Supreme Court

Binds all courts beneath it

Criminal Division:

Bound by decisions of the Supreme Court

Binds all courts beneath it

Usually bound by its previous decisions, except for some limited exceptions: a) Where its own previous decisions conflict b) Where its previous decision has been implicitly overturned by the Supreme Court c) Where its previous decision was made *per incuriam* (through carelessness) d) Where it was an interim decision by two judges (***Boys v Chaplin [1968]***) e) Where one of its previous decisions is inconsistent with a subsequent decision of the ECHR	All the exceptions which apply to the Civil Division also apply to Criminal Division The Court of Appeal also have a wider discretion where the liberty of the individual is at stake

3) The High Court

- In its appeal function, the High Court is bound by its own decisions.
- In its 'first instance' function, cases are not binding (but are generally followed)

4) Crown / County / Magistrates

Have no binding authority

5) Court of Justice of the EU

Is not bound by its own previous decisions → part of a civil law system

- Decisions of the ECJ are no longer binding in English law but are very highly persuasive on matters of Retained EU Law

6) European Court of Human Rights

Is not bound by its own previous decisions but judges and commentators do carefully consider what has been said by previous judges

7) Privy Council

Decisions of the Judicial Committee of the Privy Council are persuasive authority, but not binding

Distinguishing:

When the facts of a case are significantly different from earlier ones, **the judge is not required to follow earlier precedent**

- When faced with a binding statement of law, an advocate can argue that the authority is not relevant to the situation because there are material factual distinctions between the precedent and the present case
- Can also distinguish the point of law → this is when they argue that the legal question answered by the precedent is not the same as that asked in the present case

Civil Procedure Rules = the permission to appeal will only be given if the court considers that the appeal has a real prospect of success or if there is some other compelling reason why the appeal should be heard

- If a defendant is convicted, they are able to appeal against the conviction and/or the sentence on a point of law or fact

Permission for appeals are generally decided on points of law, not fact (recognising that the court may have got the law wrong)

Affirming = when a higher court confirms it agrees with the appeal before it from a lower court

Applying = when a court indicates that it is adopting statements or reasoning from other decisions

Departing = Where a court of one level disagrees with a previous decision, in another matter, by an equal court

Overruling = When a judge disagrees with the statement of law made by a judge in a lower court. Whilst the outcome of the earlier decision remains the same, it will not be followed in the new case

Reverse **=** when a decision of a lower court is appealed to a higher one, the judges in the higher court can *reverse* the decision if they believe the law has not been interpreted accurately

The Constitution

A Constitution usually defines a state's fundamental political principles, establish the framework of the government of the state and guarantee certain rights and freedoms to the citizens

- Unwritten constitution = made up of a number of different sources, such as statute and case law (what the UK has)
- Federal constitution = decision of power between the central and regional government.
- Unitary constitution = single sovereign legislative body, with power concentrated at the centre

- Entrenched/rigid = constitution may be changed only by following a special procedure

The core principles on which the UK constitution is based:

a) The rule of law
b) The separation of powers
c) The sovereignty of Parliament

Sources of the Constitution

The UK constitution is unwritten or uncodified → made up of 4 different sources

Acts of Parliament:

The test for a constitutional statute:

a. The statute must condition the legal relationship between citizen and state in some general, overarching manner or
b. The statute must change the scope of fundamental constitutional rights

Key Examples:

- Magna Carta 1215: first assertion of the limits on the powers of the Monarch and of the rights of individuals
- Bill of Rights 1689: imposed limitations on the powers of the Crown in its relationship with Parliament
- Acts of Union 1706-7: united England and Scotland under a single Parliament of Great Britain
- Parliament Acts 1911 and 1949: altered the relationship between the House of Lords and House of Commons → will of HoC would prevail
- Human Rights Act 1988: incorporated ECHR into domestic law → allows citizens to raise alleged breaches of their human rights before domestic courts
- European Union (withdrawal) Act 2018 and European Union (withdrawal agreement) act 2020: ended supremacy of EU law and introduced retained EU law

Case Law:

- Residual freedom = citizens are free to do or say whatever they wish unless the law clearly states that such an action or statement is prohibited
- Established through the common law that actions taken by state officials must have a legal basis if they are to be lawful (***Entick v Carrington)***
    The exercise of power by the state had to have clear legal authority
    State officials do not have exemption from legal accountability
- Habeas Corpus = an individual who has been detained by the state has the right to have the legality of that detention tested before a court

- Right to having a fair hearing is a fundamental constitutional principle (developed through common law)
- Parliamentary Sovereignty is a common law doctrine accepted by the judiciary
    - **Enrolled Act**: once an Act of Parliament has been entered onto the parliamentary roll, the **courts will not question the validity of the Act or hold the Act to be void** → cannot deem it unconstitutional
- Judicial review - enables the court to ensure that the Government and other public bodies exercise the powers that have been granted in the proper way

Royal Prerogative:

Some powers which the govt exercises are derived from royal prerogative:

What remains of the absolute powers that were exercised by the monarch and have not been removed by Parliament

Most of the powers are by convention exercised by the PM and other govt ministers on the Monarch's behalf

Acts of Parliament can remove prerogative powers (e.g. Crown Proceedings Act 1947 & Fixed Term Parliaments Act 2011)

- Where statute and the Royal prerogative come into conflict, **statute will prevail**

The judiciary is responsible for **deciding the extent of the royal prerogative**

- Through case law, courts have established that new prerogative powers cannot be created or the scope of existing powers extended

Key Areas:

Foreign Affairs:	Domestic Affairs:
• Declarations of war and the deployment of armed forces overseas • Making treaties • The recognition of foreign states	The summoning of Parliament The appointment and dismissal of the Prime Minister The giving of Royal Assent to bills The dissolution of Parliament Defence of the realm The exercise of the prerogatives of pardon and mercy Granting public honours The setting up of public bodies to disburse funds made available by Parliament

Non-judiciable areas:

a) Making international treaties
b) Control of the armed forces

c) Defence of the realm
d) The dissolution of Parliament
e) The prerogative of mercy
f) Granting public honours

Constitutional Conventions:

Non-legal source of the constitution:

- 'Rules of constitutional behaviour which are considered to be binding upon those who operate the constitution but which are not enforced by the law courts …. nor by the presiding officers in the House of Commons

Key Examples:

- Monarch plays no active role in matters of government
- Monarch will not refuse Royal Assent to a bill that has been passed by the HoC and HoL
- The Monarch can legally dissolve Parliament at will, but will normally do so only on the advice of the PM
- All govt ministers will be members of either the HoC or the HoL
- Individual Ministerial Responsibility
- Collective cabinet responsibility → cabinet collectively responsible to Parliament for the actions of the Govt as a whole & govt must retain the confidence of the HoC
    - Cabinet must be united in public support of government policy. Cabinet minister must resign if they wish to speak out in public against a policy
- HoL will not reject legislation which gives effect to an important manifesto commitment of the democratically elected govt
- UK govt will normally only legislate on a matter that has been devolved to the Scottish Parliament, Senedd Cymru or Northern Ireland Assembly if the relevant legislature has given its consent
- Members of the judiciary do not play an active part in political life
- Ministers and MoP do not criticise in public individual members of the judiciary

Not Enforced by the Courts:

- In *Miller*, the Supreme Court reaffirmed that the courts cannot enforce conventions as they operated in the political sphere alone

The Rule of Law and Separation of Powers

The Rule of Law

The rule of law is a doctrine that forms a key element of the UK constitution

- Laws should be enacted properly and should be clear. Laws should not be applied arbitrarily, no one is above the law and no one may be punished other than in accordance with the law

- **Formal** = the rule of law should focus on the form of law and procedures for making it
    - Morally neutral
- **Substantive** = rule of law should not be confined to procedural elements, but should extend to the protection of fundamental rights

Application:

- The Right to Liberty
- The Right to a Fair Hearing
- Access to Justice
- Equality before the Law

Traditional Definitions:

AV Dicey in *An Introduction to the Study of the Law of the Constitution (1885)* **produced a classic definition of the rule of law:**

- Legal Certainty: citizens should be able to rely on laws that are both made and set out clearly
    - Like cases should be treated in like ways
    - State officials have no exemption from legal control or accountability and are subject to the ordinary law of the land
    - The law does not operate retrospectively
- Personal Liberty: citizens should be detained and subject to punishment only if they have broken the law
- Due process of law: citizens have a right to fair procedures for determining civil or criminal liability

Modern Interpretation:

Joseph Raz's work, *The Authority of the Law (1979)* has been influential in contemporary thinking regarding the rule of law (**formal approach**):

a. It should be open and clearly stated
b. Not have retrospective effect
c. Be made by proper procedures
d. Be relatively stable
e. Provide for open and fair hearings
f. Be administered by an independent judiciary

Lord Bingham in *The Rule of Law (2010) (***substantive approach***):*

- Expanded to include adequate protection of human rights
- The state must comply with its obligations in international law

Separation of Powers

- Whilst there is no formal separation of powers in the UK, a partial separation of powers exists, with an **informal system of checks and balances**
- There should be no overlap between the branches (in terms of functions or personnel)

Monarch:

The Monarch is part of all three branches of state, although the role is largely ceremonial

- The government is 'His Majesty's Government' (but royal prerogative means most acts are exercised by the govt on his behalf)
- Monarch is part of the legislature as must give Royal Assent before a bill can become an Act of Parliament (always gives this, although legally can refuse)
- Monarch is the head of the judiciary → King's Judges and King's Court (but does not exercise any judicial power)

Executive & Legislature:

The House of Commons Disqualification Act, 1975 supports a limited separation of powers between the executive and legislature:

- Section 1 = disqualifies certain members of executive (civil servants, members of the armed forces and police) from being MPs
- Section 2 = limits the number of government ministers who may sit in the House of Commons to 95

BUT: govt ministers can also be MPs (ministers are either from HoC or HoL

Elective Dictatorship?

Once a general election takes place, the Government can generally act as it pleases and get Parliament to enact is legislative programme in full

- First Past the Post = in built majority in HoC
- Government has significant control over the parliamentary timetable
- Most of the bills considered by Parliament are introduced by govt ministers
- Government Whips pressure on backbenchers
- Henry VIII powers (enable Government to amend or repeal primary legislation without reference back to Parliament)
- Salisbury Convention means HoL will not reject a bill that gives effect to a manifesto promise

Effective Parliamentary Scrutiny?

- Questions → time set for MPs to put oral questions to ministers and the PM
- The standing orders of the HoC provide for emergency debates on matters of urgent consideration
- General Committees
- Select Committees → appointed to examine the expenditure, administration and policy of the main govt departments
- Parliamentary and Health Service Ombudsman

Executive & Judiciary:

Section 3 of the CRA 2005 = govt is under a duty to uphold the independence of the judiciary and that individual ministers should not seek to influence particular decisions through any special access to judiciary

Judicial independence is secured in the UK through:

a) **Appointment** → judicial appointments done through the Judicial Appointments Commission which is impartial
b) **Tenure** → senior judges hold office 'during good behaviour' and will only be dismissed following a vote by both Houses of Parliament
c) **Salary** → determined by an independent body and are paid from the Consolidated Fund (immune from political interference)
d) **Immunity** from civil action → judges have wide-ranging immunity from claims in tort in respect to their judicial actions
e) **Constitutional conventions** → members of the executive do not criticise judicial decisions & members of judiciary do not engage in party political activity
f) **The sub-judice rule** → parliament will refrain from discussing matters currently being heard or waiting to be head by the courts
g) **Contempt of court laws** → ensures no outside interference with administration of justice

The judiciary does not have the power to declare actions of the executive to be unconstitutional but can examine the legality of a decision or action

Legislature & Judiciary:

a) S 1 of ***House of Commons (Disqualification) Act 1975*** → holders of judicial office are disqualified from membership of the House of Commons
b) Constitutional convention that MPs will not make a criticism of a particular judge and judiciary will not become involved in political activities
c) Sub-judice rule → parliament will refrain from discussing details of cases before the courts

Parliamentary Supremacy

Parliamentary functions:

1. Scrutinising the work of the Government
2. Passing legislation
3. Debating the key issues of the day
4. Approving the funding necessary for the Government to carry out its statutory duties and legislative proposals
5. Providing the personnel for Government

The Legislative Process

- There are 650 Members of Parliament (sitting in the House of Commons)
- House of Lords Act 1999 → 92 hereditary peers remain, otherwise appointed as life peers under the Life Peerages Act 1958
- The Dissolution and Calling of Parliament Act 2022 has now replaced the FTPA, making dissolution a royal prerogative power
- A session of Parliament (typically a year long) ends when Parliament is 'prorogued' by Royal Decree

Types of Bills:

Public Bills:

Public bills alter the general law (law concerning the public as a whole). Two forms:

a) Government bills → bills submitted to Parliament as part of the Government's legislative programme
b) Private members' bills → bills introduced by MPs or Lords who are not government ministers

- Process: first reading → second reading → committee stage → third reading → proceedings in the HoL → Royal Assent

Private Bills:

Relate to matters of individual, corporate or local interest and affect particular persons and or a particular locality

House of Lords:

The HoL is often described as being a 'revising chamber' → they will use its considerable expertise to make small changes to legislation

- The Lords' role is constrained by the Parliament Acts 1911 and 1949 which ensures that ultimately, the will of the Commons must prevail
- Money bills passed by the Commons can receive Royal Assent one month after being sent to the Lords and will become law even if lacking consent
- Other public bills can receive royal assent after it has been rejected by the Lords in each of 2 successive sessions

Delegated Legislation:

Delegated legislation = every exercise of power to legislate that is conferred by or under an Act of Parliament

- The provisions of an Act of Parliament often confer upon ministers a power to make delegated or subordinate legislation
- Parliament are unable to amend delegated legislation and it can often come into effect without either House voting for it

Most commonly used procedures:

Affirmative resolution procedure → the instrument either cannot come into effect, or ceases to have effect, unless one or both Houses passes a resolution approving the instrument

Negative resolution procedure → the Government is required to 'annul' the instrument if either House passes a resolution rejecting the instrument within a specified period after it is 'laid before Parliament'

Parliamentary Sovereignty

Classic definition provided by AV Dicey:

a) Parliament is the supreme law-making body and may enact or repeal laws on any subject
b) No Parliament may be bound by a predecessor or bind a successor
c) No other person or body may question the validity of an Act of Parliament or declare the Act to be unlawful

Key Examples:

- Enrolled Act Rule → once an Act of Parliament has been entered onto the Parliamentary roll, the courts will not question the validity of that act or hold that Act to be void
- Statute may override international law (***Cheney v Conn [1968]***)
- Statute may override constitutional conventions (***Madzimbamuto v Lardner- Burke [1969]***)
- Statute may alter the constitution (e.g. Parliament Acts, Human Rights Act and EU Withdrawal Act)
- Statute may operate retrospectively (***Burmah Oil Co v Lord Advocate [1965]***)
- Statute may abolish or curtail aspects of the royal prerogative
- If a later Parliament expressly repeals the content of an Act made by an earlier Parliament, that earlier Act will no longer be valid

- Implied Repeal - where a later Parliament passes an Act that contradicts the contents of an established Act but does not expressly repeal it
    - May not apply to constitutional statutes → should be expressly repealed

Limitations?

The Acts of Union: The Acts of Union 1706-07, make explicit provision for the preservation of the separate Scottish legal system and the Church of Scotland

Devolution

Doctrine of Implied Repeal

Manner and Form theory → whether a Parliament can bind its successors as to the procedure to be adopted when repealing legislation enacted by that earlier Parliament

- E.g. through referendums

Henry VIII Powers:

- Permits the relevant government minister to amend or even repeal the relevant statute by delegated legislation

Human Rights:

It was not until the enactment of the Human Rights Act that individual citizens could bring a claim for breach of their rights under the ECHR before domestic courts:

- ***Section 2***: although domestic courts must 'take into account' judgements of the ECHR, they are not bound to follow such judgements (although domestic courts do normally follow them)
- ***Section 3:*** primary and secondary legislation must be interpreted in accordance with Convention rights 'so far as it is possible to do so'
- ***Section 4***: where a court cannot interpret legislation in a manner that makes the legislation compliant with Convention rights, the courts may make a declaration of incompatibility (this does not invalidate or affect the operation of the offending Act)
- ***Section 10***: when a declaration of incompatibility has been made, creation of a 'fast track' procedure that the government may use to amend the relevant legislation if there are 'compelling reasons' to do so (not obliged to)
- ***Section 19***: a statement of compatibility or non compatibility must be made before the second reading of the bill

Bill of Rights

In the Queen's Speech of May 2022, govt set out proposals for a British Bill of Rights to replace the HRA. Set to:

Clarify the primacy of UK case lover of ECtHR
Limitations on UK courts ability to 'alter legislation contrary to its ordinary meaning'
A requirement for the claimant to prove they have suffered 'significant disadvantage' before they can bring a human rights claim
Provisions making it harder for foreign criminals to avoid deportation (not able to rely on the right to family life to avoid deportation)
Expanding press freedom of speech

Devolution and Parliamentary Privilege

Devolution

The United Kingdom is a unitary state. Although it comprises 4 countries, the **Westminster Parliament is ultimately sovereign**

- The UK Parliament has delegated certain powers to the devolved legislatures, it can legally revoke them

Scotland

The Scotland Act 1978 provided for the creation of a devolved assembly, following a referendum

The Referendums (Scotland and Wales) Act 1997 allowed for a referendum on the issue

The Scotland Act 1998 established the Scottish Parliament and Scottish Government

- S 63A of the Scotland Act 1998 → the Scottish Parliament and Scottish Government are a permanent part of the constitutional arrangements of the UK (can't be abolished without a referendum)

Scottish Parliament

The Scottish Parliament has 129 members (MSPs) → 73 are constituency members, 57 are regional

- Elected under FPTP
- 16 and 17 year old's can vote
- Elections take place every 5 years (***Scottish Elections (Reform) Act 2020***)

Devolved Matters

The 1998 Act devolved to the Scottish Parliament all matters, *other than reserved matters* (reserved powers model)

- This includes significant tax-raising powers (e.g. Scottish Landfill Tax and Scottish Rate of Income Tax)

Provisions outside its legislative competence are those that:

a) Would form part of the law of any territory other than Scotland
b) Relate to reserved matters
c) Modify certain enactments
d) Are incompatible with the ECHR
e) Would remove the Lord Advocate from their position as head of the system of criminal prosecutions and investigation of death

⟶ The Advocate General, the Lord Advocate or the Attorney General may refer to the Supreme Court to question whether a bill or any of its provisions are within the Parliament's legislative competence

The Sewel Convention

Convention that Westminster would not normally legislate on devolved matters in Scotland, without the consent of the Scottish Parliament

- Scottish Parliament typically give consent through Legislative Consent Motions (LCMs)
- Statutory recognition in the Scotland Act 2016
- But does not affect parliamentary sovereignty
    - Whilst the UK Parliament will not normally legislate on a devolved matter, without their consent, it has the competence to do so as the Convention is not legally enforceable

Wales

Wales Act 1978 → provided for the creation of a devolved assembly in Wales, if Welsh voters supported it in a referendum

- Very narrow majority following referendum through the Referendums (Scotland and Wales) Act 1997

Government of Wales Act 1998 → established the National Assembly of Wales

- Originally a conferred Powers Model → limited the competence of the National Assembly to those powers specifically granted to it
- ***Wales Act 2017*** → now a reserved powers model

Government of Wales Act 2006 → split the Legislature (Senedd Cymru) and the Welsh Government in 2

- Can only be abolished following a referendum

Welsh Parliament (Senedd Cymru)

- Acts of the Assembly are known as Acts of the Senedd
- Assembly Members are known as Members of the Senedd (60 MSs (incl 20 regional))
- Proportional Representation
- 16 and 17's can vote
- Elections every 5 years
- Similar restrictions apply to the Senedd's legislative competence and the Scottish Parliament
- The Sewel Convention also applies to Wales

Northern Ireland

Following 'the Troubles', negotiations between the British and Irish governments and the main Northern Irish political parties resulted in the Good Friday Agreement, 1998

A unified Ireland will only be brought about with the consent of the majority in both areas (north and mainland)

Northern Ireland Assembly

The Northern Ireland Act 1998 established the Northern Ireland Assembly

- Follows the reserved powers model (referred to instead as ability to legislate on 'transferred matters' → all matters except reserved and excepted matters)
    - Excepted = matters remaining with the UK Government
    - Reserved = NI Assembly can legislate with the consent of the Secretary of State (may be devolved in the future)
- Assembly comprises 90 members (MLA's) → proportional representation
- Elections every 5 years

Northern Ireland Executive

The Northern Ireland Act 1998 provides for power-sharing between the different communities (Nationalists, Unionists and Other)

- The First Minister is the nominee of the largest political party of the largest political designation
- The Deputy First Minister is the nominee of the largest political party of the next largest political designation

→ Have equal status. When one resigns the other must do as well

Role of the Supreme Court

There are 3 ways in which the question whether legislation passed by a devolved legislature is outside its legislative competence can come before the Supreme Court:

a) Through a reference by a devolved or UK law officer to the Supreme Court
b) Through an appeal from certain higher courts
c) Through a reference from certain appellate courts

- Devolved legislation is justified as long as it relates to a matter that has been devolved (does not solely have to relate to that matter, can be overlaps with a reserved matter
- Acts of the devolved legislatures can normally be challenged on the grounds that they exceed the legislative competence of the legislature

The continuing relationship:

The Joint Ministerial Committee:

- Set of committees that consist of ministers from the UK and devolved governments
- Provide central coordination of the overall relationship between UK and devolved nations
- Considers non-devolved matters that affect devolved responsibilities
- Consider devolved matters if it is beneficial to discuss their respective treatment in the different parts of the UK
- Keep the arrangements for liaison between the governments under review
- Consider disputes between the Governments

Sub-Committees of the JMC:

- JMC Europe and JMC EU Negotiations were set up as a forum to involve the devolved administrations in agreeing a UK approach to the UK's withdrawal from the EU
- JMC Europe met as a form for discussions on EU policy matters that affect devolved policy areas

United Kingdom Internal Market Act 2020:

Ensures no internal trade barriers in the UK

The mutual recognition principle provides that goods and services which can be legally sold in one part of the UK can also legally be sold in other parts

- E.g. Scotland could not exclude goods which are lawfully produced to English standards

Principle of non-discrimination prohibits devolved governments from enacting regulations that discriminate directly or indirectly between goods produced in, and services provided from, other parts of the UK

Parliamentary Privilege

The main privileges of the House of Commons are:

a) Freedom of Speech
b) The right to control its own composition and procedures (exclusive cognisance)

Freedom of Speech

- ***Article 9 of the Bill of Rights 1689***: freedom of speech and debates or proceedings in Parliament 'ought not to be impeached or questioned in any court or place out of Parliament'
    - Privilege encompasses ancillary matters such as words spoken or written and actions taken outside the core proceedings themselves, but which are of necessity connected to those proceedings
    - Also includes official reports of proceedings and committee proceedings
- Allows parliamentarians to carry out their functions without fear of civil proceedings or criminal prosecutions
- Also have immunity from contempt of court → allows them to disclose facts in debates which should not otherwise by lawfully disclosed

Exclusive Cognisance

- Parliament has sole control over all aspects of its own affairs → to decide for itself what procedures it should adopt, whether any of its procedures have been breached and the following consequences
- Courts will generally not question the validity of an Act, on the basis that correct procedures were not followed (***Pickin v British Railways Board [1974] AC 765***)
- Right to regulate own affairs includes:
    - Disciplinary powers over MPs
    - Right to punish anyone for contempt of Parliament (usually through a reprimand)

Retained EU Law

The Original EU System

EU Law Institutions:

The Council of the European Union

Otherwise referred to as 'The Council'

- Made up of one Government Minister from each state
- Membership changes according to the topic up for discussion
- Has a decision making role → uses a qualified majority voting system (legislation is passed where there is a majority of 55% of the member states who represent at least 65% of the EU)

The European Council

Council of each Head of State / Head of Government

- Makes key political decisions and establishes policy guidelines on how to implement decisions

The European Commission

Made up of commissioners selected by each Member State

- Prepares and drafts new EU law and ensures member states comply with their obligations
- Runs the EU day-to-day
- Once selected, commissioners must be independent of national loyalties

The European Parliament

Directly Elected EU Institution

The European Court of Justice (ECJ)

The ECJ is the highest legal court in the European system

- Has supreme authority on EU law (interpret EU law to make sure it is applied in the same way across all EU states) & can solve disputes between national governments and EU institutions
- The ECJ operates under a civil law system → based on a written code (type of rule book setting out the law)
  - ***The Treaty of the Functioning of the European Union*** sets out the law in general terms (framework treaty) → sets out a basic framework of legal principles
- If there is a dispute about what a piece of EU law means, the ECJ will interpret that EU law is using a purposive approach
  - What the idea behind the law actually is and then interpret the law accordingly

5 Key Functions:

1) Interpret EU law
2) Enforce EU law
3) Declare EU law invalid
4) Ensure the EU takes action
5) Sanction an EU institution

EU Law:

How it is made:

There are 2 main ways for EU Law to be made:

1) Through the ordinary legislative process (most common method)
    - The Council and Parliament will ask the Commission to put forward proposals for new legislation → the commission is then responsible for drafting this legislation
    - Ordinary legislative procedure gives a significant role to the European Parliament → can propose amendments and veto draft legislation

2) Special Legislative Procedure:
    - Consists of the consultation procedure and the consent procedure
    - Consultation procedure → where the council must merely consult with the european parliament (can choose to ignore them)
    - Consent procedure → new law can be passed when the european parliament and the council agree (European Parliament can only accept or reject a proposal, no amendment rights)

Direct Applicability & Direct Effect

Directly Applicable = the EU law automatically forms part of the National Law, *without the member states having to do anything*

Direct Effect = the EU law gives rights to individuals which they can enforce in their national courts

Individuals enforce their rights through the national court, not the ECJ

Just because an EU law is directly applicable, does not mean it will have direct effect → further tests that have to be complied with

Treaty Articles and EU Regulations are **directly applicable** → they form part of national law without the member state having to do anything

They will have **direct effect** when they meet certain requirements: it is clear, precise and unconditional (the member state governments do not have to set up another body before you can have the EU law by right)

Vertical Direct Effect = the EU law can be enforced against the state (E.g. government or public sector organisation)

Horizontal Direct Effect = EU law can be enforced against a private individual

Types of EU Legislation

EU Treaties

They lay down the objectives of the EU, the rules for EU institutions, how decisions are made and the relationships between the EU and its member countries

- Directly applicable and have direct effect

Regulations

Legal acts that apply automatically and uniformly to all EU countries as soon as they enter into force, without needing to be transposed into national law.

- Directly applicable and automatically binding

Directives

Directives set out objectives / goals that all EU states must achieve

- Up to individual countries to devise their own laws on how to reach these goals (have to be implemented into national legislation)
- Member states usually have up to 2 years to implement the directive into national legislation (can then use the national legislation to bring a claim)

There are certain circumstances which allow a directive to have direct effect:

a) Where they are clear, precise and unconditional, **and**
b) The directive deadline for implementation has expired

- If this is the case, will only have vertical direct effect (not horizontal)
- Although, the ECJ has given a wide interpretation of what constitutes public sector → emanations of the state (3 criteria):
    a) Provides a public service under a statutory duty (the organisation has been set up by a statute or national law → created by govt)
    b) Under the control of the state (the industry it operates under is subject to state rules and regulations)
    c) Has special powers (something the government or public organisation would normally do)

Decisions

Decisions are directly binding to those that they are addressed to

Recommendations

Allows EU institutions to make their views known and to suggest a line of action without imposing any legal obligation on those to whom it is addressed • Not binding

Recommendations
Allows institutions to make a statement in a non-binding way • Often while laws are being made, the various committees will give an opinion from their specific regional / economic and social viewpoint • Not binding

Retained EU Law

Statute Overview

- In accordance with the ***European Communities Act (ECA) 1972***, in many instances, EU law had supremacy over UK law (if there was a conflict)
- Repeal of the ***ECA*** by the ***European Union (Withdrawal Agreement) Act (EUWA) 2018***
    - The Withdrawal Agreement entered into force on 1 Feb 2020. There was a transition period from Oct 2019 to Dec 2020 where the UK was still largely treated as a Member State → EU law remained in full force in the UK
    - The ***EUWA*** aimed to provide legal continuity by creating the concept of retained EU Law

    EU law as it existed at the date of the UK's exit would be preserved as a new category of English law
- ***The European Union (Withdrawal Agreement) Act 2020*** implemented the withdrawal agreement into UK domestic law (as it was considered an international treaty) and amended parts of the EUWA
- ***The European Union (Future Relationship) Act (EU(FR)A) 2020*** implemented the ***Trade and Cooperation Agreement*** into domestic UK law
    - Automatically amends UK statute's existing at the time the act came into force as giving effect to the ***TCA***
    - The ***TCA*** provides for free trade in goods and limited mutual market access for services, cooperation in a range of policy areas, provisions about fisheries and UK participation in some EU programmes

What is retained EU Law?

Retained EU law is a snapshot of EU law that was in force in the UK immediately before 'implementation period completion day' and which continues in force

- Notwithstanding law which was repealed with effect from IP completion day (e.g. exit from the customs union, single market and provisions around free movement)

There are 3 main categories of retained EU law:

a) EU-derived domestic legislation
b) Direct EU legislation
c) Rights etc arising under ***s 2(1) of the ECA 1972***

EU-derived domestic legislation

Section 2 of the EUWA 2018 preserves certain 'EU-derived domestic legislation' made under the ***ECA 1972***

- Comprises of the laws that the UK adopted in order to implement its **obligations** under EU law
- EU-derived domestic legislation will mostly be secondary legislation enacted by the UK Government
    - The UK government enacted the Working Time Regulations 1998/1833 to implement the Working Time Directive
- Will sometimes be an Act of Parliament
    - Parts of the Equality Act 2010 were enacted to implement EU anti-discrimination Directives

Status

Section 7(1) of the EUWA 2018: EU law retained as EU-derived domestic legislation has the same status as it had pre-IP completion day (either as primary or secondary legislation)

Direct EU Legislation

Section 3 of the EUWA 2018 converts certain 'direct EU legislation' into UK law so far as 'operative' immediately before 'IP completion day'

- EU law that has direct effect in the UK, without it needing to be implemented by domestic legislation
    - Includes regulations which are directly applicable and binding on all member states
    - Certain types of decisions and directives that have direct effect
    - Regulation (EC) 261/2004 ([2004] OJ L46 / 1) → protects air passenger rights → continues now

Status

Direct EU legislation is split into 2 categories:

a) Retained direct 'principle' EU legislation (includes most EU regulations)
   - Must be amended or repealed by primary legislation or in limited circumstances through secondary legislation:
     i) Where primary legislation has granted ministers a Henry VIII power
     ii) Where ministers are using powers under the ***EUWA 2018*** to correct deficiencies in retained EU Law

b) Retained direct 'minor' EU legislation (e.g. EU tertiary legislation and decisions)
   Amended or repealed in the same manner as ordinary domestic secondary legislation

Rights etc arising under s 2(1) of the ECA 1972

Section 4(1) of the EUWA 2018 preserves certain rights, powers, liabilities, obligations, restrictions, remedies and procedures recognised and available in UK law immediately before IP completion day

- Aims to ensure that any remaining EU rights and obligations that don't fall within the scope of ***ss 2*** and ***3*** become part of retained EU law
  - Directly effective rights contained within EU treaties → e.g. the right for men and women to receive equal pay under Article 157 of the ***Treaty on the Functioning of the European Union*** (***TFEU***)
- Essentially a residual category of EU rights and obligations

Other Aspects:

Non-implemented directives:

Directives which have *not* been implemented as EU-derived domestic legislation (or have been implemented incorrectly), can be used **vertically** against the state or state bodies

- Where **rights** arising under Directives have already been **recognised** by a UK or EU court or tribunal **before IP completion day** → the right (not the directive) become retained EU Law
  - E.g. a Directive that prohibited discrimination on the grounds of race, disability, religion or sexual orientation could provide a directly effective right not to be discriminated against, even if that particular Directive had not been the exact subject of case law
- If the rights is of a kind that has *not* been recognised by a court, excluded from retained EU law

Retained EU Case Law

Retained EU case law consists of retained domestic case law and retained EU case law

- Retained domestic case law = principles and decisions laid down by UK courts and tribunals, before the end of IP completion day, in relation to retained EU law
- Retained EU case law = principles and decisions laid down by the Court of Justice of the European Union before IP completion day in relation to retained EU law

The judgements of the CJEU remain binding on all UK courts below the level of Court of Appeal

Retained General Principles of EU Law

Include principles such as proportionality, equality, fundamental rights and subsidiarity

- No general principle of EU law will be retained unless it was recognised as such by EU case law before IP completion day
- Even where retained, failure to comply with a principle cannot give rise to a right of action
- Many of the general principles have been incorporated into the ***Charter of Fundamental Rights of the European Union ([2000] OJ C364/1) (the Charter).*** But this charter does not form part of retained EU law

Exclusion of State Liability

The EUWA excludes the principle of state liability (Francovich damages)

- No right for individuals to claim damages from a Member State for its failure to implement a Directive at all or properly, or for other breaches

Interpretation of retained EU Law

Section 6(3) of the EUWA 2018:

Questions on the meaning of retained EU law which **remain 'unmodified'** on or after IP completion day (by UK law), will be determined by UK courts in accordance with relevant 'retained case law' and 'retained general principles of EU law'

Section 6(6) of the EUWA 2018:

Questions on the meaning of retained EU that **has been modified** on or after IP completed day (by UK law) can be determined in accordance with relevant retained case law and retained general principles of EU law if doing so is **consistent with the intention of the modifications**

The principle of indirect effect has been **carried over** into retained EU Law

- This is where courts had to read UK legislation in such a way as to make it compliant with EU law
    - ***Re Allied Wallet [2022] EWHC 402 (Ch)*** → applied indirect effect to retained UK regulations originally made to implement a directive (the regulations were interpreted in a manner consistent with the Directive)

Correcting 'deficiencies' in retained EU law

Section 8 of the EUWA 2018 grants *temporary powers* for UK Government ministers and devolved administrations, to **make secondary legislation that corrects deficiencies in retained EU law**

Deficiencies include:

Provisions that have no practical application after the UK has left the EU

Provisions on functions that during the UK's membership of the EU, were carried out in the EU on the UK's behalf

Provisions on reciprocal arrangements of rights between the UK and other EU Member States that are no longer in place or are no longer appropriate

Any other arrangements or rights, including through EU treaties, that are no longer in place or no longer appropriate

EU references that are no longer appropriate

E.g. where EU legislation requires governments of Member States to consult with the European Commission before taking certain action or the legislation contains references to the UK being a Member State

- Regulation 261/2004 states that it applies to passengers departing from, or arriving at, an airport in a Member State
    - UK Government corrected the deficiency so that the Regulation applies to passengers departing from, or arriving at, an airport in the UK to ensure it makes sense now that the UK is no longer a Member State.

Supremacy of retained EU law

There is a limited form of supremacy of retained EU Law:

- Where a conflict occurs between a provision of retained EU law and a piece of pre-IP completion day legislation that is not retained EU law, then the retained EU Law will prevail

Challenges to retained EU law

- Primary legislation that falls within EU-derived domestic legislation, can only be challenged on the grounds that it contravenes another provision of retained EU law that should prevail over it
- Secondary legislation that falls within EU-derived domestic legislation can be challenged on the same basis, as well as on the same public law grounds that apply to any other secondary legislation
- No provision of retained EU law can be challenged on or after IP completion day on the basis that an EU instrument was invalid
- Retained direct principal EU legislation can be subject to a declaration of incompatibility under the HRA 1998 (but will not be invalid)
- Retained direct minor EU legislation can be subject to a declaration of incompatibility under the HRA 1998 and declared invalid

UK Courts and Retained EU Law

Applying retained EU Law

Approach to applying retained EU Law set out in ***Lipton & Anor v BA City Flyer Ltd [2021] EWCA Civ 454***:

1. It is necessary to determine the **status** of any relevant EU regulation and whether it has become retained EU law
2. Then necessary to consider whether any domestic UK legislation has **amended** it
3. Retained EU law should be given a **purposive construction**
4. UK courts should take into account **pre-IP completion day case law** of the CJEU
5. UK courts should take into account **general principles** of EU law that have been recognised in case law before IP completion day
6. Necessary to analyse whether retained EU law has been **amended or superseded by the TCA** and the EU(FR)A 2020

Departing from retained EU Law

- Originally, ***s 6(6)*** of the ***EUWA 2018*** provided that in deciding whether to depart from any retained EU case law, the Supreme Court or the High Court of Justiciary must apply the same test used for departing from its own case law
- ***S 6(5A)-(5D) of the EUWA 2018*** gave the Government the power to make regulations by extending the ability to depart from retained EU case law to the Court of Appeal
- Courts are likely to take a cautious approach (***TuneIn Inc v Warner Music UK Ltd [2021] EWCA Civ 441***)

The Brexit Freedoms Bill

May 2022 Queen's Speech, Government announced plans for a Brexit Freedoms Bill to enable the Government to take advantage of the benefits of leaving the EU.

Henry VIII Powers

- The bill is planned to make it easier to amend or remove outdated retained EU law and get rid of burdensome 'red tape'
- Changing outdated laws by primary legislation would take many years
- Enabling the Government to change retained EU laws by delegated legislation will enable it to capitalise on Brexit freedoms more quickly
- Critics point that many EU legislation received thorough scrutiny by the elected European Parliament and was supported by the UK govt

Ending principle of supremacy

- Want to end provision whereby retained EU legislation has priority over UK legislation enacted before IP completion day
- Critics argue that altering the effect of the EUWA 2018 several years after it was passed could lead to unpredictable and unforeseen consequences
- Retained EU law remains an important source of the rules governing consumer rights, data protection, health and safety, VAT, employment law and financial services

Retained EU case law

- Looking to expand power to depart from retained EU case law to courts below the Court of Appeal
- By allowing first instance courts to depart from Retained EU case law, would avoid unnecessary appeals
- Bar Council believes that extending the power would create legal uncertainty

The Withdrawal Agreement

The Withdrawal Agreement **set out the terms for the UK's exit** from the EU (1 Feb 2020).

Does not cover the long-term future relationship between the two sides

Sought to protect both UK and EU citizens who exercised their right of free movement before the end of the transition period

The European Union (Withdrawal Agreement) Act 2020 incorporated the Withdrawal Agreement into domestic UK law

Areas that will be enforceable after 31 Dec 2020:

- Citizens' Rights → (protects rights of EU and UK citizens to live in either jurisdiction → retain the right to live there & their children)

These rights have direct effect → can be relied on *even* if national legislation implementing those decisions is defective

Questions about EU citizens' rights in the UK can therefore be submitted to the CJEU until the end of 2028

- Financial settlement → (UK agreed to abide by the financial commitments it made as a Member State)
- The Northern Ireland Protocol
- Governance and Dispute Resolution → (will seek to resolve any disputes through a joint committee before being referred to an arbitration panel)

Application of the Agreement:

- Article 4 states that the provisions of the Agreement and the provisions of EU law that it incorporates will have the same effect in UK law as they produce within the EU
- Able to rely on the provisions that meet the criteria for direct effect under EU law
- Section 7A of the ***EUWA 2018*** gives supremacy to the Withdrawal Agreement in the same way as the old ECA 1972

  Although Parliament can pass any Bill which overrides these provisions
- Whether UK citizens or EU citizens are eligible for permanent residence depends largely on whether they satisfy the criteria set in relevant EU legislation

- Individuals and businesses should be able to rely on the direct effect of the Withdrawal Agreement's provisions in national courts where those provisions are sufficiently clear, precise and unconditional

The EU Settlement Scheme:

- Requires EU citizens resident in the UK to obtain pre-settled or settled status to retain their right to live in the UK
- Settled status is available to EU citizens who have been continuously resident in the UK for 5 years or more
  - Once they have settled status, they can spend up to 5 years in a row outside the UK
- Pre-settled status is available to EU citizens who have been resident in the UK for fewer than 5 years (allows them to stay for another 5 years, from the date they obtained pre-settled status)
  - Can spend up to 2 years outside the UK
  - Cumulative absences exceeding 6 months in a rolling 12 month period can break continuous residency

Free Movement of People

Under Article 21 of the ***TFEU***, the Union citizen has the right to move and reside freely within the territory of the Member States (subject to limitations)

Article 45 of the ***TFEU*** allows for free movement of workers

- The EU national worker has an absolute right of residence so long as they remain in work.
- The right not to be discriminated against as regards conditions of work
- An EU national has a right of entry to look for work and a reasonable period of residence to find it.
- Article 45(3) permits derogations on grounds of public policy, public security and public health

- Article 45(4) does provide for a public service exception, where the posts involves the exercise of official authority and functions related to safeguarding the general interests of the State' (Case 149/79 *Commission v Belgium*).

Regulation 883/2004: Social security rights are guaranteed to EU nationals from the host State.

Directive 2004/38

- ***Article 5(1)***: allows Union citizens the right to enter another Member State simply on production of their passport or national identity card
- ***Article 6(1)***: right of residence up to 3 months in the host State (no conditions)
- ***Article 16(1)***: a right of permanent residence after 5 years
- ***Article 7(1)***: right of residence for longer than 3 months for:
    a) Workers and self-employed (***Article 7(1)(a)***)
    b) Persons with sufficient resources to support themselves & family (and comprehensive sickness insurance) (***Article 7(1)(b)***)
    c) Students with sufficient resources to support themselves & family & sickness insurance (***Article 7(1)(c)***)
    d) Family members of the Union citizens referred to in Articles 7(1)(a)–(c). (***Article 7(1)(d)***) (even if those family members are not Union citizens).
        - The rights of family members are contingent on the Union citizen's rights

If the worker becomes involuntarily unemployed, Directive 2004/38 will continue to guarantee them a right to reside in the host State

If they become voluntarily unemployed, they would be disqualified from social security benefits.

If a worker becomes permanently disabled or reaches retirement age, their right of residence continues under this Directive as well.

Family Members:

***Article 2(2)* of *Directive 2004/38* provides that the following are family members:**

- Spouse (***Article 2(2)(a)***)
- Registered partner (if the legislation of the host Member State treats registered partnerships as equivalent to marriage) ((***Article 2(2)(b)***)
- Direct descendants (under 21) / dependants of the spouse / registered partner (***Article 2(2)(c)***)
- Dependent direct relatives in the ascending line and those of the spouse or registered partner (eg parents). (***Article 2(2)(d)***)

Article 3(2)(b):

- The host State must facilitate their entry and residence of other family members (eg non-dependent children over 21 and parents), in accordance with its national legislation

- Covers 'the partner with whom the Union citizen has a durable relationship, duly attested'
- A partner of a Union citizen does not qualify as a family member

Their Rights:

Family members have the right to accompany the migrant Union citizens and have the following rights:

- The right to enter the host State on production of their passport (***Article 5(1)***)
- A right of residence of up to three months in the host State when accompanying or joining a Union citizen (***Article 6(2)***)
- A right of residence for more three months when accompanying or joining a Union citizen covered by Article 7(1)(a)–(c); (***Articles 7(2)***)
- A right of permanent residence after five years (***Article 16(2)***)

Effects of Separation:

- The rights of a spouse are not dependent on their residing with the worker, and thus can terminate only if the worker leaves the host State.
- ***Article 12(3) of Directive 2004/38*** gives a spouse (or registered partner) who has custody of minor children in education a right to remain following the Union citizen's departure, but it is silent about the position where no children are involved

Effects of Divorce:

- ***Directive 2004/38*** provides for the spouse (or registered partner) to remain in the country if they have resided for three years, or if they have been awarded custody or access to children, or alternatively if the court considers that allowing them to remain is warranted in the circumstances.

Enforcement of Rights:

- If an EU national or a family member is refused entry or residence rights, they will be allowed to invoke their EU rights before the appropriate immigration authority or court, or as a defence in criminal proceedings where deportation is being considered.
- If an EU national believes that they have been discriminated against in relation to employment, they should follow the appropriate national procedure in the host State to obtain a suitable remedy

Tort Law

Negligence (Duty of Care and Breach)

Negligence = carelessness

- A **Tort of Negligence** = a breach of a legal duty of care, owed to a claimant, that results in harm to the claimant, undesired by the defendant

There are 3 elements which a claimant has to prove in negligence cases:

1) Did the defendant owe the claimant a duty of care?
2) Was the defendant in breach of that duty?
3) Did the defendant's breach of duty cause damage/harm to the claimant?

Duty of Care

- A defendant will be liable, *only* if they are under a legal duty to take care for the person who is injured

1) Is it an established duty station?

Established Duty Station = where it is already clear from case law that a duty of care is owed (usually when there is a relationship between the parties)

Case Law Examples:
a. Doctor and Patient (***Cassidy v Ministry of Health***) b. Employer and Employee (***Wilsons & Clyde v English***) c. Road users to other road users and pedestrians (***Nettleship v Weston***) d. Occupier to visitors (***Occupiers' Liability Act 1957***) e. Occupier to trespasser (***Occupiers' Liability Act 1984***) f. Manufacturer to end user (***Donoghue v Stevenson***) g. Where a defendant's actions have created a dangerous situation where it is reasonably foreseeable that someone may attempt a rescue, the defendant owes a duty of care to the rescuer (***Baker TE Hopkins and Son Ltd [1959]***)

2) Or is it a novel duty station?

→ When the court has to decide whether or a not a duty of care should be imposed

'The Neighbour Principle' (Donoghue v Stevenson)

- ***Donoghue v Stevenson [1932]*** sets out the test for establishing if a duty of care exists in a novel situation

  <u>*Case Overview:*</u>
  - Donoghue drank half a ginger beer, before realising there were the remains of a decomposed snail inside. Her friend had bought her the drink so she had no contractual relationship with the seller (which would have fallen under the established duty of care)
  - This led to the creation of the **'neighbour principle'**

The Neighbour Principle:
- 'You must take reasonable care to avoid acts or omissions which you can reasonably foresee would be likely to injure your neighbour'
- **Legal definition of 'neighbour'** = persons who are so closely and directly affected by my act that I ought reasonably to have them in my contemplation as being so affected when I am directing my mind to the acts or omissions which are called in question'

→ The Caparo Test

- The neighbour principle was redefined in ***Caparo Industries plc v Dickman [1990].*** The HoL set out a three part test to determine if a duty is owed in novel situations:

1) Reasonable Foresight of Harm to the Claimant:

Is it **reasonably foreseeable** that the **defendant's actions *will* affect** this **particular claimant?**

In ***Bourhill v Young [1943]***: it was found that harm to the claimant was *not* reasonably foreseeable. Claimant sued the estate of the dead motorcyclist whose negligence had caused a car crash for the shock and miscarriage that she suffered as a result of witnessing the crash

- Whilst the motorcyclist owed a duty of care to the car it hit in the accident (damage to the driver of a vehicle on the road is foreseeable). Claimant was not a foreseeable victim so no duty of care

2) Sufficient Proximity of Relationship between the Claimant and Defendant

3) It's fair, just and reasonable to impose a duty:

- In ***Marc Rich v Bishop Rock Marine Co Ltd [1996]***: the claimant's valuable cargo was lost at sea when the ship carrying it sank. Made a claim against a ship classification society, NKK who had inspected the ship and deemed it satisfactory
  - BUT was an independent and non-profit making entity, created and operating for the sole purpose of promoting the safety of lives and ships at sea
  - Satisfied the first 2 conditions but court found it would not be fair, just and reasonable to impose a duty

No duty for an omission to act

General Rule:

The general rule is that **you do *not* owe a duty to the world for your omissions** (i.e. for doing nothing to prevent harm)

E.g. there is no duty to rescue someone whom you see in danger → if you do rescue someone, you are liable in Negligence only if you *positively* make the situation worse

Stovin v Wise [1996]: the Highway Authority knew that a road junction was dangerous but failed to exercise its powers to reduce the danger → accident occurred

- Held that the authority owed no duty of care to road-users to alleviate the danger

Exceptions - Special Relationship rule:

Where there is a **special relationship**, one party may have **a duty to take positive action to safeguard another**

- There is a duty to act positively in tort if a person has some sort of power or control over the other person or object (e.g. a driving instructor isn't just a regular passenger)

  Case Law example:

  - ***Home Office v Dorset Yacht Co Ltd [1970]*** → a group of incarcerated young offenders are left unsupervised by the officers in charge and board a yacht where they collide with another causing damages
    - A duty of care is owed by the Home Office → liable for the negligent acts of its employees
    - Was due to an omission act from the offices but they had control over the boys

  - ***Barrett v Ministry of Defence CA 1994:*** Barret, naval airman on remote base in Norway was very drunk and collapsed unconscious → friends found him and put him to bed

- Continued to check on him. Went to check later and found he had died by choking on his vomit
- His widow sued the Ministry of Defence as vicariously liable for the negligence of those who looked after him
- Court of Appeal found that as soon as his friends found him, they assumed responsibility → Barrett wasn't solely responsible for his own death

BUT: Policy Considerations:

- In some cases of negligently caused harm, the courts declined to find that the defendant owed the claimant a duty to take care, **because of policy**:
  - ⇒ The floodgates argument, deterrence, resources (e.g. no insurance), public benefit (e.g. safety), or upholding the law

- Public body liability is the only area where the type of defendant is taken into account in terms of whether recovery is appropriate
  - Often felt that political, moral and economic reasons justify the non-imposition of a private law duty on public bodies
  - Making public bodies pay compensation would be through tax-payer money

- A general exclusionary rule operates, often preventing a duty of care from arising:
  Where the actions of the public body are not direct
  Do not cause these 'easily recognised' harms
  Do not make the situation worse
  - ***East Suffolk Rivers Catchment Board v Kent [1941]***: public bodies would be liable only for the negligent exercise of statutory power where doing so had made matters worse

The Police:

Duty of Care to Public at Large:

Hill v Chief Constable of West Yorkshire [1989]: police were exonerated from liability after failing to properly investigate previous murderers in an area where the claimants daughter was then murdered
- Held that the police do not owe a duty of care to any individual, but the public at large
- If the duty had been imposed, the duty owed to the public would be too wide → every time the police failed to apprehend a criminal, they would be liable in a civil claim
- Obiter comments by Lord Keith: 'there is another reason why an action for damages in negligence should not lie against the police in circumstances such as those of the present case, and that is public policy'
  - ➢ The general duty of public duty which motivates police forces

won't be appreciably reinforced by the imposition of a duty of care

- ➢ May lead to the exercise of a function being carried on in a detrimentally defensive frame of mind
- ➢ Significant diversion of police manpower and attention from suppression of crime to defending negligence cases

Unless they have assumed responsibility:

Kirkham v Chief Constable of Greater Manchester Police [1990]: after arresting Kirkham (who had recently attempted suicide twice), police failed to pass on the information to the prison authorities (despite Kirkham's wife telling them). Kirkham committed suicide whilst on remand

Here, the police had assumed a responsibility towards the prisoner → proximity

If a prisoner dies or is injured in custody there is an enquiry → carry a lot of public attention → courts may take public view into account

Or harm a third party:

Robinson v Chief Constable of West Yorkshire Police [2018]

Supreme Court held that where a third party is injured or has suffered damages due to the negligence of a police officer, the police would be liable (if the damage or injury caused to a third party was reasonably foreseeable)

Here, if the police have themselves created the damage, no immunity

Fire Service	Ambulance Service
Duty of Care to Public at Large: ***Capital & Counties plc v Hampshire County Council and other cases [1997]:*** the Court of Appeal said that the fire service owes no private duty of care to individuals calling in an emergency - There is no obligation to respond *and* no obligation to take care having done so, *unless* there is a negligent positive act on the part of the fire service which makes the situation worse than it would have been if the fire service failed to respond	**Duty of Care to Individuals to Respond:** ***Kent v Griffiths [2001] CA***: The ambulance service owes a duty of care to individuals in certain circumstances & has a duty to respond to an emergency call. - Distinguished from fire service as an extension of the National Health Service who have a duty of care towards its patients - Seen as providing a service to individuals, rather than public at large

Coastguard:	Education Authorities:
Duty of Care to Public at Large: ○ ***OLL Ltd v Secretary of State for Transport [1997]***: the coastguard owes no duty to respond to calls from people in trouble at sea, only a duty not to make the situation worse when they do	○ ***Phelps v Hillingdon London Borough Council and other cases [2001]***: an authority owes a duty of care in respect of the provision of an education appropriate to a child's needs and there where this fails to materialise due to the negligence of a teacher or other employee, the authority could be liable according to the principles of vicarious liability

Human Rights as an avenue for tortious redress?
Where the defendant is a public body, the **HRA may provide a direct alternative** to a claim in court ● Provision 6 of the HRA provides that it is unlawful for a public authority to act in a way which is incompatible with a Convention right ● Under the HRA, a victim is able to bring proceedings against the public authority and the court can provide remedy for such a breach ● Courts are also considered private bodies so they must also ensure that their judgements are compatible with Convention rights → allows human rights to have an indirect influence on the development of the law of tort *Case Law Example:* ○ ***Osman v UK [1999] ECtHR***: human rights violations occurred when UK domestic courts refused to consider their negligence claim against the police - Whilst the ECHR found that the decision was accurate, the way the decision had been made was a violation of Article 6 rights - Decided that if there was serious negligence alleged against a public body's acts or omissions, coupled with serious harm attributable to that negligence, a case against a public body should not necessarily be struck on policy grounds - Overturned in ***Z and others v UK [2001] and TP and KM v UK [2001] ECtHR***

Breach of Duty of Care

The defendant must be at fault by **failing to come up to the standard** required by law **for fulfilling the duty.**

Two stage test:

a) The court will determine the standard that the defendant was expected to reach
b) The court will then assess whether the defendant has breached that standard

The Standard of a Reasonable Person

This is a **question of law** → assessment of how the defendant ought to have behaved

- The defendant must meet the standard of 'the reasonable person' → i.e. take as much care as would be taken by an average person

  → ***Blyth v Birmingham Waterworks (1856)***: Alderson B → 'Negligence is the omission to do something which a reasonable man ... would do, or doing something which a prudent and reasonable man would not do'

- It is an objective and impersonal test
  - ***Glasgow Corp v Muir [1943]***: Lord MacMilan - 'the issue to be decided is not 'what did this defendant foresee? But what would a reasonable person have foreseen in the particular circumstances'

Exceptions

→ There are **3 special standards** where it is considered unfair to measure the defendant's conduct against that of a reasonable person:

1) The Skilled Defendant:

Instead of being compared to a reasonable person, they are compared to a reasonable person with the same degree of skill

<u>Case Law Examples:</u>

- ***Bolam v Friern Hospital Management Committee [1957]***: doctors must meet the standard of their profession.
  - Found that the defendant would not be in breach of their duty, as long as their actions were supported by a reasonable body of professional opinion
  - This applies to anyone who exercises a special skill
- In ***Bolitho v City and Hackney Health Authority [1997]***: the court acknowledged that in some cases it cannot be demonstrated that the body of opinion relied on by the defendant is reasonable or responsible → it will always be the court to make the final decision on whether a skilled defendant acted reasonably

2) The Under-Skilled Defendant:

Inexperience *will not* be a relevant consideration in deciding whether a defendant has been negligent

<u>Case Law Examples:</u>

- *Wilsher v Essex Area Health Authority [1987]*: a junior hospital doctor must show the level of competence benefitting a doctor holding the same post
- *Nettleship v Weston [1971]*: a learner driver is expected to reach the standard of the reasonably competent driver

3) The Child:

It is unfair to expect a child to satisfy the standard reasonable person test without modification

A child defendant will be expected to show such care as can reasonably be expected of an ordinary child of the same age (***Mullin v Richards [1998]***)

The younger the child is, the less likely they are to foresee harm to others

Breach of the Reasonable Standard

This is a **question of fact** → assessment of the degree of care expected of a reasonable person

Magnitude of the risk:

Assessing the Risk of Injury:

- How aware should the defendant have been about the risk of injury?

<u>*Case Law Examples:*</u>

- ***Bolton v Stone [1951]***: The claimant was injured after a ball from a neighbouring cricket pitch flew into her outside her home. The cricket field had necessary protections (17 foot gap between the ground and surrounding fence)
  - Balls going over the fence were rare
  - Considered that the likelihood of harm was low → not in breach of a duty of care

Severity of Injury:

Will also assess the likelihood that an injury would be especially severe

- If a defendant knows that a particular individual runs a risk of suffering greater damage than normal, may have increased obligations

<u>*Case Law Examples:*</u>

- ***Paris v Stepney Borough Council [1951]***: claimant was blind in one eye and employed in a garage but no safety goggles were provided → hit by a piece of metal and blinded in other eye

  Defendant argued that it was not normal practice to provide safety goggles

  BUT because claimant was already blind, magnitude of the harm was greater → a reasonable person would take additional steps to protect that employee

Practicability of precautions:

How easy would it be to take precautions and **how much would they cost**?

Were the usual precautions taken?

Might be in breach if the risk of injury could have been substantially reduced at a low costs to the defendant

Great expenses do not excuse defendant where risk of injury is great (i.e. if there is foreseeability of risk, then the defendant is usually required to pay the additional cost to ensure safety)

The defendant's purpose:

If the defendant's **behaviour is in the public interest → less likely to be held liable**

<u>*Case Law Examples:*</u>

- ***Watt v Hertfordshire County Council [1954]***: claimant worked for the fire department & answered a call about a woman trapped under a lorry. The usual vehicle which transported heavy equipment was unavailable → his boss told him to take it unsecured on the back of a truck
  - Claimant injured when equipment fell on him
  - Could of Appeal concluded that because it was an emergency situation, combined with the high social utility of saving a women's life → fire department not in breach

Proving Breach of Duty

The **burden of proving** that the defendant has breached the duty of care lies with the **claimant** → must prove on a 'balance of probabilities' (more likely than not)

- Usually through witness evidence (either first-hand or expert)

Res Ipsa Loquitor

Where there's no direct evidence as to how the defendant actually behaved, causation can be inferred from the facts, if the injury is of the kind that does normally occur *without* negligence

'The thing speaks for itself' (***Scott v London and St Katherine Docks Co (1865)***

Three conditions:

The cause of the accident is unknown to the claimant

The accident would not normally happen without negligence

The thing causing the damage must be under the control of the defendant / someone who the defendant is responsible

→ Defendant then has to provide a reasonable explanation for how the accident could have occurred without negligence (***George v Eagle Air Services Ltd***)

The Civil Evidence Act 1968

- ***S 11 of the Civil Evidence Act 1968***: a defendant who has been convicted of a *criminal offence* is presumed, in any *subsequent civil proceedings*, to have committed that offence
- Helps in cases which involves careless conduct → the claimant can rely on the conviction (in the criminal court) as evidence that the careless conduct did take place (in the civil court of tort)

Negligence (Causation & Defences)

Causation

Causation deals with 3 questions:

1) Was the defendant's negligence a cause of the claimant's harm
2) Was there an intervening act?
3) Was the damage too remote?

Causation in Fact

The 'but for' test:

As a matter of fact, was the defendant's negligence a cause of the claimant's damage?

But for the defendant's breach of duty, would the harm to the claimant have occurred?'

Case Law Examples:

Barnett v Chelsea & Kensington Hospital [1969]: Barnett went to hospital complaining about severe stomach pains and vomiting. Doctor told him to go home and contact his GP. Barnett died 5 hours later from arsenic poisoning.

- Was always going to die → even if the doctor had properly examined him, could not have done anything to save him
- Established the but for test

- ***Holston v East Berkshire Area Health Authority [1987]:*** claimant fell from a tree and was injured, then treated negligently by a doctor → decided that there was a 75% chance that their medical condition would be the same, irrespective of the medical attention received → no causation

Material Contribution?

Where there may be **multiple causes for a claimant's loss**, the claimant *doesn't* need to show that the defendant's breach of duty was the *only* cause of the damage to the claimant, or even the main cause. Just has to show that it **materially contributed to the damage**

Case Law Examples:

Bonnington Castings Ltd v Wardlaw [1956]: the defendant was negligent in exposing the claimant to dust from equipment which hadn't been maintained. Two causes of the dust → still able to establish causation as he could show that the breach of duty materially contributed to the disease

- ***Wilsher v Essex Area Health Authority [1988]:*** claimant failed to establish that the defendant's negligence was the cause of his damage as there were several possible alternative causes of his blindness

  Here, the defendant's negligence could not be shown to have made a material contribution to the claimant's harm (or to have increased the particular risk)

Established Injuries:

- Where the claimant (or their property) has already suffered damage, a later defendant who causes a subsequent injury should be liable only to the extent that they make the claimant's damage worse
  - ***Performance Cars v Abraham [1962]***: defendant negligently collided with a Rolls Royce causing the car to need a partial respray → same part of the car had already been damaged in an earlier accident (would have needed a respray anyway)
    - Court held that the defendant did not have to pay damages → no causation

Material Increase in Risk (scientific uncertainty):

- ***Sienkiewicz v Greif (UK) Ltd [2011]:*** decided that the principle of material increase in risk is to be limited to cases of scientific uncertainty (currently mesothelioma is the only one)
- Previously, had extended this material contribution to cover situations where the defendant's breach of duty had caused a material increase in the risk of suffering harm (***McGhee v National Coal Board [1973]***)

Proportionate Damages:

If the defendant has only *contributed* towards the claimant's injury, may only have to pay proportionate damages:

- ***Holtby v Brigham and Cowan (Hull) Ltd [2003]***: the claimant developed asbestosis from exposure to dust while at work → disease had developed over a period of time (working for multiple companies), but only sued one employer.

  Court found the defendant to be liable BUT was only asked to pay proportionate damages (according to length of time of employment)

- Where the injury has multiple causes but the damages cannot be divided proportionately, the claimant is entitled to recover damages in full from either party
    - ***Civil Liability (Contribution) Act 1978***: where two or more people are responsible for the same damage, the act gives the court the power to apportion the damage between them, according to each person's share of responsibility

Intervening Act?

A '*novus actus interveniens*' (new intervening act) breaks the chain of causation

By a third party:

Whether or not the chain of causation has been broken is often a question of fact, which depends on the judgement the court makes about the circumstances of the case

- The chain of causation is unlikely to be broken by an action which the defendant ought to have foreseen as a likely consequence of their negligence (e.g. negligent medical treatment typically doesn't break the chain, unless grossly negligent)

Case Law Examples:

An instinctive reaction / intervention by a third party in a moment of alarm does not break the chain (***Scott v Shepherd (1773)***)

The negligent intervention of a third party can break the chain (***Knightley v Johns [1982]***)

Likely to break the chain where the intervening conduct is reckless or intentional (***Lamb v Camden London Borough Council [1981]***)

An Act of God / Natural Disaster will break the chain if unforeseeable (***Humber Oil Terminal v Sivand***)

By the claimant:

- Where the claimant does something after the defendant's negligent act which causes the claimant to suffer further harm
- To break the chain, the act must be entirely unreasonable in all the circumstances

Case Law Examples:

McKew v Holland & Hannen & Cubitts (Scotland) Ltd [1969]: defendant's negligence had weakened the claimant's leg, leaving it with a tendency to give way.
The claimant then descended a steep staircase with no handrail and leg gave way

- HoL held the the claimant had acted unreasonably and broken chain

Wieland v Cyril Lord Carpets Ltd [1969]: claimant injured her neck due to the defendant's negligence. Fitted with a neck collar which made it hard to use her glasses. Injured herself further when she fell down stairs

- This did not break the chain of causation → claimant had acted reasonably

○ ***Corr v IBC***: a claimant's suicide would not break the chain of causation where it was not a voluntary act, but the result of impaired mental function due to depression caused by the initial injury

- Only breaks the chain where it was a 'voluntary and informed decision to take his own life'

By another Tort?

<u>*Case Law Examples:*</u>

Baker v Willoughby: claimant was run over and badly damaged leg. Before the trial, he was shot in the same leg by a different person (required amputation)

- The shooting did not remove the negligent driver's liability → the driver had done enough damage to still be liable for the reduced mobility and loss of income from the initial damage (the shooter then liable for the further damage caused)

Jobling v Associated Dairies: employer negligently caused claimant to suffer a slipped disc. 4 years later, claimant developed a degenerative disease which left him disabled (would have occurred without the split disc)

- Employer only liable up until the second event occurred (so for just the first 4 years)

Remoteness (Legal Causation)

A **damage can be too remote and the defendant is *not* held responsible for it** → operates to limit the liability of the defendant

The Wagon Mound (No 1) sets out the test for remoteness:

1) Reasonably Foreseeable?

Is the damage of such a kind that the reasonable person would have foreseen it

2) Similar in Type?

It is not necessary to foresee the precise way in which the damage is caused, just that **the type of damage is reasonably foreseeable**

Case Law Examples:

Hughes v Lord Advocate [1963]: defendant negligently left lit paraffin lamps unattended → two young boys (claimants) climbed into the unattended manhole with the lamps → caused an explosion → bad burns suffered
  - Whilst it was not foreseeable that a paraffin lamp would be knocked down the hole and explore, the type of injury (burning) was foreseeable

- ***Tremain v Pike [1969]***: defendant negligently allowed rats to proliferate his farm → claimant (employee) came into contact with the rats and contracted a rare condition caught by contact with rat's urine
  - Court decided injury was not foreseeable → type of injury that was foreseeable would be a bite from a rat, not the rare condition
- ***Corr v IBC Vehicles Ltd [2008]***: defendant had caused an injury to an employee, leading to his suicide → accepted owed the claimant a duty of care and was in breach, causing physical & psychological injures → disputed liability for the suicide
  - Held that the employer was liable → enough that it was reasonably foreseeable that her husband would suffer some form of depression
  - The suicide was not a break in the chain of causation as was not a completely voluntary and conscious act (as depressed)

3) The Egg-Shell Skull Rule:

A defendant **must take your victim as you find them**

- If the claimant suffers a particular disability or has a particular condition, they can recover in full for their losses, even though the defendant could not have foreseen the full extent of harm

Case Law Examples:

- ***Robinson v Post Office [1974]***: claimant suffered injuries as a result of defendant's negligence → saw a doctor who gave him an anti-tetanus injection → had an allergic reaction → defendant at breach for the original injury and the allergic reaction

Defences

A negligence claim may still fail if a defendant **can successfully raise a defence**

Voluntary Assumption of Risk

'Volenti non fit injuria'

- Operates as a complete defence for the defendant, preventing the claimant recovering at all for the defendant's breach of duty
- For it to succeed, a defendant must establish that:

    The claimant had full knowledge of the nature & extent of the risk, **and**

    That the claimant willingly consented to accept the risk of being injured due to the defendant's negligence

    - The claimant freely consented to run the risk of injury

Road Users:

→ Very few cases likely to succeed with a *volenti* defence

<u>*Case Law Examples:*</u>

Nettleship v Weston [1971]: learner driver crashed with friend in the car → the defence of *volenti* did not stand ('knowledge of the risk of injury is not enough, nor is a willingness to take the risk of injury. Nothing will suffice short of an agreement to waive any claim for negligence'.)

Dann v Hamilton [1939]: Hamilton was drunk driving, Dann willingly got in the car knowing that he had been drinking (aware of the risk that he might drive carelessly) → crashed. Sued for injuries. Defence of *Volenti non fit Injuria* used.

- Not accepted → 'complete knowledge does not by itself imply consent to waive liability for the risk' → voluntarily getting in the car did not mean the claimant waived all liability for any injury then sustained
- Knowledge that there is a risk of negligence is not the same as authorising possible negligence

Morris v Murray [1990]: Murray drove a helicopter drunk with Morris as a passenger → defence was held.

The drunkenness of the pilot was so extreme and glaring that the claimant could be said to have accepted the risk of his negligence

→ **Since the passage of the Road Traffic Act 1988,** any defence of *volenti* for motor incidents cannot be relied on, where it is a **passenger suing a driver**

Employers

- For *volenti* to be successful, the claimant's consent must be freely and voluntarily given → cannot be as a result of fear or duress
- Consent cannot apply in a relationship where the claimant can't truly decide voluntarily whether or not to assume the risk
- E.g. if an employee refuses to carry out a task, they risk losing their job

Case Law Examples:

- ***Smith v Baker [1891]***: claimant injured when a heavy crane lifting stones dropped on him → just because the claimant had continued to work, knowing the risks, did not mean he consented in law to the risk

Rescuers

Rescuers often act under moral compulsion. **Not assumed to have voluntarily assumed risk of injury if:**

a) They were acting to rescue persons or property endangered by the defendant's negligence
b) They were acting under a compelling legal, social or moral duty
c) Their conduct was reasonable and a natural and probable consequence of the defendant's negligence

Case Law Examples:

- ***Haynes v Harwood [1935]***: policeman (Haynes) was injured as a result of the negligence of Harwood → sued. He did not voluntarily agree to take the risk, but did it as part of his official duty

Defence of Illegality

- *Ex turpi causa non oritur actio* → '**no action arises from a disgraceful cause**'
- If a claimant was involved in an illegal enterprise at the time they were injured, can provide a defence

Case Law Examples:

- ***Ashton v Turner [1981]***: claimant and defendant escaping from a burglary they had just carried out. Defendant's negligent driving caused them to crash → claimant injured → defence of illegality applied

- ***Pitts v Hunt [1990]***: both underage, Hunt driving motorcycle without a licence and drunk. Pitts encouraging him.

  Held that it was an example of *ex turpi causa* → the reckless driving, which was the cause of the claimant's injuries, was an inherent part of their joint criminal enterprise.

  Also no duty of care owed by the deceased to the claimant as it arose directly from the joint illegal enterprise

  Extreme case → may not always apply

- *Gray v Thames Trains Ltd [2009]*: claimant injured in a rail crash, caused by negligence of defendant → suffered from PTSD leading to a personality change → later stabbed a stranger to death. Accepted that 'but for' the accident & PTSD, would not have stabbed stranger
    - Defence argued that the killing was a voluntary and deliberate act
    - Tied up with own criminal conduct → defence of illegality applied

Contributory Negligence

- If a defendant cannot rely on any of the above defences, may be able to raise the partial defence of contributory negligence, on appropriate facts (*Law Reform (Contributory Negligence) Act 1945*)

Comprises 2 elements:

Carelessness on the claimant's part

That carelessness has contributed to the claimant's damage

Proving Contributory Negligence:

In order to prove contributory negligence, the court will assess:

a. **Culpability**
b. **Causation** → i.e. extent to which the claimant's carelessness has caused or contributed to the loss suffered
    - The issue is not who caused the accident, but who caused the damage

<u>*Case Law Examples:*</u>

- ***Froom v Butcher [1975]:*** in a road accident, the claimant wasn't wearing a seatbelt and so their damages were reduced by 25% (even they did not cause the accident, but did contribute to the damage)
- ***Capps v Miller [1989]:*** Same tariff as laid down in ***Froom v Butcher*** extended to failure to wear crash helmets on a motorcycle
- ***Owens v Brimmell [1997]:*** Passengers who accept lifts from a driver they know to be drunk will have damages reduced if injured

Reasonable Person Test:

- The reasonable person test is also applied for contributory negligence → the court will decide whether the claimant has failed to take reasonable care for their own safety, with their behaviour measured against that of an ordinary reasonable person in the circumstances
- When the defendant's negligence causes the claimant to put themselves in a dangerous situation to try and save themselves → was the claimant's actions a reasonable response to danger

<u>*Case Law Examples:*</u>

Sayers v Harlow UDC [1958], as a result of the defendant's negligence, the claimant became trapped in a public lavatory owned by the defendant. After unsuccessfully calling for assistance, the claimant thought that she could get out by climbing over the door. In trying to get down, she slipped, fell and sustained injury.

- The court found that the defendant was liable for the injuries, as the claimant had not taken any risks disproportionate to her 'necessities'
- BUT: claimant's damages were reduced by one quarter for contributory negligence (should have appreciated that she could not rely entirely on the toilet roll holder to support her weight).

Exceptions - children:

As a matter of law, there is **no age below which a child cannot be contributorily negligent**

- But, the older the child, the more likely a court is to make a finding of contributory negligence
- Determine whether an ordinary child of the claimant's age would have taken more care for their safety

Case Law example:

- ***Gough v Thorne [1966]***: claimant only 13½ → 'a judge should only find a child guilty of contributory negligence if he or she is of such an age as reasonably to be expected to take precautions for his or her safety'

Exceptions - rescuers:

Baker v TE Hopkins & Son Ltd [1959].

- A rescuer will be judged against the standard of a reasonable rescuer with allowance made for the emergency situation in which they may find themselves
- Will likely only find a rescuer contributory negligent if they've shown a 'wholly unreasonable disregard for his or her own safety' (rare)

Exceptions - workers:

Cases where a claimant is injured at work, partly because of their employer's negligence but also as a result of their own carelessness

Court will take into account all the relevant circumstances → courts are prepared to make findings of contributory negligence against careless workers

Its effects:

It does not defeat a claim completely (***Section 1(1) of the Law Reform (Contributory Negligence) Act 1945***)

- Where there is a finding of contributory negligence, the claimant's damages are to be reduced
    - The court will calculate the full amount of damages which would have been payable had it not been for the claimant's contributory negligence. Will then make an appropriate reduction to take the contributory negligence into account

Damages should be reduced:

a) To such extent as the court thinks just and equitable
b) Having regard to the claimant's share in the responsibility for the damage

Remedies

Compensatory / Nominal Damages:

The aim of damages in tort is to **put the claimant in the same position that they would have been *if the tort had not been committed***

Nominal Damages:

- Where a tort is **actionable per se** (e.g. the tort of trespass to the person and the tort of trespass to land), the claimant **does not need to prove any actual damage or loss** in order to establish a claim
- Whilst an award of compensatory damages is not appropriate (as the claimant has not suffered any actual damage), the court recognises that their rights have been infringed by an award of **nominal damages**
    - Beneficial when a tort claim is introduced for aims that are not compensatory

Compensatory Damage:

Key Terms:

Mitigation of Loss = the claimant should be no worse off, but also no better off (i.e. they should not be able to profit from the incident). The claimant thus has a duty to mitigate → they must take all reasonable steps to keep the losses they are claiming to a minimum

- → *E.g.* a claimant who unreasonably refused medical treatment would not be able to recover damages for harm which the treatment could have avoided
- → E.g. a claimant who loses their job as a result of a defendant's negligence, but who is still capable of working, should look for alternative employment

One Action Rule = a claimant can bring only one claim based on one set of facts

- Once an award of damages has been made, a claimant *cannot* go back to court with a second claim if the injury worsens

Special Damages = losses which are capable of being calculated precisely at the time of the trial and which are stated in the form of a calculation

General Damages = losses which are not capable of being calculated precisely and are therefore left to the court to determine (no definitive figure can be placed on them)

- Includes pain, suffering, loss of amenity and losses incurred after trial

Non-Pecuniary Losses:

Non-Pecuniary losses are not capable of being calculated in money terms. They cover past, present and future pain, physical and mental anguish, fear of surgery etc…

- Can also covers the anguish of knowing that your life expectancy has been shortened due to the accident (***Administration of Justice Act 1982, s 1(1)(b)***)

Pain and Suffering

Covers both physical and mental anguish (past, present and future)

The test for awarding non-pecuniary losses is subjective → the claimant must be aware of the injuries to be able to claim for pain and suffering (***Wise v Kaye [1962]***)

If they were unconscious, they cannot recover damages for pain and suffering for that period

Loss of Amenity

Loss of amenity = the effects of the injury on the claimant's enjoyment of life (e.g. changing to a less enjoyable job / no longer able to do hobbies)

A claimant who was very active prior to the accident will receive more under this head of damage than a claimant who was inactive

This is an objective test → **able to recover whether conscious or not** (i.e. could still recover if in coma/unconscious) (***West v Shephard [1964]***)

Measuring Damages:

- To assess the amount of damages owed, courts will consider the individual facts of each case
- The Judicial College publishes a set of guideline figures for awards of damages for personal injuries
- Lawyers will also turn to practitioner texts like *Kemp and Kemp on Damages*, which contain thousands of cases in which damages have been awarded → used as a rough guide for damages their client should obtain (estimation)

Pecuniary Losses:

Pecuniary losses = ***capable*** **of mathematical calculation** in **money terms**

Medical Expenses

The claimant is able to **recover any medical expenses that have been incurred**

- For medical damages incurred post-trial (general damages), the court will base its assessment on the annual cost of treatment and the number of years the treatment is likely to continue
- A claimant is able to recover the reasonable cost of private medical treatment
  - ***s 2(4) of the Law Reform (Personal Injuries) Act 1948***: a claimant cannot be found to have failed to mitigate their loss by paying for private treatment, rather than obtaining free treatment under the NHS

Services provided to the claimant

A claimant is able to recover the cost of services relating to their medical care (e.g. help with housework/nursing care) as long as they can prove that the need for these services is related to the injury (***Schneider v Eisovitch [1960]***)

- It does not matter who renders these services (e.g. freely by a relative) → still able to receive damages
- Where a claimant's spouse (or other relative) has given up paid employment to care for them, the claimant can recover the cost of that care

<u>*Case Law Example:*</u>

- ***Housecroft v Burnett [1986]***: the cost is assessed according to the loss of earnings suffered by the carer (with the costs not exceeding the commercial rate for providing these services)
  - Where care is provided for free and the carer was not previously employed, court will determine amount owed based on the facts

Loss of Earnings Pre-Trial

Are considered to be special damages

- Must ascertain net earnings (i.e. after deduction of tax and national insurance) as compensation should be the same sum of money that they would have taken home if they could work (this included a deduction in pension contributions)
- If the claimant regularly earned overtime or bonuses, these should be included
- Also any perks of the job are included (e.g. company car, reduced mortgage rates, share options etc…)

Loss of Earnings Post-Trial

Are considered to be general damages

- Seeks to determine how much the claimant would have been capable of earning in the future, if the accident had not occurred:

The Multiplicand:	The Multiplier:

The court will ascertain the claimant's **net annual loss of earnings**
- Will take into account if the claimant was likely to have increased earnings (by promotion)
- Will *not* take into account inflation
- The net figure (post tax etc) is the multiplicand
	The court will then calculate **how long the claimant will lose this money** (the period of future loss)
	- If the claimant is unable to work again, the period will be based on their pre-accident working life expectancy
	- *Discount Rate*: Takes into account the interest that the claimant could earn on damages by reducing the multiplier rate
	  - Solicitors use Ogden tables to find an appropriate multiplier, based on the client's age and rate of interest
	    - From Aug 2019, the prescribed discount rate to be taken into account by the courts is minus 0.25% (so that claimants are treated as risk averse investors)
	  - Will also take into account contingencies of life (i.e. possibility that claimant would have been made redundant anyway)

Loss of Earnings - The Lost Years

The Lost Years = the additional years that the claimant would have worked, had their life expectancy not been shortened

- Occurs where a living claimants life expectancy has been reduced (as a result of the defendant's negligence)
- Allows a claimant to recover damages for their financial losses (loss of earnings pre and post trial whilst alive) and also, to recover damages for the lost years, (the amount they might have earnt if they would have lived, but for their injuries)

When you calculate the loss of earnings figure for the period after the claimant is expected to die, you must deduct the amount which the claimant would have spent on themselves

This deduction is generally set at 25% for a person married with dependent children and at 33% for those with no dependents (***Harris v Empress Motors***)

Case Law Example:

Pickett v British Rail Engineering [1980]: claimants whose life expectancy has been shortened by the incident could recover loss of future earnings for lost years

Loss of Earnings - Children

If a child is injured in an accident and will never be able to work in the future, court **will still award a sum for future loss of earnings**

BUT, virtually impossible to predict what a child's earnings might have been

Multiple ways to assess including looking at parents earnings, at the national average, specific potential of the child

Loss of Earning Capacity

Where a claimant is **injured** and **suffers from a continuing disability**, **but is still able to work** (potential disadvantage of finding a future job / being paid less)

Only relevant where the claimant is still in their original job

Speculative damages → judge must be satisfied that there is a real risk of the claimant losing their job & then put a monetary value on this chance

Referred to as the ***Smith v Manchester Corporation*** award (***Smith v Manchester Corporation)***

Exceptions to net deductions:

There are **some payments which a claimant is allowed to keep in full** (e.g. without having to deduct for tax/insurance) and are *not* deducted from the damages which the claimant receives:

a) Insurance payments
b) Ill-health pensions
c) Charitable payments

- If these sums were deduced, it would discourage people from protecting themselves by insurance
    - ***Social Security (Recovery of Benefits) Act 1997***: for state benefits received, they are deducted from the claimant's damages and then the defendant is required to pay it back to the State (ensures state isn't bearing the costs of the defendant's negligence). **Three heads of damages affected by the Act are**:
        1) Compensation for lost earnings

2) Compensation for cost of care
3) Compensation for loss of mobility

Alternative to the Lump Sum Approach:

- ***s 32A of the Senior Courts Act 1981***: occurs where there is a chance that at some point, the injured claimant will develop further disease or deterioration in physical/mental condition (as a result of the defendant's negligence)
    - Damages are first assessed on the assumption that the injured person will not develop the disease or suffer from deterioration
    - Further damages will be provided in the future if the claimant does develop these symptoms
- ***Damages Act 1996, s 2***: in some circumstances, the court will award damages for personal injury as periodic payments, rather than as a lump sum

Damages on Death

Key Terms:

Estate = the property belonging to the dead person
Will = document where a person sets out their wishes as to the distribution of their estate on death
Intestate = a person who has died without leaving a will
Executors = people appointed under the will to administer the distribution of the estate according to the deceased's wishes
Administrators = people who administer the distribution of the estate in an intestacy
Personal Representatives = term encompassing both executors & administrators
Beneficiaries = people either named in the will or who satisfy the rules of intestacy & who inherit all or part of the deceased's estate
Dependants = people for whom the deceased used to provide for financially

The limitation period to bring a claim under either Act is 3 years

The Law Reform (Miscellaneous Provisions) Act 1934

Deals with getting money for the Estate

Where a claimant dies before they have received an award of compensation or the defendant dies prior to the settlement, **the cause of action will survive**

- Does not create any new cause of action, but allows existing causes to continue
- So can claim for pain, suffering, loss of amenity, any property damage
- Where the claimant died instantly, and did not have the opportunity to start a claim, the estate can bring a claim on their behalf

Where a defendant dies before claims can be settled, **the Act limits *loss of income* to the *period up to death***

Except for reasonable funeral expenses (if they have been paid for by the estate), any money that the estate has had to pay out because of the death will not be taken into account

Non-pecuniary losses such as pain and suffering and loss of amenity will **end at the date of death**

The Fatal Accidents Act 1976:

Deals with getting money for dependants

Recognises the numerous levels of dependency that exist in modern life → allows dependants to sue for the death of the person on whom they were dependent

Must be able to show that, had the deceased survived, they would have been able to bring a claim against the defendant

There are 3 possible claims:

A claim on behalf of the dependants for loss of dependency

Who can claim:

Section 1: a person must fall within these class of dependants:

i) Wife or husband of deceased
ii) Anyone who was living with the deceased in the same household immediately before the date of death and had been living with them in that household for at least 2 years & was living during that period as wife / husband
iii) Any parent or other ascendant
iv) Any person who was treated by the deceased as his parent
v) Any child or other descendant
vi) Step-children
vii) Brother/Sister/Uncle/Aunt of the deceased

→ ***They must be financially dependent and on the statutory list in order to claim***

What can they claim:

Provides compensation for **pecuniary losses only** → must be able to show that they had a reasonable expectation of pecuniary benefit from the deceased (i.e. were financially dependent on them)

Can include cost of replacing services provided by deceased (e.g. childcare)

Calculating the claim:

- The court needs to assess the future pecuniary benefits which the defendant would have received from the deceased:
    - ***S 3(3)***: the amount of damages *does not* take into account chances of the spouse remarrying
    - ***S (4)***: the amount that the dependants would receive from any *will is not taken into account*

Multiplicand:

- The multiplicand is based on the **deceased's net annual earnings** (taking into account that part of these earnings would have been spent on themselves)
- The deceased's own living expenses are deducted from their earnings (conventional deduction is 25% for a married person with children and 33% without children)
- Other contributions aside from income will also be included (e.g. perks of the job and services provided to the household)

Multiplier:

- The multiplier is based on the **period of loss to the dependent** (i.e. until the deceased would have ceased work)
- A short multiplier is applied for children of the deceased → you would expect the period of dependency to cease when the child reaches 18 (unless still in full time education)

A claim for damages for bereavement

***S 1(A)*: the only people who can claim damages for bereavement are:**

a) The wife, husband or civil partner of the deceased
b) The parents of a minor who was never married / had a civil partner

The amount of bereavement damages is currently £15,120 (fixed sum)

A claim for funeral expenses

S 3(5): funeral expenses, where they have been paid for by the dependants can be rewarded

Negligence (Psychiatric Harm & Economic Loss)

Limited duty stations = situations were a duty of care may not be owed but can occasionally occur (usually relating to psychiatric harm and economic loss)

- If the law allowed for such claims to fall under a tort of negligence, the number of claimants and the extent of their claims would be indefinite → floodgates

Pure Economic Loss

- **Pure Economic Loss** = financial damage suffered due to a negligent act, not accompanied from any physical damage to a person or property
    - The defective quality of the product
    - The cost of replacing the defect / product
- Exclusionary Rule = losses which are purely economic and not consequential on the claimant's personal injury cannot generally be claimed for

Acquiring a defective product:

- Pure economic loss can include economic loss caused by acquiring a defective item of property → *no duty of care is owed here in tort*
- E.g. if person A receives a gift from person B but that gift is then faulty. Person A has no contact with the retailer so cannot sue in Contract, but will also not be able to sue in tort for the cost of replacing the faulty item

  If they were allowed to sue in cases like this, the law of tort would interfere with and undermine the law of contract

Liability for a defective product *only* occurs where *the defect caused damage to persons or other property* (i.e. leads to consequential economic loss):

- Where a claimant has suffered personal injury or damage to other property (as a result of a faulty item), the law more readily accepts that there is a sufficient close relationship between claimant and defendant for a duty of care to arise

    - ***Murphy v Brentwood DC [1990]:*** defendant local authority had negligently approved plans for the footings of a house → claimant purchased the property and then it began to subside due to defects in the footings → claimant forced to sell property at a loss
        - Damages suffered were purely economic so the defendant was not liable in negligence → did not cause damage to persons or other property

Economic loss unconnected to personal injury / physical damage

- **You can subdivide this type of pure economic loss into two categories:**
    a) Economic loss caused by damage to the property of a third party
    b) Economic loss caused where there is no personal injury or physical damage to the property

Economic loss caused by damage to the property of a third party:

General Rule:

If B negligently damages property belonging to a third party and causes A loss, there is not a sufficiently close relationship between them → B does not owe A a duty of care and A cannot recover their losses from B → situation of pure economic loss

Case Law example:

- ***Spartan Steel & Alloys Ltd v Martin & Co (Contractors) Ltd [1973]***: defendants negligently damaged an electricity cable which directly supplied energy to the claimants' factory. As a result of the power supply failure, items of 'loss':
  a) The damage to the melt which was already in the furnace (poured out) → **recoverable** as constituted physical damage to property
  b) The profit lost as a result of the damaged melt → **recoverable** as a consequential economic loss following on from physical damage
  c) The loss of profit during the hours the electricity was cut off → classed as pure economic loss so **not recoverable** (economic loss caused by damage to the property of a third party - the electricity supplier)

- ***Muirhead v Industrial Tank Specialities Ltd and others [1985]:*** Muirhead planned to store lobsters in tanks bought from Industrial Tanks, the motor for the tanks had been supplied by ITT (UK) Ltd. Motor failed and some lobsters died → sued ITT (based on ***Donoghue v Stevenson***)
  - Liable for the dead lobsters - damaged property
  - Liable for the lost profit on the dead lobsters (consequential economic loss)
  - Can't claim for the expense of trying to correct the faulty pump or the cost of replacing the pumps (pure economic loss)

Economic loss where there is no personal injury or physical damage to property:

Economic loss where there is no personal injury or physical damage to property can be:

a) Caused by negligent actions, or
b) Caused by negligent statements

Negligent Actions:

Case Law example:

- ***Weller & Co v Foot and Mouth Disease Research Institute [1966]***: Virus escaped from defendant's premises and affected cattle making them unsaleable → claimant (a cattle-auctioneer) brought an action for loss of profit he would have made had the cattle not been affected
  - Unable to recover its losses as was not caused by property damage (the claimant did not own any of the cows) → pure economic loss & no duty owed

Negligent Statements:

***Candler v Crane Christmas* [1951]:** 'a duty of care could arise when negligent words caused pure economic loss'

- ***Hedley Byrne & Co Ltd v Heller & Partners Ltd:*** a duty of care arises in a case of negligent statements causing pure economic loss where:
    a) There is an assumption of responsibility by the defendant
    b) Reasonable reliance by the claimant

  Restated criteria in *Caparo Industries plc v Dickman*
    The adviser knew the purpose for which the advice was required
    The adviser knew that the advice would be communicated to the advisee
    The adviser knew that the advisee was likely to act on the advice, without independent inquiry (it induced them)
    The advice was acted on by the advisee to its detriment

→ Will also consider whether reliance on the statement was reasonable (similar to the but for test)

<u>*Case Law example:*</u>

- ***James McNaughton Papers Group Ltd v Hicks Anderson & Co (a firm) [1991]***: company accountant owed no duty of care to a prospective takeover bidder who relied on his rushed draft → insufficient proximity of relationship → did not know the accounts would be communicated to the bidder for that transaction

- ***Morgan Crucible Co plc v Hill Samuel Bank Ltd [1991]***: claimant bidding to take over a company (that company advised by defendants). Defendants negligently misrepresented to the third party → loss for the claimants
    - Issue was whether a party advising a company owed a duty of care to other companies to ensure that the advice was accurate
    - Duty did exist → proximity of relationship

- General rule, no duty of care owed for advice given in a social situation (no assumption of responsibility), except for:
    - ***Chaudhry v Prabhakar [1989]***: claimant & defendant friends → defendant gave advice about purchase of a car (car unusable) → duty of care existed as the defendant had more experience and knowledge & claimant made it clear they were relying on defendants skill and judgement

→ Extension of Special Relationship:

Negligent Statement to a Third Party	Negligent Provision of Professional Services
Spring v Guardian Assurance plc [1994]: claimant's former employer provided a reference to his prospective new employers (prepared negligently) → not employed as a result Duty of care was owed → responsibility by former employer to take care in providing the reference Negligent statements made to a third party which was relied on to the detriment of the claimant	→ Only where there has been an assumption of responsibility: ○ ***White v Jones [1995]***: client instructed a solicitor to draft a new will (negligently delayed in drafting) → client died before new will made → claimant would have been a beneficiary under new will (loss of prospective inheritance) Duty of care was owed → the solicitor undertook a responsibility towards the potential beneficiaries ○ ***Henderson v Merrett Syndicates Ltd***: claimant (investors in Lloyds Insurance Syndicates) brought actions against defendants (underwriters of the syndicates) for substantial losses - Court held it was permissible to sue concurrently in contract and tort - No specific statements made, but owed a duty not to cause pure economic loss by the negligent provision of professional services

Excluding Liability:

Liability can be excluded using a disclaimer, *if*:

a) Reasonable steps are taken to bring the exclusion notice to the claimant's attention *before* the tort was committed
b) The wording of the notice must cover the loss suffered by the claimant

- The ability of a defendant to exclude liability is limited by the ***Unfair Contract Terms Act 1977*** and the ***Consumer Rights Act 2015***:

UCTA:
The UCTA Deals with Business to Business Relations Section 2 deals with a defendant's ability to exclude liability for negligent acts or omissions - ***S 2(1):*** Defendant cannot exclude liability for death or personal injury resulting from negligence

- For other loss or damage, can exclude or restrict liability *only* if the exclusion satisfies the requirements of reasonableness ***(s 2(2))***
    - ***S 11(3):*** should be fair and reasonable to allow reliance on the exclusion notice, having regard to all the circumstances

- ***Smith v Eric S Bush; Harris v Wyre Forest District Council [1989]***: exclusion notices did not satisfy the requirements of reasonableness:
    - Were the parties of equal bargaining power
    - Would it be reasonably practicable to obtain the advice from an alternative source (cost and time considerations)
    - How difficult is the task being undertaken for which liability is excluded
    - What are the practical consequences (money at stake, can parties bear the loss involved)

Consumer Rights Act:

Deals with a defendant's ability to exclude liability for negligent acts or omissions

- ***S 65(1)***: Defendant cannot exclude liability for death or personal injury resulting from negligence
- For other loss or damage, can exclude or restrict liability only if the exclusion satisfies the requirements of fairness (s 62)

Tort of deceit?

Another option for a claimant who has relied on a false statement is to sue in tort of Deceit instead

Whilst Negligence provides a remedy for loss caused by carelessness, tort of Deceit provides a remedy where the defendant's actions were intentional

Harder to establish than a claim in Negligence. Requirements:

a) The defendant made a false statement of fact (by words or conduct)
b) The defendant made the statement knowing that it was false (or might be)
    - Knew the statement was false
    - Was reckless as to whether the statement was true or fale
    - Made the statement without believing it to be true
c) The defendant made the statement intending that the claimant would act on it
d) The claimant did act upon the statement and then suffered damage

Pure Psychiatric Harm

Pure psychiatric harm is caused **without any physical impact or injury** to the claimant

- The court has developed specific rules which define more narrowly the kinds of pure psychiatric harm for which a duty of care can be owed:

The injury must be:

Caused by a sudden shock; and either

A medically recognised psychiatric illness or
A shock induced physical condition (e.g. miscarriage or heart attack)
- No duty of care in relation to harm caused by a gradual build up of events

Primary Victims:

Primary Victim = was in the actual area of danger or reasonably believed they were in danger
- Provided the risk of physical injury was foreseeable, risk of psychiatric harm doesn't have to be foreseeable

<u>*Case Law Example:*</u>

Page v Smith [1995]: Claimant involved in a crash due to the defendant's negligence → suffered no physical injuries but resulted in chronic and permanent exhaustion (had suffered from chronic fatigue syndrome before but now permanent)
- Claimant was considered a primary victim
- Owed a duty of care in relation to their pure psychiatric harm

Dulieu v White & Sons [1901]: claimant was a pregnant bar-maid working in a public house → defendant negligently crashed into the building → claimant suffered severe shock, resulting in a miscarriage
- Held to be a primary victim as she reasonably feared for her own physical safety & the defendant's negligence created a foreseeable risk of physical harm

Secondary Victims:

In order for secondary victims to be owed a duty of care, certain requirements must be met (established in ***Alcock v Chief Constable of South Yorkshire Police):***
- The case involved claims by the relatives of the victims of the Hillsborough football stadium disaster (spectators crushed and many killed/injured due to negligence of the Police). Claims made by relatives of the victims who witnessed the event (live and on TV) - suffered pure psychiatric harm

1) Foreseeability of Psychiatric Harm

If the claimant is a secondary victim, they must demonstrate that **psychiatric injury was a foreseeable consequence** of the defendant's negligence

Court will ask 'if an ordinary person in the claimant's position witnessed these events, is it foreseeable that they would suffer a psychiatric injury?'

⇓

2) Proximity of Relationship

The claimant must have a close relationship of love and affection with the person who is endangered by the defendant's negligence

- This is presumed in a relationship of parent / child, husband / wife and fiancé's
- If the claimant falls outside the categories of close tie presumption, the claimant must prove that a close relationship of love and affection exist
    - HoL have held that a normal passer-by might be able to claim for psychiatric harm if the incident witnessed was particularly horrific
- Defendant can adduce evidence to the court to rebut the presumption of love and affection, where the claimant was not actually close to the victim

⇓

3) Proximity in Time and Space

The claimant must be present at the accident or its immediate aftermath

They must see or hear the accident, or its immediate aftermath, with their own senses

Case Law Example:

- ***McLoughlin v O'Brian [1982]***: claimant was at home when her husband and children were in a car accident (caused by defendant's negligence). Was told and driven to the hospital 2 hours after crash took place
    - Argued that the impact of what she heard and saw caused her severe shock resulting in psychiatric illness
    - Court held that a duty was owed → extended to those who weren't at the site of the incident but came upon the 'immediate aftermath' (the claimant witnessed her family in the same conditions that they were in at the site of the crash)

⇓

4) Proximity of Perception

McLoughlin v O'Brian: shock must come to the claimant 'through sight or hearing of the event or its immediate aftermath' - cannot be compensated if the event is communicated by a third party

Case Law Example:

- ***Alcock v Chief Constable of South Yorkshire Police:*** claimants who suffered shock as a result of witnessing the live TV broadcasts were not able to show a duty of care → what the claimants did see was not equivalent to seeing and hearing the event or its immediate aftermath
    - The broadcast did not show the suffering of identifiable individuals
    - Held that a live tv broadcast may be sufficient to render the tortfeasor liable to claimants in shock if the 'impact of the simultaneous television pictures

would be as great, if not greater, than the actual sight of the accident'

Liverpool Women's Hospital NHS Foundation Trust v Ronayne [2015]: claimant's wife suffered a series of complications after undergoing a hysterectomy at the defendant's hospital (negligence) → claimant suffered psychiatric injury as a result of the 'shock' of his wife's rapid deterioration over the course of 36 hours

- Held that his psychiatric illness was not caused by a shocking event (the sudden appreciation by sight or sound of a horrifying event, which violently agitates the mind' (Lord Acknew in Alcock)

***RE and others* v *Calderdale and Huddersfield NHS Foundation Trust* [2017]:** A grandmother was able to recover damages as a secondary victim for the psychiatric harm she suffered after witnessing the traumatic and chaotic birth of her granddaughter → held that the event was sufficiently shocking

Rescuers:

As the law stands, a rescuer does not hold a special status different from other accident victims who suffer only pure psychiatric harm

<u>*Case Law Example:*</u>

- ***White v Chief Constable of the South Yorkshire Police [1999]:*** police officers at the Hillsborough disaster (suffered psychiatric harm) → involved in rescue activities but never at risk of physical injury
  - Psychiatric harm came from being exposed to shocking events and scenes during the course of their employment as police officers, whilst acting as rescuers
  - HoL did not accord a special status to employees or rescuers → rescuers should be treated in the same way as any other victim
- ***Chadwick v British Railways Board [1967]***: two trains crashed, Chadwick lived near to disaster and went to help → asked to crawl into debris and give injections to the wounded → suffered pure psychiatric harm → held that a duty of care was owed
  - Primary victim = in the area of danger and at risk of physical injury

Breach of Duty and Causation of Damages:

Generally, a defendant in cases of pure psychiatric harm admit that they **fell below a reasonable standard of care and so in breach of a duty** (argument usually about whether a duty was owed)

A damage is too remote when it is **not a reasonably foreseeable consequence** of the defendant's negligence

If a person is particularly vulnerable to psychiatric harm, can rely on the egg-shell skull rule in relation to causation of damage

Evaluation and Reform:

The English law of liability for psychiatric illness has attracted severe criticism

- Criticism of the practicality and consistency of the legal principles in question

HoL in ***White v Jones*** found that 'the search for principle' in this area of law has been 'called off' and is a 'patchwork quilt of distinctions which are difficult to justify'

Employers' & Vicarious Liability

Employers' Liability

The Common Law Duty of Care:

Personal in Nature:

- The duty owed by employer to employee is 'personal to the employer' → it is a non-delegable duty
- An employer cannot escape liability for negligence by saying that it delegated its performance to someone else, whom it reasonably believed to be competent
- The employee does not have to identify exactly who was to blame for the accident, but can simply allege that a given event proves the employer breached its personal common law duty

Lord Wright in ***Wilsons & Clyde Coal Co Ltd v English [1937]*** saw the employer's common law duty as comprising **3 separate duties to take reasonable steps to provide:**

a) Competent Staff
b) Adequate Material
c) A Proper System of Work and Supervision

Competent Staff:

An employer owes an employee a duty to provide the employee with competent fellow workers.

- Arises where an employer knows, or ought to know, about the risks a particular worker is posting to fellow workers (***Waters v Commissioner of Police for the Metropolis [2002]***)
  This risk can be psychological as well as physical harm → takes into account bullying

  Case Law Example:
  - ***Hudson v Ridge Manufacturing Co Ltd [1957]:*** employer liable for failing to prevent the independent dangerous actions of an employee (was known to have a reputation for playing tricks and pranks and had been told to stop before)
  - Where it is a one-off practical joke, by someone not prone to such activity, employer is not liable (***Smith v Crossley***) (but may be vicariously liable)

Adequate Material:

Equipment covers **anything provided by an employer for the purpose of its business**. Duty is relevant in 2 situations:

Where an employer does provide plant and or equipment to their employees, but it is inadequate in some way

Where an employer does not in fact supply all the plant and equipment needed for the job

- ***S 1 of the Employer's Liability (Defective Equipment) Act 1969***: where an employee is injured as a result of defective equipment at work, they can sue the employer for breach of its duty to provide adequate plant and equipment *instead of* the manufacturer

A Proper System of Work and Supervision:

An employer must **devise a safe system and take reasonable steps to ensure it is complied with**

- Includes the physical lay-out of the job, the sequence in which the work is carried out and the provision of training, warnings, notices, safety equipment and the issue of special instructions

In ***Latimer v AEC Ltd [1953]***, a 4th duty was added:

A Safe Place of Work:

An employer must take reasonable steps to provide a safe place of work

- Applies, regardless of where the employees are at work → an employer must assess premises to which their employees are sent for dangers and then, if such dangers are found, devise and implement a system of work so as to eradicate or minimise those dangers (***General Cleaning Contractors v Christmas [1953]***)

Stress:

The duty to provide a safe system of work can extend to an employee who has suffered stress, as a result of work (***Walker v Northumberland County Council [1995]***)

- A duty can be owed to an individual employee if the 'threshold question is satisfied' as established in ***Hatton v Sutherland [2002]*** and then approved in ***Barber v Somerset County Council [2004]***
    a) An employer *does not have* to inquire about an employees' mental health → can take what they are told at face value

b) Where an employee wishes to remain in a stressful job, and the only alternative is demotion or dismissal, the employer is *not in breach* for allowing the employee to continue

c) The threshold question to determine whether a duty would arise was whether injury to health through stress at work was reasonably foreseeable
   - The court will consider the nature and extent of the work done by the employee (e.g. was it over demanding in terms of type or amount / was there a high degree of absenteeism or sickness in that department)
   - Signs from the employee themselves

d) Employers who offer confidential counselling advice services are *unlikely* to be found in breach of their duty

Breach / Causation / Defences:

Proving Breach of Duty:

- An employer will be in breach of its duty if it **fails to meet the standard of care to be expected of a reasonable employer in its position**
  - To be in breach, the risk must be known to the employer
- The court will assess the standard of care to be expected by looking at all the circumstances of the case, including the magnitude of the foreseeable risk and the cost and practicality of precautions (***Latimer v AEC Ltd)***

<u>*Case Law Example:*</u>

Paris v Stepney Borough Council [1951]: the council was required to take extra precautions for the claimant's safety as they knew he had only one eye and therefore risked total blindness if that eye was damaged

Causation:

The usual tests of causation apply (but for, *novus actus interveniens* and remoteness) are all considered

Defences:

- The defence of *volenti* will often fail → difficult to show that the employee freely consented to run the risk of injury caused by the employer's negligence (***Smith v Baker***)
- Careless employees can have damages reduced for contributory negligence, except:
  - May make allowances for employees working in noisy conditions and doing repetitive work (***Caswell v Powell Duffryn Associated Collieries Ltd [1940]***)

Statutory Health and Safety Regulations

Regulations governing health and safety in the workplace are made under the ***Health and Safety at Work etc Act 1974 (HSWA 1974)*** → cover a vast range of issues arising in the workplace, including:

Obligations to carry out risk assessments
Provision of information and training for employees
Provision and maintenance of work equipment
Provision of personal protective equipment
Lifting and handling
Noise at work
Lifting in the workplace

Breach of these regulations are a criminal offence

Such regulations can no longer be relied upon as the basis for a claim for breach of statutory duty → although may still be relevant in assessing breach of duty

- Where a particular risk is covered by statutory health and safety regulations, the content of those regulations will be highly relevant in establishing breach of duty → act as a guide to the standard which a reasonable employer ought to meet

Vicarious Liability

- A claimant can sue either the employer (vicariously liable) or the employee (primarily liable) or both (jointly liable)
    - Employer is generally a safer option as more chance they can pay (as a result of the ***Employers' Liability (Compulsory Insurance) Act 1969***)

There are 3 essential elements for vicarious liability to exist on the part of an employer:

1) The worker must be an employee or in a relationship akin to employment
2) The employee must have committed a tort
3) The employee's tort must have been committed in the course of their employment

Must be an Employee

- Must distinguish an employee (employed under a contract of service) from an independent contractor (employed under a contract for services)
    - Point of contention when an employer sets up a contractual relationship with the worker so that the worker is defined as a self-employed independent contractor

Various Claimants v Catholic Child Welfare Society and Others [2012]: sets out guidelines for establishing if there is a relationship of employment:

The employer is more likely to have the means to compensate the victim than the employee and can be expected to have insured against that liability

The tort will have been committed as a result of activity being taken by the employee, on behalf of the employer

The employee's activity is likely to be part of the business activity of the employer

The employer will have created the risk of the tort being committed by the employee (by hiring them)

The employee will have been under the control of the employer

In the Course of Employment

- An employer is vicariously liable for an employee's torts, only if they were committed **'in the course of the employee's employment'**
- As set out in the book ***Torts***, by Sir John Salmond, an employer will be vicariously liable for:
  a) Wrongful acts which it has authorised
  b) Wrongful and unauthorised modes of carrying out an authorised act

<u>*Case Law Examples:*</u>

Poland v Parr [1926]: an employee pushed a man away who was trying to steal from his employers property (whilst off-duty) → was in course of employment

As the man was protecting his employer's property, he had implied permission to push away the thief

- ***Century Insurance v NI Road Transport Board [1942]***: An oil tanker driver decides to have a cigarette whilst unloading his tank of oil at a garage forecourt. He throws away the match he uses to light the cigarette, which causes a fire.
  - Within the course of employment → doing an authorised act (unloading oil) in an unauthorised way (whilst smoking).

Harrison v Michelin Tyre Co Ltd [1985]: An employee (acting carelessly), loses control of a wheelbarrow he is pushing, colliding with a colleague & injuring him.

- In the course of employment → the employee is doing his job (pushing the wheelbarrow) but in a careless way.

- ***Warren v Henleys Ltd [1948]***: an employee, who was insulted by a customer and punched him in the face to retaliate, was not acting in the course of his employment.
  - The retaliation was a personal act not authorised or connected with his employment.

Acts prohibited by the employer?

Rose v Plenty [1976]: 'it depends very much on the purpose for which it is done. If it is done for the employer's business, it is usually done in the course of his employment, even though it is a prohibited act'

Case Law Example:

- ***Twine v Bean's Express (1946)***: van driver gave a lift to a hitch-hiker, despite being prohibited by his employer from giving lifts (passenger then died as a result of the driver's negligence)
    - Outside course of employment as was not acting within the scope of his employment
    - The act did not further the employer's business

Intentionally committed torts?

Intentionally committed torts are often also criminal acts → unlikely for an employer to be held vicariously liable for such acts (neither authorised acts, nor unauthorised ways of doing authorised acts)

Exception where there is a close connection:

Lloyd v Grace, Smith & Co [1912]: a conveyancing clerk used his position to fraudulently transfer property into his own name

- The fraud stemmed from an act that his employer had authorised him to do and so it fell within course of employment

- ***Lister and others v Hesley Hall Ltd [2001]***: held that an employer can be vicariously liable for an intentional wrongful act committed purely for an employee's benefit where there is a close connection between the work they had been employed to do and the acts in question

Further guidance in ***Mohamud v WM Morrison Supermarkets plc [2016]***:

a) What function or field of activities has been entrusted by the employer to the employee (the nature of the job)
b) Whether there was a sufficient connection between the position in which they were employed and their wrongful conduct to make it fair and just for the employer to be held vicariously liable

Case Law Example:

- ***WM Morrison Supermarkets plc v Various Claimants [2020]***: were the actions of the employee so closely connected with acts they were authorised to do that, for the purpose of the liability of their employer to third parties, it may fairly and properly be regarded as done by them while acting in the ordinary course of their employment

    The employee's motive is taken into account

Frolic Cases:
If an employee is acting outside their course of employment when they commit a tort, they are said to be 'on a frolic of their own' (***Joel v Morison (1834)***) ***Hilton v Thomas Burton (Rhodes) Ltd [1961]***: It will be a question of degree in each case whether an employee's departure from their authorised route is sufficient to put them 'on a frolic of their own' - Taking into account geographical divergence and departure from the task set <u>*Case Law Example:*</u> ○ ***Harvey v RG O'Dell Ltd [1958]***: stopping for lunch was held to be reasonably incidental to ones work

Employer's Indemnity:

- Where an employer has paid out compensation to someone, they have a right at common law to claim an indemnity (i.e. its full loss) from the employee who actually committed the tort (***Lister v Romford Ice & Cold Storage Co Ltd [1957]***)
- BUT there is a gentleman's agreement not to pursue such claims for an indemnity, unless there was evidence of collusion or willful misconduct on the part of the employee

Occupiers Liability

The topic of occupiers' liability is governed by two statutes:

The Occupiers' Liability Act 1957

- Governs an occupiers' duties to 'visitors'
- There is quite a wide liability (only slight differences with common law Negligence)
    S1(1): covers 'dangers due to the state of the premises' and 'things done or omitted to be done on [the premises]'

The Occupiers' Liability Act 1984

- Governs an occupiers duties to others (mostly trespassers)

Liability of Occupiers to Visitors (1957)

To fall within the Occupiers' Liability Act 1957, a claimant must:

a) Establish they have suffered loss due to the state of the premises
b) Identify the occupier
c) Prove they are a visitor
d) Establish that the occupier failed to take reasonable care for the claimant's safety

Who is an occupier?

Wheat v E Lacon & Co Ltd [1966] 1 All ER 582:
'An occupier is someone who has a sufficient degree of control over premises'

- This means, someone who is not an owner of the premises, but has sufficient control over them, can be defined as an 'occupier'
  - In ***Wheat v E Lacon***, the Richardsons' were managers of the pub and occupied the rooms above (didn't own it) → still held to be occupiers
  - An independent contractor, working on another persons premises, could constitute an occupier
    - Where a contractor is not an occupier, can use common law of Negligence (***AC Billings & Sons Ltd v Riden [1958]***)
- There can be more than one occupier of the same premises

Who is a visitor?

Under the ***1957 Act***, a visitor is a person who has **express or implied permission** to be on the occupiers' land
- This includes persons who enter under the terms of a contract and persons who enter in order to exercise any right conferred by law
- A person who exceeds their express or implied permission *becomes* a trespasser

What is a premise?

S 1(3)a of the ***1957 Act***: premise has a very wide definition. It **includes open land as well as fixed or moveable structures**. Also includes vessels, vehicles or aircraft

The Common Duty of Care

The duty owed by an occupier to visitors under the ***1957 Act*** is called the ***'common duty of care'***

S 2(2): the duty is to take such care as is reasonable in all the circumstances to see that the visitor is reasonably safe in using the premises for the purpose for which they are permitted to be there
- The duty is directed towards the visitor's reasonable safety, rather than towards the safety of the premises

Breach of the Common Duty of Care

- An occupier must reach the standard of the reasonable occupier and will be in breach of duty if they have failed to reach this standard
- ***S 2(2)***: 'all the circumstances of the case must be considered in deciding what 'reasonable care' is
- **The court is likely to take into account:**

a) The nature of the danger
b) Purpose of visit and type of visitor
c) Seriousness and magnitude of injury risk
d) Cost and practicability of steps required to avoid the danger
e) How long the danger has been on the premises
f) Any warning of the danger

Special Visitors

S 2(3) of the ***1957 Act*** specifies the type/nature of the visitor as a factor which is relevant in determining the standard of care expected of an occupier

Singles out two categories of visitor relating to the degree of care expected on the part of the occupier:

Children:

S 2(3)a: **child visitors require a higher degree of care** from the occupier than other visitors as they cannot be expected to appreciate dangers which would be obvious to an adult

- Where the danger is an allurement (temptation), the occupier should take additional precautions to safeguard a child's safety (***Glasgow Corporation v Taylor [1922]***)
  ⟶ further increases the standard of care
- Occupier will have complied with their duty to a very young child, if they make the premises reasonably safe for a child, who is accompanied by the sort of expected guardian (***Phipps v Rochester Corporation [1955]***)

  Case Law Example:
  - ***Bourne Leisure Ltd v Marsden [2009]***: a 2 ½ year old drowned in a pond situated within the boundaries of a holiday park. Pond surrounded by a 2-foot fence. Claimants argued that the park should have done more to warn the parents of the danger of the pond
    - Court of Appeal found that as the pond was an obvious feature of the park, and the danger it presented to very young children was obvious, the park had not breached the common duty of care

Skilled Visitors:

S 2(3)b: visitors coming onto the premises to **exercise their skills also require a lower degree of care**

- 'An occupier may expect that a person, in the exercise of his calling, will appreciate and guard against any special risks ordinarily incident to it, so far as the occupier leaves him free to do so'

Case Law Example:

Roles v Nathan [1963]: an occupier can reasonably expect the skilled visitor to appreciate and guard against any risks which are part and parcel of their job

Adequate Warnings

An adequate warning will mean the occupier has complied with their common duty of care and will not be in breach

- ***S 2(4)a***: the mere fact that a warning was given will not necessarily suffice to enable the occupier to escape liability → the crucial issue is whether the warning was sufficient to enable the visitor to be reasonably safe (question of fact)

  The court will take into account:

  a) The nature of the warning (how specific it was)
  b) The nature of the danger (was it a hidden or obvious danger)
  c) The type of visitor (adult or child)

- An occupier need not warn of every danger - there is no obligation to warn of a danger which would be obvious to a particular visitor

Independent Contractors

Provided the occupier satisfies the three provisos found in ***s 2(4)(b)*** of the ***1957 Act***, the occupier will have discharged their common duty of care and if injury then results from the faulty workmanship of the contractor, the occupier is not liable (instead, the visitor must look to the contractor for recompense)

1) Reasonableness

It must be **reasonable for the occupier to engage the contractor** to do the task

- ***s 2(4)(b)*** applies only to 'work of construction, maintenance or repair

2) Competent contractor

The occupier must **take steps to satisfy themselves** that the contractor they choose **is competent**

- An occupier can obtain references and make enquiries locally and of Trade Associations to ascertain the contractor's competence

3) Checking the contractors work

The occupier must have taken **reasonable care to check that the contractor's work** was done properly
- Only expected to make such checks as are reasonable in all the circumstances of the case

  <u>*Case Law Example:*</u>
  - ***Haseldine v Daw & Son Ltd [1941]***: landlord of a block of flats engaged a highly reputable firm of hydraulic engineers to maintain the lifts. A visitor is injured when a lift malfunctions due to the contractor's negligence
    - The servicing of a lift is work of a technical nature which an occupier could not reasonably check themselves → occupier discharges their duty by entrusting the work to the contractor without the need to check the work for themselves
  - ***Woodward v The Mayor of Hastings [1945]***: a child at school slips on a step which a cleaner had negligently left in an icy condition
    As no specialist knowledge is required to recognise that an icy step is dangerous, by not checking the contractor's work, the occupier has not discharged their duty of care and so would be liable.

→ So, as long as an occupier has done all that reasonable care required of them, they will not be in breach of duty

Causation / Remoteness / Defences

The normal Negligence rules of causation and remoteness (***Jolley v Sutton London Borough Council [2000]***) apply

Defences

Voluntary Assumption of Risk

S 2(5) preserves the common law defence of *volenti* (applies the same principle as usually done in negligence)
- The claimant must know of the precise risk that causes the injury and show by their conduct that they willingly accept the legal risk
- Just because an occupier places a warning sign (e.g. all visitors enter at their own risk), does not necessarily allow defence of *volenti* → does not make visitors aware of the precise nature of any risks before they encounter it (not specific enough)

Excluding Liability

S 2(1) allows an occupier to **rely on an exclusion clause or notice to escape liability**
- But the notice must cover the liability in question and the occupier must have taken reasonable steps to bring it to the visitors' attention (***White v Blackmore [1972]***)

The impact of the UCTA and CRA:
- ***S 2(1)*** of the 1957 Act must be read subject to the provisions of ***UCTA*** and ***CRA***, **for business occupiers and traders** (private occupiers are not subject to these provisions)
  - Private occupiers (such as ordinary householders) can display a prominent notice excluding liability to visitors
- Any attempt to exclude liability for negligence causing death or personal injury is void
- An occupier can exclude liability for a visitors property under ***s 2(2) of UCTA*** provided it is reasonable, in all the circumstances, for the occupier to rely on the exclusion term/notice (will take into account ***Smith v Eric Bush*** guidelines to assess reasonableness)

The normal rules of contributory negligence apply.

Liability of Occupiers to Trespassers

Lord Dunedin in ***Robert Addie & Sons (Colliery) Ltd v Dumbreck [1929] AC 358*** defined a trespasser as 'one who goes upon land without invitation of any sort and whose presence is either unknown to the proprietor or, if known, is practically objected to'

Under the ***Occupiers' Liability Act 1984***, the terms 'occupier' and 'premises' have the same meaning as the 1957 Act

Who is owed the duty?

S 1(1)a: the duty is owed to **people other than visitors** (those who have implied or express permission to be on the premise)
- Irrelevant whether the entrant is unaware that they are trespassing

The act also covers 3 other types of entrants:

People entering under an access agreement or order under the National Parks and Access to the Countryside Act 1949

People who enter land pursuant to the Countryside and Rights of Way Act 2000

People who exercise private rights of way over land

S 1(7): a person using a public right of way (a highway) is excluded from protection under the Act

What is the duty?

The duty owed by an occupier to a trespasser does not arise automatically, but is subject to **certain conditions** (all 3 must be met)

Awareness of the danger

s1(3)(a): if the **occupier is aware of the danger or has reasonable grounds to believe it exists**

Vicinity to the danger

s1(3)(b): if the occupier **knows or has reasonable grounds to believe** that the other is **in the vicinity of the danger** concerned or that he may come into the vicinity of the danger

Case Law Example:

- ***Donoghue v Folkestone Properties Ltd [2003]***: at the time of the year (winter) and time of day (night), the occupier did not have reasonable grounds to believe a trespasser would be swimming off Folkestone harbour

Reasonable grounds to believe = requires actual knowledge of facts which would lead a reasonable occupier to be aware of the danger or presence of the trespasser

Risk requires protection

s1(3)(c): the risk is one against which, in all the circumstances of the case, he **may reasonably be expected to offer the other some protection**

The court will look at all the circumstances of the case in assessing whether it is reasonable to expect the occupier to have offered the trespasser some protection under ***s1(3)(c)***.

Will look at:

The nature and extent of the risk → was it an obvious or hidden danger / magnitude of danger (more serious the risk, likelier that occupier needs to safeguard)
The type of trespasser → adult or child, deliberate or inadvertent trespasser
The cost and practicality of precautions

Case Law Example:

- ***Rhind v Astbury Water Park [2004]***: the occupier did not have reasonable grounds to believe that there was any obstruction in the lake

There are also certain other restrictions on the duty owed:

Restricted to state of the premises

The 1984 act is concerned with liability **due to the state of the premises** (not the trespassers own conduct)

Case Law Examples:

- ***Tomlinson v Congleton Borough Council [2003]***: claimant dived into a shallow lake → held that it was a natural and obvious feature of the premises. The only risk was diving into it (so arose out of the claimant's own conduct)
- ***Revill v Newbery [1996]***: defendant fired a shotgun towards a trespasser intending to frighten them off → trespasser was injured. 1984 act not applicable here
  Trespasser was injured by an 'activity' not the state of the premises

Restricted to personal injury

Ss 1(4) and ***(8)*** limit the duty owed **only in respect to injury**

- ***S 1(9)*** defines injury as 'anything resulting in death or personal injury' (can cover both physical and mental impairments) → means that the duty under ***s 1(3)*** does not cover damage to a trespasser's property

Breach of duty?

***S 1(4)*:** the duty is to take such care as is reasonable (only liable if fall below the standard of the reasonable occupier)

The following factors are likely to be relevant:

a) The nature of the danger
b) The age of the trespasser
c) The nature of the premises (how dangerous are they)
d) The extent of the risk
e) The cost and practicability of precautions
f) The nature and character of the entry
g) The gravity and likelihood of injury
h) The foreseeability of the trespasser (the more likely people are to trespass, the more precautions need to be taken)

Warnings

- ***S 1(5):*** a warning will often be inadequate for children
- ***S 1(5):*** where a warning is not adequate, an occupier should also put an obstacle round the danger to prevent the trespasser coming into physical contract with the danger

Causation / Remoteness / Defences

Causation and remoteness are dealt with in the same was as common law Negligence

S 1(6): Voluntary Acceptance of Risk is the same as the common law defence

- Used in ***Ratcliff v McConnell and another [1999]***: defendants were able to establish that the claimant was aware of the risk of diving into a partly drained swimming pool with very shallow water and willingly accepted that risk

- Usual principles of contributory negligence apply

Excluding Liability

- The 1984 Act is silent as to whether or not liability can be excluded → open to debate
- As the Act does not expressly state that the occupier can exclude liability, it is interpreted to mean that they cannot
- The provisions of ***UCTA*** or ***CRA 2015*** do not apply under the 1984 Act

Cases of Illegality:

- Some trespassers will enter onto land for some criminal purpose
- If such a trespasser is injured in their attempt to commit a serious crime and the occupier is found to have breached a duty owed under ***s 1(3)***, **the defence of illegality will not hold** (would thwart Parliament's intention to provide safety net protection to trespassers) (***Revill v Newbery***)

Product Liability

A cause of action for defective products can lie in one of three areas of law:

a) The tort of Negligence
b) Under the Consumer Protection Act (CPA) 1987
c) Contract Law

Liability for Defective Products (Negligence)

The Narrow Rule - Donoghue v Stevenson:

- The narrow rule considers the circumstances in which a manufacturer of a product would owe a duty of care to the consumer

To show a duty of care under the narrow rule, the claimant must establish that:

The defendant is a manufacturer

The item causing damage is a product

The claimant is a consumer

The product reached the consumer in the form in which it left the manufacturer with no reasonable possibility of intermediate examination

Loss it covers:

☑ Any injury to **persons or damage to property** done by the defect in the product

✗ If the only loss is the defective quality of the product, the reduction in value of the product or the cost of replacing the defect / product → classed as **pure economic loss**

Duty of Care:

1) Who is a Manufacturer?

A manufacturer can include any person who works in some way on a product before it reaches the consumer, **including**:

- Repairers of products (***Haseldine v Daw & Sons Ltd [1941]***)
- Installers of products (***Stennett v Hancock [1939]***)
- Occasionally, suppliers of products (***Andrews v Hopkinson [1957]***)
    - Where they ought reasonably to inspect or test the products which they supply
    - If they knew of a defect/danger

2) What is a Product?

Wide interpretation → **a product covers almost any items which is capable of causing damage**

- Can also include items supplied with the product (e.g. packaging, containers, labels)

3) Who is a Consumer?

A consumer is the **ultimate user of the article** as well as **anyone whom the defendant should reasonably have in mind** as likely to be injured by the defendant's negligence

4) Intermediate examination?

If there is a **reasonable possibility of immediate examination**, then the 'manufacturer' of the product will not owe a duty under the narrow rule

- Generally, reasonable possibility means likelihood of examination

Case Law Example:

Kubach v Hollands [1937]

Claimant was injured after chemicals in a school experiment exploded

Manufacturer was not liable as the chemicals were provided with an express warning that it was to be tested before use

Had expected the test to be carried out so there was a 'reasonable possibility' of an intermediate examination (no duty)

The school were not liable as although they had supplied the chemical to Kubach, it did not owe a duty as a supplier

- They had not been warned of any problem with the chemical or need to test before use

The intermediate supplier of the chemical to the school owed the duty

- They had knowledge of the need to test before use

Breach of Duty:

The duty is to exercise reasonable care

- Will be determined by looking at all the circumstances, including the magnitude of the foreseeable risk, the gravity of potential injury and the costs and practicalities of precautions

Proving Breach of Duty:

The onus of proving breach of duty is on the claimant

Often hard to prove breach of duty in a manufacturing process that you were not apart of

Daniels v R White & Sons [1938]: despite presence of carbolic acid in claimant's lemonade, failed to show that there was any problem with the manufacturing process

Claimants have been prepared to 'infer' breach of duty from facts that the claimant is able to prove

Grant v Australian Knitting Mills [1936]: claimant suffered severe dermatitis due to sulphur in underwear supplied by the defendant

- Whilst claimant couldn't show a specific problem in the manufacturing process, court inferred that the chemical would not have been present in the underwear, had the defendants taken reasonable care (inferred a breach of duty)

Also in ***Carroll v Fearon [1998]***

→ The claimant must prove some facts on which the court can base its inference. But once the inference arises, as with *res ipsa loquitur*, the court will infer breach of duty (unless the defendant can rebut the inference by pointing to a later problem)

Causation and Remoteness:

The typical **factual causation** rules apply (but for and intervening act)

- ***Evans v Triplex Safety Glass Co Ltd [1936]***: the windscreen of the claimant's car shattered 12 months after it was fitted → claimant injured by shard of glass
  - The claimant was not able to establish any casual link between the defendant's negligence and disintegration of windscreen as too much time had passed

Court will then take into account **remoteness (Wagon Mound test)**

Defences:

Voluntary Assumption of Risk

Where a claimant is **aware of a defect** in a product and **still decides to continue with the use** of the product, there is scope for the defendant to argue *volenti*

- 'The man who consumes or uses a thing which he knows to be noxious cannot complain in respect of whatever mischief follows because it follows from his own conscious volition in choosing to incur the risk or uncertainty of mischance' (***Grant v Australian Knitting Mills***)
- The claimant's conduct must indicate a willing acceptance of the risk (often difficult to prove)

Contributory Negligence

- Often easier to prove than *volenti* → where the defendant continues to use a product despite believing its faulty

Consumer Protection Act 1987

A claim under the CPA 1987 provides an additional cause of action to a claim in Negligence

- Aimed to increase the protection of consumers by ensuring that someone can be found liable in relation to defective products

Establishing a Claim:

Section 2(1) of the CPA 1987 states that anyone who can establish the following is able to sue:

a) That they have suffered damage
b) Caused by

c) A defect
d) In a product

Unlike in Negligence, the claimant **does not have to be a foreseeable victim**

Suffered Damage:

Section 5 of the CPA 1987 defines damage as

- ***S 5(1):*** Death or personal injury (no limit)
  - Personal injury = 'any disease and any other impairment of a person's physical or mental condition'
- ***S 5(4):*** Loss or damage to private property *if* it exceeds £275 (full amount can then be recovered)
- Act is silent on whether you can claim for consequential economic loss, but is likely that you could as per the aims of tort

Won't be liable for

- The loss or damage to the product itself (can't include the cost of repairing or replacing the defective product itself)
- ***S 5(3):*** Damage caused by a defective product to *business* property
  - The goods must be of a description of property ordinarily intended for private use, occupation or consumption or intended to be used in such a way

Caused By:

The claimant has the burden of proving causation, with the usual 'but for test'

BUT: rather than looking at the defendants breach of duty, only has to prove that the defect caused the actual damage (direct consequences test) → **liability is strict**

- **The defendant will be liable without proof of any fault on their part (*A v National Blood Authority*)**

Act is silent on remoteness

A Defect:

Claimants must prove that they have suffered damage caused wholly or partly by a defect in a product

- ***Section 3(1)* and *(2)* of the *CPA 1987* defines a defect as 'unsafe'**
- The safety of the product is not such as persons generally are entitled to expect (consumer expectation test)

Takes into account:

a) The whole get-up and presentation of the product
b) What the expected use of the product is

c) The age of the product

<u>*Case Law Example:*</u>

A v National Blood Authority [2001]: the consumer expectations for blood products were that the blood would be free from viruses

- The blood was defective under the CPA (despite reasonable care being taken)

Of a Product

Section 1(2) of the CPA defines a product as 'any goods or electricity and includes a product which is comprised in another product whether a component or raw material'

Who is Liable?

There are 4 categories of potential defendants:

The producer of the product (manufacturer) (***S 2(2)(a))***

An 'own-brander' (***S 2(2)(b))***

An importer (***S 2(2)(c))***

A supplier (under certain circumstances) (***S 2(3)***

The Producer (S 2(2)(a))

The manufacturer of the product will be the usual defendant

Where a component part of a product is faulty, both the manufacturer of the part and the manufacturer of the whole product are liable

The 'Own-Brander' (S 2(2)(b))

Occurs where a person who, by putting their name or trademark on the product, held themselves out as being its producer

The Importer (S 2(2)(c))

A person who **imported** the product into the UK (from outside) in order to supply it to another person

The Forgetful Supplier (S 2(3))

A supplier (e.g. retailer) is only liable where they are **unable to meet a victim's request to identify any of the other people involved in the chain of supply**

Defences

It is on the defendant to establish one of the defences in *s 4 of the CPA 1987:*

1) The defect was attributable to compliance with **legal requirements** ***(S 4(1)(a))***
   Compliance with a legal requirement will absolve a produce from liability, only if the defect was an inevitable result of compliance

2) The defendant did not **supply** the product to another ***(S 4(1)(b))***
   Where the manufacturer has not supplied the product to the party, could use as a defence (e.g. if product acquired through theft)

3) The defendant supplied the product otherwise than in the course of business ***(S 4(1)(c))***
   - E.g. where a defective product is sold by one friend to another

4) The defect **did not exist when** the defendant supplied the product ***(S 4(1)(d))***
   - If the defendant can show that the defect was caused by misuse of the product or by fair wear and tear

5) A **manufacturer of component parts** is not liable for a defect in the finished product which is wholly attributable to the design of the finished product, or to compliance with the instructions given by the manufacturer of the finished product ***(S 4(1)(f))***

6) **Development risks** (or 'state of the art')
   - A defendant must prove that the state of knowledge, at the time the product was supplied, amongst producers of the product in question, was not such as to allow a producer of the product to discover the defect ***(S 4(1)(e))***
   - Sets the standard of knowledge for this defence as that of 'other producers' in the market
   - Defendant essentially able to rely on this defence in any case where they had acted as a 'reasonable producer'
   - In case law, used more of a narrow interpretation → producer is judged against the highest standard of knowledge that is accessible anywhere in the world (***Commission v UK [1997]***)
   - This defence only applies to defects/risks that could not have been foreseen (***A v National Blood Authority [2001]***)

7) Partial **contributory negligence**:
   - ***S 6(4):*** contributory negligence applies where the claimant is partly responsible for their loss or damage

<u>No Exclusion of Liability:</u>

- ***S 7*****: a defendant can't exclude, limit or restrict their liability in any way**

Main differences between negligence and CPA

CPA	Claim in Negligence
Strict liability	Claimant must establish the defendant's negligence in order to succeed
Can't recover business property & minimum claim for damage to private property is £275	Can recover all damage to other property
Claimant does not have to be a foreseeable victim	Must establish duty of care owed
Narrow list of defendants (narrow definition of producer) - Does cover importers and own branders (not covered in Negligence)	Wider class of potential defendants (includes repairers and installers)
Can't exclude liability under CPA	Can exclude liability as long as reasonable

Land

Where claimants suffer loss on their own premises, potential claims:

In private nuisance

In trespass to land

Under the tort known as the rule in ***Rylands v Fletcher***

There are 3 ways in which a defendant may interfere with the use of a claimants land:

1) Dispossession
2) Direct Interference with Possession
3) Indirect Interference with Land

Dispossession

Where the defendant moves on to the land themselves and takes possession of it (or part).

- Effectively dispossessed the claimant who was *originally* on the land
- Will have to bring an action to recover possession of the land

Examples:

a) Squatters
b) Travellers park caravans on part of an industrial estate
c) Student protestors occupy buildings on a university campus

Direct Interference with Possession

Where the claimant remains in possession, the defendant might interfere with that possession

- The claimant needs to be able to bring a court action *to stop the interference* (could be through an injunction or a declaration of their rights)
- The tort to provide a remedy for this kind of interference is trespass to land

Examples:

a) Using a path or driveway without permission where there is no right of way
b) Coming on to land and taking things
c) Dumping rubbish on land without permission

Indirect Interference with Land

A person's use of land can be interfered with by things done elsewhere, not on that land

- Claimant needs to be able to bring an action *to stop the interference* and obtain compensation for any damage caused
- The tort to provide a remedy is private nuisance

Examples:

a) An industrial process carried out on the defendant's neighbouring land causing toxic fumes which kill plants on the claimant's land
b) Tree roots which grow from the defendant's neighbouring land underneath the claimants land
c) Noisy activities on the defendant's land, which interfere with the claimant enjoying the use of their land

Private Nuisance

Private Nuisance = 'an unlawful interference with a person's use or enjoyment of land, or some right over, or in connection with it' (***Winfield & Jolowicz on Tort (18th edn), p 712***)

Potential Claimants

Only a person with the right to exclusive possession of land can sue in private nuisance (i.e. a right to exclude everyone else) (***Hunter v Canary Wharf [1997]***)

☑ Includes an **owner-occupier**

☑ A **tenant** of land (proprietary interest in the leasehold title)

☑ A **landlord** who owns land, but has parted with possession to a tenant, but permanent damage has been done to their property

☒ **Children** of the owner-occupier

☒ **Guests** staying in property legally owned by another person (including hotel guests)

☒ A live in **housekeeper**

Potential Defendants

There are 3 potential defendants:

a) The **creator** of the nuisance
b) The **occupier** of the land from which the nuisance originates
c) The **landlord**

The Creator

The **original creator of the nuisance remains liable** for it, *even* if the land is now occupied by someone else

The creator did the first wrong and therefore remains responsible (subject to remoteness)

The Occupier

The **current occupier** of land will be **liable for nuisances they have created** (either a positive act or failing to take steps)

Will also be liable for nuisances created by other people when:

The nuisance was created by an employee acting in the course of their employment

The nuisance was created by an independent contractor, *provided* the nature of the work carried a special danger of the nuisance being created

Matania v National Provincial Bank: the risk of nuisance was inevitable due to the substantial alteration work being carried out by the contractor

The nuisance was created by a visitor, predecessor in title or trespasser, or arises through some natural occurrence (provided the occupier has adopted the nuisance or continued it)

Occupiers ***'adopt'*** a nuisance if they make use of the thing which constituted the nuisance

- Occupiers ***'continue'*** a nuisance if, once they know or ought reasonably to know of its existence, they fail to take reasonable steps to end the nuisance (often take account of defendant's financial resources)

Case Law Example:

- For visitors (***Lippiatt v South Gloucestershire CC [1999]***)
- For predecessors in title (***St Anne's Well Brewery Co v Roberts (1928)***)
- For natural events (***Leakey v National Trust [1980]***)
- For trespassers (***Sedleigh-Denfield v O'Callaghan [1940]***)

The Landlord

General Rule: where a nuisance arises on premises which are let to a tenant, the landlord is ***not*** liable (tenant considered the proper defendant as in occupation)

Exceptions:

a. Where the landlord has expressly or impliedly authorised the nuisance (i.e. the nuisance is the inevitable result of the letting)
   - ***Tetley v Chitty [1986]***: local council let a piece of land to a go-kart club for use as a racing track. The nuisance was the inevitable result of this letting

b. Where the nuisance existed at the start of the letting and the landlord knew or ought reasonably to have known of it

c. Where the landlord has covenanted (i.e. promised) to repair the premises (or has the right to enter to do so). Fails to make the repairs, giving rise to the nuisance (***Payne v Rogers (1794)***)

The damage which is recoverable:

The claimant must prove that they have suffered damage:

Hunter v Canary Wharf [1997]:

☑ Physical damage to land or buildings *is* recoverable (including crops / plants growing in the land)

☑ Interference with the quiet enjoyment of the land

✗ *No* claim for personal injury in private nuisance → (should use Negligence)

✗ Damage to personal property (although in ***Halsey v Esso Petroleum***, were allowed recovery on the basis that such losses flow as a consequence of the personal discomfort caused by the nuisance)

→ Where the claimant can prove recoverable damage, then the defendant would be liable for any consequential losses flowing from this as well (e.g. loss of profits ***Andreae v Selfridge & Co Ltd [1938]***)

Main Elements

The claimant must show:

- There there is an interference with the claimant's use and enjoyment of land or some rights they enjoy over it; and
- That the interference is unlawful

Interferences

There are 3 types of interferences within private nuisance (*Hunter v Canary Wharf [1997]*):

1) Nuisance by encroachment on a neighbour's land
2) Nuisance by direct physical injury to a neighbour's land
3) Nuisance by interference with a neighbour's quiet enjoyment of his land (referred to as interference with personal comfort or loss of amenity)

- To be actionable in nuisance, the interference had to be something that ***materially interfered*** with '**ordinary comfort**' (not just 'elegant or dainty modes … of living')
    - The loss of prospect (a view) from your home is not an actionable interference (***Aldred's Case (1610)***)
    - Disruption to TV reception caused by a new building was not an actionable interference in private nuisance (***Hunter v Canary Wharf [1997]***)
        - General principle at common law is that anyone may build whatever he likes upon his land.

That are unlawful

In tort, unlawful means substantial and unreasonable (does not usually mean criminal)

- You have to tolerate a certain amount of noise, smells etc as part of everyday life
- BUT you should not be expected to tolerate substantial and unreasonable interferences

The courts will attempt to balance the right of one person to do what they are lawfully entitled to on their land, against their neighbour's right to enjoy their land free from interference. (***Sedleigh-Denfield v O'Callaghan [1940]***)

- Courts find encroachment onto a neighbour's land to be unlawful without further consideration

It will be a **question of fact in every case** whether the claimant can show that the interference is unreasonable. May take into account:

Duration and Frequency

The **overall duration of an interference** will be an important factor & as well as **how often it occurs** (frequency)

- The longer the interference has lasted, the *more likely* it is that the court will consider the interference unreasonable
- An isolated incident is *unlikely* to give rise to liability in nuisance
    - Will only constitute an actionable private nuisance if it emanates from some continuing state of affairs on the defendant's property (***Spicer v Smee [1946]***)

Excessiveness of conduct / extent of the harm

- The courts will have regard to **how *excessive* the defendant's conduct is** → viewed objectively
    Physical damage is typically considered excessive (unless trivial)
- The courts will also look at **the *extent* of the harm** (the impact on the claimant) → viewed subjectively

Case Law Example:

- ***Matania v National Provincial Bank Ltd [1936]:*** the noise caused by substantial renovation work carried out on behalf of the defendant (lasting from 8am to 5pm each day) was found to be excessive

Character of the Neighbourhood

The courts will sometimes take into account the **character of locality** in order to decide whether particular interference is unlawful

- The character of a neighbourhood is *only relevant* to an interference which causes personal discomfort and inconvenience (not physical injury to property) (***Halsey v Esso Petroleum Co Ltd [1961]***)
- Thesinger LJ in ***Sturges v Bridgman (1879)***: 'what would be a nuisance in Belgrave Square would not necessarily be so in Bermondsey'
- Will take the activities of the defendant into account when assessing the character of a locality, but only to the extent that those activities do not constitute a nuisance (***Coventry v Lawrence [2014]***)

Public Benefit?

A defendant may argue that their activity is ***reasonable* as it benefits the public**

Courts hold that the interest of the public *should not* deprive an individual of their private rights → public benefit rarely a relevant factor (may come into play when considering remedies)

Case Law Example:

> ***Adams v Ursell [1913]***: Defendant's argued that a 'smelly chip shop' provided a valuable source of hot food to the local community → court held was a nuisance

Malice?

Where a defendant's **nuisance is motivated by malice**, *more likely* to make an interference unlawful

- ***Hollywood Silver Fox Farm v Emmett [1936]***
- ***Christie v Davey [1893]***

Abnormal Sensitivity of the Claimant?

The courts will look at the impact of nuisance on the *normal use of neighbouring land*, **ignoring any abnormal sensitivity of the claimant** (***Robinson v Kilvert (1889)***)

- The claimants sensitivity is relevant as regards remedies, but not liability → where the claimant can show that the interference is unlawful against a normal user, they can recover for all losses (even if greater than usual) (***McKinnon Industries v Walker [1951]***)

Causation and Remoteness

The claimant must prove that the **unlawful interference caused their damage** (usual 'but for' test and intervening acts apply)

The same test for **remoteness of damage** (the Wagon Mound test) applies in Nuisance →

- Whether the kind of damage which occurred was reasonably foreseeable to someone in the defendant's position at the time the relevant acts were done
  - ***Cambridge Water Co ltd v Eastern Counties Leather plc [1994]***: the type of harm (contamination of water) was not reasonable foreseeable as at the time of the defendant's actions, the properties of the chemical were unknown

Defences

Effective Defences

Effective defences enable the defendant to escape lability

Prescription
Where the defendant can show that there has been a **continuing nuisance for a period of at least 20 years against the claimant** ● The defendant has essentially 'acquired' the right to commit the nuisance <u>Case Law Example:</u> ***Sturges v Bridgman (1879)***: whilst the defendant had made noise in the property for more than 20 years, had not been an actionable nuisance for the entire period (only once the claimant built a consulting room nearer the noise)

Statutory authority
Where a statute permits a defendant to commit a nuisance ● Can rely on the defence of statutory authority if it can show that the nuisance was an inevitable result of doing what the statute authorised ● Mostly used by public authorities acting under statutory powers <u>Case Law Example:</u> ○ ***Allen v Gulf Oil Refining Ltd [1981]***: an oil company (authorised by statute to construct an oil refinery) could plead statutory authority as a defence to complaints about noise and vibrations from the refinery Nuisances are inevitable from implicit authorisation by statute

Contributory Negligence
Usual tort rules apply

Consent
Where the defendant can show that the **claimant has specifically agreed to accept the interference**

Act of God / Nature

Where an interference on the defendant's land **results from a 'secret unobservable process of nature'**, the defendant will not be liable in nuisance (unless they adopt or continue it)

- ***Wringe v Cohen [1940]*** → subsidence under or near the foundations of the defendant's house

Necessity

Two elements:

a) A situation of necessity exists because of an imminent danger to life and limb; and
b) The defendant's actions were reasonable in all the circumstances

- *Can't be used* if the circumstance giving rise to necessity were of the defendant's own making
- Threat to property can very rarely count

Case Law Example:

- ***Southport Corporation v Esso Petroleum [1956]***: defendant's oil tanker ran aground, danger of loss of lives of the crew. Master discharged 400 tons of oil into the sea to prevent this (polluted river)
    - Whilst nuisance had been committed, defence of necessity as life and limb were at risk

Ineffective Defences

Claimant 'came to the nuisance'

Provided a claimant uses their property for essentially the same purpose as their predecessors before the nuisance started, the defendant *cannot* rely on the defence that the claimant 'came to the nuisance'

- Where a claimant builds on their land or changes the use of the property after the defendant had initially commenced the activity, claim for nuisance will fail
- But may still be a relevant factor in deciding whether to give an injunction

Public Benefit

- *Can't* be used as a defence
- Might be taken into account when deciding to grant an injunction

Contributory actions of others

It is no defence that the nuisance results from the separate actions of several people

- The defendant can't argue that their act alone would not constitute an actionable nuisance

Planning Permission

The mere granting of planning permission *does not legitimise a nuisance* (***Wheeler v Saunders [1995]***)

- The grant of planning permission can operate to change the character of the neighbourhood
    - ***Gillingham BC v Medway Docks Co Ltd [1992]***: planning permission for a former naval dockyard to be converted into a container port → the level of noise was now not considered unlawful as the character of the locality had been changed to an area that was a container port

      When deciding unlawful interference, must consider the character of the neighbourhood as it was *after* the grant of the planning permission

- Where planning permission places limits on the frequency and intensity of noise, may be relevant in assisting the claimant's action (***Coventry v Lawrence [2014]***)

Remedies

There are 2 principle remedies for private nuisance:

a) Damages
b) Injunction

Damages

Damages will be awarded for **any loss which the claimant has already suffered by the date of the trial**. Including:

a) Physical damage to the claimant's land

- A claimant will generally be awarded damages to reflect the cost of repairing damage to their property or (where not possible), the loss in value of the land in question

b) Personal discomfort

- Suggested that personal discomfort should be valued by looking at the loss of amenity value of the land in question (***Hunter v Canary Wharf***) → i.e. land with nuisance being worth less

Injunctions

Injunction = an order of the court which **restrains the commission of or continuance of some wrongful act in the future**

- Where common law remedy *is not sufficient* (e.g. for future breaches)
- Is an *equitable remedy* → discretion of the court
    - Could instead grant damages in lieu of an injunction to cover future breaches (where the claimant receives damages as compensation for future interference with their rights)

1) **Prohibitory Injunction**

   Forbids the defendant from persisting in some wrongful act

2) **Mandatory Injunction**
    - Where the court orders the defendant to take some positive action to rectify the consequences of what they have done

3) **A '*quia timet*' Injunction**
    - Courts can be prepared to grant either a prohibitory or a mandatory injunction *quia timet* → i.e in anticipation of the commission of the tort (prevents claimant suffering damage)
    - Claimant must show:
        a. They are almost certain to incur damage without the injunction; and
        b. Such damage is imminent; and
        c. The defendant will not stop their course of conduct without the order of the court

When to grant an injunction?

Guidelines established in ***Shelfer v City of London Electric Lighting Co [1895]***:

The court *may not* grant an injunction where:

a) The harm suffered by the applicant is
    i) Small; and
    ii) Capable of being quantified in financial terms; and
    iii) Capable of adequate compensation by damages; and

b) It would be oppressive to the defendant to grant the injunction

The fact that those tests are not all satisfied does not mean that an injunction has to be granted

Public interest may be a relevant consideration

Previous authorisation in planning permission may influence court

Case Law Example:

- ***Miller v Jackson [1977]***: injunction refused → public interest in playing cricket should prevail over the private interest of the claimants. Had also bought their house knowing about the cricket club
    - Took into account public benefit and that the claimants 'came to the nuisance' in deciding whether to grant an injunction

- ○ ***Kennaway v Thompson [1981]***: the public benefit of the power boat racing was not sufficient to deprive the claimant of an injunction → granted a prohibitory injunction to restrict the club's racing activities and the noise levels of boats

Also a third remedy used:

Abatement
Involves the removal of the interference by the victim • Except for in emergency situations, must give prior-warning (***Lemmon v Webb [1895]***) 　○ ***Mills v Brooker [1919]***: branches of a tree from defendant's garden overhung into claimants drive. Claimant exercised remedy of abatement by cutting down the branches themselves 　　- Did not need to notify the defendant in advance as did not need to enter their land to remove the nuisance 　　- BUT did have to return the branches as were considered defendant's property

Main differences between Private Nuisance and Negligence

Private Nuisance	Negligence
Type of claimant → only someone with a proprietary interest in the land affected by the interference can sue	Type of claimant is wider (don't have to show that the use or enjoyment of the claimant's land has been affected)
Requires continuity → an isolated interference *will not* constitute private nuisance	Any isolated act or omission is enough
For unlawful interference → whether the defendant's use of the land is unreasonable	Whether the defendant's act is unreasonable (standard of a reasonable person)
Willing to take into account defendant's financial means, if hazard has arisen naturally on the land	Financial resources are *irrelevant*
Can still be liable even if they have exercised reasonable care (use of land, not the defendant's act is relevant)	Defendant only liable if they have fallen below the standard of the reasonable person
Can sue for tangible *and* intangible damage	*Can't* sue for intangible damage

Personal injury *doesn't* seem to fall under scope (and personal property)	*Can* claim for personal injury
Injunction as a remedy	Injunction *not* a remedy

Rylands v Fletcher

Rylands v Fletcher (1868):

Created a tort that covers a situation where there is an escape of something dangerous in the course of a non-natural use of land

↪ The occupier of the land is liable for the damage caused as a result of the escape, irrespective of fault (strict liability)

- Protects claimants from interferences due to isolated escapes from a neighbour's land

Main Elements

The elements of the tort are:

a) The defendant brings onto their land for their own purposes something likely to do mischief
b) If it escapes
c) Which represents a non-natural use of land
d) It causes foreseeable damage of the relevant type

Defendant brings onto their land for their own purposes something likely to do mischief

The thing or substance brought onto land **need not be dangerous *in itself*, but must be capable of causing damage if it escapes** (e.g. water/cattle/sewage/electricity)

- Must be shown that the defendant had done something which they recognised or, ought to have reasonably recognised, as giving rise to an exceptionally high risk of danger or mischief if there should be an escape (***Transco v Stockport Metropolitan Borough Council [2003]***)
    - Increased the requirement of a risk of mischief from likely to 'exceptionally likely'

An Escape

There must be an escape of a 'thing likely to do mischief' (isolated escape from land)

- The substance or item causing damage must actually move from the defendant's premises to a place outside the defendant's occupation or control
    - ***Stannard (t/a Wyvern Tyres) v Gore [2012]***: Tyres stores on the defendant's land caught fire and destroyed the claimant's premises → claim failed as the tyres themselves had not escaped (just the fire, which had not itself been brought onto the defendant's land)

Non-natural use of land

Where the thing that causes damage by its escape is not 'naturally' on the defendant's land

- The use of land must be extraordinary or unusual according to the standards of the day (***Transco v Stockport Metropolitan Borough Council***)
    - The use of land for normal industrial purposes is not generally a non-natural use'
- Question of fact on each case

Causes foreseeable damage of the relevant type

4th requirement added in ***Cambridge Water Co Ltd v Eastern Counties Leather plc [1994]***:
Damage suffered must be reasonably foreseeable (same as ***Wagon Mound***)

Defences

1) Escape caused by the unforeseeable act of a stranger
2) Escape caused by an 'act of God' which *couldn't be reasonably foreseen*
3) Statutory authority
4) Consent (voluntary assumption of risk)
5) Contributory Negligence

→ In reality, Rylands v Fletcher is rarely used

Public Nuisance

Public Nuisance = an act or an omission that endangers the life, health, property or comfort of the public, or obstructs the public in the exercise or enjoyment of rights common to all His Majesty's Subjects

- Usually enforced by public officers / bodies (Attorney General / local authorities)
- *Can* be used in tort where *individuals* have suffered particular harm

Elements of Tort of Public Nuisance

The elements of the tort of public nuisance are:

a) Unreasonable conduct that materially affects the reasonable comfort and convenience of a 'class of His Majesty's subjects'; and
b) The claimant has suffered particular harm

Unreasonable Conduct

Unreasonable conduct that materially affects the reasonable comfort and convenience of a 'class of His Majesty's subjects'

- Whilst a private nuisance only affect particular individuals, public nuisance affects 'His Majesty's subjects' more generally
- Number of people that need to be affected is a question of fact per case
  - Must be a representative cross-section affected

Claimant has suffered particular harm

Must have suffered 'particular' damage over and above that suffered by the public at large

- Can include personal injury, property damage and loss of profit

Case Law Example:

Castle v St Augustine's Links [1922]: a car driver was struck by a golf ball from a nearby golf course (routinely occurs). The class of persons affected are highway users and the public's right to use the highway has been affected. Claimant has also suffered particular damage (personal injury)

Trespass to Land

'The intentional direct interference with the claimant's possession of land'

- It is actionable per se → do not need to prove tangible loss
- Seeks to protect the claimant's rights, rather than to provide compensation for damage

The Claimants:

A claimant must be in possession of the land, but they don't need to own it

- Includes an owner-occupier or tenant under a lease
- Generally, a person who merely has a personal right to use land will not have possession (but will depend on facts of the case)
- A squatter has the right to possession of the land they occupy → can use trespass against anyone apart from persons with a better right to possession (legal owner / earlier trespassers) (***Delaney v TP Smith Ltd [1946]***)

Elements:

A trespass can be committed by:

Entering upon the claimant's land

Acting in excess of one's permission to be on the claimant's land (***The Calgarth [1927]***)

Bringing anything into direct contract with the land (e.g. throwing a ball over)

Damaging the land (e.g. breaking off a branch of a tree)

Land:

Land includes:

a) The surface of the land
b) Any building on the land
c) Any plants in the land
d) The sub-soil beneath the land (***Bocardo v Star Energy UK Onshore Ltd [2010]***)
e) Airspace is limited to 'such height as is necessary for the ordinary use and enjoyment of his land and the structures on it' (***Bernstein v Skyviews & General Ltd [1977]***)
    - Included a sign on the defendant's land which projected over the boundary of the claimant's property (***Kelsen v Imperial Tobacco Co Ltd [1957]***)
    - Cranes on the defendant's land which swung across the claimant's property (***Anchor Brewhouse Developments Ltd v Berkeley House (Docklands Developments) Ltd [1987]***)

Direct Interference

Trespass to land requires direct interference

- Requires the interference to flow almost immediately and without any intervention from the actions of the defendant

Intentional Interference

Trespass requires an intentional act

- The act (which constitutes the trespass) must be voluntary
    - No trespass is committed if someone throws you onto land (***Smith v Stone (1647)***)
- The defendant doesn't need to know they are trespassing or intend the consequences of their act
    - Will have trespassed if you thought you were on your own land, but innocently strayed onto your neighbours (***Basely v Clarkson (1681)***)
- A trespass *can* be committed by Negligence (***League Against Cruel Sports Ltd v Scott [1986]***):
    - A master of staghounds releases the hounds, knowing there is a real risk that they may enter or cross prohibited land (failure to exercise proper control)
        - Although considered to be an *exception to the general rule*

The measure of damage will be the same as in Negligence (***Network Rail Infrastructure Ltd v Conarken Group Limited; Network Rail Infrastructure Ltd v Farrell Transport Ltd [2010]***)

Causation / Remoteness:

- Where there is no tangible damage, don't have to show causation / remoteness
- If the claimant has suffered tangible damage to their land, must show that the defendant caused it ('but for' and intervening act)
- Direct consequences test for remoteness → the defendant is liable for all direct consequences of their tort, even those that are unforeseeable (***Re Polemis [1921]***)

Defences:

1) **Justification / Consent**
    - You would be justified in entering someone else's land if:
        a) You had the owner's permission to do so (licence to enter)
        b) You were permitted by the law to do so

2) **Necessity**

Remedies:

Order for possession

Where someone dispossesses the person who is entitled to occupy the land, **the person entitled to possession can bring a claim to recover the land**

- Must prove they have a right to immediate possession

Case Law Example:

- ***McPhail v Persons Unknown (1973)***: on application for possession against trespassers, once the right to possession is established, the court has no jurisdiction to delay the order and must grant immediate possession

- ***Malik v Fassenfelt [2013]***: defendants were squatters who had entered onto the claimant's land as trespassers and established a home (improved the land to a better condition)
  - Claimant was the owner of the land (private individual)
  - Held that Article 8 of the ECHR was applicable → defendant's right to a home
  - BUT: applying Article 8 to the facts, claimant was still entitled to an order for immediate possession

Injunction / Damages

a. A claimant who is subjected to continuing interference with their possession may seek an injunction to prevent the trespass continuing in the future
b. Could also seek damages for the past interferences they have already suffered
   Actionable per se so even where no tangible damage has been caused

→ **The successful party will also recover their legal costs from the losing party**

- Where the costs are more substantial than the damages won (e.g. where nominal damages are awarded), can still recover legal costs if they brought proceedings legitimately in order to protect their legal rights

Administrative and Human Rights

Introduction to ECHR

The UK was a signatory to the *European Convention on Human Rights*

Bound as a matter of international law to comply with the Convention → ratified in 1951

Judgements of the ECtHR are binding on the UK as a matter of international law

Procedure

There are 2 ways in which proceedings may commence:

a) **State applications**
- Proceedings may be brought against the UK by another signatory state

b) **Individual petitions**
- Individuals who allege that their Convention rights have been breached may start their own proceedings against the UK in Strasbourg
- Must be shown that any domestic remedies which exist have first been exhausted
- The petition must be made within four months of the final UK decision
- The body in breach must be a public body

Two-stage process

Two mains stages:

a) **The admissibility stage:**
- A single-judge formation will declare an application inadmissible (if obvious from the outset)
- No right to appeal against its decisions

b) The merits stage:
- 3 Member Committee → cases covered by well-established case law of the Court
  - They will rule on the admissibility and where the case *is admissible*, give a final decision or judgement

- Chamber of 7 judges → other cases heard by this chamber, which rule on the admissibility and give judgement by a majority
  - The judgement becomes final after 3 months
  - During this time, the applicant may ask for the case to be referred to the Grand Chamber for fresh consideration (their judgement is final)

Remedies

- Individual decisions are only binding as a matter of international law under the Convention and have no direct binding force in domestic law
- The Committee of Ministers of the Council of Europe are responsible for ensuring that states comply with judgements of the ECtHR
- The Court relies on the willingness of states to abide by the Convention and accept its judgements
    - Dec 2020: Council of Europe (oversees the ECHR), passed a resolution which expressed 'profound concern' at the govts failure to enforce judgements by the ECtHR

General Principles

Subsidiarity:

Principle which states that human rights should primarily be protected at national level and the system under the ECHR is subordinate to this

Living Instrument:

The ECHR has to be generously interpreted in the light of its aim of protecting human rights, the understanding of which **may change with evolving social conditions**

- The ECtHR *does not* operate a strong system of precedent

Margin of Appreciation:

National authorities are *in principle* better placed than the ECtHR to **evaluate local needs and conditions** (***Protocol 15 (ECHR)***)

- Where member states *legitimately* reach different conclusions on a particular issue, the ECtHR will respect the judgement of a member state as to what the public interest requires
- The state's margin of appreciation is subject to the supervision of the ECtHR (reviews whether it is compatible with the ECHR)

Extent of the margin of appreciation varies depending on context

a) Important principles / general consensus as to meaning = no / narrow margin
b) Where there are diverging views = wider margin

Case Law Example:

- ***Handyside v UK (1979)*** → ECtHR held that the UK hadn't breached Article 10 when its obscenity laws prohibited publication of a sex education manual for children
- ***SAS v France (2014)*** → claimant challenged a ban on wearing clothing designed to conceal the face in public (breached right to private life & right to manifest religion / belief)
  - As views on this topic could differ in a democratic society (little agreement) → states had a wide margin of appreciation

Protection from Discrimination:

Article 14 → all of the rights and freedoms set out in the ECHR must be protected and applied without discrimination

- To rely on this right, a victim must show that the discrimination has affected their enjoyment of one or more of the other rights in the Convention

Derogations:

Article 15 → a state **may derogate** from part of the Convention '**in time of war or other public emergency threatening the life of the nation'**

- For the period of the derogation, the State is not bound to apply the specified provisions
- Must only be to the extent that it is strictly necessary
- No derogation is possible in respect of ***Article 3 (torture)***, ***4(1) (slavery)***, ***7 (retrospectice criminal offences)*** or ***2 (right to life)***, except in respect of deaths resulting from lawful acts of war
- A UK court will not be able to enforce Convention rights where a derogation is in operation

Human Rights Act 1998

Main Sections

Section 1 → incorporates and gives effect to the Convention Rights

- Article 2 - 12 and 14 of ECHR
- Article 1 - 3 of the First Protocol
- Article 1 of the Thirteenth Protocol

Section 2 → domestic courts must 'take into account' judgements of the ECtHR, but are not bound to follow them

Section 3 → 'so far as it is possible to do so, primary and subordinate legislation must be read and given effect in a way which is compatible with the Convention rights'

Section 4 → High Court and higher courts may declare an Act of Parliament to be incompatible with Convention rights

- *Does not* affect the validity or bind the parties to the proceedings (political pressure to change the law)

Section 6 → unlawful for a public authority to act in a way which is incompatible with Convention rights

Section 6(3) → Court is a public body

Section 7 → a person who claims that a public authority acted contrary to ***s 6*** may 'bring proceedings against the authority' or 'rely on the Convention right ... in any legal proceedings'

Section 8 → a court in civil proceedings may award damages, where a public authority unlawfully infringes a Convention right, if it is necessary to 'afford just satisfaction' to the injured party

Section 10 → creates a 'fast track' procedure for changing legislation

- Where UK legislation is in breach, the Govt may make a 'remedial order' changing UK law
- Delegated legislation which then has to be approved by Parliament, under the 'affirmative procedure'

Section 19 → a Minister introducing future legislation must make a written statement stating that the bill is compatible with Convention Rights or that it is incompatible but still wishes to proceed

Act of Public Authorities

Section 6(1) → it is unlawful for a public authority to act in a way which is incompatible with Convention rights

Doesn't apply where, as a result of an Act of Parliament, the authority couldn't have acted differently or the authority is giving effect to, or enforcing, provisions of an Act which are incompatible with the Convention

Adds a ground of challenge in judicial review of administrative acts

If a decision maker is a public body under the traditional principles of judicial review, it will also be a public authority for the purpose of a decision which breaches a Convention right

Enforcement against private individuals

The court is a public authority and therefore has a duty to apply the Convention → horizontally as Convention rights can affect relations between private citizens

Absolute Rights

Convention rights are normally divided into 3 types:

Absolute Rights → states must uphold at all times (no interference)

Limited Rights → can only be limited in clearly defined and finite situations

Qualified Rights → require a balance between the rights of the individual and wider public interest (may be interfered with to protect an important general interest / right of others)

Generally:

- Articles 2-7 (absolute and limited rights) cover the most fundamental human rights (contain no or narrow express exceptions)
- Article 8-11 and Article 1 of Protocol 1 cover qualified rights which can be overridden in the public interest

Article 2 - Right to Life

Article 2 is an absolute right, with exceptions that define its scope

Substantive Obligation:

1) It prohibits the state from taking life **and**
2) Places on the state a positive duty to protect life

Positive Duty?

☑ State must put in place effective criminal law provisions to deter the commission of offences against the person, backed up by law enforcement machinery

☑ May be a positive obligation on the authorities to take preventive operational measures to protect an individual whose life is at risk from criminal acts of another individual

- Only where the authorities knew or ought to have known of the existence of a real and immediate risk to the life of an identified individual from the criminal acts of a third party and they failed to take measures within the scope of their powers which, judged reasonably, might have been expected to avoid that risk

✗ Has been held *not* to protect embryos by preventing their destruction, when one party withdraws their consent to implantation

✗ Right to die *can't* be read into the right to life

Procedural Duty:

Places a procedural obligation on the state to investigate when individuals have been killed as a result of force (***McCann v UK***)

In ***Da Silva v United Kingdom (2016)***, the ECtHR stated that for an 'effective investigation':

a) It was necessary for the persons responsible for carrying out the investigation to be independent from those implicated in the events
b) It must be adequate, that it must be capable of leading to the establishment of the facts so determining whether the force used was or was not justified in the circumstances and of identifying and punishing those responsible
c) The nature and degree of scrutiny necessary would depend on the circumstances but would need to be stringent where death was at the hands of a state agent
d) The investigation must be accessible to the family
e) There must be a sufficiently element of public scrutiny
f) It must be carried out promptly

Derogation?

No derogation is possible, except in respect of deaths resulting from lawful acts of war

Article 2(2) allows the use of force that results in the deprivation of life, but only if certain conditions are met:

1) Use of force must be no more than absolutely necessary
2) Must be in pursuit of one or more of 3 objectives:
   The force is used in defence of any person from unlawful violence
   Force is used to effect a lawful arrest or to prevent the escape of a person lawfully detained
   The force is used in action lawfully taken for the purpose of lawfully quelling a riot or insurrection

Article 3 - Freedom from Torture

Article 3 → Freedom from Torture, Inhuman and Degrading Treatment

- **No limitations or exceptions**

Substantive Obligation:

- **Torture** = the 'deliberate inhumane treatment causing very serious and cruel suffering' (***Ireland v United Kingdom [1978]***)
- **Inhuman treatment** = treatment or punishment 'likely to cause actual bodily injury or intense physical and mental suffering' (***Ireland v United Kingdom [1978]***)
- **Degrading Treatment** = 'treatment which humiliates or debases an individual showing a lack of respect for, or diminishing, his or her human dignity or arouses feelings of fear, anguish or inferiority capable of breaking an individual's moral and physical resistance' (***Pretty v UK)***

States have an obligation to ensure that non-state actors (such as parents or guardians) do not punish children at a level at which Article 3 will be engaged

Asylum:

<u>*Case Law Example:*</u>

- ***R (Limbuela) v Secretary of State for the Home Department [2005]*** → 3 asylum seekers were refused support on the ground that they had not claimed asylum as soon as reasonably practicable after arriving in the UK
  - Prohibited from taking employment & so reliant on charity for food
  - Court stated that Art 3 would be breached if an asylum seeker, with no means or alternative support is 'by the deliberate action of the state, denied shelter, food or the most basic necessities of life'
    - Take into account gender, age and health, support available, length of time

Deportation:

- ***Immigration Act 1971*** allows the Government to deport those who are lawfully in the UK, but aren't UK citizens (if they have been convicted of a serious offence or their presence is not conducive to the public good)
  - **Removal** → where those who are not in the UK lawfully are removed
  - **Extradition** → anyone living in the UK being sent to another country in order to be tried for a criminal offence allegedly committed in that country

Would be a violation of Art 2 / 3 if an individual were to be deported to, removed to or extradited to a country where there was a real risk they might be killed, tortured or treated in any other way that may violate these articles

Procedural Duty:

Similar procedural obligations to Article 2

Article 4 - Freedom from Slavery

Substantive Obligation:

- **Slavery** = the status or condition of a person over whom any or all of the powers attaching to the right of ownership are exercised
- **Servitude** = an obligation of the person who is the 'serf' to live on the property of another and an inability for that person to change that condition
- **Forced Labour** = work or service that an individual was forced to do against their will

- Circumstances to consider are the type of work involved, the penalty or burden to be imposed if the work was not carried out and the level of hardship or oppression to which the individual was subjected

- **Human trafficking** = the recruitment or movement of people for exploitation by the use of threat, force, fraud or the abuse of vulnerability
  - States are under a positive obligation to enact and enforce laws to prohibit and punish trafficking

Certain forms of work *don't* constitute forced or compulsory labour (*Article 4(3))*:

✕ Work ordinarily done by convicted prisoners as part of their sentence

✕ Compulsory military service

✕ Work required in an emergency or calamity threatening the life or wellbeing of the community

✕ Any work or service that forms part of normal civic obligations

Article 7 - Punishment According to Existing Law

A person cannot be charged with a criminal offence for conduct that was *not* a crime when they committed it

- It's also a violation for the courts to impose a heavier penalty than was applicable at the time the offence was committed
- *Does not* preclude the gradual clarification of the principles of criminal liability on a case-by-case basis, provided that the development is consistent with the essence of the offence and could be reasonably foreseen (***SW v United Kingdom; CR v United Kingdom (1996) 21 EHRR***)

<u>*Exception*</u>:

- ***Article 7(2):*** people *can* still be prosecuted retrospectively for conduct that was 'criminal according to the general principles of law recognised by civilised nations', even if the conduct was not criminal at the time it was carried out
  - Essentially to ensure that Nazi's could be prosecuted

Article 12 - Right to Marry

The right extends to transsexual people (***Goodwin v United Kingdom (2002) 35 EHRR***)

Subject to national laws on marriage, including those that make marriage illegal between certain types of people

✕ Article 12 does not require the state to recognise same-sex marriage (***Oliari v Italy (2017) 65 EHRR 26***)

Any restrictions can't be arbitrary and must not interfere with the essential principle of the right

- Prohibiting the marriage of a father-in-law to a daughter-in-law in the Marriage Act 1949 violated Article 12 (***B v United Kingdom (2006) 42 EHRR***)

Article 3 of Protocol 1 - Right to Free Elections

Requires states to hold free elections at reasonable intervals, by way of secret ballot (absolute)

- BUT governments have a wide margin of appreciation and can decide what *type* of electoral system to adopt
  - A blanket ban on all serving prisoners to vote was not compatible with ***Article 3 of Protocol 1*** (***Hirst v UK (No 2) (2006) 42 EHRR***)
    - UK govt agreed to allow prisoners who are released on temporary licence or on home detention curfew to vote

Article 1 of Protocol 13 - Abolition of Death Penalty

Ratified by UK in 2003 and came into force in 2004

Limited Rights

Article 5 - Right to Liberty and Security

The purpose of ***Article 5*** is to ensure that **no one is deprived of their liberty in an 'arbitrary fashion'**

- ***Article 5(1)***: 'everyone has the right to liberty and security of person. No one shall be deprived of his liberty save in the following cases and in accordance with a procedure prescribed by law'
- The most significant ways in which the state may lawfully restrict the liberty of an individual are:
  - Arrest and detention
  - Imprisonment after conviction
  - Detention of mentally ill in hospitals
  - Detention of foreigners (asylum and deportation)

Procedural Standards:

Article 5 lays down procedural standards that must be followed before a person is deprived of their liberty:

Article 5 requires:

a) Breach, or reasonable suspicion of breach, of some known law (***Article 5(1)(a) and (c)***)
b) The giving of reasons for arrest and charge (***Article 5(2)***)

c) A trial within a reasonable time (***Article 5(3))***

d) The availability of judicial review of the legality of detention (***Article 5(4))***

e) The right to compensation for breach of Article 5 ((***Article 5(5))***

Defining deprivation:

Deprivation of Liberty = 'the difference between deprivation of and restriction upon liberty is one of degree or intensity, and not one of nature or substance' (***Guzzardi v Italy (1981)***)

- It is necessary to look at *the level of restriction* placed on the applicant, rather than their specific nature

Case Law Example:

- ***Secretary of State for the Home Department v JJ [2007]***: SoS used statutory powers to make control orders over 6 people of Iranian and Iraqi nationally (suspected them of involvement in terrorist related activity)
    - Called to wear an electronic tagging device, to remain within their specified residence (except between 10am and 4pm where they could go to restricted urban areas) and to permit Police to search premise at any time. Couldn't meet anyone without pre-arrangement with Home Office
    - Adopting approach taken by ECtHR in *Guzzardi*, HoL held that the right to individual liberty connoted the physical liberty of the person → right to liberty had been violated
    - A person may be deprived of their liberty without being detained in prison, but needs to be a significant element of physical containment, together with significant restrictions on the life that can be lived when not so confined

Kettling:

Kettling is the practice of **containing a group of people in a particular area for a limited period of time** in the interests of public order

Austin v UK (2012): 4 people were contained within a police cordon for 6-7 hours during an anti-capitalism demonstration

- Court did not find a breach → ***Article 5*** was not concerned with mere restrictions on liberty of movement
- Difference between a deprivation of liberty and a restriction upon it was one of degree
- Context was significant → police had no alternative to use a cordon to avert the risk of injury / damage → court unable to identify a point at which a restriction on their freedom of movement became a deprivation of their liberty
    - Containment was the least intrusive measure the police could use

Exceptions:

Article 5(1)(a)-(f) outlines 6 situations **where an individual may lawfully be deprived of their liberty:**

a) When an individual is sent to prison after being convicted of a criminal offence
b) When an individual is arrested or detained in order to ensure that the individual complies with a court order
c) When an individual is arrested on reasonable suspicion of having committed a criminal offence, to prevent them from committing an offence or to prevent them from fleeing after having committed an offence
    Reasonable suspicion = requires an existence of some facts of information which would satisfy an objective observer that the person concerned may have committed the offence (***O'Hara v UK (2002)***)
d) When a minor is detained for the purposes of educational supervision
e) When someone is detained to prevent the spreading of an infectious disease or someone who is mentally ill is detained for their own protection or the protection of others
f) The detention of individuals in connection with asylum, deportation or extradition

BUT → must take place in accordance with a procedure prescribed by law

- Can't be carried out in an arbitrary manner (***Saadi v United Kingdom (2008)***):
    Detention has to be carried out in good faith (closely connected to above purposes) → objective
    The length of the detention should not exceed that reasonable required for the purpose pursued
    Proper records of the reason for the detention must be kept
    The detention must be lawful within the terms of the national law of the state concerned

PACE:

The Police and Criminal Evidence Act 1984 (PACE):

Section 24 of Pace:

An arrest may be made in relation to 'any offence';
Where a police officer has 'reasonable grounds' to believe that an arrest is necessary for one of the reasons specified in ***S 24(5)***

Section 28 of Pace:

The police must tell the arrested person that they are under arrest and the reasons for the arrest as soon as practicable

Section 37 of Pace:

The arrested person must normally be taken to the police station as soon as practicable where they will be brought before the custody officer
The custody officer may authorise detention of the arrested person if:

a) There is insufficient evidence to charge them and detention is necessary either to secure or preserve evidence relating to the offence or to obtain evidence by questioning

Initial period of detention = 24 hours
Extended detention can be authorised by a police officer of at least the rank of superintendent, where they have reasonable grounds to believe that:

a) The offence the person has been arrested for is an indictable offence (trial by jury)
b) The detention of that person without charge is necessary to secure or preserve evidence relating to an offence for which they are under arrest or to obtain such evidence by questioning them; and
c) The investigation is being conducted diligently and expeditiously

→ Can then authorise detention up to 36 hours

- If they wish to detain for more than 36 hours, must apply to the magistrates' court for a warrant for further detention (can then grant up to 36 hours further)
- The overall period of detention may not exceed 96 hours in total

Article 6 - Right to a Fair Trial

Absolute as to a fair trial, limited in relation to the trial being in public

Article 6(1):

- 'In the determination of his civil rights and obligations or any criminal charge against him, everyone is entitled to a fair and public hearing within a reasonable time by an independent and impartial tribunal established by law'
- Judgement shall be pronounced publicly *but* the press and public *may be excluded* from all or parts of the trial in the interests of morals, public order or national security in a democratic society, where the interests of juveniles or the protection of the private life of the parties so require
    - Or to the extent strictly necessary in the opinion of the court in special circumstances where publicity would prejudice the interests of justice

Article 6 will only be invoked where a case concerns an individual attempting to assert a substantive legal right that is recognised in national law

Criminal Trials:

The ECtHR set out a number of criteria that had to be applied by a court when deciding whether a legal process constitutes the determination of a criminal charge (***Engel v The Netherlands (1979–80)***)

First determine whether the national law of a state classifies a matter as being criminal (if yes, Article 6 applies)

If not, the court must then determine whether the proceedings against an individual are similar to a criminal trial

Do the proceedings require a finding of guilt or innocence to be made

What was the purpose behind the proceedings → if to impose punishment, likely to be criminal

Procedural Standards:

There are certain elements which must be met when criminal charges are brought against an individual:

a) **Access** to the court

b) **Independent and impartial** tribunal

The imposition of a sentence is part of the trial and so should be imposed by an independent and impartial tribunal (not the Home Secretary) (***R (on the application of Anderson) v Secretary of State for the Home Department [2002]***)

c) **Public trial** and decision announced publicly:

Exclusion when:

i) Required in the interests of morality, public order or national security

ii) Required in the interests of juveniles or the protection of the private life of the parties

iii) There are special circumstances that would prejudice the interests of justice

d) Take place within a **reasonable time:**

Custody time limits ensure that defendants who are remanded in custody have their trials heard within a reasonable time → can't be held in custody for longer than 6 months prior to their trial (can be extended)

e) Trial should be **conducted in a fair way**

- Defendant should be able to participate effectively in their trial (at least in their presence and should be able to follow and understand the proceedings)
    - ***T v United Kingdom (2000) 30 EHRR 121***: steps taken to ensure the trial of 2 11-year old boys (in an adult Crown Court) were not sufficient to allow them to understand the trial
- Court accepts that national laws *may allow* the use of **evidence obtained illegally or improperly**
    - ***Khan v United Kingdom [2000] ECHR***: Using a bugging device to obtain evidence did not violate ***Article 6***
        - The domestic courts have the discretion to exclude the evidence under ***s 78 of PACE*** if they thought it unfair

        Evidence that is unlawfully obtained is still admissible, provided that it's relevant to an issue and is not unreliable
    - Courts will refuse to allow evidence that has been obtained through oppression, or as a result of something said or done which is likely to render it unreliable (***s 76 PACE***)

Article 6(2) and 6(3):

Article 6(2): everyone charged with a criminal offence shall be **presumed innocent until proven guilty**

- Strict liability offences do not breach Article 6(2) (***Salabiaku v France (1991) 13 EHRR***) → permissible provided they are reasonable
- The right to silence can be read into the presumption of innocence
- No rule to prevent adverse inferences to be drawn from silence (but would be a breach if convicted on the basis of their silence alone) (***Murray v United Kingdom (1996) 22 EHRR***)

Article 6(3): series of **minimum rights that apply to those charged** with a criminal offence:

a) **To be told promptly and fully the detail of the case against them**

Must be given in a language that the defendant understands
Prosecuting authorities must supply details of their case
It was a breach of Article 6 to rely on closed material in a terror suspect hearing to justify the decision to make a control order (***Secretary of State for the Home Department v AF [2009]***)

b) **To have sufficient time and facilities to prepare their defence**

Need time to contact witnesses who may assist their defence / obtain documents

c) **To defend themselves** either personally or with the assistance of a lawyer, who should be provided by the state where the individual doesn't have sufficient means to pay for legal assistance and the interests of justice so require

d) **To call witnesses in their defence** and to **cross-examine witnesses** who have given evidence against them

e) To have an **interpreter provided** free where necessary

Contempt of Court:

Contempt of Court Act 1981:

Where a newspaper comments on a court case which has not yet been decided, there is a danger that the report will influence a jury / pressure the judge

Liability for contempt of court is strict → no intention to interference with the court proceedings needs to be shown

Only applies to **communications addressed to the public at large** or sections of the public

Proceedings must be active

For criminal, this is when the defendant is arrested
For civil, when arrangements for the hearing are made

The publication must create a **substantial risk** that the proceedings will be **seriously prejudiced** (***Attorney General v News Group Newspapers [1987]***)

I.e. whether there is a substantial risk that it will be read and remembered
Takes into account whether the publication is local or national and proximity of the trial (in ***Attorney-General v NGN***, 10 months was too far)

Any **defences**?

Section 3 provides a defence for 'innocent publication' → publisher didn't know and had no reason to suspect that the proceedings were active

Section 4 provides a defence for contemporary reports of proceedings, provided that they are fair and accurate and published in good faith

5. Section 5 protects **discussions in good faith of public affairs** or matters of general public interest, if the risk of **prejudice was merely incidental**

Includes social media

Common Law Contempt:

Intentional contempt remains an offence at common law → where the publication was calculated to impede or prejudice the administration of justice

- Often difficult to prove
- Also an offence at common law to impede the judicial process in the courtroom → e.g. holding a demonstration, shouting or otherwise interfering with the proceedings

Qualified Rights

Justified Interferences

1) Qualifications must be express

Only restrictions on qualified rights which are expressed in the ECHR are recognised

- Must be used for the purpose for which they have been prescribed (***Article 18***)
- Can only be relied upon if it is prescribed by law, had a legitimate aim and is necessary in a democratic society
- Can't be applied in a discriminatory fashion (***article 14***)

2) Qualifications must be prescribed by law

A govt **can rely on a Convention qualification to justify a restriction** on a Convention right, only if **provisions of that state's law actually take advantage of the qualification**

- E.g. not possible for UK govt to justify infringement of the right to respect for private life (e.g. by phone tapping), on the basis that it was needed for the prevention of crime (***Article 8***), unless UK law clearly permitted the infringement
- The law must be accessible and sufficiently precise to enable the citizen to regulate their conduct

Case Law Example:

- ***Malone v UK (1985)*** → ECtHR held that English law on phone tapping was not clear enough at the time to provide a sufficient legal basis for a restriction on the right to respect for private life
- ***R (on the application of Purdy) v DPP*** → absence of a crime-specific policy relating to assisted suicide, meant that the statutory offence of assisted suicide was not in accordance with law for purpose of Article 8(2)

3) Legitimate Aims:

Qualifications **must be justified by reference to the aims specified for each right**. Interests of society may justify restrictions on the rights of individuals:

a) Interests of national security, public safety or the economic wellbeing of the country
b) The prevention of disorder of crime
c) Protection of health or morals
d) Protection of the rights or freedoms of others
e) Prevention or disclosure of information received in confidence
f) Maintaining the authority and impartiality of the judiciary

3) Necessary in a democratic society (proportionate)

Qualifications are **usually required to be necessary in a democratic society**

There must be a pressing social need

The interference with the Convention right must be proportionate

Proportionality test in ***Bank Mellat v HM Treasury (No 2) [2013]:***

1. Is the objective of the measure complained of sufficiently important to justify the limitation of a fundamental right
2. Is the measure rationally connected to the objective
3. Could a less intrusive measure be used
4. Having regard to these matters & to the severity of the consequences, has a fair balance been struck between the rights of the individual & the interests of the community

Article 8 - Respect for Private and Family Life

Article 8:

1. Everyone has the **right to respect for his private and family life, his home and his correspondence**
2. There shall be *no* interference by a public authority with the exercise of this right, except such as in accordance with the law and is necessary in a democratic society in the interests of:
   - National security
   - Public safety
   - The economic well-being of the country
   - For the prevention of disorder or crime
   - For the protection of health or morals
   - For the protection of the rights and freedoms of others

Private Life:

Issues within the scope of private life include:

- Bodily integrity
- Personal autonomy
- Sexuality
- Personal information

Fingerprints and DNA:

S and Marper v the United Kingdom (2009)

- ECtHR held that the retention of fingerprints and DNA (permitted by statutory provision) invoked Article 8
- 'The retention constitutes a *disproportionate interference* with the applicant's right to respect for private life and cannot be regarded as necessary in a democratic society

Supreme court in ***R (on the application of GC) v The Commissioner of the Police of the Metropolis [2011]***:

- Ruled that a blanket policy of retaining biometric data was not compatible with Article 8

→ Protection of ***Freedom Act 2012*** → includes provisions requiring the deletion of some DNA profiles from the DNA database

Photographs:

Wood v Metropolitan Police Commissioner [2009]

- Court of Appeal held that the decision by police officers to retain photographs of an arms trade protestor involved in a peaceful protest breached his right to privacy
- Although the police were justified in taking the photograph, their retention was not proportionate

Vaccination:

Allette v Scarsdale Grange Nursing Home Ltd [2022]

- Care assistant claimed she was unfairly dismissed from her job when she refused to have a vaccination against COVID
- The employment instruction had the legitimate aim of protecting the health and safety of others and was proportionate given the risks posed

Deportation (no family life ties):

- Article 8 may be engaged when the main issue is the consequence for physical or mental health of removal
- Threshold for establishing this is high → must show that the violation of rights would be so flagrant ***(R(Razghar) v Secretary of State for the Home Department)***

Family Life:

Typical situation where an individual argues that their deportation, removal or extradition will *disproportionately* damage family ties and relationships they have in the UK

Uner v The Netherlands (2007)

- ECtHR held that the deportation, removal or extradition of an individual *could* engage the right to respect for their family life under ***Article 8(1)***
- Factors to take into account for proportionality:
  a) The length of time the individual had been in the country
  b) The seriousness of the offences that the individual had committed
  c) Details of the particular family circumstances of the individual (age of children)

d) The interests of the children
e) The seriousness of the difficulties that the family may experience in the receiving country
f) The nature of the ties that the individual has with expelling & receiving country

- Found that there wasn't a violation:
  - Uner had only lived with his partner and child for a short period. Still had social and cultural ties with Turkey
  - His offences of manslaughter and assault were very serious in nature

Norris v Government of USA (No 2) [2010]:

- Concerned extradition of a British national on charges of obstruction of justice
- Supreme Court emphasised that only where some quite exceptionally compelling feature, or combo, is present will interference with family life consequent upon extradition be disproportionate to the objective the extradition serves
- Public interest for extradition will always be a powerful consideration (great weight attached)

H(H) v Deputy Prosecutor of the Italian Republic, Genoa [2012]

- A lengthy delay since the crime was committed may reduce the weight to be attached to the public interest and increase the importance of family life
- BUT public interest in extradition will outweigh family unless consequences on family life would be exceptionally severe

Article 9 - Freedom of Thought, Conscience and Religion

Article 9:

Everyone has the **right to freedom of thought, conscience and religion**; this right includes **freedom to change his religion or belief and freedom**, either alone or in community with others and in public or private, **to manifest his religion or belief**, in worship, teaching, practice and observance

Freedom to manifest one's religion or beliefs shall be subject only to such limitations as are prescribed by law and are necessary in a democratic society in the interests of

a) Public safety
b) For the protection of public order
c) Health or morals
d) For the protection of the rights and freedoms of others.

✅ **Freedom of thought, conscience and religion = <u>absolute</u> (*Kokkinakis v Greece (1994)*)**

❌ **The right to *manifest* a religion or belief = qualified**

Religion:

At Work:

Eweida and others v United Kingdom (2013)

- Four separate applicants argued that their respective employers had either imposed restrictions on dress or dismissed them in violation of their rights under ***Article 9***

  Eweida not allowed to wear a cross necklace (employer was British Airways)
  - Her cross was discrete and would not have detracted from her professional appearance (didn't impact corporate brand)

  Chaplin not allowed to wear a cross (NHS prohibited wearing necklaces to reduce risk of injury to patients)

  Protection of health and safety was more important → hospital managers better place to make assessments on safety than the court

  Lavelle refused to be designated as a registrar of civil partnerships (against same sex marriage) → disciplinary proceedings and lost her job
  - National authorities should be given a wide margin of appreciation for striking a balance between competing Convention rights

  MacFarlane employed at a marriage guidance organisation → didn't want to provide counselling to same-sex couples → disciplinary proceedings
  - Wasn't a breach

At School:

- ***Williamson v Education Secretary [2005]***: parents of children at a christian school (who had a policy of corporal punishment, in line with their faith) argued that the legislation banning it breached their rights
  - HoL held that this belief could be interfered with, in pursuit of a legitimate aim and proportionate
  - Legitimate aim was to protect the rights of others

- ***R (on the application of Begum) v Headteacher, Governors of Denbigh High School [2006]:*** schoolgirl had been excluded from her school for failure to comply with dress code → wanted to wear a jilbab to school
  - Found there had been no breach → school acted in a proportionate manner
  - Had chosen to attend a school outside her catchment area → could have easily attended another school which permitted wearing a jilbab
  - The school had tried to devise a uniform policy which respected Muslim beliefs in an inclusive, unthreatening and uncompetitive way

Article 10 - Freedom of Expression

Article 10:

- 'Everyone has the **right to freedom of expression**. This right shall include freedom to **hold opinions and to receive and impart information and ideas without interference by public authorities and regardless of frontiers**. This article shall not prevent States from requiring the licensing of broadcasting, television or cinema enterprises
- The exercise of these freedoms, since it carries with it duties and responsibilities, may be subject to such formalities, conditions, restrictions or penalties as are prescribed by law and are necessary in a democratic society:
  a) In the interests of national security
  b) Territorial integrity or public safety
  c) For the prevention of disorder or crime
  d) For the protection of health or morals
  e) For the protection of the reputation or rights of others
  f) For preventing the disclosure of information received in confidence
  g) For maintaining the authority and impartiality of the judiciary.

Political Advertising

Ban on the broadcasting of political advertising in the ***Communications Act 2003***

- ***Animal Defenders v United Kingdom (2013)***: they campaigned against the use of animals in commerce, science and leisure → tv advertisement was blocked
  - ECtHR rejected their argument that it was a violation of ***Article 10***
  - Pursued the legitimate aim of preserving the impartiality of broadcasting → protecting the democratic process
  - Margin of appreciation was narrow

Hate Speech

Free speech that is offensive, shocking or disturbing is protected by ***Article 10*** and shouldn't be restricted

Jersild v Denmark (1995): expression of outright racist views would not be protected by ***Article 10*** as such views went beyond what was offensive, shocking or disturbing

Norwood v United Kingdom (Admissibility) (Application no 23131/03) (2005): convicted for an offence of causing alarm or distress (poster outside his flat saying 'Islam out of Britain'

- His application to ECtHR was rejected → the views he sought to express were aimed at undermining others & were incompatible with the values that underpinned the ECHR

Restraints in England and Wales

1) **Defamation** → false statement exposing someone to hatred, ridicule or contempt
2) **Misuse of private information** → information will be private if, in the circumstances, an individual would have 'a reasonable expectation of privacy'
3) **Official secrets** → Official Secrets Act 1989
4) **Threatening, insulting or abusive words or behaviour** → s 4, 4A and 5 of the Public Order Act 1986
5) **Incitement to racial and religious hatred**
6) **Obscenity** → The Obscene Publications act 1959
    - An article is obscene if its effect, taken as a whole, such as tends to deprave and corrupt persons who are likely in all the circumstances to read, see or hear the matter which it contains
7) **Terrorism Act 2006** → criminal offence to encourage terrorism by directly or indirectly inciting or encouraging others to commit acts of terrorism
8) **Contempt of Court**

Article 11 - Freedom of Assembly and Association

Article 11:

- Everyone has the right to **freedom of peaceful assembly and to freedom of association with others**, including the right to form and to join trade unions for the protection of his interests
- No restrictions shall be placed on the exercise of these rights other than such as are prescribed by law and are necessary in a democratic society:
    a) In the interests of national security or public safety
    b) For the prevention of disorder or crime
    c) For the protection of health or morals
    d) For the protection of the rights and freedoms of others.
- This Article shall not prevent the imposition of lawful restrictions on the exercise of these rights by members of the armed forces, of the police or of the administration of the State.

Freedom of Assembly:

Conduct will fall within scope of ***Article 11*** if it is a 'peaceful assembly'

- ***Tabernacle v Secretary of State for Defence [2009]***: a byelaw which prevented the appellant from camping in the vicinity of the Atomic Weapons Establishment violated the rights of free expression and association guaranteed by Articles 10 and 11

Freedom of Association:

Designed to protect an **individual's right to participate with other people in an organised way** in pursuit of a common aim

- The state may lawfully limit the exercise of the right to freedom of association provided that limitation is prescribed by law, is in pursuit of a legitimate aim and is proportionate to that aim

Case Law Examples:

- ***United Communist Party of Turkey v Turkey (1998)***: In July 1991, the constitutional court made an order dissolving the Party, based on the inclusion in its name of the constitutionally prohibited word 'communist' and the alleged encouragement of Kurdish separatism
  - The Court found that the dissolution of the Party was permitted under Turkish law and arguably had a legitimate aim – national security.
  - But was disproportionate → ***Article 11*** therefore had to be viewed in the light of the protection of freedom of expression as guaranteed by ***Article 10.***
- ***Refah Partisi (the Welfare Party) v Turkey (2003)***: Turkey's state counsel applied for the dissolution of the party on the grounds that the activities were contrary to the principle of the separation of the state from religious institutions as set out in the Turkish constitution, and also because some of its members had called for the establishment of an Islamic state and the imposition of sharia law in Turkey.

  The Court found that the dissolution of the Refah Partisi *did not* violate ***Article 11***

  The model of society and government that Refah Partisi wished to introduce would undermine the very basis on which the ECHR rested.

  Posed an immediate danger to Turkish democracy

Article 1 of Protocol 1 - Right to Peaceful Enjoyment of Possessions

Article 1 of Protocol 1:

- Every natural or legal person is entitled to the **peaceful enjoyment of his possessions**. No one shall be deprived of his possessions **except in the public interest** and **subject to the conditions provided for by law** and by the **general principles of international law.**
- The preceding provisions shall not, however, in any way impair the right of a State to enforce such laws as it deems necessary to control the use of property in accordance with the general interest or to secure the payment of taxes or other contributions or penalties.
- This Article guarantees the right to peaceful enjoyment of possessions (both land (realty) and personal property).

Only interference which affects the financial value of property or possessions will engage the right to 'peaceful enjoyment' of them

- A 'deprivation of property' under this Article will not be considered to be in the public interest unless the owner receives compensation.

Article 2 of Protocol 1 - Right to Education

Article 2 of Protocol 1:

- No person **shall be denied the right to education**. In the exercise of any functions which it assumes in relation to education and teaching, the state shall respect the rights of parents to ensure such education and teaching in conformity with their own religious and philosophical convictions.

Belgian Linguistic (1979–80) → the rights protected are:

A right of access to educational institutions existing at a given time. It does not require the Government to provide or subsidise any particular type of education;

A right to official recognition of the studies a student has successfully completed.

Schools are allowed to use admission policies so long as they are objective and reasonable.

The right did not preclude disciplinary measures such as expulsion or temporary exclusion, though to be lawful any such measures had to be foreseeable, had to pursue a legitimate aim and had to be proportionate to that aim (***Ali v United Kingdom (2011)***)

Conflict of Rights

The ECHR does not lay down any strict hierarchy of rights → **courts have to determine priority on a case-by-case basis**

Absolute and Qualified

Article 2 and 3

Protection of identity:

- ***Venables and Thompson v News Group Newspapers Ltd [2001]***: had been convicted (aged 11) for the murder of a toddler → granted injunctions protection them from being identified upon release
    - Publication of such information would cause lives to be in danger

- Also in ***Carr v News Group Newspapers Ltd [2005]*** and ***D v Persons Unknown; F v Persons Unknown [2021]***

Article 6

Where a newspaper comments on court proceedings, may interfere with ***Article 6*** (right to a fair trial)

Contempt of Court Act 1981:

- Liability for contempt of court is strict

Common Law Contempt → intentional contempt (calculated to impede or prejudice the administration of justice)

Qualified

Main area of conflict is between ***Article 10*** and ***Article 8***

S 12(4) of the Human Rights Act 1998 is drafted so as to prevent claims of breach of privacy from unduly restricting the freedom of the press

- Courts must have particular regard to the right to freedom of expression
- Where proceedings relate to journalistic, literary or artistic material, the court must consider the extent to which the material is already in the public domain, whether the publication would be in the public interest and any relevant privacy code

Campbell v Mirror Group Newspapers Ltd [2004]:

Naomi Campbell took the Mirror Group to court after publishing that she was receiving treatment for her drug addiction, the details of such treatment and photographs of her leaving a Narcotics meeting

1) **Did her complaint come within the scope of Article 8?**
    - Appropriate test was whether the claimant had a reasonable expectation of respect for her private life in the particular circumstances (reasonable person of ordinary sensibilities placed in the position of the claimant)

2) **Balance Article 8 and Article 10:**
    Which should assume the most importance would depend on the facts of the case
    a. First look at the comparative importance of the actual rights being claimed in the individual case
        - Political, artistic or impression speech is deserving of protection
        - Stories about intimate details of a celebrity's private life attract less protection
    b. Justifications for interfering with or restricting each of those rights
    c. Applying proportionality test to each

- HoL found that the photographs of Campbell attending a Narcotics Anonymous meeting had far greater effect than just words → invaded her right to private life
- ***MGN Ltd v United Kingdom (Application No 39401/04)*** → ECtHR upheld decision
    - Lack of compelling need for public to have the information

ZXC v Bloomberg LP [2022]:

- Central factor = assessment of the contribution which the publication of the relevant information would make to a debate of general interest
- Take into account role press plays as a 'public watchdog'

Axel Springer AG v Germany (2012)

1. Contribution to a debate of general interest
2. How well known is the person concerned and what is the subject of the report
3. The prior conduct of the person concerned
4. The method of obtaining the information and its veracity
5. If publication had been restrained, the severity of any sanction imposed

Photographs:

Von Hannover v Germany (No 1) (2005):

- Princess Caroline of Monaco → photographs taken of her by the paparazzi were in breach of her Article 8 rights
- ECtHR ruled that the decisive factor was the contribution that the published photos and articled made to a debate of general interest
    - Photos and articles related exclusively to details of her private life, *not* official role

Von Hannover v Germany (No 2) (2012):

- Publication of Caroline and her husband skiing on holiday with an accompanying article about the health of her father
- Information about Prince Rainer's health was a matter of public interest due to his status → public were legitimately interested in how his children 'reconciled their obligations of family solidarity with the legitimate needs of their private life'
- Link between photograph and article were close enough to justify the publication
- Photos must contribute to a genuine debate of general interest

Murray (by his Litigation Friends) v Express Newspapers [2008]:

- Article 8 rights of JK Rowling's 8 year old son → photograph had been taken with a long-range lens (without consent)
- Arguable that the appellant had a reasonable expectation of privacy (objective test)
    - Law should protection children from intrusive media attention

RocknRoll v News Group Newspapers Ltd [2013]:

- Judge granted an injunction to Kate Winsley's husband, preventing publication by a newspaper of photographs which had been posted by a friend on Facebook

Other case law:

Mosley v News Group Newspapers [2008]:

- Head of Formula 1 racing → right to privacy had been infringed after News of the World published a story alleging that he had engaged in a Nazi-themed sado-masochistic orgy with a group of prostitutes
- Issue was whether there was sufficient public interest to justify publication
    - Held there wasn't → newspaper failed to demonstrate that the activities did have a Nazi theme

LNS v Persons Unknown [2010]:

- High Court overturned a 'super-injunction' which had prevented a newspaper from reporting on an alleged extramarital affair of John Terry
- The injunction was not necessary or proportionate having regard to the level of gravity of the interference with Terry's private life

Ferdinand v MGN Ltd [2011]:

- Rio Ferdinand claimed that a newspaper article about his relationship with a woman breached his privacy
- Court found that as Ferdinand had stated he was a family man, there was a public interest in demonstrating that this image was false (also England captain)

PJS v News Group Newspapers Ltd [2016]

- Sun on Sunday proposed to publish the story of PJS's sexual encounters with AB → sued for breach of confidence, breach of privacy and asked for an injunction to prevent publication
  - Necessary to protection himself, his partner and young children
- Held that there was a need to impose an injection to stop a 'media storm' (especially to protect the children)
- Held that the publication of private sexual encounters 'will on the face of it constitute the tort of invasion of privacy' → 'repetition on further occasions is capable of constituting a further tort of invasion of privacy'

Note:

- In these cases, one of the parties have been a private body (can only bring a claim under HRA against a public body)
- Provided that the claimant has another cause of which which they can use to bring a case (e.g. breach of confidence or misuse of private information)
- → The court will then be a public authority so when it decides on the case, it will need to act compatibly with any relevant Convention Rights

Public Order

English judges have traditionally acknowledged that a 'right' to protest exists (***Hubbard v Pitt***)

Enshrined in Human Rights Act:

Article 10 = right to freedom of expression

Article 11 = right to freedom of assembly and association

- Can be limited under the Convention 'for the protection of the rights of others', for the 'prevention of disorder or crime'
- The state may infringe freedom of assembly if it doesn't take positive measures to protect the exercise of the right (***Plattform 'Ärzte für das Leben' v Austria***)
  - This doesn't require the state to ensure that there is a right to assembly on private land, unless this has the effect of preventing any effective exercise of the right to freedom of expression (where there is nowhere else to meet) (***Appleby v United Kingdom***)

Basic approach of the law = processions and meetings are **prima facie lawful, unless they amount to crimes or torts**

- In examining 'lawful excuse' courts need to decide if an activity causing an obstruction is itself lawful and whether it is reasonable
- As processions and meetings are prima facie lawful, the police usually need specific powers to control them

The Public Order Act (POA) 1986 (amended by the *Police, Crime, Sentencing and Courts Act 2022*)

Processions

Public procession = a procession in a public place (*s 16)*

Public place = any highway or any other place that the public may lawfully access on payment or otherwise (*s 16*)

1) Advance Notice

Any person organising a 'public procession' for any purposes in *s 11(1)(a), (b), and (c)* must give the police at least 6 clear days' notice of the date, time and route of the proposed procession (*s 11(1) POA*). These purposes are:

a) To demonstrate support for or opposition to the views or actions of any person or body of persons,
b) To publicise a cause or campaign
c) To mark or commemorate an event

S 11(4): organisers must deliver the notice to a police station in the police area where the procession will start

Exceptions

- Doesn't apply to funeral processions or to customary or commonly held processions in a given police area (*s 11(2)*)
- Occasions where it is not reasonably practicable to give notice

Offences

Only the organisers will be guilty of an offence if:

a) They do not give the required notice *(s 11(7)(a))*
   - **Defence** = if the organisers did not know and did not have any reason to suspect that s 11 had not been complied with *(s 11(8))*

b) If the procession differs from what the notice specified *(s 11(7)(b))*

- **Defence** = if the departure from the details arose from circumstances beyond the organiser's control or from something done with the agreement of the police or by their direction ***(s 11(9))***

2) Imposing Conditions (*s 12*):

The **police have powers to impose conditions upon public processions**, provided that a senior police officer reasonably believes that (***s 12 POA***):

Serious disorder / damage / disruption:

The march will result in *serious* public disorder, *serious* damage to property, or *serious* disruption to the life of the community ***(s 12(1)(a))***

- E.g. significant delay to the delivery of a time-sensitive product to consumers
- Prolonged disruption to any essential goods or services (e.g. food or health services)

Impact of noise:

The noise generated may result in serious disruption to the activities of an organisation which are carried out in the vicinity of the procession or it may have a significant relevant impact on persons in the vicinity of the procession ***(s 12(1)(aa))***

- Where persons cannot carry out those activities for a *prolonged period of time* ***(s 12(2C))***
- **'Relevant impact'** = noise may result in intimidation or harassment of people of reasonable firmness or may cause such people to suffer alarm or distress (***s 12(2D))***
    - Should take into account the likely number of people who would be affected and the likely duration and intensity of that impact upon them (***s 12(2E)***)

Purpose of organisers:

The purpose of the organisers is to intimidate others with a view to compelling them not to do something that they have a right to do, or to do something that they have a right not to do ***(s 12(1)(b))***

Intimidation = more than being a nuisance or causing discomfort (***Police v Reid***)

What conditions?

The conditions that senior police officer may impose are those that **appear to be necessary to prevent such disorder, damage, disruption or intimidation**

Imposed by:

The identity of the 'senior police officer' with the power to impose conditions **depends on the circumstances**

For conditions imposed during the procession = must be the most senior police officer present at the scene and must be given verbally ***(s 12(2)(a))***

For conditions imposed in advance = must be the chief officer of the police ***(s 12(2)(b))***

- Must be provided in writing
- Must provide sufficient reasons for the demonstrators to understand why the conditions have been imposed and so the court can assess whether the belief that the procession may resulted in the listed consequences is reasonable ***(R (Brehony) v Chief Constable of Greater Manchester Police)***
- Must take into account Article 11 → any conditions imposed must be proportionate

Offences under s 12:

Section 12 of the POA 1986 creates the offences of:

a) Organising or taking part in a public procession and failure to comply with a condition imposed under ***s 12(1)*** where they ought to know that the condition has been imposed ***(s 12(4) and (5))***
b) Inciting a participant in a public procession to commit an offence under ***s 12(5) (s 12(6))***

Have a defence if they can show that their failure to comply with the conditions was due to circumstances beyond their control

- Burden of proof is on the defendant to prove the defence on the balance of probabilities

3) Power to prohibit processions (*s 13*):

Section 13(1) of the POA 1986 allows a chief officer of police to **apply for a prohibition order** in respect of public processions if they reasonably believe that the powers in ***s 12*** are insufficient to prevent a risk of serious public disorder ***(s 13(1))***

- The order can ban all processions or processions of a particular class, such as political marches
- There is no power to ban a specific individual procession
- Can be challenged via judicial review ***(Kent v Metropolitan Police Commissioner (1981) The Times)***
    - Although courts are reluctant to quash these decisions

Admin:

- Must apply to the local authority which then makes an order with the Home Secretary's consent
- Doesn't apply to London → the Commissioner of Police for the City of London or the Commission of Police of the Metropolis makes the order and then the Home Sec consents ***(s 13(4))***
- Order can be for any period not exceeding 3 months
- Must be in writing ***(s 13(5))***

Offences under s 13:

- Organising or taking part in a public procession, knowing it is prohibited under ***s 13 (s 13(7) and (8))***
- Inciting a participant to take part in a public procession that is prohibited under ***s 13 (s 13(9))***

Public Meetings

Public Assembly = an assembly comprising two or more persons in a public space that is wholly or partly open to the air (***s 16 POA***)

Must be in a location to which the public or any section of the public has access and which can be fairly described as a scene

(***R (on the application of Baroness Jones and others) and others v Commissioner of Police of the Metropolis)***

General Rule = no requirement to obtain permission to hold a meeting

BUT local or private Acts of Parliament may lay down a requirement for permission (e.g. Trafalgar Square Byelaws 2012)

A meeting on private land requires the permission of the owner

Imposing conditions on public assemblies:

Section 14 POA: a senior police officer can impose conditions on any public assembly if they reasonably believe that:

a) It may result in serious public disorder
b) Serious damage to property
c) Serious disruption to the life of the community
d) The noise generated may result in serious disruption to the activities of an organisation which are carried out in the vicinity of the procession
e) The noise may have a significant relevant impact on persons in the vicinity of the procession
f) That the purpose of the organisers is the intimidation of others

The conditions that the senior police officer may impose are **those which appear necessary to prevent such disorder, damage, disruption, impact or intimidation**

No power to ban public assemblies, can impose conditions limiting the duration of the meeting.

Offences under s 14:
Offences: a) Organising or taking part in a public assembly and failing to comply with a condition imposed under ***s 14(1)*** where they knew or ought to know the condition has been imposed ***(s 14(4) and (5))*** b) Inciting a participant in a public procession to commit an offence under ***s 14(5) (s 14(6))*** **Defences:** • Organisers and participants have a defence if they can show that their failure to comply with the conditions was due to circumstances beyond their control • Also a defence to prove that the conditions are invalid (e.g. if it is a very small gathering)

One-Person Protest

Section ***14ZA*** allows the police to impose conditions on a one-person protest where:

a) The senior police officer reasonably believes that the noise generated by the person carrying out the protest may result in serious disruption to the activities of an organisation which are carried out in the vicinity of the protest, **or**

b) It may have a significant relevant impact on persons in the vicinity of the protest

Police may impose conditions as appear necessary to prevent such disruption or impact

Same conditions as ss 12 and 14

Trespassory Assemblies

S 14A POA 1986 → introduces the power to ban trespassory assemblies

- 'An assembly to be held at a place or on land to which the public has no right of access or only a limited right of access' ***(s 14A(1))***
- Assembly means an assembly of 20 or more persons', and land means 'land in the open air' ***(s 14A(9))***

Imposing conditions on trespassory assemblies:

The chief officer of police must reasonably believe that it is **intended to hold a trespassory assembly**

a) **Without the permission of the occupier** or outside the terms of any permission or right of access; **and**

b) Which **may result in serious disruption to the life of the community** or significant damage to the land, building or monument which is of historical, archaeological or scientific importance.

May then apply to the local authority for an order prohibiting for a specified period the holding of all trespassory assemblies in the district or part of it (and then consent from Home Sec)

There are strict time and geographical limits on the scope of the order → can't last for more than 4 days and can't apply to an area greater than 5 miles' radius from a centre

S 14C gives a constable in uniform who reasonably believes that a person is on their way to a trespassory assembly the power to stop that person and direct them not to proceed in the direction of the assembly.

Offences:
Offences: • Organising or taking part in an assembly knowing it to be prohibited ***(s 14B(1) and (2))*** • Incitement to organise or participate in an assembly if the person knows it is prohibited ***(s 14B(3))***.

Common Law

Police also have common law powers to prevent a breach of the peace

Breach of the peace = whenever harm is actually done or likely to be done to a person or in his presence to his property or a person is in fear of being so harmed through an assault, an affray, a riot, unlawful assembly or other disturbance.' ***(R v Howell)***

Powers of Police:

The police have a variety of powers they can use to prevent a breach of the peace:

Power of arrest (also to prevent a breach of peace)

Powers to take steps falling short of arrest (e.g. ordering people to move away)

Can attend and disperse a gathering if they reasonably fear a breach of the peace

- Common law powers of entry without a warrant to prevent a breach of the peace ***(s 17(6) of the Police and Criminal Evidence Act 1984)***

The police don't need to wait until actual violence occurs and can take preventative action to prevent gatherings that could result in a breach of the peace (***Duncan v Jones***)

Impact of HRA:

- ***R (Laporte) v Chief Constable of Gloucester***: police apprehended a group of 120 anti-Iraq War campaigners who were travelling to a demonstration (transported them back to London). HoL held that:
    - The powers to prevent a reasonably apprehended breach of the peace are only available when a breach is 'imminent'
    - Relied on the ECHR principle of proportionality → police action had been premature → could have taken less drastic action
- BUT the police can, in limited circumstances, take drastic action to prevent a breach of the peace, even if it adversely impacts innocent bystanders (***Austin & Others v The United Kingdom***)

Judicial Review

Judicial Review = the mechanism by which the courts ensure public bodies act within the powers that they have been granted

- Court makes sure that public bodies make decisions in the 'right way' (not the merits of the decision)
- Concerned with the 'decision-making process', looking at whether the decision-maker has stayed within their powers and followed a fair procedure

If the court finds against a public body, it will not substitute its own decision → court will refer the matter back to the public body to make the decision again (in a lawful manner)

Justification?

Ultra vires theory:
- 'Beyond the powers'
- Judicial review *upholds the supremacy of Parliament* → ensure public bodies do not act beyond the powers conferred upon them by Parliament

Common law theory:
- Judicial review arises from the common law
- Justification lies in the principles of *good and fair administration*

Modified ultra vires theory:
- In carrying out judicial review, courts are upholding Parliamentary supremacy, as it's Parliament that grants discretionary powers to public bodies
- Assert that the courts ensure that such discretionary powers are exercised fairly and *in accordance with the rule of law*

Powers which can be reviewed?

Powers under statute and delegated legislation:

- Most powers exercised by public bodies are those which have been given to them by statute
- Government Ministers have also been given powers under statute to make delegated legislation

→ The use of these powers can be reviewed by the courts to ensure public bodies have acted lawfully

Prerogative powers:

Any executive powers (including prerogative powers) could be reviewed, provided the subject matter of those powers were suitable for review by a court (***CCSU v Minister for Civil Service***)

- There are certain prerogative powers which are considered non-justiciable

The Court Proceedings

Judicial review is dealt with by the Administrative Court (specialist court within the High Court)

1) Pre-Action Protocol:

Before starting proceedings, the claimant should follow the Pre-Action Protocol for Judicial Review (except in very urgent cases)

- Should send a letter before making a claim to the decision-maker → gives them 14 days to reconsider
    - Aim is to try and avoid unnecessary legal proceedings
- Courts will take into account any failure to follow the Protocol when awarding costs.

2) Permission Stage:

- It is at the permission stage that the court considers whether the claimant has standing and whether the claim was begun in sufficient time
- The court must *not* grant permission to apply for judicial review where the improper conduct complained of would be highly likely not to have resulted in a substantially different outcome for the claimant (***S 31(3C) of the Senior Courts Act 1981 (inserted by the Criminal Justice and Courts Act 2015***)

3) The hearing:

The substantive hearing is before a judge in the Administrative Court
The hearing is usually confined to arguments on points of law

Valid Claim?

A claim for judicial review can **only be brought against a public body** and can **only be used to challenge a public law decision**

1) Procedural Exclusivity?

The principle of procedural exclusivity requires that, in a 'public law case', the judicial review procedure should normally be followed, rather than the ordinary private law procedure

- As a general rule, it would be contrary to public policy and an abuse of process of court to allow a claimant to seek to enforce public law rights by way of ordinary action, rather than judicial review ***(O'Reilly v Mackman)***

What is a Public Body?

2-stage test to determine what constitutes a public body ***(R v Panel on Takeovers, ex p Datafin)***

a) **Source of power test**
    - Public body if the body making a decision has been set up under statute or delegated legislation, or derives its power under a reviewable prerogative power

If this isn't met, second stage:

b) **Nature of power test:**

May still be a public body, if the body making the decision is exercising a public, governmental, function

Governmental = what the situation would be if the body didn't exist

- If govt would step in and create a body with similar functions = public body

Exception - combo cases:

An exception to the 'procedural exclusivity' principle is where a case involves both private and public law

- Where a claim is based on a mixture of private rights and public law grounds, the public law element may be raised in private law proceedings (***Roy v Kensington Family Practitioner Committee***)
- A public law issue may be raised as a defence in private law proceedings → collateral challenge (***Wandsworth London Borough Council v Winder*** and ***Boddington v British Transport Police*** → for criminal cases*)*

2) Sufficient Interest?

The court will deem a claimant to have standing to bring a judicial review claim, only if they have 'sufficient interest in the matter to which a claim relates' (***s 31(3) of the Senior Courts Act 1981***) (***R v Inland Revenue Commissioners, ex p The National Federation of Self-Employed and Small Businesses Ltd***)

The question of standing is closely linked to the merits of the case

Courts are unlikely to reject a valid judicial review claim simply on the grounds of a lack of standing

Pressure Groups?

Factors to take into account when deciding if a pressure group has sufficient standing to bring a claim for judicial review (***R v Secretary of State for Foreign Affairs, ex p World Development Movement Limited***):

a) The need to uphold the rule of law
b) The importance of the issue raised
c) The likely absence of any other responsible challenger
d) The nature of the alleged breach of duty
e) The role of the pressure group

3) Within Time?

A claimant seeking judicial review **must start their claim within the given time limits**

1) **For general claims** = should be filed promptly and within a maximum of 3 months after the ground to make the claim first arose (***CPR r 54.5***) (***Finn-Kelcey v Milton Keynes Borough Council and MK Windfarm Ltd***)
2) **Planning Acts cases** = 6 weeks from the date of the decision (***r 54.5***)
3) **Public Procurement cases** = 30 days

Time limits in the Rule are without prejudice to any statutory provision which shortens the time limit (***Rule 54.5(3)***)

A court can refuse a claim where it feels there has been 'undue delay' (***s 31(6) of the Senior Courts Act 1981***)

Courts do reserve a discretion to extend the time limit, but only for good reason (***R v Stratford-upon-Avon DC, ex p Jackson***)

- For the judge to conclude whether the merits of allowing a claim outweighed the undue delay and prejudice that would be caused by granting the permission (***Hardy v Pembrokeshire CC***)

Even if permission was granted and the case proceeded to a full hearing, a remedy could be refused if the application had been made outside the three-month time limit (***R v Dairy Produce Quota Tribunal, ex p Caswell***)

4) Ouster Provisions?

Ouster clauses are inserted by Parliament into Acts where it **wishes to exclude any right of challenge once a decision has been made by a public body**

Full ouster clauses

A full ouster clause = purports to allow no right of challenge at all and attempt to exclude the courts from playing any role in review of the decision

- **BUT** won't protect decisions that were never legally valid (*ultra vires*) (***Anisminic v Foreign Compensation Commission***)
- The courts treatment of ouster clauses was 'a natural application of the constitutional principle of the rule of law' (***R (Privacy International) v Investigatory Powers Tribunal***)
    - To date, no legislation has been passed containing a full ouster clause with sufficiently 'clear and explicit words' to be upheld by the courts when challenged

Partial ouster clauses

A partial ouster clause provides **some opportunity for a decision to be challenged by way of judicial review**

- E.g. by substantially limiting the time frame for review (***R v Secretary of State for the Environment, ex p Ostler***)
    - The courts have no discretion to grant an extension, even if there are good reasons for delay (***Smith v East Elloe Rural District Council***)
- Courts have tried to find an appropriate balance between the statutory context and the inferred intention of the legislature on the one hand, and the rule of law (***R (Privacy International) v Investigatory Powers Tribunal***)

Other statutory remedies

The provision of an adequate statutory remedy for an aggrieved party (e.g. right of appeal) may impliedly oust the courts' judicial review jurisdiction (***R v Epping and Harlow Commrs, ex p Goldstraw***)

- Where a claimant had failed to make a proper use of an appropriate statutory procedure for obtaining a remedy, the court would not generally exercise its discretion to allow an application for judicial review

Grounds for Review

There are 3 grounds of domestic judicial review (*CCSU v Minister for Civil Service*):

a) Illegality (substantive)
b) Irrationality (substantive)
c) Procedural impropriety

And 2 'European' grounds:

Breach of the European Convention on Human Rights
Breach of retained EU law

Illegality

An action is illegal if it is beyond the powers of the public body in question either:

a) Because the powers claimed do not exist
b) Because they are exceeded or abused in some way

Acting without legal authority:

Public authorities cannot act without legal authority (***R v Richmond-upon-Thames LBC, ex p McCarthy and Stone (Developments) Ltd***)

- A public law decision maker will act unlawfully if it *acts ultra vires* → outside the limits of its jurisdiction

Rule against delegation:

General rule that decision-making powers, once given by Parliament, can't then be further delegated (***Vine v National Dock Laboir Board***)

- E.g. administrative duties which can't be delegated

Exceptions:

a) The Carltona principle:

Government Ministers sub-delegating decision-making powers to civil servants in their departments *was allowed*

As individual Ministerial responsibility means government Ministers are ultimately responsible for their departments, they act through their civil servants in taking decisions

BUT: wouldn't apply if it was clear from the wording of the statute that the decision was one for the Minister alone (***R v Adams***) → i.e *'only'* that secretary can make the decision

b) S 101, Local Government Act 1972:

- Local authorities may delegate decision-making powers to committees (or an individual officer), provided they make a formal resolution to do so

Fettering of discretion

If Parliament provides a public body with a discretionary power, the courts will not permit that body to 'restrict' or 'fetter' such discretion (i.e. adopting an over-rigid policy)

- Decisions taken must represent a true and proper exercise of the discretion conferred by Parliament

Fettering can occur in 2 ways:

a) Acting under the dictation of another (***Lavender & Sons Ltd v Minister of Housing and Local Government***)

b) Applying a general policy as to the exercise of discretion in too strict a manner (***British Oxygen v Minister of Technology***)
   - Anyone who has a statutory discretion must not shut his ears to an application and must be always willing to listen to anyone with something new to say
   - Decision makers may formulate policies provided they are consistent with the statute granting the power and applied in such a way that the decision maker can consider each case on its merits

Using powers for an improper or unauthorised purpose

Public bodies will be acting illegally if they use their powers for an improper or unauthorised purpose

- ***Congreve v Home Office***: Home Secretary announced an increase in TV licence fees from £12 to £18 → sought to revoke the licences of those who had acquired a new (and cheaper one) just before

  Home Office had no authority to revoke the licences (aim was to raise revenue in a way not provided for by Parliament)

Dual purposes

Situations were a public authority arrives at a decision based on more than one consideration (one which is relevant to the purpose of the power it's exercising, but the other is irrelevant)

→ Primary purpose test (***Westminster Corporation v LNWR***):

- Where there are dual purposes behind a decision, provided the permitted purpose is the 'primary' purpose → decision should stand

→ Material influence test (***R v Inner London Education Authority, ex p Westminster City Council***):

- Was the authority pursuing an unauthorised purpose, which materially influenced the making of its decision?

Taking account of irrelevant considerations

A public body must both disregard irrelevant considerations and take into account relevant considerations when exercising its powers

Robert v Hopwood: Poplar Borough Council paid its employees such wages as 'it saw fit' → generous minimum wage, applied to female workers in the same way as male workers

- District Auditor ordered the Council to make good the financial losses caused by paying its employees so generously
- HoL found the Council had taken account irrelevant considerations (socialist philanthropy and feminism) and had disregarded relevant considerations (wage levels in the labour market and burden on ratepayers)

Padfield v Minister of Agriculture: Minister of Agriculture had the discretionary power to order an investigation into complaints made about the Milk Distribution Board

Number of farmers made a complaint → Minister refused to order an investigation

HoL held that the Minister had taken into account an irrelevant consideration (potential political embarrassment for the Minister) in deciding not to exercise his discretion to order an investigation

Errors of Law

Errors of law which affect a decision will always be amenable to judicial review (***Anisminic Ltd v Foreign Compensation Commission***)

Errors of Fact

Some errors of facts are amenable to judicial review:

a) Jurisdictional errors of fact (***R v Secretary of State for the Home Department, ex p Khawaja***)
   - Decisions based on alleged errors of fact, which go to the root of a public body's capacity to act are reviewable
     - In ***Ex p Khawaja***, Home Sec made an order for removal of Khera as he was an 'illegal entrant' → got a central fact wrong → he had not tried to hide his entry into the UK
       - Was a jurisdictional error as the Home Sec wouldn't have been able to rely on the Act if Khera had been legally in the UK

b) Material error of fact leading to unfairness (***E v Secretary of State for the Home Department***):
   - 4 conditions would need to be satisfied to give rise:
     a) There must have been a mistake as to an existing fact (incl a mistake as to the availability of evidence on a particular matter)
     b) The fact must be uncontentious and objectively verifiable
     c) The person seeking review must not have been responsible for the mistake
     d) The mistake must have played a material part in the decision-maker's reasoning

Irrationality

Require proof of a very high degree of unreasonableness

Wednesbury principle:

- Test = whether the decision-maker came to a conclusion that was 'so unreasonable that no reasonable authority could ever have come to it' (***Associated Provincial Picture Houses Ltd v Wednesbury Corporation***)

NOW:

→ To be irrational, a decision needed to be 'so outrageous in its defiance of logic, or of accepted moral standards, that **no sensible person could have arrived at it**' (***CCSU v Minister for Civil Service***)

<u>*Case Law:*</u>

- ***Wheeler v Leicester City Council [1985]***: Leicester City Council opposed sporting links with South Africa (apartheid period). 3 players from Leicester rugby club were selected by England to tour South Africa
  - Club said it was up to players to decide whether to travel
  - Council decided to ban the club from using council-owned recreation ground
  - HoL: the club couldn't be punished as it had done nothing wrong → not illegal for players to go to SA

- ***R (on the application of Gardner and another) v Secretary of State for Health and Social Care [2022]***: case bought by the children of 2 residents of care homes who died of Covid in 2020

- Court held it was irrational not to have advertised in the policy document issued by the Sec of State that, where an asymptomatic patient was admitted to a care home, they should be kept apart from other residents for 14 days
    - Drafters had failed to take into account the risk to vulnerable residents from non-symptomatic transmission which had been highlighted by the Chief Scientific Adviser

Procedural Grounds

Procedural grounds focus not on the decision itself, but on the **procedure followed in *arriving* at the decision under review**

- They are about the steps leading to and the circumstances surrounding the tribunal's decision, rather than the decision itself
- Where someone breaches a statute which confers decision-making powers and procedural requirements, they are '**procedurally *ultra vires***'
- Other requirement are derived from the doctrine of 'procedural fairness' / rules of natural justice

Rules of Natural justice

The rules of natural justice are common law rules

- Comprise any requirement of procedural fairness which the courts impose as a matter of common law, rather than by applying an Act of Parliament

There are 2 rules of natural justice:

The rule against bias
The right to a fair hearing

→ Don't apply where the decision-maker has a legislative, rather than a judicial function (***Bates v Lord Hailsham***)

The rule against bias:

A decision-maker should have no personal interest in the outcome of their decision

- The application of this rule depends on whether the interest of the decision-maker is 'direct' or 'indirect'

Direct Interests:

Where the interest is direct, the court is normally obliged to automatically 'quash' the decision as bias of the decision-maker is presumed

- An interest which may lead to financial gain is a direct interest (***Dimes v Grand Junction Canal Proprietors***)
- Also can be non-pecuniary interests where the decision-maker is involved in promoting the same cause as a party to the case (***R v Bow Street Metropolitan Stipendiary Magistrate, ex p Pinochet Ugarte***)

Indirect Interests:

- E.g. where it is a relative of the decision-maker who has the interest

→ The reviewing court cannot quash the decision automatically → has to investigate the relationship between the indirect interest and the decision and decide whether the decision should be quashed on the basis of apparent bias

Use this test (***Porter v Magill***):

- ➢ Would a **fair minded and impartial observer** conclude that there had been a real possibility of bias?

<u>*Case Law:*</u>

- ***R v Pintori*** → appellant was convicted of possession of a Class A drug after a police raid. After trial, became apparent that one of the jurors was a civilian working for the police who knew some of the officers involved in the raid
  - Found that there was a real possibility that the juror and therefore the jury as a whole were biassed against him (could influence their decision)

The right to a fair hearing:

There is a duty on decision-makers to **act in good faith and listen fairly to both sides** (***Board of Education v Rice***)

- What is required to be done in order to achieve 'fairness' will depend partly upon the nature of the claimant's interest
- Will likely take into account how much the claimant had to lose (the nature of their interest)

Every claimant is entitled to a hearing which is fair and reasonable in all the circumstance (***Lloyd v McMahon***)

- There was a discretion to refuse to allow witnesses to be called or cross-examined, but that discretion must be exercised reasonably and on proper grounds (***R v Hull Prison Board of Visitors, ex p St Germain (No 2)***)

3 categories of claimant, depending on the nature of their interest (***McInnes v Onslow-Fane***):

Forfeiture Cases:

Where the claimant had the most to lose (involve the claimant having been deprived of something they previously enjoyed)

- Claimants should know the case against them and have the right to reply at each stage of the decision-making process (***Fairmount Investments Ltd v Secretary of State for the Environment***)

Case Law Example:

- ○ ***Ridge v Baldwin***: Ridge was the Chief Constable of Sussex → accused of conspiracy to obstruct the course of justice (acquitted) → trial judge still criticised Ridge for not having set a good example to his junior officers (he was then dismissed)
  - Applied for judicial review of the decision to dismiss on the grounds of procedural unfairness
  - HoL held that outcome was of special importance as Ridge stood to lose (or forfeit) his pension rights as well as livelihood

Legitimate Expectation Cases:

Where the claimant seeks the renewal or confirmation of some licence / membership / office / state benefit which they held previously

The express promise / existence of a regular working practice might give rise to **2 different types of legitimate expectation:**

Procedural legitimate expectation → a decision maker has failed to follow a normal procedure

- ○ ***R v Liverpool Corporation, ex p Liverpool Taxi Fleet Operators***: City Council had promised 300 Liverpool taxi licence holders they would be consulted if the Council granted new licences → challenged when they didn't
- ○ ***R (Save Britain's Heritage) v Secretary of State for Communities and Local Government***: legitimate expectation that the SoS would provide reasons for refusing to call in a planning application (previous promises had been made)

Substantive legitimate expectation → a decision maker has led someone to believe they'll receive a benefit:

There are 3 possible outcomes in these cases (*R v North and East Devon Health Authority, ex p Coughlan*):

a) Court may decide that the public authority is only required to bear in minds its previous policy or other representation
   - Must give this the weight it thinks right (but no more) when deciding to change course
b) Court may decide that the promise or practice induces a legitimate expectation of being consulted before a particular decision is taken (procedural from above)

c) Court may decide that to frustrate the legitimate expectation is so unfair that it would amount to an abuse of power
   - Court will weigh the requirements of fairness to the individual against any overriding public interest for the public body in changing its policy
   - Only arises where the public body had made a *specific undertaking*, directed at a *particular individual*, that the relevant policy would be continued (***R (on the application of Niazi) v Secretary of State for the Home Department***)

→ The nature of a fair hearing depends on the expectation that the decision maker created

Application Cases

First-time applicants who seek a licence / membership / office which they had not held previously

- Applicants are merely entitled to have their cases heard honestly and without bias
  - Unless a refusal casts doubt on their good character, entitled to know the gist of the case against them (***ex p Benaim and Khaida***)

Case Law Examples:

- ***McInnes v Onslow-Fane***: McInnes made 6 applications to the Boxing Board of Control for a licence → application refused on each occasion (no oral hearing or reason)
  - Found for Boxing Board as McInnes was a first time applicant

Exceptions:

Where a decision that has been made is **merely preliminary**

Lewis v Heffer → decision to suspend (not dismiss) meant option for judicial review not available → final decision hadn't been made yet

National security concerns:

CCSU v Minister for Civil Service → the right of the trade union to be consulted before a change was made to the T&C's of staff at GCHQ yielded to considerations of national security

R (on the application of Begum) v Secretary of State for the Home Department: Judicial review for refusal of re-entry to UK to appeal stripping of citizenship → requirements of national security prevailed

The right to reasons:

The law does not recognise a general duty to give reasons for an administrative decision (***R (on the application of Hasan) v Secretary of State for Trade and Industry***)

EXCEPT:

Decision appears aberrant:
Where a decision it taken which, in the absence of reasons, looks 'aberrant' (completely wrong) <u>*Case Law Example:*</u> ○ ***R v Civil Service Appeal Board, ex p Cunningham:*** was granted a much lower award of compensation for the Civil Service Appeal Board than usual (£6,500 v £15,000) ○ Should give a reason where the decision 'cries out for explanation'

Important right at stake:
<u>*Case Law Example:*</u> ○ ***R v Secretary of State for the Home Department, ex p Doody***: important for applicants, serving a life sentence for murder → only able to hear about parole once served a minimum period of imprisonment (the tariff) Set by Home Sec who decided not to follow recommendations and set a longer tariff

Imposed by statute:

Procedural ultra-vires

The wording of legislation can sometimes place statutory procedural requirements on decision-makers

- Such statutory procedural requirements are classified as being 'mandatory' or 'directory'
- Only in reference to statutory procedure, not policies

Mandatory:
Failure to comply with a mandatory requirement renders the **decision invalid** on grounds of procedural *ultra vires* <u>*Case Law Example:*</u> ***Bradbury v London Borough of Enfield***: s 13 of the Education Act 1944 required local education authorities to give notice to the public if they closed down existing schools / changed nature of a school

- Enfield failed to provide the required notice to the public when it carried out a major reform of local schools

Directory:

Failure to comply with a directory requirement does not necessarily render the **decision invalid**

Case Law Example:

- ***Coney v Choyce***: s 13 of the Education Act specifically required that notice should be given to the public in a local newspaper, in some conspicuous places and at or near the main entrance of the school concerned. The Authority did comply with the first two notice requirements but not with the third.

- Whether a requirement is mandatory or directory depends on context → court discretion to decide

To decide if a statutory requirement is mandatory or directory will often take into account:

The extent to which the public authority had attempted to comply with the procedural requirements
Whether or not a claimant is substantially prejudiced by non-compliance with an important procedural safeguard

In ***R v Soneji***, Lord Steyn suggested that courts should instead consider the consequences of non-compliance with a statutory procedure

- The court should put itself in the position of those who had enacted the legislation
- Would Parliament have intended the consequence of non-compliance with the relevant statutory requirement to be the invalidity of the decision that had been taken?

Remedies:

Judicial review remedies are discretionary

- The court must refuse a remedy if it appears to the court to be highly likely that the outcome to the claimant would not have been substantially different if the conduct complained of had not occurred (***S 31(2A) of the Senior Courts Act 1981***)

Public law remedies

Prerogative orders are the main court orders that a judicial review claimant can seek:

a) A quashing order
b) A prohibiting order
c) A mandatory order

→ Only available against public bodies

Quashing Order

A quashing order **'quashes' a decision which is ultra vires** (ie deprives the decision of legal effect)

- The court doesn't usually substitute its own decision but remits it to the decision-maker who must reconsider the decision in light of the court's judgement
- **Suspended quashing orders (SQO)** = won't take effect until the date specified in the order but, once it does take effect, that effect can be retrospective
- **Prospective quashing order (PQO)** = removes or limits any retrospective effect of the quashing order
- When deciding whether to make a SQO or PQO, court will take into account (***s 1, Judicial Review and Courts Act 2022***):
  - The nature and circumstances of the unlawfulness in question
  - The detriment to good administration that would result from exercising or failing to exercise the power
  - Any other matter that appears to the court to be relevant.

Prohibiting Order

A prohibiting order will **order a public body to refrain from illegal action** (rare)

Mandatory Order

A mandatory order is designed to **enforce the performance by public bodies of their duties**.

- E.g. to consider an application

Private law remedies

Declaration

A declaration is a court order confirming, but not changing, the legal position or rights of the parties.

Injunction

The Administrative Court can award damages on a claim for judicial review where the claimant is seeking other relief (eg a quashing order) and damages could have been awarded in a civil claim (***s 31(4) of the Senior Courts Act 1981***)

- The claimant must have a private law cause of action (eg in tort or contract) or a claim for breach of a Convention right.
- Damages cannot be awarded just because the claimant has a ground of challenge (***Dunlop v Woollahra Municipal Council*** and ***R v Knowsley MBC, ex p Maguire***)

Equity and Trusts

Introduction

Defining Equity

Equity is a body of law in its own right

- Includes not only trusts but also equitable remedies such as injunctions, dealings with land and mortgages, the administration of deceased persons, partnerships and the setting aside of written instruments

Defining Trusts

'A trust is the relationship which arises wherever a person called the trustee is compelled in equity to hold property for the benefit of some persons (beneficiaries) or for some object permitted by law, in such a way that the real benefit of the property accrues, not to the trustee, but to the beneficiaries or other objects of the trust (***Keeting and Sheridan, The Law of Trust***)

a) There is a **binding obligation** placed **on a person** - a **trustee**
b) To **look after property for** the benefit of another - **a beneficiary** (or for a purpose permitted by law)

Express Trusts:

- A settlor can <u>expressly</u> and <u>intentionally</u> create a trust
- They define the benefit the beneficiaries are to receive from the property

Legal and Equitable Interests

A trust allows the ***separation*** **of control of property from its enjoyment and use**

- The trustee has management and control of the property subject to the trust
- BUT the beneficiary is the 'real' owner → they enjoy the benefit of the property
- Equity recognises that when a trust is created:
  The trustees hold the legal title or interest in the trust property; and
  The beneficiary has an equitable interest in the trust property (a beneficial interest)

Legal Interests held by the trustee:
The trustee holds the legal title, allowing them to manage the trust property

- BUT in contrast to an outright owner, trustees are obliged to hold the property for the benefit of those possessing the equitable title
- The beneficiaries get the benefits *indirectly* by enforcing the trust obligation against the trustee

Equitable Interests held by the beneficiary

The equitable interests give beneficiaries two rights:

a) **Personal** → have a personal right to enforce the trustee's duties and seek compensation for breaches (enforceable against the trustee, personally)
b) **Proprietary** → have an ownership interest in the trust property itself
    Can be enforced against the trustee and successors in title
        Only a bona fide purchaser for value who has no notice of the beneficiaries' rights is *not* bound (would instead sue the trustees for any loss)
    The proprietary nature means that it is itself an item of property which can be sold or given away

Types of Trusts

Fixed Trusts

The terms of the trust define the share of the trust property which the beneficiary will receive:

- The trustees have no discretion as to how the trust property is to be allocated between the beneficiaries

'On trust for X for life, remainder to Y'

- **X = the life tenant**, who has a life interest → (limited trust as only receives the income from the trust, not the capital)
- **Y = the remainderman**, who has an 'interest in remainder'
- Creates a successive interest
    - When X dies, the trustees will transfer the trust property itself to Y & the trust will come to an end (absolutely entitled → receives the income and the capital)

On trust for A if A attains 21 but if A dies before then, for B:

A's interest is conditional on A attaining 21 (trustee will look after trust property for A till then)
If A dies before turning 21, A's interest fails and B becomes entitled

On trust for Z where Z is an infant or cannot manage their affairs for some other reason

- Trust is used to ensure that the property is managed by trustees for the benefit of Z

On trust for C where C is an adult with full mental capacity

- Bare trust → trustees hold on trust for a sole adult beneficiary possessing full mental capacity absolutely
- Unusual type of trust as the trustee must handle the trust property as the beneficiary dictates
- The beneficiary can end the trust at any time and become the legal owner (***Saunders v Vautier***)
- The above trusts can convert into a bare trust once the person becomes an adult with full mental capacity
- Examples: transferring a portfolio of company shares to a discretionary portfolio manager

Discretionary Trusts

Gives the trustees a discretion as to:

a) The **amounts** any beneficiary may receive **and / or**
b) Whether particular beneficiaries **receive anything at all (*Mettoy Pension Trustees Ltd v Evans [1990]*)**

- E.g. where a settlor gives property to the trustees 'to hold on trust for such of my children and in such shares as my trustees think fit'
- No individual has an equitable interest under a discretionary trust until the trustees exercise their discretion in that individual's favour
    - Until then, they are called 'objects' rather than beneficiaries

Beneficial Interests

A beneficial interest may described as any, or all of:

Vested or Contingent
In Possession or In Remainder
Absolute or Limited

Where a beneficiary's interest is vested, in possession and not limited in enjoyment = **absolutely entitled** (a sole adult beneficiary can bring the trust to an end)

Vested and Contingent Interests

Is my interest unconditional?

- If vested = yes
- If contingent = no

Vested interest = a beneficiary has a vested interest if that beneficiary exists and *doesn't* have to satisfy any conditions imposed by the terms of the trust before becoming entitled as of right to trust property

Contingent Interest = a beneficiary has a contingent interest if it is *conditional* upon the happening of some future event *that may not happen*, or if the beneficiary is not yet in existence

- If the condition is satisfied, the beneficiary's interest *then becomes vested*
- If the condition is *not* satisfied the settlor can provide for what should happen by a substitutional gift
  If they don't → resulting trust → property returns to the settlor
  The trustee will hold the trust property on a resulting trust for the settlor

Interests in possession and interests in remainder

When will I benefit?

- If in possession = now
- If in remainder = later

Interest in possession = a beneficiary has an interest in possession if they can enjoy that interest immediately

Interest in remainder = a beneficiary has an interest in remainder if they *cannot* enjoy it immediately, but instead, has to wait until some other beneficiary's right to enjoyment expires (postponed interest)

- Difference between in remainder and a conditional interest
  - E.g. if someone's interest was reliant on the death of another person, it is not conditional → the death will happen at some point (vested, but in remainder)

Absolute and Limited Interests

What do I get?

- **If an absolute interest** = income *and* capital
- **If a limited interest** = income *only*
  - E.g. if shares, only able to get the dividends from the shares
  - Never able to use the actual product (that remains controlled by the trustee's), but can receive the income benefit accrued (e.g. dividends, interest on money in savings, rent from property)

The Law of Succession

When a person dies **their estate** (all property which that person had a vested interest in) is **dealt with by their personal representatives**

- The PR's *automatically* become legal and beneficial owners of the property forming the estate of the deceased when they die
  They can then pass on legal and beneficial title to the beneficiaries
- When the PR is named in the will, referred to as executors
  - Obtain a Grant of Probate (confirmation of their authority)
- Where there is no executor, statutory rules govern who will be PR (referred to as administrators)

- Obtain a Grant of Letters of Administration (authorisation to deal with the estate)

Wills

A person who makes a will is described as testator (testatrix if female)

Requirements for a valid will:

Made in writing; and

Signed by the testator (with 2 witnesses who also sign) (***s 9 Wills Act 1837***)

A will may be altered by a later document (**a codicil**) → signed and witnessed

Gifts

- **A devise** = gift of freehold land (realty)
- **A legacy / bequest** = gift of personal property or personalty (cover everything other than realty)
- **Specific gifts / legacies / devises** = gifts of an asset or group of assets which are distinguished in the will from all other assets of the same kind (e.g. my car / my shares)
- **Pecuniary legacies** = gifts of money
- **Residuary Gift** = a gift of what remains (after debts / tax / specific legacies / devises / pecuniary legacies)
- **Gift on trust** = property given to trustees to hold on the beneficiary's behalf

Failure of Gifts

- **Ademption** = where the specific gift fails because the testator no longer possesses the specified property when they die
- **Lapse** = where the beneficiary dies before the testator

  Lapsed specific or pecuniary gifts falls into the residuary estate

  A lapsed residuary gift passes under the intestacy rules
- If a will is witnessed by a beneficiary or their husband / wife, the will is valid but the gift to the beneficiary fails (***s 15 of the Wills Act 1837***)

Revocation of Wills

A will may be **wholly or partly revoked by the testator at any time before their death**.

Can be revoked by:

The marriage or civil partnership of the testator

The destruction of the will with an intention to revoke

The making of a new will which deals with the same property as the first will

The Intestacy Rules

Intestacy rules apply to:

The whole estate if the deceased made no will at all, or

To the residuary estate if the will contains no residuary gift or it has failed or been revoked

Estate is shared between the deceased's relatives, in accordance with a specified order of entitlement (statutory next of kin)

Creating Express Trusts

Method of Creating the Trust

Voluntary settlement = a term to describe the methods of gratuitously benefiting someone

Can be done in 3 ways ***(Milroy v Lord (1862))***:

a) **Outright gift** to the donee (making a 'perfect' gift)
b) **Transfer to trustees** to hold on trust for the person to be benefited
c) **Declaration of self as trustee** for the person to be benefited

Declaration of Trust

Must make a valid declaration of trust → a valid trust can *only* exist if the settlor intends to create a trust and defines the relevant property and beneficiaries clearly

The 3 certainties test - ***Knight v Knight***

a) Certainty of intention to create a trust
b) Certainty of subject matter
c) Certainty of objects

Must also:

- Comply with the beneficiary principle
- Satisfy the rules against perpetuity
- Complete any formalities for express declarations of trust

The Three Certainties Test

Certainty of Intention:

Must be an intention on the part of the settlor or testator to create a trust

- Necessary to examine the words used by the owner
  - Did they intend to impose trustee-like duties on the recipient of the property (or themselves)
  Yes if they wanted to impose a legally binding obligation on the holder of the property to deal with the property in a certain way
- 'Equity looks to intent rather than form' → more concerned with the substance of the transaction, than the form it takes (conduct can infer intent)
  - ***Paul v Constance [1977]***: Constance lived with (but not married to) Mrs Paul → after receiving compensation for an injury, opened an account in Constance's sole name
    - Parties treated the account as their joint money → 'the money is as much yours as mine'
    - Court accepted these words and the course of conduct → express declaration of trust
- Insufficient to use 'precatory' words → e.g. 'hoping that' / 'believing that' / 'expecting' (***Re Adams and Kensington Vestry (1884)***)

Certainty of Subject Matter:

Must be a clear description of the trust property and the respective interests of beneficiaries:

a. **The settlor must identify the trust property clearly** (***Palmer v Simmonds***)
   - ***Re London Wine Company (Shippers) Ltd***: buyers of wine stored in a warehouse, but not segregated from the general stock of wine couldn't establish a trust as the subject matter was uncertain
     - Settlor had to identify which chattels (out of the collection) they intended to form the subject matter of the trust
   - ***Hunter v Moss [1994]***: shares of the same class in the same company are indistinguishable from each other → the settlor doesn't have to stipulate exactly what shares they mean
   - ***Re Lewis's of Leicester Ltd [1995]***: placing money in a separate account meant it had been segregated from general money
   - ***Mac-Jordan Construction Ltd v Brookmount Erostin Ltd [1992]***: money held on trust had not been placed in a separate bank account → not been segregated from ***Brookmount's*** other funds
   - ***Re Golay [1965]***: Must give a workable formula for calculating the amount → a beneficiary given a 'reasonable income' was sufficiently objective to provide an 'effective determinant' for the court to decide the amount to give

b. **The beneficial interests must be certain** → what type of interest each beneficiary has and what shares they will enjoy

- *Don't have to with a discretionary trust* → beneficiaries' shares are regarded as certain if they are determined by the trustees
- Where a trust is made for a group of beneficiaries and the settlor hasn't specified the shares each member is to receive, assumed to be equal
- Must make clear whether the beneficiary has a life / absolute / contingent interest

→ If a trust fails because of a lack of certainty of subject matter, there is a resulting trust back to the settlor (or estate if in a will)

Certainty of Objects:

Must be sufficient identification of the beneficiaries (the objects)

- More problematic where there is a trust for a 'class' of objects (where settlor gives a general description of the beneficiaries but doesn't name them)
- Where a trust fails due to uncertainty of objects, the trustees hold the trust property on a resulting trust for the settlor (or their estate)

Where there is a fixed trusts:

1. **Complete list test** → must be possible to draw up a comprehensive list of each and every beneficiary (***IRC v Broadway Cottages Trust [1955]***)
    1. The description of beneficiaries must have 'conceptual certainty'
    2. Must also have 'evidential certainty' → must identify each and every member of the class
        - ***OT Computers v First National Tricity Finance [2004]***: set up 2 bank accounts. One was held on trust for 'urgent suppliers' → held to be void as objects were uncertain
            - Not possible to draw up a complete list of every beneficiary of this fixed trust

Where there is a discretionary trust:

- **Given postulant' test** → The trust is valid if it can be said with certainty that any individual is or is not a member of the class → (***McPhail v Doulton***)
- The settlor must have laid down sufficient criteria in the description of objects so that it is clear what sort of person will qualify
- The burden is on the claimant to prove they are in the given class of objects
    - A discretionary trust for 'relatives' of employees and ex-employees was valid → satisfied the given postulant test as was possible to say of any individual whether they were or were not a relative (***Re Baden's Deed Trust (No 2)***)
        The term 'relative' was conceptually certain
        Whilst could be evidential uncertainty, won't make the trust fail

BUT: administrative unworkability / capriciousness:

- Administrative unworkability = where the definition of beneficiaries is so hopelessly wide as not to form 'anything like a class' (***McPhail v Doulton***) → e.g. a trust for 'everyone in the world'

- ◦ ***R v District Auditor, ex p West Yorkshire Metropolitan CC:*** A Council creating a discretionary trust for some of the inhabitants of West Yorkshire (2.5m people) was invalid → the size of the class of objects was administratively unworkable
- Capriciousness = irrational

The Beneficiary Principle

Trusts must have ascertainable human beneficiaries

Except:

- If the purpose is regarded as charitable (considered a public trust & the Attorney-General will enforce the trust on behalf of the public)
- Legacy in a will to maintain a pet

Rules against Perpetuity

The law will only tolerate trusts that last for an acceptable period:

a) Rules against remoteness of vesting

- Relevant to contingent interests and discretionary trusts
- A contingent interest is *void* unless it vests within the 'perpetuity period'
  - If came into effect before 1st April 2010 = vest within 80 years ((***Perpetuities and Accumulations Act 1964)***
  - If came into effect after 1st April 2010 = vest within 125 years (***Perpetuities and Accumulations Act 2009***)

b) Rules against inalienability:

- Applies to trusts for non-charitable purposes
- Will be void if the trust capital is not freely alienable (prevented from being transferred) within the relevant perpetuity period (21 years)

Correct Formalities

Trusts of Personalty:

- No written formalities to observe → can be oral

Trusts of Land:

S 53(1)(b), Law of Property Act:

- Trusts must be evidenced in writing

- Must contain the terms of the trust and be signed by the person able to declare the trust

Constituting a Trust

What type of property

Property = anything a person can 'own':

a) **Real Property (realty)** = freehold land
b) **Personal Property (personalty)** = all property *except* freehold land:
   i) Chattels (things in possession)
   ii) Things in action (debts, copyrights, shares, bank accounts)
   iii) Leasehold land

Expectancies

- An expectancy is not property (as there is no proprietary interest)
- It is a mere hope of ownership of property in the future (e.g. legacy under the will of someone who is alive)
- You can't transfer that which you do not own
- It is possible to conclude a binding contract to transfer such future property

Transfer legal title

In order to validly constitute a trust, the settlor must transfer the legal title to the trustee

UNLESS:

- **Settlor declares themselves as trustee** → constitution of the trust is automatic (already hold the legal title to the trust property)

Land

The transferor must execute a deed (***s 52(1) Law of Property Act 1925***) which satisfies ***s 1 of the Law of Property (Miscellaneous Provisions) Act 1989***

a) Stated / signed as a deed
b) Signed in the presence of a witness (who also signs)

Must then be sent to the Land Registry to register the transferee as the new legal owner

Shares in a company

There are 2 parallel methods of transfer of the legal ownership:

a) **Shares outside the *CREST system***
   - Shares in private companies will be outside the ***CREST system***

   1. Transferor signs stock transfer form
   2. Transferor hands completed stock transfer form and share certificate to transferee
   3. Transferee sends both docs to the company to be registered (legal title doesn't pass till registration)

b) **Shares within the *CREST system***
   - Under the ***CREST*** computerised share transfer system, owners of shares in public quoted companies may dispense with share certificates
   - Their shareholdings are recorded electronically by an organisation (which is a member of ***CREST***)
   - Transfers are recorded electronically on the instructions of the shareholder
   - Registration and transfer of legal title is immediate

Money

Bank notes are a form of **'bearer'** instrument
- The possessor / bearer has the rights conferred by the instrument
- Transfer of those rights is achieved by delivery of the note to the transferee

Cheques:
- A cheque is a revocable instruction to the donor's bank to pay the amount of money indicated to the donee upon presentation of the cheque
    - Donor can revoke by 'stopping the cheque' before presentation

Credit cards
- Are a mandate to the bank to pay the shop → instruction is immediate

Chattels

Title to chattels is passed by physical delivery of the asset to the transferee (or by deed)

- ***Jaffa v Taylor Gallery Ltd (1990) The Times***: the transfer of a picture to trustees was valid without physical delivery (the deed setting up the trust vested title in them)

Digital Assets

- Digital assets covers a wide range of asset types (ranging from NFTs to social media accounts)
- Cryptocurrency was to be treated as property

Exceptions

GENERAL RULE:
If the correct procedure *hasn't* been followed, the court will not 'save' an invalid trust (*Richards v Delbridge (1874)*)

- 'Equity will not assist a volunteer' (*Milroy v Lord)*

There are 3 exceptions:

Every effort exception
Strong v Bird
Choithram v Pagarani

Every Effort Test:

As established in ***Milroy v Lord*** in order to render a **voluntary settlement valid and effectual**, the **settlor must have done everything which was necessary to be done (every effort test)**

- Where the donor has failed to transfer the legal title, the transfer may be regarded as complete in equity if the donor has put the property beyond their recall
  - I.e. they have done everything within their control (***Re Rose [1952]***)
  - Only outstanding matters are the actions of the third parties

Strong v Bird:

Only where the donor has died

Four conditions must be met for the rule in *Strong v Bird* to apply:

a) The settlor intends to create an immediate trust to the trustee, but the trust is invalid because they fail to comply with the appropriate formality for transferring the legal title to the relevant property

b) The intention must be to make an immediate trust, not one condition on an event in the future

c) The intention to give must continue unchanged until the donor's death
   - ***Re Gonin [1979]***: mother allegedly attempted to give a house and garden to her daughter, but failed to sign a deed
     - She subsequently sold a part of the garden → indicated she still considered herself the owner

d) The settlor dies and the trustee is appointed the donor's executor or administrator

Choithram v Pagarani:

Choithram International SA v Pagarani

- An imperfect transfer to trustees is perfected if the settlor is also *one of* the trustees
- Only directly relevant where a settlor is setting up a trust and they are to be one of several trustees. When the settlor makes the declaration of trust, but doesn't successfully transfer the subject matter of the trust to all the trustees, equity will save the invalid gift
  - Their conscience is affected and so Equity will not allow them to revoke the gift

Gifts

There are 4 requirements for a valid outright gift:

a) The donor must have the necessary **mental capacity** to make a gift
b) The donor must have the **intention** (by words or conduct) to make a gift
c) The donor must ensure there is **certainty of subject matter and objects**
d) The property must be transferred to the donee in the **correct manner**

Mental Capacity:

The donor must be able to **understand the nature of the transaction and its consequences** (varies depending on the nature of the gift)

Re Beaney [1978]: a mother, suffering from senile dementia, made a gift of her house (her only substantial asset) to one daughter (disinheriting her other 2 children)
- The required degree of understanding was high
- Had to understand the claims of all potential donees (did not have such understanding)

Intention to Make the Gift
The donor must have the **intention, manifested by words or conduct, to make the gift** • Can usually be inferred from the circumstances (no need for express words) • Often the intentions of the donor have to be ascertained by the court from the circumstances

Certainty of Subject Matter and Objects
The subject matter of the gift must be certain • If the gift is by deed, the wording must be sufficiently certain • The donee (the object of the gift) must also be certain

Transferred in the correct manner
Must be transferred using the method appropriate to that type of property

In the absence of fraud or other invalidating cause, the donor has ***no* right to demand the return of a gift** (once it has been given)

- The donee now has complete control of the property

Commercial Trusts

- **A person is insolvent if they have insufficient assets to meet their debts**
  All the bankrupt's assets will vest in a trustee in bankruptcy (a representative of the creditors), whose job it is to distribute the bankrupt's assets among the creditors according to the statutory order of priority

For companies = liquidation

- The liquidator is the equivalent to the trustee in bankruptcy → gather in the company's assets and use them to repay the creditors of the company
- Must follow a prescribed order of payment for the distinct types of creditors
  1. **Secured Creditors** (those with a charge over some of the company's assets) & **Preferential Creditors** (e.g. employees)
  2. **Ordinary creditors** (i.e. unsecured and non-preferential)
     - Share available assets 'pari passu' → in proportion to the amounts they are owed

Customer Prepayments

- If a supplier goes into liquidation before delivering goods or services to a customer who has prepaid, the customer is a lowly unsecured creditor (little chance of recovering their money)
- The customer can choose to create a trust for this prepayment → ask for your money to be held on trust until you receive the goods
    - As a trustee of the money, the company would be obliged to keep it separate from its other funds

The company could also declare a trust over the customer money, pending delivery (usually in the T&C's)

- Beneficial as a director who knew or ought to have concluded that there was no reasonable prospect that the company would avoid going into insolvent liquidation is required to take all possible steps to minimise the potential risk to the company's creditors (***s 214, Insolvency Act 1986***)
    - If a court is satisfied that the necessary steps were not taken, it can order the errant director to contribute personally to the insolvent company's assets

Case Law Example:

Re Kayford [1975]

- A mail order company credited customer payments to a separate account (in order to keep them safe). BUT didn't use the words 'Trust' or 'Customer' in the name
- Able to infer certainty of intention to create a trust (didn't have to state expressly that the bank account was held 'on trust'
    - Was certain as the directors had paid the trust property into a separate bank account

Preference of Creditors:

A preference occurs if a company does anything or suffers anything to be done which puts one of its creditors in a better position on the company's insolvency than it would otherwise have been (***s 239 of the Insolvency Act 1986***). **IF**:

a) Such a preference occurs within 6 months before the onset of the company's insolvency (or 2 years if the creditor is connected to the company); **and**
b) The company was influenced by a desire to put the creditor in a better position

→ The court can make an order putting the parties in the same position as they would have been if there had been no preference

'A declaration of trust over the money of existing customers is an unlawful preference' (***Re Farepak Food and Gifts Ltd [2006]***)

- A trust created for new customers = fine
- A trust created for existing payments = unlawful preference

Purpose Trusts

General rule: 'every trust must have a definite object. There must be somebody in whose favour the Court can decree performance' (***Morice v Bishop of Durham (1804)***)

- → i.e. there must be a beneficiary

Exceptions:

a) Charitable Trusts
b) Denley trusts
c) Trusts for the care or maintenance of specific animals (***Re Astor*** and ***Re Dean***)
d) Trusts for the maintenance of graves and sepulchral monuments (***Re Astor*** and ***Re Hooper)***

→ Trusts of imperfect obligation' as there is nobody to enforce them

- Nobody can compel the trustees to carry out the purpose → can't go to court to enforce
- If the trustees do not carry out the purpose specified, the residuary beneficiaries can go to court and claim the money

The aim of a purpose trust is not to give trust property or money beneficially to anyone

- There are *no* beneficiaries who will take a share of the trust property

Requirements

Certainty of Objects:

In order to be valid, the purpose trust must be stated in terms:

'Which embody definite concepts and the means by which trustees are to try to attain them must also be prescribed with a sufficient degree of certainty' (***Re Astor's Settlement Trusts***)

- **Charity trusts do *not* need to meet the objects rule**
- For Denley trusts, it is thought that they must satisfy the given postulant test & it can't be administratively unworkable (***R v District Auditor ex p West Yorkshire Metropolitan CC***)

Perpetuities:

For non-charitable purpose trusts, must meet the **rule against inalienability**:

a) Be limited in duration to 21 years, **or**
b) Allow the trustees to spend all the trust capital on the purpose and thereby end the trust at any time

- Charitable trusts are an *exception* to perpetuity rule

Charitable (Purpose) Trusts

There are 3 requirements to make a purpose trust charitable:

a) It must have a charitable purpose
b) It must have sufficient public benefit
c) It must be *exclusively* charitable

Charitable Purpose

Section 2(1) of the Charities Act 2011 provides that a charitable purpose is a purpose which:

a) Falls within ***section 3(1)***

Section 3(1) Charities Act 2011:

Section 3(1) of the Charities Act 2011 **provides:**
A purpose falls within the subsection if it falls within any of the following descriptions of purposes -

a) The prevention or relief of poverty
b) The advancement of education
c) The advancement of religion
d) The advancement of health or the saving of lives
e) The advancement of citizenship or community development
f) The advancement of the arts, culture, heritage or science
g) The advancement of amateur sport
h) The advancement of human rights, conflict resolution or reconciliation or the promotion of religious or racial harmony or equality and diversity
i) The advancement of environmental protection or improvement
j) The relief of those in need by reason of youth, age, ill-health, disability, financial hardship or other disadvantage
k) The advancement of animal welfare
l) The promotion of the efficiency of the armed forces of the Crown, or the efficiency of the police, fire and rescue services or animal services

Public Benefit

Section 2(1) of the Charities Act 2011 provides that a charitable purpose is a purpose which has sufficient public benefit

Benefit Aspect:

The benefit aspect:

The purpose must be beneficial, and any detriment or harm must not outweigh the benefit.

If the benefit is not obvious, the Charity Commission will require evidence

There is no presumption of benefit → it must be proved (***s 4(2)***)

The Public Aspect:

The public aspect:

The purpose must be of benefit to the public in general, or to a sufficient section of the public and must not give rise to more than incidental personal benefit

The opportunity to benefit must not be unreasonably restricted

- **Restrictions must be legitimate, proportionate, rational and justifiable** given the nature of the organisation's charitable aims

☑ Geographical restriction are acceptable if related to the aims

☑ No objection if benefits are restricted according to charitable need (youth, age, poverty, disability)

☑ Restricting to personal characteristics (religion / gender) is acceptable

Personal nexus test not relevant to trusts for the advancement of religion

☑ Trusts for the relief of poverty are charitable (relief of poverty is so altruistic that the public benefit may be inferred) (***Re Scarisbrick [1951]***)

- **Not subject to the personal nexus test**

✗ Restricting the benefits to a particular geographical area was not objectionable BUT, further limiting the trust to another group within that area was (a class within a class) (***IRC v Baddeley [1955]***)

✗ Can't be restricted to those who have a personal nexus (familial relationship to given individuals - ***Re Compton [1945]***) or employment by a common employer (***Oppenheim v Tobacco Securities Trust Co Ltd [1951]***)

Unless for the relief of poverty

✗ Whilst charities can charge fees for the benefits they provide, they can't exclude a considerable number of people who can't afford to pay the fees

- Private schools must make more than a token provision for the less well-off

(*Independent Schools Council v Charity Commission for England and Wales [2011]*)

Exclusively Charitable

A trust must be exclusively charitable (***s 1, Charities Act 2011***)

- Question of degree
- Charities *are* permitted to engage in activities which are ancillary to the main charitable purposes (means of achieving their main purpose)
    - University student union voicing disagreement with and lobbying against Government policy regarding tuition fees would be acceptable (***Webb v Doherty 1991***)
    - ***McGovern v AG (1982)*** → courts held that the Amnesty International Trust was not exclusively charitable → combined charitable purposes with non-charitable purposes (procuring the abolition of torture / inhuman or degrading treatment)

Denley Trusts

Re Denley's Trust Deed [1968]

- A plot of land was transferred to trustees, to be held on trust to be maintained and used for the purpose of a sports and recreation ground for the benefit of employees of a particular company and for such other persons as the trustees might allow
- Whilst the trust was expressed as a purpose, it was directly or indirectly for the benefit of individuals (the employees)
- This benefit was sufficiently tangible to allow them to go to court to enforce the trust (so was valid)
- Must meet the requirements for a purpose trust

Quistclose Trusts

A Quistclose Trusts exists when a lender **intends to create a trust of the loan monies**, if:

a) The monies are *not* to be regarded as part of the borrower's general assets; **and**
b) *Cannot* be spent in *any way* the borrower wishes (***Twinsectra v Yardley [2002]***)

- 'For a quistclose-style trust to be created, there must be an intention to create a trust on the part of the transferor, ascertained objectively … by words or conduct and not innermost thoughts' (***Bellis v Challinor [2015]***)

Barclays Bank v Quistclose Investments Ltd [1970]

- Quistclose lent money to Rolls Razor Ltd on condition that they would use the money to pay dividends to its shareholders
- Before the dividends were paid, RR went into liquidation

- Barclays, an unsecured creditor, argued that the money formed part of RR's assets available to unsecured creditors. Quistclose claimed money was held on trust
- HoL: held a trust existed with Quistclose as the settlor and RR the trustee
  - Two-tier trust: RR held the loan money on a primary trust to pay dividends to shareholders
  - Should the purpose prove impossible → secondary trust to return money to Quistclose

Re EVTR Ltd (1987):
- Payment of loaned money to be used for new computer equipment was held on a Quistclose trust, even though the money was not held separately from general funds
- Payment into a separate bank account was a useful indicator of intention to create a trust, but it wasn't essential

Implied Trusts

Resulting Trusts

Resulting Trusts are implied where a person transfers property or money to another, in circumstances where it is unclear who owns the beneficial interest

The presumption is that the *transferee holds the property or money on a resulting trust for the transferor*

A resulting trust arises in 2 circumstances: (***Westdeutsche Landesbank Girozentrale v Islington London Borough Council [1996]***)

a) Incomplete disposal of trust's equitable interest
b) Voluntary transfer trust / purchase money resulting trust

1) Incomplete Disposal

Incomplete Disposal of a Trust's Equitable Interest

Resulting trusts of this type arise when:
a) The settlor transfer property to trustees on trust; **but**
b) Does *not* dispose of all or part of their equitable interest

→ The trustees will hold the property on a resulting trust for the settlor

<u>Example</u>:
a) Trust does not name a beneficiary who attains a vested interest
b) Attempted trust lacks certainty of objects
c) Attempted trust doesn't define beneficial interests with sufficient certainty

d) Attempted trust offends the rules against perpetuity
e) Attempted trust offends the beneficiary principle

2) Voluntary Transfer / Purchase Price

a) Voluntary transfer

A voluntary transfer occurs where X transfers property (which they own) to Y, for **no consideration**

Resulting Trust?

Where there is ***no* evidence of the transferor's intention,** the **presumption** is that the **transferee holds the property on resulting trust** for the transferor

Case Law Example:
Thavorn v Bank of Credit and Commerce International [1985]
- A women opened a bank account, in the name of her nephew (under 18)
- Gave instructions to the bank that she alone was to operate the account
- Held that the presumption was of a resulting trust → no evidence of intention to benefit the nephew

Presumption is less likely to apply for land:

No presumption of a resulting trust after a voluntary transfer of land (***Lohia v Lohia [2001]***) (***Kahan v Ali [2002]***)

S 60(3) Law of Property Act → where a voluntary transfer of land occurs, the presumption of resulting trust will not apply

b) Purchase price:

Where **X provides purchase money** for property **to be purchased *either***:
a) In the name of Y, or
b) In the names of X and Y (e.g. X provides contributions to the house deposit that is in Y's name)

Resulting Trust?

→ **Presumption that Y holds the legal title on a resulting trust for X and Y**

- Under a resulting trust, each would have an equitable interest, proportionate to their contributions (you get what you pay for)

To form a resulting trust, payments must be part of the purchase price & made at the time of the initial purchase (***Curley v Parkes [2004]***):

☑ Payment of the whole, or part of the deposit

☑ Other contributions to the purchase price, at the time of the purchase

✗ Payments of legal fees

✗ Payments of mortgage instalments and other outgoings after the date of the purchase

✗ Lending money for the deposit

Case Law Example:

- ***Abrahams v Trustee in Bankruptcy of Abrahams (1999)***: Mr and Mrs A both members of a National Lottery syndicate (15 members in total). Mrs A paid £2 per week for both of them
    - Continued to do so after they had separated
    - Syndicate won money → held that Mr A held his shares on a resulting trust for Mrs A
- ***Parrott v Parkin [2007]***: X and Y purchased a yacht, but was registered in Y's sole name (X contributed 55% of the purchase price) → held that Y held the yacht on a resulting trust for X

Or an advancement?

Presumption of advancement = where the person making the voluntary transfer or providing the purchase money is regarded as being under an **obligation** to provide for the other party

- Does *not* create a resulting trust
- Instead considered to be a gift

Requirements:

☑ **Applies in 3 situations:**

Where a father makes a voluntary transfer or purchases property in the name of his child (***Bennet v Bennet (1879)***)

- Child must be born to parents who are married to each other
- Weak presumption (especially if child is over 18 and independent) → 'judicial instrument of last resort' (***McGrath v Wallis)'***

Arises when a person in loco parentis makes a voluntary transfer or purchase property in the name of the child (***Bennet v Bennet (1879)***)

A person is in loco parentis if they have taken on a father's responsibility to provide financially for the child during their infancy

A widowed mother / single parent with financial responsibility might be regarded as in *loco parentis*

When a husband / fiancé makes a voluntary transfer or purchases property in the name of his wife (***Pettitt v Pettitt [1970]***)

Rebuttable:

→ **These presumptions can be rebutted:**

Case Law Examples:

- ***McGrath v Wallis [1995]:*** unemployed father and son both provided some of the purchase money to buy a house (in son's name only). When the Father died, the son claimed that the father's contribution was a gift (presumption of advancement)
    - Rejected as the reason why it was in son's name was because of a technicality (mortgage lenders didn't lend to Father's age group)

Marshal v Crutwell (1875): husband transferred his bank account into the joint names of himself and his wife

- Presumption of advancement rebutted by evidence that the reason for doing this was convenience (not a gift)

Warren v Gurney [1944]: father purchased a house in his daughter's name at the time of her wedding.

Rebutted presumption of a gift

Father had retained the title deeds until his death

There was also evidence that the father intended his son-in-law to repay the cost of the house

- ***Loosemore v McDonnell [2007]***: father-in-law supplied £110,000 towards the purchase of a matrimonial home for his son and daughter-in-law
    - Moved in with the couple (required 24 hour care)
    - When marriage ended, question of if it was a gift or loan
    - At time of purchase, father-in-law had confirmed he claimed no interest in the money → clear evidence that it was a gift

- ***Fowkes v Pascoe (1875)***: Expect a resulting trust, rather than a gift, when property is put in a solicitors' name

Admissible?

☑ Must be by evidence of acts done / statements made at, or before, the time of transactions

✗ Can't rely on subsequent self-justifying statements or acts (***Shephard v Cartwright [1955]***)

Constructive Trusts (Family Home)

Constructive trusts arise by operation of law, whenever the circumstances are such that it would be unconscionable for the owner of property to asset his beneficial interest (***Paragon Finance v DB Thakerer & Co [1999]***)

- The courts prefer to use constructive trusts when determining cohabitees' rights in their family home
- Used to establish present interests in property (not future interests)

Joint Legal Ownership

Where parties have purchased the home in their joint names, the **legal title *must* be held as joint tenants**

- The beneficial interest can be held as joint tenants / tenants in common

Where a trust is not expressly stated, but the legal interest was conveyed into joint names, there was a prima facie case that both the legal and beneficial interests in the property were joint and equal (***Stack v Dowden [2007]***)

Where a party wants to claim greater equitable interest in the property / assert their interest

→ Onus of proof is on the party seeking to change this presumption:

Establishing the Constructive Trust:

Must prove that the parties held a common intention that their beneficial interest would be different to their legal interests

Quantifying the Equitable Interest:

☑ The **only remedy** for a constructive trust is a **beneficial interest**

Court will look at the whole course of dealings between the parties to ascertain what shares were intended (***Midland Bank v Cooke [1995]***)

- A mathematical calculation, based on the proportion of purchase price contributed, isn't the correct approach

In most cases**, where the legal title was jointly held (but no agreement as to the beneficial interest),** the appropriate **division would be an equal one**

Rebuttable Presumption:

BUT: presumption can be rebutted (unusual circumstances) →

Either entitled to the shares which were agreed at the time the property was acquired; **or**
Entitled to the share which the court considers the parties intended each to own (regard to whole course of dealings) (***Stack v Dowden***):

i) Advice and discussions at the time of the purchase
ii) The purpose for which the house was acquired
iii) The nature of the relationship
iv) Whether resources were pooled
v) Contributions to mortgage payments
vi) Payment of outgoings such as council tax and utilities
vii) Repairs, insurance and payment for improvements.

→ The court is seeking to ascertain the intention of the parties, rather than imposing what they believe is fair and reasonable (***Fowler v Barron***)

Sole Legal Owner

(Common Intention Constructive Trust):

Establishing the constructive trust:

There is a **presumption** that the **sole legal owner** *also* owns the **equitable interest** (***Stack v Dowden***)

BUT: the claimant will obtain an equitable interest under a constructive trust if:

1) Common Intention:

There must be a **common intention** between the parties that both parties were to have an interest.

Either by:

a) **Express Agreement:**
   - ***Grant v Edwards [1986]***: there was express common intention where the legal owner had told the claimant that her name would have been on the legal title, but for the fact that it might prejudice her divorce proceedings

     Curran v Collins [2015]: giving an excuse why the claimant's name isn't on the title does not necessarily constitute an express common intention

b) **Inferred from conduct:**
   - **Conduct** = direct contributions to purchase price (initially, or by payment of mortgage instalments) (***Lloyds Bank v Rosset [1991]***)
   - Doubts on whether non-financial acts will lead to interference (e.g. household expenses)
     - Expenses will be regarded as indirect contribution to purchase price if the payments are substantial *and* made pursuant to an agreement that the parties will share the mortgage and expenses equally (e.g. one pays mortgage, one pays expenses) (***Le Foe v Le Foe and Woolwich plc***)
       - Seems like not only has there got to be a substantial financial act, also done with understanding

2) Claimant acted to their detriment:

The **claimant must have acted to their detriment** as a result of that common intention:

- ***Lloyds Bank v Rosset:*** claimant had to show that they had 'significantly altered their position in reliance on the agreement'
- ***Grant v Edwards:*** claimants substantial contribution to household expenses and bringing up the children amounted to a sufficient detriment

Quantifying Equitable Interest:

☑ The **only remedy** for a constructive trust is a **beneficial interest**

Court will look at the whole course of dealings between the parties to ascertain what shares were intended (***Midland Bank v Cooke [1995]***)

- A mathematical calculation, based on the proportion of purchase price contributed, isn't the correct approach

- Court will consider financial and non-financial factors
- Will take into account the ***Stack v Dowden*** factors:
    i. Advice and discussions at the time of the purchase
    ii. The purpose for which the house was acquired
    iii. The nature of the relationship
    iv. Whether resources were pooled
    v. Contributions to mortgage payments
    vi. Payment of outgoings such as council tax and utilities
    vii. Repairs, insurance and payment for improvements.

→ The court is seeking to ascertain the intention of the parties, rather than imposing what they believe is fair and reasonable (***Fowler v Barron***)

- Party's intention was to be objectively inferred from conduct and dealings (***Jones v Kernott)***

An initial agreement can also change over time (***Jones v Kernott***):

- ***Gallarotti v Sebastianelli:*** two friends bought a flat together → sole name of S but both made cash contributions (S provided largest) → rest in mortgage under S name. Initially agreed to a 50% share in the flat → when realised contributions unequal, G agreed to pay more of mortgage repayments
    - G did not end up paying more → court held the 50:50 sharing agreement ended → inferred agreement that beneficial ownership would reflect financial contributions

Proprietary Estoppel

1. Establishing the Equity

The legal owner must have **behaved in such a way** that the **claimant believes** they have, or **will get** at some point in the future, **some rights** in relation to the property (the expectation).

The claimant has acted to their detriment in consequence of this belief
- The promises don't have to be the sole reason for the claimant acting to their detriment
- Onus on the claimant to show the casual connection
- Can include looking after ill family member (***Greasley v Cooke***)

It would thus be unconscionable for the legal owner to insist on their strict legal ownership

Active Assurance?
Pascoe v Turner [1979]: ○ Legal owner of a house repeatedly told his unmarried partner that the house was hers ○ He was estopped from denying her an interest in the house, after she made improvements, repairs and decoration in reliance on his assurances

Inwards v Baker [1965]:

- A father persuaded his son to build a bungalow on the father's land → then unconscionable for the father to claim that, as the bungalow was on his land, it belonged to him

Passive Assurance?

Passive assurance = where the legal owner stands back and lets the claimant act to their detriment, in the belief that they are entitled to an interest in the property

Gillett v Holt [2001]:

- G worked for H for nearly 40 years (little pay) → refused offers of alternative employment because H repeatedly assured G that he would leave his entire estate to him

Thorner v Major [2009]:

- Worked for a farmer with no pay. Farmer made various oblique remarks which led to the claimant to hope and then expect that he would inherit the farm on his death

Satisfying the Equity

→ Do what is necessary to avoid an unconscionable result

- Originally, the remedy should be the minimum to satisfy the equity
- Now focus is on what is fair and proportionate as between the parties (***Joyce v Epsom and Ewell BC***)
    - Claimant's expectation is likely to be the starting point (***Davies v Davies***)
    - Can be a proprietary interest but also a monetary award

Court will take into factors such as (*Jennings v Rice*):

a) The extent of the detrimental reliance;
b) Any unconscionability, including misconduct by the claimant as well as by the defendant;
c) Any alteration in the defendant's finances;
d) Financial obligations owed by the defendant to others;
e) The effect of taxation;
f) Any benefits the claimant has derived from the situation, such as rent-free accommodation;
g) Whether the proposed remedy is practical;
h) Proportionality – is the remedy proportional to the detriment suffered?

Trust Duties and Powers

Appointment / Retirement / Removal

Appointment

A trustee may be a private individual, a professional person or a Trust Corporation

- A private trust of pure personalty can have any number of trustees
- Trusts of land can have a *maximum* of 4
- Charity Commission usually requires at least 3 trustees for a registered charity

The settlor / testator will normally appoint the original trustees

- Thereafter, they have no further power to appoint new trustees
  UNLESS: they expressly reserve that power in the trust instrument
- A trustee can disclaim their appointment, provided they do so before they have done any act showing acceptance

Appointing new trustees

S 36, Trustee Act 1925:

3 circumstances in which new trustees can be appointed:

Where a trustee is dead / remains out of the UK for more than 12 months / desires to be discharged / refuses or is unfit to act / is an infant

- Another trustee can be appointed in their place

Where a trustee has been removed under a power contained in the instrument containing the trust

- Another trustee can be appointed in their place

Where there are not more than 3 trustees

- Can appoint an additional trustee (not obligatory unless by trust instrument / statute)

Can be appointed by:

The people nominated for the purpose of appointing new trustees by the trust instrument, or
Where N/A, the current trustee(s)
Personal representatives of the last surviving or continuing trustee

The number of trustees can't be increased beyond 4 by virtue of any such appointment

Vesting of trust property in new trustees

S 40, Trustee Act 1925:

Where by a deed a **new trustee is appointed** to perform any trust, then:

a) If the deed contains a declaration by the appointer to the effect that any estate or interest in any land subject to the trust, or in any chattel or to recover any debt or other thing in action, **shall vest in the persons who become or are the trustees** for performing the trust
   - The **deed shall operate without any conveyance or assignment**, to vest in those persons as joint tenants and for the purposes of the trust the estate interest or right to which the declaration relates

Power of court to appoint new trustees

S 41, Trustee Act 1925:

1) The **court may**, whenever it is expedient to **appoint a new trustee** or new trustees, and it is found **inexpedient, difficult** or **impracticable** to do so **without assistance of the court**, make an order appointing a new trustee (either in substitution or in addition to any existing trustees)

Retirement

Retirement of a trustee (no new appointment):

S 39, Trustee Act 1925:

1) Where a trustee is desirous of being discharged from the trust and after his discharge there will either be a trust corporation or at least 2 persons to act as trustees to perform the trust
   - Then, if that trustee *by deed* declares he is desirous of being discharged
   - And his co-trustees *by deed* deed consent to the discharge of the trustee, and to the vesting in the co-trustees alone of the trust property
   - The trustee desirous of being discharged shall be **deemed to have retired** from the trust and shall, by deed, be discharged **without any new trustee being appointed** in their place

Removal

At instance of beneficiaries

S 19, Trusts of Land and Appointment of Trustees Act 1996

In the case of a trust where:

a) There is no person nominated for the purpose of appointing new trustees
b) The **beneficiaries under the trust are of full age, capacity and absolutely entitled**

2) The beneficiaries may give a direction of *either or both* of the following:
   a) A **written direction to a trustee to retire** from the trust and
   b) A **written direction to the trustee for the time being to appoint** by writing to be a trustee the person specified in the direction

Ending a Trust - Saunders v Vautier

Where there is more than one beneficiary, the beneficiaries can end the trust by calling for a transfer of trust property to themselves or to other trustees if **all the beneficiaries under the trust who could possibly become entitled** (are all absolutely entitled): (***Saunders v Vautier***)

a) Are in existence and ascertained
b) Are 18 or older and sound in mind
c) Agree

Powers of Trustees

When deciding whether trustees have power to do something, it is advisable to **look at the trust instrument first** → it may modify, extend or exclude the statutory powers

The law gives the trustees powers that enable them to **apply trust money for the benefit of the beneficiaries** *before* they have **become entitled to possession** of their share of the trust fund

a) **The power of advancement** allows trustees to apply part of a beneficiary's share of trust capital before that beneficiary is strictly entitled to receive it
b) **Power of maintenance** allows them to apply the income of the trust fund for minor beneficiaries

Power of Advancement

Section 32 of the Trustee Act 1925:

Useful when beneficiaries need trust capital earlier than they are strictly entitled to it

- It is a way of **releasing** part of the beneficiary's **entitlement to trust capital early**

→ The beneficiary has **no 'right' to an advancement**

Must be cautious when approached by parents of a young beneficiary ***(Re Pauling's Settlement Trust)***

- If there is reason to suppose that the beneficiaries are unlikely to use the money for the purpose for which it was advanced, trustees should apply the money directly for the purpose

When it can be used:

☑ **For the advancement of benefit** = 'any use of the money which will improve the material situation of the beneficiary' (***Pilkington v IRC***)

☑ Only if they have an **interest in Capital**

How it can be used:

☑ Must **bring advance into account (*s 1(b) Trustee Act 1925)***

☑ Must seek **written consent** of **beneficiary with** a **prior interest**

☑ The beneficiary has **no 'right' to an advancement** → always at trustee's discretion (even if 18+)

✗ **Can't prejudice** any persons entitled to any prior life / other interest in the money paid (*unless* they are of full age and consent in writing) (***s 1(c) Trustee Act 1925***

✗ For trusts created before 1 Oct 2014 → can only receive an advancement of **one half of their share (*s 1(a) Trustee Act 1925*)**

Once received this figure, the trustees can't give them a further advancement if the trust fund increases in value (***Re Marquess of Abergavenny's Estate Act Trusts***)

☑ For trusts created after 1 Oct 2014 → can receive an advancement of full amount of their share (***Section 9 of The Inheritance and Trustees' Powers Act 2014)***

Power of Maintenance

Where the **beneficiaries** are **<u>infants</u>**, trustees have a discretion to **apply trust income** for the **infant's maintenance, education or benefit** (*s 31, Trustee Act 1925*)

☑ **Beneficiary must have an interest in income**

☑ **Under 18** = trustees have a discretion to apply trust income for the beneficiaries maintenance, education or benefit and a duty to accumulate any income not so used

- Before 1 Oct 2014 → amount = 'reasonable amount'
- After 1 Oct 2014 → amount = 'as they see fit' (***Section 8 of the Inheritance and Trustees' Powers Act 2014)***

☑ **18 + with an immediate vested right** = trustees are under a duty to pay trust income to the beneficiary as it arises

- Their discretion whether to apply it for maintenance, education or benefit *ceases* when the beneficiary reaches 18

☒ Subject to prior interests

- I.e. if there is a life tenant

☒ 'So far only as a contrary intention is not expressed in the instrument' (***s 69(2))***

A direction in the trust instrument to accumulate the income will be treated as a contrary intention (***Re Turner's Will Trusts***)

☒ A beneficiary under a discretionary trusts has *no* individual right to the trust property or its income

Section 31 of the Trustee Act 1925:

Where any property is held by trustees in trust for any interest (vested or contingent), then, *subject to any prior interests*:

i) During their infancy, the trustees may (at their discretion), pay a reasonable income to his parent or guardian, or apply towards his maintenance, education or benefit.

   - ***Section 8 of the Inheritance and Trustees' Powers Act 2014*** amends to 'as they see fit' instead of reasonable amount (post 1 Oct 2014)

If, when they reach 18, they don't have a vested interest, the trustees shall pay the income of that property under subsection 2 of this section to him, until he either attains a vested interest or dies, or until failure of his interest

2) During the infancy, the trustees shall accumulate all the residue of that income by investing it, and any profits shall be held:

   If any such person:

   a) Reaches 18, marries or forms a civil partnership under that age and his interest in such income during his infancy is a vested interest, or
   b) On reaching 18, marriage, civil partnership, they become entitled to the property in fee simple, absolute or determinable or absolutely

Controlling the Trustees

Once the trust is set up, the settlor has *no further say* in its affairs

⟶ Responsibility for supervising the activities of the trustees **lies with the beneficiaries**

It is possible for the settlor to provide for the beneficiaries to play an active role in the trust by inserting an appropriate provision in the trust instrument

To perform duties

☑ Beneficiaries can compel the trustees to perform their duties, if necessary **by court action**

✗ **BUT**: trustees are under **no duty to exercise a power** and the beneficiaries cannot force them to do so

Cannot dictate how they perform their duty (this is in the trustees' discretion)

E.g. can insist they perform their duty to invest in authorised investments, but cannot tell them which company to invest in (that is discretionary)

With discretionary trusts, can apply to the court to ensure that the trustees select and object, but the question of which beneficiary should be selected is a discretion

Improper discretion:

☑ The court will intervene in the exercise of a power or discretion if its 'improper' (***Tempest v Lord Camoys***)

Court *will* intervene to prevent the exercise of the discretion in favour of a non-object

Will intervene where there is a capricious exercise of the trustee's discretion → i.e. it's 'irrational, perverse, or irrelevant to any sensible expectation of the settlor' (***Re Manisty's Settlement***)

✗ **BUT**: Trustees must not simply do what the settlor tells them to do. They must exercise their autonomy (***Turner v Turner***)

To see Trust Documents:

☑ Beneficiaries are allowed to see trust documents (***Schmidt v Rosewood Trust***)

- The courts have a discretion to order disclosure, even of confidential documents

✗ But they cannot demand documents that contain trustees' deliberations on a discretion or power (***Re Londonderry's Settlement***)

- This includes a letter of wishes from the creator of a discretionary trust to the trustees (***Breakspear v Ackland***)

  UNLESS:

  - Where beneficiaries have a legitimate expectation that a discretion will be exercised in their favour, they are entitled to be warned if trustees decide to change their policy (***Scott v National Trust***)
  - Pension schemes → as members pay for their benefits

Duties of Trustees

Standard of Care?

In fulfilling trustees duties, they **must exercise the appropriate standard of care**

- Traditionally this meant using such care as would a prudent man of business (***Speight v Gaunt***)
- A higher standard of care is expected of professional trustees
- There is a statutory standard of care in relation to duties involving investment and associated matters (***the Trustee Act 2000***)

Basic Duties

1) **On taking up office,** trustees owe duties to:
   a) Ensure they are properly appointed
   b) Become familiar with terms of the trust
   c) Inquire into past business of the trust to discover previous breaches of trust and to take appropriate action to remedy past breaches
2) There is a duty to **keep trust property in the joint names of all trustees** → prevent misappropriation of property
3) Duty to **invest in authorised investments**
4) Duty to **provide information** → trustees must keep trust accounts showing how the trust fund is invested and what money is going in / out

5) Trustees are ***not* under a duty to exercise powers** (only a duty to consider to exercise them)
    Don't have to explain to beneficiaries why they decided not to exercise a power / why they exercised it in a certain way

6) There is a duty to **act in the best interests of all beneficiaries** and to act **impartially** between them (e.g. between life tenant and remainderman)

7) Trustees are under a duty to **play an active role in the administration of the trust** → passive trustees can be liable for the defaults of the active trustees
    - Decisions to exercise powers should be taken unanimously

Liability for actions of other trustees:

✗ **Trustees are not vicariously liable for the acts of their co-trustees**

☑ **BUT: may be liable for failure to be active in the affairs of the trust:**

a) Trustees are liable if they leave trust property in the hands of their co-trustees
    - Trust property should be vested in the names of all the trustees to reduce the risk of theft

b) Trustees are liable if they leave the affairs of the trust in the hands of a co-trustee without enquiry

c) Trustees are under a duty to watch over, and, if necessary, to correct the conduct of their co-trustees ***(Styles v Guy)***

d) Trustees are liable if they are aware that a co-trustee is committing a breach of trust, but do nothing to stop it happening

Investments

Aim of investments

- A person may **invest money in order to produce income / capital growth**
    - **Income** = regular receipts
    - **Capital growth** = the profit investors see when they sell the investment for more than they paid for it
- To strike a fair balance between a life tenant and remainderman, the trustees must ensure that the trust investment produce capital growth and income
    - Income only = accounts with banks, building societies etc.
    - Capital returns only = antiques, land
    - Income and capital = shares, govt stocks

Investments under the Trustee Act 2000

Trustees have a **duty to invest trust money only in authorised investments**
- If the trustee instrument is silent, statute governs what the trustees can invest in

The Trustee Act 2000 gives trustees:
a) Unfettered powers to invest and
b) Powers to employ experts to manage the trust investments

→ Applies to all trusts, whether created before or after (*s 10*)

Beneficiaries can only recover compensation from trustees if their breach of duty has **caused loss to the trust** (***Nestle v National Westminster Bank***)

Authorised Investments

S 3 of the Trustee Act 2000:
- Trustees can make any investment that they could make if they were absolutely entitled to the assets of the trust
    - They can choose to invest in anything at all
    - Investment = if it's expected to produce income or capital growth (***Harries v Church of England Commissioners***) (a car is a depreciating asset so wouldn't count)
    - Can also lend money (provided they obtain a mortgage over the borrower's land)

Section 8:
- Trustees can purchase freehold or leasehold land as an investment
    - Can purchase a property and let the beneficiaries live there

Specific Investment Duties

S 4 of the Trustee Act 2000:
When exercising a power of investment, trustees may have regard to the 'standard investment criteria':

a) **Suitability**:
Must decide whether its appropriate for the trust to invest in public company shares
Must be satisfied that the particular investment proposed is a suitable example of its type (in respect to the interests of the beneficiaries)

b) **Diversification**

- Must consider the need for diversification of investments as far as is appropriate to that trust

c) **Advice** (*s 5*)

Trustees must obtain and consider proper advice about the way they should exercise their power of investment, having regard to the standard investment criteria unless the trustees reasonably conclude that in the circumstances it is unnecessary or inappropriate to do so

Not obliged to follow the advice they receive, but must give that advice proper consideration

d) Review:

- Must from time to time review trust investments and consider whether they should be varied

Statutory Duty of Care:

S 1 of the Trustee Act 2000:

- Trustees must exercise **such care and skill as is reasonable in the circumstances**
  - Will vary according to the trust (e.g. size)
  - The standard expected depends on the special knowledge or skill the trustee has
  - A higher standard is expected of a professional trustee acting in the course of their business
- For **investments**, trustees must exercise the same standard of care as would a reasonable business person when investing for someone for whom they felt **morally bound** to provide
  - A trustee's failure to keep pace with inflation and average performance of company shares over a particular period was *not* a breach of its duty of care (***Nestle v National Westminster Bank***)
  - A trustee is *not* liable for an investment decision unless it is one which no reasonable trustee (with similar knowledge and skill) would make (***Wight v Olswang (No 2)***)
  - Also not liable for just one bad investment → court will look at the performance of the whole trust
- Trustees' performance is judged according to investment policies at the time

Investment duties under general law

- Trustees are **subject to fiduciary duties** not to place themselves in a position where their personal interests conflict with their duty to the trust and not to make an unauthorised profit
- Trustees must put aside their social, moral and political views when deciding how to invest → duty to act in the best interests of the beneficiaries (***Cowan v Scargill***)
- **4 circumstances when trustees may take ethical considerations into account:**
  a) Where an investment in an ethical concern yields as good a return as investment in a less ethical company
  b) If the beneficiaries are all adults with very strong views against an ethical concern (rare)

c) For charitable trustees to invest in a company whose objects are directly opposed to the purpose of the charity (***Harries v Church of England Commissioners***)
d) The settlor can provide in the trust instrument or will that trustees are not to invest in certain sectors

Delegation

Traditionally, equity would *not* allow trustees to delegate their powers to an agent (***Turner v Corney)***

Current law: 'the law is not that trustees cannot delegate: it is that trustees cannot delegate unless they have authority to do so' (***Pilkington v IRC***)

Collective Delegation:

Collective delegation = where **all the trustees** want to **delegate *some* of their functions**

Delegable functions?

☑ Can delegate most functions which **relate to the administration of the trust:**

- Trustees can delegate decisions such as whether to sell or lease trust land and whether to sell or replace trust shares
- The receipt of dividends on trust shares and the preparation of tax returns can be delegated (***s 11(2)***)

✗ **BUT**: Trustees *cannot* **delegate the power to appoint new trustees** (***s 11(2)(C))***

✗ *Can't* **delegate 'dispositive' powers or discretions** which involve the distribution of trust capital or income among beneficiaries

- For discretionary trusts, trustees *cannot* delegate any functions relating to whether (or in what way) any assets of the trust should be distributed (***s 11(2)(a)***)
- This includes powers to give capital and income to beneficiaries under powers of maintenance and advancement

→ Where delegation is permitted, trustees can pay the agent reasonable remuneration out of the trust fund (***s 32***)

Protections

- ***Section 13(1) and (2)***: any agent appointed must comply with the conditions attached to those functions (e.g. seeking advice)
- ***Section 15***: there are special restrictions on appointing an agent to fulfil asset **management functions**:

  Must enter into a written agreement with the agent (***s 15(1)***)

- The agent should agree to observe the terms of the policy statement (***s 15(2)(b)***)

Trustees must provide the agent with a written policy statement to ensure the agent does not adopt an inappropriate investment strategy (***s 15(2) and (4)***)

- Must set out the investment objectives of the trust and how the agent is to exercise the delegated functions
- Should ensure the functions are exercised in the best interests of the trust (***s 15(3))***

- ***Section 16***: permits the vesting of trust property in nominees
- ***Section 21 and 22***: trustees must regularly review the performance of agents and nominees
- ***Sch 1, para 3***: the s 1 duty of care applies to delegation
- ***S 12(3)***: trustees cannot appoint a beneficiary, *unless* the trust is of land

Liability of trustees for defaults of agents:

- Where an agent causes loss to the trust, the trustees may be able to sue the agent for negligence or breach of contract and hold any damages on trust for the beneficiaries
- **Trustees are not vicariously liable for the defaults of their agents**:
  - The beneficiaries would have to show that the trustees have breached their duty of care as regards the initial appointment or review (***s 23***) *and* this caused loss to the trust (would then be able to sue trustees)

Individual Delegation:

If a trustee is going abroad for a time / ill for a prolonged period, they ***should* appoint an agent to take over their duties while they are unable to act as a trustee**

- Make the appointment by executing a formal document (power of attorney)
- Can either give the attorney unlimited powers to do any act which you were capable of, or can delegate specific acts

Section 25, Trustee Act 1925:

1) A trustee may, by power of attorney, delegate the execution or exercise of all or any of the trusts, powers and discretions vested in him as trustee either alone or jointly with any other person.

2) A delegation under this section:
   b) Continues for a period of 12 months or any shorter period provided by the instrument

4) Before or within seven days of giving a power of attorney, the donor shall give written notice of it.
   - Must specify the date on which the power comes into operation, its duration, the donee of the power, the reason why the power is given and if only some are delegated, the trusts, powers and discretions delegated to:

a) Each person who under the instrument creating the trust has power to appoint a new trustee
b) Each of the trustee

BUT: failure to comply with this subsection shall not invalidate any act done or instrument executed by the done

7) The donor of a power of attorney shall be liable for the acts or defaults of the done in the same manner as if they were the acts or defaults of the donor

- Again, can't delegate distributive duties (***s 11(2)(a), Trustee Act***)
- It is possible to appoint a sole co-trustee to be an attorney

Fiduciary duties

Breaches of Fiduciary Duty

Is there a 'fiduciary' relationship?

The relationship between trustee and beneficiary is fiduciary
→ Trustees are subject to certain negative obligations to prevent them acting in their own interests when making decisions for the trust (***Bray v Ford***)

- 'A fiduciary is someone who has undertaken to act for or on behalf of another in a particular matter in circumstances which give rise to a relationship of trust and confidence' ***(Bristol and West Building Society v Mothew)***

Types of Fiduciary Duties:

- **Status-based fiduciaries** → fiduciary label attaches to their office (e.g. personal reps, agents, partners, directors and senior employees with access to confidential info)
- **Fact-based fiduciaries** → where the courts decide that a fiduciary relationship exists (***LAC Minerals Ltd v International Corona Resources Ltd / Murad and another v Al Saraj and another)***

Did the fiduciary breach their duties?

A trustee will breach their fiduciary duty when they **place themselves in a position** where their **duty to the trust conflicted with their interest**

Trustee as a Purchaser

2 possible situations:

a) The trustee purchases trust property from themselves and their co-trustees

b) The trustee purchases the equitable interest of a beneficiary

Trustee purchases trust property:

Where a **trustee buys property from themselves and the other co-trustee:**

- They will be acting on both sides of the transaction
- Conflict between their duty to get the best price for the property and their personal interest in buying the property for a low price
- Where the settlor anticipates that a trustee may wish to purchase trust property, the trust instrument should authorise the transaction in question

Self-dealing rule:

- Courts are *unwilling* to consider whether the trustee has gained an unfair advantage (***Ex p Lacey***)
- The sale is **voidable** by the beneficiaries within a reasonable time
    - If they decide to avoid the sale, they must refund the price and expenses in return for the property

To ensure the sale the trustee could:

a) Seek a court order authorising it

b) Seek the consent of the beneficiaries

Trustee purchases the equitable interest of a beneficiary

E.g. where the trustee purchases the life interest or remainder from a beneficiary

There is a presumption of undue influence

A beneficiary can avoid such a transaction, *unless* the trustee can show that it was **fair** and there was **no undue influence** (**fair-dealing rule**)

Trustees must ensure that:

a) They disclose all material facts to the beneficiaries *before* the purchase

b) The transaction is fair and honest

c) They can show that they took no advantage, and that the beneficiary exercised an independent judgement and was not the subject of undue influence

Competition with Trust

Where a trustee includes a business and a trustee sets up their own business in competition, the trustee is accountable for any profits made out of the competing business

- Can get an **injunction** to prevent the trustee from carrying on the competing business (***Re Thomson***)

Unauthorised Remuneration of Trustees

Trustees can recover out-of-pocket expenses from the trust fund (e.g. cost of travelling to trustees' meetings (***s 31(1)(a), Trustee Act 2000***)

Basic rule → **trustees *cannot* demand payment** for their **services unless *authorised* by**:

a) **Charging clause** in the trust instrument
b) **Beneficiaries' consent** → if the beneficiaries are all *sui juris*, they can agree to pay the trustees remuneration
   - Unless the agreement is fair and the trustee makes full disclosure of all relevant facts, the beneficiaries can set it aside later
c) **Court order** → court has inherent jurisdiction to authorise remuneration
   - Courts should order remuneration if it's in the interests of the beneficiaries (e.g. if they need the trustees skills and fees aren't excessive)
d) **Trustee Act 2000** → law permits professional trustees to charge fees
   i) ***S 29(2)(a) of the Trustee Act 2000*** → necessary for the trustee to act in a professional capacity
   ii) ***S 28(5)*** → the trustees act 'in a professional capacity' where they act in the course of a profession or business which consists of or includes the administration of trusts, or particular types of trusts or particular aspects of such administration
   iii) ***S 29(2)*** → a trustee who is not a trust corporation can charge fees, only if all the other trustees agree in writing
      - *Can't use this act if a sole trustee*
   iv) ***S 29(5)*** → can't use this act if 'any provision about trustees' entitlement to remuneration has been made by the trust instrument'
   v) ***S 29(3)*** → Able to charge 'reasonable' remuneration → considering the nature of the services, the trust, the attributes of the trustee who is seeking to charge

Incidental Profits:

Trustees must account to the trust for any **personal profit they gain from the use of the trust property**, or from **exploiting information or an opportunity** that arose by virtue of the trusteeship

Remuneration from a third party

E.g. where a trustee receives **commission after entering a certain transaction**

- Trustee will have to account for the commission, unless the trust instrument authorises trustees to keep it (***Williams v Barton***)

Where a **trustee becomes a director in a company that the trust has shares in**

- If they would have been appointed as a director, *regardless* of the shares votes the trust had, *don't have to account* → became a director independently of the trust shareholding (***Re Gee***)
- If they were voted as a shareholder, *because of* the trust's shares → became a director by virtue of being a trustee → *will have to account* to the trust for the salary (***Re Macadam***)
- If they became a director *before* they became a trustee, can keep salary (***Re Dover Coalfield Extension***)

Renewal of trust leases

Keech v Sandford:

Trustee held a lease on trust for an infant → lease expired → landlord refused to renew the lease in favour of the trust → granted the lease to the trustee personally

Trustee had to transfer the lease to the trust and account for the profits they had made

Trustee was strictly liable for breaches of fiduciary duty

- Courts will not inquire into the merits of individual cases (deterrent and evidential difficulties (he said she said))

Extended to renewals of trust leases as well (***Don King Productions Inc v Warren and Others***)

Use of information and opportunities

A trustee is accountable for **profits made out of information or opportunities that they receive by virtue of being a trustee**

Boardman v Phipps → Boardman (trust's solicitor) and T (testator's son) were acting as proxies for 2 active trustees. Attended a shareholders meeting for a private company where they gained valuable information

- Purchases shares in the company in their own name (had gained authorisation from the 2 active trustees)

  - Held that the trustees had not authorised the profit correctly → when they consented, they did not have all the information before them
- Defendants found liable for breach of fiduciary duty → found to be fiduciaries as purported to act for and represent the trust in their negotiations (self-appointed agents)

Authorisation?

There are steps which trustees can take to authorise a personal profit

☑ Trustee could obtain the consent of all the beneficiaries (if they are *sui juris*) and the consent must be fully informed and given freely

Remedies?

The exact nature of the remedy for breach of fiduciary duty **depends on the facts**
Common objective is to strip the trustee of any possible profit or personal gain

Beneficiaries have an option of a personal claim or a proprietary claim to the property representing the profit (***FHR European Ventures LLP v Cedar Capital Partners LLC***)

Personal remedy = fiduciaries must 'account for' any unauthorised profit which they make (e.g. commission, money from information gained etc…)

- Requires a trustee to pay compensation equal to the amount of the unauthorised profit from their own funds (even if trust has not had a loss)

Proprietary claim = action to recover property which you own

- E.g. to recover shares
- Useful in bankruptcy situations → has priority over the fiduciary's creditors

Two sets of tracing rules:

a) Common law
   - If a company brings a common law action, can only use common law tracing rules
   - Can identify an asset through changes in form
   - BUT cannot identify the claimants property, once it has been mixed with other property ***(Taylor v Plumer)***
   - Also breaks down where funds are transferred between banks electronically ***(Agip (Africa) Ltd v Jackson)*** → common law tracing can *only* follow a physical asset

b) Equitable:
   - Can identify the company's property, even after mixing or an electronic transfer (as above)

Remedies against Trustees

A breach of trust occurs if a trustee does any act which the ought not to do and / or fails to do any act which they ought to do

Beneficiaries have 2 options:

a) **Personal claim** → if the breach of trust has caused loss to the fund → beneficiaries can sue the trustees for compensation
b) **Proprietary claim** → claiming the return of property owned by the trust

Personal Claim	Proprietary Claim
☑ The defendant does *not* hold any trust property nor its replacement	☑ The defendant trustee is bankrupt • A personal claim would make the beneficiaries ordinary creditors on the defendant's bankruptcy • A proprietary claim would allow the beneficiaries to recover their property in full (ahead of the creditors) - The unauthorised profit will be held on a constructive trust for the beneficiaries
☑ The trust property misappropriated by the trustee has gone down in value	☑ Where the property representing the missing trust fund has increased in value • If only did a personal claim, would just be granted the initial expense
	☑ Where the breach took place some time ago • Personal claims are often statute barred after 6 years (proprietary claims are not subject to statutory limitation)

Personal Claims

Establishing the Claim

In order to sue a trustee for compensation for breach of trust, a beneficiary *must prove*:

a) The trustee has breached one of their duties; **and**
b) That breach has caused loss to the trust

The court will then:

Order the trustee to restore the trust fund to the value it would have had, *but for* the breach; **and**

Will order the trustee to pay interest at the rate of 1% above minimum lending rate (or the rate allowed on the court's short-term investment account)

As a general rule, the courts do *not* allow a trustee to set-off the profit made on one breach of trust against the loss incurred on another breach

- Set-off is permitted where the profit and loss arise from the same breach or 'transaction' (***Bartlett v Barclays Bank Trust Co Ltd***)

Contribution and Indemnity:

Where 2 + trustees are ***both* guilty of a breach of trust** causing a loss, they are **jointly and severally liable**

- Beneficiaries can choose to sue both of them or one only for the entire loss
- May both be guilty where one has caused the loss and the other has failed in their duty by acting as a passive trustee, e.g:
  - Trustees are liable if they leave the affairs of the trust in the hands of a co-trustee without enquiry
  - Trustees are under a duty to watch over, and, if necessary, to correct the conduct of their co-trustees ***(Styles v Guy)***
  - Trustees are liable if they are aware that a co-trustee is committing a breach of trust, but do nothing to stop it happening

A trustee who is sued for the entire loss could either:

Claim a Contribution:

A trustee could claim a contribution from their co-trustees who are in breach of trust under the ***Civil Liability (Contribution) Act 1978***

- The court may order such a contribution as is just and equitable having regard to the extent of each trustee's responsibility for the loss
- (Probably where they can't claim the full sum back)

Seek an indemnity:

Seek an indemnity under equitable rules from their co-trustees who are in breach:

- E.g. where a co-trustee fraudulently obtained a benefit from the breach

- Where the co-trustee received trust property and used it for their own benefit ***(Bahin v Hughes)***
- Where a trustee blindly follows the advice of a co-trustee who is a solicitor, can recover a full indemnity (***Re Partington***)
    - Would have to prove that the solicitor exerted such a controlling influence that they did not exercise their own judgement ***(Head v Gould)***

Defences

There are 4 defences for trustees:

a) Knowledge and consent of beneficiary
b) ***S 61 of the Trustee Act 1925***
c) Express exemption clause
d) Limitation and laches

Knowledge and consent of beneficiaries:

'The beneficiaries need not know that what he is concurring in is a breach of trust, provided that he fully understands what he is concurring in' ***(Re Pauling's Settlement Trust)***

- Beneficiaries must be an adult and give consent freely with full knowledge of the relevant facts
- ***S 62 Trustee Act 1925***: where a trustee commits a breach of trust at the instigation / request / consent in writing of one beneficiary, the court has a discretion to impound some / all of the beneficiary's equitable interest to meet the claim
    - Court will consider whether the beneficiary benefited / intended to benefit from breach

S 61 of the Trustee Act 1925:

Section 61 provides that the court **can relieve trustees of liability if**:

a) They acted honestly and reasonably; and
b) Ought fairly to be excused in respect of the breach and omitting to obtain directions of the court ***(Santander UK PLC v RA Legal Solicitors)***

- Courts are reluctant to grant relief to professional trustees (***Bartlett v Barclays Bank Trust Co Ltd (No 2))***
    - Even if they have taken advice (***National Trustee Co of Australia Ltd v General Finance Co)***
- Courts are also unlikely to relieve breaches committed as a passive trustee → would encourage trustees not to be active in trust business

Exemption Clause:

The person creating the trust can include a clause relieving trustees of liability

Limitations:

Actions in respect of any breach of trust **cannot be brought after the expiration of 6 years** from the **date on which the cause of action accrued *(s 21(3) of the Limitation Act 1980)***

- Where the beneficiary is in remainder, the time doesn't start to run until their interest falls into possession

BUT, under *s 21(1)* won't apply:

a) To a fraudulent breach of trust to which the trustee was a party / privy
b) To recover from the trustee trust property in the possession of the trustee, or previously received by the trustee

Laches:

The equitable doctrine of laches (where there is no statutory limitation period (***s 36 (2) Limitation Act)*** → court will not allow a claimant to succeed where it would be inequitable

Claimants who have acquiesced in the breach for a prolonged period, resulting in the defendant acting to their detriment, may be barred from claiming

Preventing a Breach - Injunctions:

Injunction = equitable remedy in the form of a court order which either compels or restrains a party from doing a particular act

- Failure to comply = contempt of court

Types of Injunctions:

Perpetual prohibitory injunction → awarded after a full-trial case

Mandatory injunction → orders the performance of an act

Interim search order → made without notice to the defendant (to try and obtain evidence)

- Claimant must prove that they have a strong *prima facie* case and that there is a risk of serious potential damage
- Must be clear evidence that the defendant has incriminating evidence and that there is a real possibility that it will be destroyed if the court refuses the injunction

- Claimant must provide an undertaking to pay damages if they lose the case

Freezing order → prevents the defendant from dissipating or removing assets from the jurisdiction
Must have a strong case and give an undertaking in damages

Proprietary Claims

Beneficiaries can bring proprietary claims to recover:

a) Trust property which a trustee has misappropriated, or
b) To acquire an unauthorised profit which a trustee holds on a constructive trust.

Possible because the beneficiaries have an equitable interest in the property

Only possible if the trustee *still* holds the trust property or replacement property

Tracing:

Where the trustee has stolen trust property and then **changed its form** → equitable tracing enables the claimant to identify the trust property through its changes of form

Clean Substitution

The trustee may exchange the trust property for another asset in a clean substitution

Beneficiary can either (*Re Hallett's Estate*):

a) Take the property which has been acquired with the trust property
b) Take a charge over the acquired property for the amount belonging to the trust (equitable lien)
    - Allows the beneficiary to insist that the property is sold and then use the funds to be paid back the amount that was taken (only allowed to recover the amount that was taken, doesn't matter if property has increased in value)

Purchase with mixed funds:

Where a trustee buys an asset using part of their own money and part trust funds

Beneficiary could elect to either (*Foskett v McKeown*):

Claim a **proportionate share of the asset** (corresponding to the proportion of the misapplied trust fund to the purchase price of the asset)

- More advantageous where the mixed asset has increased in value

Enforce a lien (charge) upon the asset to secure their personal claim against the trustee for the misapplied money

Would be for the precise amount of money taken from the trust (plus interest)

Is a secured debt so has priority over ordinary creditors if bankrupt

Withdrawal from Mixed Account:

When a trustee mixes trust money with their own personal funds in a bank account and makes withdrawals

1. Held that a trustee is deemed to spend their own money first → any balance remaining in the account belongs to the trust (***Re Hallett's Estate***)
2. New approach in ***Re Oatway*** → aims to protect the innocent party's money
    - The wrongdoer's money is deemed to be spent on what has been dissipated
        - The beneficiaries' claim had to be satisfied from any identifiable part of the mixed fund before the trustee could set up their own claim
    - Beneficiaries can gain a lien over the property, equal to the trust money spent on them
3. As ***Re Oatway*** didn't deal with an asset which had increased in value, can use ***Foskett McKeown*** → beneficiary should be entitled to a proportionate share of the mixed asset, including any increase in value
    - But didn't deal with money passing through a mixed account → topic is open

Where an asset has been purchased, but there is also enough money left in the bank account to cover the trust fund, unclear which should be used to satisfy the beneficiary's claim

Repairing the breach?

Where a trustee *subsequently* pays their own money into account *after* they dissipate the money, this is *not* regarded as replacing the trust money (***Roscoe v Winder***)

- Beneficiaries cannot claim the additional injection unless the trustee showed an intention to restore the trust funds
- Sometimes referred to as the 'lowest intermediate balance' rule → the beneficiaries *cannot* claim anything above the lowest balance to which the account sank after the trust money was paid in

Mixing of 2 Trusts

Where a trustee mixes money from Trust Fund A and Trust Fund B, the beneficiaries of both trusts will bring claims against the mixed fund

Clean Substitution:

The beneficiaries of each trust **share ownership of the shares *pari passu*** → in the proportions as they contributed to the purchase

- *Neither* trust is allowed to claim a charge over the mixed asset for the amount of their trust fund which has been misappropriated

Purchase with mixed funds:

- The first money to be paid in is also the first money to be paid out ***(Clayton's Case)***
- Won't apply when ***(Barlow Clowes International Ltd (In Liquidation) v Vaughan)***:
  It would be impractical (difficulty / expense in ascertaining the order of payments)
  Where it would result in an injustice
  Where it would be contrary to the parties' intentions

Mixing trust fund with own account:

- First apply the rules in ***Re Hallett*** and ***Re Oatway*** to allocate withdrawals from the account
- Then apply ***Clayton*** to the balance → first in first out
- ***Barlow Clowes v Vaughan*** → 'the use of the rule is a matter of convenience and if its application in particular circumstances would be impracticable or result in injustice, it will not be applied if there is a preferable alternative'

Payments in	Account	Payments out
	£	
Ralph's own money	10,000	
White trust money	30,000	
Brown trust money	20,000	

Account	Payments out
60,000	
(10,000)	Withdrawal of £10,000
50,000	Ralph dissipates the £10,000. The rule in *Re Hallett* is applied to guilty trustees. Ralph is deemed to dissipate his own money first. None of the £50,000 remaining in the account belongs to Ralph; it is all trust money.
(20,000)	Withdrawal of £20,000
30,000	According to the rule in *Clayton's case*, the White money was the first in and is, thus, the first out. Therefore, the White trust would have a charge on Ralph's house to recover the £20,000.
(5,000)	Withdrawal of £5,000
	According to the rule in *Clayton's case*, this was White money. Thus, the painting belongs to the White trust.
25,000	The remaining balance of £25,000 belongs:
	£5,000 to the White trust
	£20,000 to the Brown trust.

Remedies against Third Parties

Trustees or fiduciaries who breach their duties may be assisted by others / may transfer property to others in breach of trust or fiduciary duty

- These people are often called **'strangers'**

May want to bring a claim against a stranger when:

a) The trustee is bankrupt
b) The trustee owns *no* assets
c) A professional stranger may have insurance
d) The trustee's whereabouts are unknown
e) Option for a proprietary claim

Personal Claim against Strangers

Strangers are liable to account as though they were trustees → only duty was to account for and restore the trust property (***Williams v Central Bank of Nigeria***)

The **beneficiaries of a trust / fiduciary relationship may sue a stranger** or third party personally **if they can establish**:

a) Accessory liability
b) Recipient liability
c) Intermeddling

Accessory Liability

Also described as 'dishonest assistance'

Liable if they **dishonestly assist a breach of trust / fiduciary duty**

Must be active assistance in the breach (***Brinks Ltd v Abu-Saleh***)
Stranger must be dishonest → requires 'conscious impropriety' (advertent conduct) (***Royal Brunei Airlines v Tan***)

- Defendant was liable if they knew they were assisting some illegal scheme (don't need to know the details / that it's a breach of trust) (***Barlow Clowes v Eurotrust)***

1) Objective standard of honesty

They must have not acted as an honest person would have acted in the circumstances

2) Subjective Factors

Will then assess how a hypothetical honesty person would have acted, knowing the facts the defendant actually knows

Take into account the defendant's experience and intelligence, and the circumstances in which the activities occur

→ Can bring a **personal claim** against the accessory liability for **compensation equal to the value of the property misappropriated** from the trust (plus interest)

- Won't be able to bring a proprietary claim as don't hold trust property themselves

Recipient Liability

Also referred to as 'knowing receipt'

Recipient liability arises when:

1) Trustee transfers trust property to a stranger in breach of trust

2) The stranger received the property for their own benefit

3) Received the property with requisite degree of knowledge

The stranger must receive the property with the requisite degree of knowledge that the transfer of the property was in breach of trust or fiduciary duty, or they later acquired that knowledge and then dealt with the property in a manner inconsistent with the trust or fiduciary duty

- The stranger is not liable *unless and until they have knowledge* of the breach of trust when they dissipated the property

Unconscionability:
It is necessary to show that the defendant's knowledge made it unconscionable for them to retain the property (wider than dishonesty) (***BCCI v Akindele***) Wilfully shutting one's eyes to the obvious or wilfully failing to make enquiries would constitute such knowledge (when it's obvious that something is wrong) Recipient liability requires 'conscious impropriety' on the part of the defendant constructive notice was not sufficient - I.e. where the defendant doesn't actually appreciate that the property is stolen, but a reasonable person would have deduced this from the facts / prompted to make enquiries (***BCCI v Akindele***)

→ Can bring a **personal claim** against the recipient liability for **compensation equal to the value of the property misappropriated** from the trust (plus interest)

Intermeddling

Referred to as a '**trustee de son tort**' (a trustee of his own wrong)

Where someone who is *not* a trustee does acts characteristic of a trustee, they will be liable for any misapplication of trust property / other loss caused to the trust just as if they had been appointed as an express trustee (***Mara v Browne***)

- Strict liability applies
- An agent of the trustee continued to collect rent from the tenants of the trust properties after his instructions ceased on the death of the trustee ***(Lyell v Kennedy)***

Proprietary Claim against Strangers

Where the trustee has transferred the property to a stranger in breach of trust, a **proprietary actions may be brought against the stranger**

- Aim would be to recover the property or its replacement

Bona Fide Purchaser

Where the stranger is a bona fide purchaser having bought the property from the trustee • A bona fide purchaser **takes the property *free* from beneficiaries' equitable interests** • Can't bring a proprietary claim against them

A Wrongdoer

Where the stranger is liable as a recipient or intermeddler (**wrongdoer**):

- Beneficiaries *can* bring a proprietary claim against them to recover trust property or its replacement
- Can also bring a personal claim
- Use the same rules as when you trace against a guilty express trustee

  Clean substitution = claim asset

  Mixed asset purchase = claim proportionate share or lien (***Foskett v McKeown***)

  Allocation of withdrawals from mixed bank account = ***Hallett / Oatway***

An Innocent Volunteer

Where the stranger is an innocent volunteer (had no knowledge or notice of the breach of trust and provided no consideration for the transfer)

- Proprietary claim can be brought against the innocent volunteer **(kinder tracing rules)**
- No personal claim can be brought against an innocent volunteer

Clean Substitution:

Able to recover the property

Purchase using mixed fund:

Purchase of an asset out of a **mixture of trust money *and* the volunteer's own funds**

- Equity has to choose between 2 innocent parties
- The trust and the innocent volunteer share the asset in proportion to their contributions to the purchase price
- Beneficiaries *not* able to elect for a lien over the mixed asset for the amount of trust money lost (disadvantage where the property has decreased in value) (***Foskett v McKeown***)

Withdrawals from a mixed fund:

Withdrawals from a current bank account containing a mixture of money belonging to the volunteer and trust

- First in first out rule applies (***Clayton's Case***) → the first payment into the account is deemed to be the first payment out

BUT: Defences:

Innocent volunteers will have a defence if they can show that tracing and the resulting proprietary claim would **produce an inequitable result** (***Re Diplock***)

- E.g. where the innocent volunteer has contributed land and the trust has contributed to improvements, tracing *does not* produce equality of treatment
  The sale of the land to satisfy the changes will deprive the volunteer of the land

Law of Organisations

Business Structures

Types of Businesses:

Incorporated Business

An incorporated business exists as a separate legal entity from its owners and managers. Including:

a) Limited Company
b) Public Company
c) Limited Liability Partnership

Have their own distinct legal personality → can assume rights and obligations

Owners are generally *not* liable for business debts

If it fails, the members lose the money they invested in the company (but no more) → they have limited liability

MA 2: Only if the shareholder has not paid the full amount that they agreed to invest can they be asked to contribute (up to the unpaid amount)

Unincorporated Business

Run by individuals who have *not* set up a separate legal entity to run the business. Including:

a) Sole Traders
b) Partnerships
c) Limited Partnerships

Have full personal liability for the debts of the business (can be made bankrupt if cannot pay)

Other Types

- **Companies limited by guarantee** = usually for organisations not seeking to make a profit (shareholder guarantees the company's debts, up to a specified amount)
- **Community interest companies** = a LLC intended for businesses that wish to use their profits & assets for the public good, not private profit
- **Charitable incorporated organisations** = allow for advantages of a corporate structure, without burden of dual regulation (Registrar of Companies & Charity Commission)
- **Overseas companies**
- **Companies established by Act of Parliament or Royal Charter** = only 45 still in existence (generally historic)

- **Joint ventures** = a commercial enterprise, undertaken jointly, by two or more parties
    - Retain their own identity, but pool their resources for a specific purpose
    - E.g. Google and NASA developing Google Earth
    - Can be governed by contract or a corporate structure (controlled jointly)

How to decide

Take into account:

- Liability
- Tax
- Formalities
- Publicity of information
- Finance

Partnership

General Partnerships

Under ***s (1) of the Partnerships Act 1890*** → a partnership comes into existence **when 2 or more persons are 'carrying on a business in common with a view of profit'**

- Partners can be individuals or companies
- The partnership **does *not* have a separate legal personality** from that of the partners

Factors which can determine if there is a partnership include:

Do the individuals all take part in the decision making
Whose names are on the title deeds of any property
How are profits shared

Partnership Agreement

The PA 1890 provides a default contract governing the relationship between the partners (unless they agree their own terms)

Can be written or oral or implied by conduct
Certain sections *can't* be overridden by agreement:

Ss 1 and 2 → govern when a partnership comes into existence
Ss 5-18 → cover the relationship between partners and third parties

Name

The name can't:

a) Include limited, 'ltd', 'limited liability partnership', 'LLP', 'Public Limited Company' or PLC
b) Be offensive
c) Be the same as an existing trademark
d) Contain a sensitive word or expression or suggest a connection with govt or local authorities, without permission

Place and Nature of Business

- Often will rent or buy premises
- Agreement may set out the partnership's place of business, area of geographical operation and nature of business

Commencement and Duration

A partnership begins when the definition in *s 1* is satisfied (commencement of business activities)

- Useful to insert a date to clarify
- Some partnership agreements can have a fixed term (usually when the purpose is to achieve a specific aim)
    - If they continue working after the expiry date, they are presumed to be partners on the same terms as before (***s 27 PA 1890***)

Work Input

- Partners may take part in the management of the business, but they are *not required to do so*
- Partnership agreements should set out each partner's working hours
- A common clause is to state that a partner must devote the whole of their time and attention to the business
- Can state that they cannot engage in any other business (also a non-compete clause)
    - Non-compete clauses can be implied by default under ***PA 1890***
- Agreement should set out holiday entitlement, sickness and maternity and paternity leave (not included in the ***PA 1890***)

Roles

Partnership agreement should set out each partner's role → can restrict what they are allowed to do

Under **common law**, partners **owe a duty of the utmost fairness and good faith** towards one another:

Ss 28-30:

a) Must be completely open with one another regarding any relevant information about the partnership
b) Must account to the firm for any private profits the have earned, without the other partners' consent from any transaction concerning the partnership
c) Must not compete with the firm → if they do so without consent, must account for and pay over all profits made in that competing business

S 24:

Must bear a share of any loss made by the business, in accordance with the terms of their partnership agreement

Indemnify fellow partners who have borne more than their share of any liability or expense connected with the partnership

Decision Making

All **decisions** in a partnership must be **taken by majority** (***s 24 PA 1890***).

Except:

a) Changing the nature of the business (***s 24 PA 1890***).
b) Introducing a new partner (***s 24(7) PA 1890***).
c) Changing the terms of the partnership agreement (***s 19 PA 1890***).

→ Must be made unanimously

Financial Input

Partners will usually all contribute a sum of money to enable it to start operating (classed as capital)

Agreement should set out the partners' initial capital contributions and whether they will be obliged to contribute more capital in the future

Can also take out a bank loan

Shares in income & capital profits and losses

Under ***PA 1890***, partners **share equally in the capital and profits** of the business (***s 24(1)***)

- Initial capital = money partners contribute to the business
- Capital profits = one-off gains
- Income profits = profits which are recurring in nature (trading profit / rent)

Often, where parties have **contributed different amounts**, they will **decide to own capital profits in those proportions**

Can be inferred from a course of conduct that the partners own capital profits in unequal shares

Partners' share of income profits will depend on their working hours (if can't agree, under s ***24(1) PA 1890*** will share equally)

Drawing and salaries

- The **income profits** which partners receive are **known as drawings**
- Partnership agreement should set out how much each partner is allowed to 'draw down' in any given period (usually a month)
    - Absence of agreement = share equally
- Sometimes also receive a salary to reflect the work they do
    - But don't have a right to remuneration ***(s 24(6))***

Ownership of assets

Partnership agreement must set out how the assets the partnership uses are owned

Building and land will have title deeds to show the legal owners

Stock and machinery won't have title deeds

Expulsion

- Under default provisions, no majority of partners may expel another partner unless the partners have expressly agreed to this
- Most partnership agreements will contain an expulsion clause (linked to poor performance)

Dispute Resolution

- Include a provision that in the event of a dispute, the partners must use arbitration / another form of dispute resolution rather than formal court methods

Dissolution

Where the contractual relationship between the partners comes to an end.

How:

PA 1890:

Under PA 1890 when:

A partner retires (***s 26***)

On expiry of a fixed term (***s 32***)

By the death or bankruptcy of any of the partners (***s 33***)

If the partners give notice of dissolution to a partner who has (by order of the court) granted a charge over their share of the partnership property, for a debt owed by them alone and not the partnership as a whole (***s 33***)

Automatically if something happens which makes it unlawful for the business of the firm to be carried on (***s 34***)

By the court:

Through an application to the court if:

a) A partner becomes permanently incapable of performing their part of the contract
b) A partner's conduct is calculated to be prejudicial to the business
c) A partner wilfully or persistently breaches the partnership agreement
d) The partnership can only be carried on at a loss
e) The court thinks that it is just and equitable to order that partnership to be dissolved

Own Provisions:

Own provisions:

- ***S 32 and 33*** can be disapplied by the partnership agreement
- **Partnership at will** = a partnership which continues indefinitely until notice is given
- No need for a notice of dissolution to be of a certain length of time or to be in writing
    - A partner can end the partnership with immediate effect orally
    - → Means most agreements should include notice provisions
        - Will often include provisions that can't retire during first year of trading
- Retirement = when a partner leaves a partnership

Effects of dissolution:

Automatic dissolution means that the partnership must end → all assets must be sold and the outgoing partner has to receive their share

Partial dissolution = where it is stated in the contract that in the event that a partner leaves, the remaining partners will continue in the partnership

- Should also be a provision setting out whether the other partners must buy the outgoing partner's share, or if it remains just an option, how it should be valued and what should be paid
- If the agreement doesn't address the issue of payment for the outgoing partner's share, they are entitled to either interest (at a rate of 5% per annum) on the value of their partnership share, until they receive their share from other partners

Goodwill:

Goodwill = a **business's reputation** and the **value of its clients and contacts**

- Commonly 2 years profit is taken as the value for goodwill
  - Beneficial to put in agreement terms that build in some time for partners to find a buyer so that it can be sold as a going concern
- If the partnership's assets are sold individually, goodwill *will not* be part of the equation

Distribution of Proceeds of Sale:

Under ***s 44,*** when a partnership is sold, the **process of sale are as follows**:

1) Creditors of the firm must be paid in full (if there is a shortfall, partners must pay the balance from their private assets)
2) Partners who have lent money to the firm must be repaid the amount of the outstanding loan
3) Partners must be paid the share of the partnership's capital to which they are entitled
4) Any surplus is shared between the partners in accordance with the terms of their partnership agreement

Restraint of Trade:

A **restraint of trade** clause will only be enforceable if it protects a legitimate business interest and is no wider than is reasonable to protect that interest (duration / geographical area / scope)

It is a blanket description which includes:

a) **Non-compete clauses** → prevent former partners from competing with the partnership business
b) **Non-solicitation clauses** → prevent former partners from soliciting business from the partnership's clients or offering employment to their employees
   - Customers / employees can approach them
c) **Non-dealing clauses** → prevent the outgoing partner from entering into contracts with clients, former clients or employees of the partnership that have just left (both ends)

Liability to Third Parties

→ **Firm will be liable to the third party under the contract if:**

There is actual authority:

S 6: firm is bound by any contract or deed entered into by partners in the firm's name, provided that their actions were authorised by the partners:

a) May have **acted jointly** in making the contract
b) **Express actual authority** → may have expressly given permission to enter into a particular transaction / instructions to enter a contract
c) **Implied actual authority** → impliedly accepted that one or more of the partners have the authority to represent the firm in a particular type of transaction (e.g. regular course of dealings which aren't objected to)

There is apparent authority:

Firm may be liable for actions which were *not* actually authorised, but which may appear to an outsider to be (agency law):

a) Where the transaction relates to business of the kind carried out by the firm (objective)
b) The transaction is for which a partner in such a firm would usually be expected to have the authority to act on (objective)
c) The other party to the transaction didn't know that the partner didn't have the authority to act (subjective)
d) The other party deals with a person whom they know or believe to be a partner (subjective)

The partner who has made the firm liable (through their apparent authority) is liable to indemnify the other partners for any liability or loss which they incur

Personal Liability

S 10 PA 1890: the firm is liable for any wrongful act or omission of a partner, who acts in the ordinary course of the firm's business or with the authority of their partners

Liability for partnership debts:

Before leaving the partnership:

Each partner is jointly and severally liable with the other partners for debts incurred by the partnership, while they were a partner (***s 9 and 17***)

- A claimant can sue any or all of the partners

After leaving the partnership:

Once a partner has left the partnership, they will remain liable for debts incurred while they were a partner

Will escape liability for any debts entered into after they had left the partnership (as long as they comply with ***s 36*** requirements):

a) Anyone with whom the firm has dealt with before must be given actual notice of the partner in question leaving (directly)
b) Anyone who hasn't had dealings with the firm must also be notified (by placing a notice in the ***London Gazette***) → acts as a notice to the world
c) Unless leaving partnership by death / bankruptcy (no notice needs)
   The estate of the deceased or bankrupt partner is not liable for partnership liabilities incurred after the death / bankruptcy

Holding Out:

Holding out = when a **creditor** of the partnership has **relied on a representation** that a **particular person was a partner in the firm**

May be able to hold that person liable for the firm's debts (***s 14***)
Even if the person had never been a partner / had retired before the contract was made
Can be oral / in writing / by conduct
Representation can be made by that person / another person (if it was made with the person's knowledge)

3 criteria:

A representation
- If made by someone else, must be with the former partner's knowledge

Reliance on the representation
The consequent giving of credit

Novation agreements:

Novation agreement = when a **retiring partner is released from an existing debt**, by entering into a **contract with the creditor and the other partners** (or an incoming partner)

- Should be consideration for the creditor's promise to release the retiring partner from the liability or contract must be executed as a deed
  - Rare as this reduces the number of people the creditor can sue if the partnership doesn't pay the debt → most common in ongoing loans, very rare for one-off debts
- Different to an indemnity which is an agreement between the retiring partner and the other partners (firm's creditors aren't party to this agreement so can still sue the retired partner who will then claim from the indemnifying partners to meet the liability)

Limited Liability Partnerships

Limited Liability Partnerships Act 2000 (LLPA 2000)

- Hybrid between a company and a partnership
- The individual partners are *not liable* for the debts of the entire LLP
  - In an LLP, each member is only liable to the extent that they contributed to the assets of the LLP (similar to that of a shareholder of a limited company)
- Members of an LLP are agents → act on behalf of the LLP in business transactions ***(s 6(1))***
- An LLP will not be bound on a contract where (***s 6(2))***:
  a) The member had no authority to enter into the contract; and
  b) The third party knew that the member had no authority / didn't know or believe that they were a member
- An LLP is a legal entity in its own right so subject to its own liabilities
- LLP's are run with the informality and flexibility given by a partnership and the partners are taxed as if the business were a partnership, rather than a company
- Individual members of the LLP must register with the HMRC as self-employed

The Limited Liability Partnerships Regulations 2001 provide a default contract for an LLP

Legal Requirements:

Members

An LLP must have at least 2 members on incorporation & 2 designated members who are responsible for filing documents at Companies House

- If at any time the number of members reduces to 1 & it carries on for more than 6 months → person is jointly and severally liable for any of the LLP's debts incurred from that period onward

Designated members have **powers similar to directors in a company**:

a) Signing and filing the annual accounts with the Registrar
b) Appointing, removing and remunerating the auditors
c) Filing the annual confirmation statement

d) Sending notices to the Registrar of Companies
e) Winding up the LLP

They also owe fiduciary duties to the LLP (duty of good faith, a duty to account for any money received on behalf of the LLP and a duty to the other members to render true accounts & full information on matters concerning the LLP)

- Considered agents (***s 6 LLPA 2000***) → limitations can be placed on their actual authority
    - Principal of apparent authority functions in same way as with general partnerships

Changing membership is governed by the LLP Agreement
If a new member joins, must deliver a notice to the Registrar of Companies within 14 days of appointment
If someone leaves, must also notify Companies House

Incorporation

- Must file form LL IN01 at Companies House with the application fee

Name

- Must end with 'LLP' or 'Limited Liability Partnership'
- Similar restrictions to those on companies
- Can change its name at any time, with the consent of all the members

LLP Agreement:

Capital and Profits

The default position under LLP Regulations is that members of the LLP share equally in the capital and profits
- No default provision regarding losses (as they are borne by the LLP itself)
    - LLP members risk losing capital contributions
- Can enter into an agreement to change these provisions

Management and Decision Making

- The default rules provide that every member may take part in the management of the LLP & members are not entitled to remuneration for taking part in management

- Changing the nature of the business & changing the terms of the contract between members can only be done by unanimous consent
- Most disputes between members relating to the day-to-day management decision can be resolved by a simple majority

Leaving the LLP

- Under LLP Regulations, members can leave the LLP by giving reasonable notice to other members
- Can't be expelled under default provisions

Limited Partnerships

There must be **at least one general partners who has unlimited liability for partnership debts**

- An LP is permitted to have a limited partner whose liability is limited to the amount they initially invest in the business (***Limited Partnerships Act 1907***)
- The limited partner must not:
    a) Control of manage the LP
    b) Have the power to take binding decisions on behalf of the LP
    c) Remove their contribution to the LP for as long as it's in business
- If they break these rules, they will lose the protection of limited liability & treated as a general partner with unlimited liability
- Must be registered with the Registrar of Companies before they can start trading

Public Company

A public company (plc) is a **company limited by shares which has complied with the requirements** of the *CA 2006*:

a) The **constitution** must state that it is a public company
b) The words '**public limited company**' or 'plc' must be included at the end of the name
c) Must obtain a trading certificate as proof that it can trade and borrow and that it's met the allotted share capital requirements
d) The company's **owners** must invest a specified minimum amount of money for use by the company (***ss 761 and 763 CA 2006***)
    Must be at least £50,000
    Each allotted share must be paid up to at least a quarter of its nominal value, plus the premium on it (***s 585 CA 2006***)

There's a set of Model Articles tailored to public companies (***Sch 3 to the Companies (Model Articles) Regulations 2008 (SI 2008/3229)***)

These apply unless the applicant provides bespoke or amended articles (*s 20 CA*)

Benefits:

- Able to raise money by offering shares to the public
- Can also apply to join the stock market (main ones are the London Stock Exchange's Main Market and the Alternative Investment Market)
    - Allows companies to raise large sums of money as investors buy the company's shares quickly and easily
- A company must reach a certain size, reputation or level of growth before being a plc
- Publicly traded companies are more regulated than private companies to protect public who may invest
- Unlisted public companies can also offer shares to the public, but because their shares are not listed, it's harder to find buyers

Converting to a Public Company:

Must pass a **special resolution** approving the re-registration of the company (*s 90(1)(a) CA*)

- Must alter the name (to include plc) and the company's articles
- Must also satisfy the share capital requirements
- A trading certificate is not required → Companies House will not re-register a private company as a public company unless it has satisfied the same conditions regarding its allotted share capital that it would have to show in order to obtain a trading certificate

Must file at Companies House:

The special resolution
An application for re-registration on ***Form RR01*** (including a statement of compliance)
The fee for re-registration
The revised articles
A balance sheet and a written statement from the company's auditors & a valuation report on any shares which have been allotted for non-cash consideration between the date of the balance sheet and the passing of the special resolution

→ Companies House will then **issue a certificate of incorporation**, proving the company's existence and status as a public company (*s 96 CA*)

Private Limited Company

Main features:

The people who set up a company are known as **promoters**

1. Companies have a separate legal personality → the people who own and run it are separate to the company itself (***Salomon v A Salomon and Co Ltd [1987]***)
2. The individuals who own the shares are not usually liable for its debts (limited to the amount they paid for the shares)
3. The business assets are owned by the company, it is managed by the directors, the company is party to the contracts and the company is liable for debts incurred

Piercing the corporate veil:

"Piercing the corporate veil" refers to a situation in which courts put aside limited liability and hold a corporation's shareholders or directors personally liable for the corporation's actions or debts.

The corporate veil can only be pierced when a person is under an existing legal obligation or liability, or is subject to an existing legal restriction which he deliberately evades or whose enforcement he deliberately frustrates, by interposing a company under his control (***Prest v Petrodel Resources Limited and others [2013]***)

- Can then only be pierced so as to deprive the company or its controller of the advantage that they would otherwise have obtained by the company's separate legal personality

Typically very rare for the court to ignore separate legal personality

Forming a Ltd

To incorporate a new company, the applicant must:

☑ Complete and submit ***Companies House form IN01*** and

☑ A memorandum of association to Companies House

- There's a list on the Companies House website of over 100 company formation agents
  - They have the requisite software to complete an application to register a company online
- Law and accountancy firms may already have a shelf company the client can use, to avoid the need to set up a company from scratch
  - Company which has already been set up (usually with 2 directors and 2 shareholders)
  - Directors and initial subscribers of the shelf company will be employees of the law firm

Certificate of incorporation:

☑ A company **comes into existence upon the certificate of incorporation being issued** (*ss 15(4) and 16(2) CA 2006*).

The certificate must state:

a) The name and registered number of the company
b) The date of its incorporation
c) Whether it's a limited or unlimited company (and if so, by shares or guarantee)
d) Whether it's a private or public company
e) Whether the company's registered office is in England, Wales, Scotland or Northern Ireland

Decisions to be Made

Name

The IN01 requires the applicant to insert the company name

- The company name must not be the same as an existing company (*s 66 CA 2006*)
    - An applicant can only register a 'same as' name if the proposed new company will be part of the same group with the existing name
- A company can't use a name which the Secretary of State for Business, Energy and Industrial Strategy ('BEIS'), would constitute a criminal offence or be offensive (*s 53 CA 2006*)
- Company's which suggest a connection with a govt department / authority must get approval from the Secretary of State for BEIS (*s 54 CA 2006*)
- Name containing certain sensitive words or expressions must be approved by the Secretary of State for BEIS

    Including words which refer to geographical areas / regulated professions
- Certain letters, characters, signs, symbols and punctuation cannot be used in the company name (under the ***Names Regs 2015***)
- The name can't exceed 160 characters, including spaces.

Companies can trade using a different name to their registered name (trading name) → don't need to register

Registered Office

Company needs a registered office (*s 86 CA 2006*) and must put address on IN01

- Must be publicly available
- Must be in the same part of the UK that they are registered

- A board resolution is required to change the company's registered office (***s 87 CA 2006***)
- Registered office is where certain records must be kept (board and general meeting minutes)

First Directors

Applicant will need to decide who the company's directors will be & **include their name and date of birth on IN01**

- Every company must have at least one director who is a natural person (human) (***s 155(1) CA 2006***)
- Directors must be over 16 (***s 157 CA 2006***)
- A director's service address (where official docs should be sent) & their residential address must be in ***IN01***
    - If directors do not want their residential address to be available to SPAs or CRAs, they can make an application for it to be kept private
    - There must be a serious risk of violence or intimidation to the director or a member of the director's family in order for Companies House to accept the application

Company Secretary

Private companies *don't* have to have a company secretary (***s 270 CA 2006***)

- If they choose to have one, their name and a service address must be inserted on ***IN01***

First Shareholders

The company's **first shareholders are called subscribers**

- Their names, addresses and details of their shareholdings must be entered on the ***IN01***
- No maximum number of shareholders

Statement of Capital

Need to **include information about the shares on the IN01**:

a) The number of shares of each type the company has and their total nominal value (share capital)
b) The name and addresses of all shareholders (subscribers)
c) Information about what rights each type of share gives the shareholder (prescribed particulars):
    - What share of dividends they receive
    - Whether they can exchange their shares for money
    - Whether they can vote on certain company matters
    - How many votes their shares entitle them to

Company Constitution

Company's Constitution (*s 17 and 29 CA 2006*) includes:

Memorandum of Association:

- Statement that the subscribers wish to form a company and agree to become shareholders (signed)
- Should be in the form set out in the ***Companies (Registration) Regulations 2008***

Articles of Association:

- Notice period for board meetings, rules for directors etc…
- Set of standard articles (Model Articles of Association) → avoid having to start from scratch
  Apply by default if don't provide their own (***s 20 CA 2006***)
- Shareholders can amend the articles by special resolution (***s 21(1) CA***)
    - Must be passed by a majority of at least 75% (***s 283(1) CA***)
    - Must file a copy of the amended articles at Companies House within 15 days of them taking effect (***s 26(1) CA***)
    - Must also file a copy of the special resolution to amend the article (***s 29 and s 30 CA***)

a) **Certification of incorporation**

b) **Current statement of capital**

c) **Copies of court orders and legislation altering company's constitution**

d) **Shareholders resolutions**

The provisions of a company's constitution bind the company and its members (***s 33 CA***)

- Normally described as creating a 'statutory contract' between the members and the company and between the members themselves

People with Significant Control

The IN01 form requires the applicant to state whether, on incorporation, there will be **someone who will count as a person with significant control** (individual or corporate body) (***s 790C CA***)

Control is deemed significant if the person:

a) Holds more than 25% of the shares in the company, or
b) Holds more than 25% of the voting rights in the company

c) Holds the right to appoint or remove a majority of the board of directors of the company.

The applicant must tick the relevant box on the form to show that the person holds:

More than 25% but not more than 50% of the company's shares/voting rights

- Can block special resolutions on their own
- If they have exactly 50%, could also block ordinary resolutions

More than 50% but less than 75% of the company's shares/voting rights

- Can block and pass ordinary resolutions on their own (but can't pass special resolutions)

75% or more of the company's shares/voting rights

Can pass special resolutions alone

→ Reflects the percentage of shares needed to block or pass ordinary or special resolutions

Post-Incorporation

Chairperson

- Under ***MA 13***, the chair has a casting vote in the event of a board resolution being tied

Bank account

- No obligation for companies to have a bank account (but is practically necessary)
- Complete a bank mandate

Company seal

- *Not compulsory* but may choose to have one to look more official
- May adopt one by board resolution (***s 45(1)***)
- ***MA 49***: where a company seal is used to execute a document, the document must also be signed by at least one authorised person in the presence of a witness who attests the signature

Change of Name

- If the company is a shelf company, the directors will want to change the name
  - ***S 77 CA 2006:*** a company changes its name by a special resolution of the shareholders or by other means provided for in the company's articles
- When a company changes its name, it must file ***form NM01*** at Companies House, along with a copy of the special resolution and the applicable fee.

- Companies House will then issue a new certificate of incorporation (***ss 80-81 CA 2006***)

Accounting Reference date

- The accounting reference date (the date up to which it must prepare its annual accounts), will be the last day of the month in which the company was incorporated (***s 391(4)***)
- To change the accounting reference date, the company will have to pass a board resolution
  - Can either extend or shorten its accounting reference date
  - Will then need to complete form ***AA01*** and file it at Companies House (s 392 CA 2006)
- The accounting reference date *cannot* be extended so that the accounting reference period lasts more than 18 months
- It *cannot* be extended less than five years after the end of an earlier accounting reference period of the company that was also extended

Auditor

All companies **must prepare annual accounts** (***s 394 CA 2006***)

Under ***s 477 CA 2006***, companies which are classed as small companies under ***s 382 CA 2006*** are exempt from audit provided that certain conditions are satisfied

Service Contracts

Service contracts are employment contracts for directors.

Will set out the terms of the director's employment, including duties, responsibilities, working hours, salary, holidays and duration of the contract and any notice period

If the service contract is to be for a guaranteed term of more than two years, it must be approved by ordinary resolution of the shareholders

Tax Registrations

Companies House will automatically notify HMRC of the registration of the new company

HMRC will then send to the company's registered office address an introductory pack concerning the tax affairs of the company.

Directors should arrange for the deduction of income tax from salaries under the PAYE scheme, and for the payment of National Insurance contributions by the employees

Most businesses, except those with a very small turnover, must register for value added tax (VAT) with HMRC

- The directors will approve the applications for tax registration at the first board meeting

Directors

Types of Directors

Director = any person occupying the position of director, by whatever name they are called (***s 250(1)***)

All companies must have at least one director (***s 154(1) CA***) who is above 16 (***s 157***)

Public companies must have at least 2 (***s 154(2) CA***)

Now every director must be a natural person (***The Small Business, Enterprise and Employment Act 2015 / s 156A CA)***

Directors are either executive directors or non-executive directors

- **Exec directors** = have been appointed to the board of directors and also have an employment contract with the company (a service contract)
- **Non-Executive Directors** = appointed to the board, without service agreements (no salary, but receive directors' fees)

The board has the power to decide what services the company's directors undertake (MA 19)

Chairperson:

Directors may appoint a director to chair board meetings by board resolution (***MA12(1)***)

- Will also have a casting vote at board meetings (***MA13***)
- Will also chair general meetings if they are present and willing to do so (***MA39(1)***)

De Facto and Shadow Directors:

- **De facto director** = acts as a director although they have never been appointed, or validly appointed (***s 250(1) CA***)
- **Shadow director** = a person who has not been formally appointed as a director, but who the directors of the company are accustomed to act in accordance with (***s 251(1) CA***)
  - Typically act in the background
  - Have a great deal of influence and control over the other directors' actions in practice

Sole Directors:

In companies with only one director, they can still validly take company decisions as they won't be entitled to call board meetings (***MA 7(2)***)

Service Contracts

The **board of directors can decide on the terms of a director's service contract**:

a) Have general powers to run a company (***MA 3***) &
b) Specific power to decide on director's remuneration (***MA 19***)

Director's service contracts must be available for inspection by shareholders during their term and until a year after termination (***s 228 CA***)

- Shareholders also have the right to inspect them without charge & within 7 days of requesting to see them (***s 229 CA***)

Long term service contracts:

Long-term service contracts (guaranteed term of 2+ years) must be approved by the shareholders by ordinary resolution (***s 188 CA***)

- It's the guaranteed term element of the contract that requires authorisation (not the overall length)
    - A ten year service contract with a notice period of 1 year doesn't need authorisation by ordinary resolution
    - A 3 year fixed term service contract with no provision for early termination would
- When the board proposes such an ordinary resolution, it must keep a copy of the memorandum setting out the terms of the proposed service contract at the registered office for 15 days prior to the general meeting & at the meeting (***s 188(5)***)
    - If the ordinary resolution is proposed by written resolution, a copy of the memorandum & written resolution must be circulated to the shareholders

Decision making

- ***MA 3*** → the company's directors are **responsible for the day-to-day running of the company**
- ***MA 5*** → the directors can delegate their powers as they see fit, so employees will be allowed to make decisions within their job description

Board Meetings:

Directors make decisions collectively in board meetings through board resolutions

- Any director may call a Board Meeting

Notice:

Directors must give notice when they call a board meeting (*MA 9*)

- Must be reasonable (***Re Homer District Consolidated Gold Mines, ex parte Smith (1888)***)
- Notice must include the time, date and place of meeting (method of communication if online) (***MA 9(3))***

Quorum:

A quorum of 2 directors must be present at all times during a board meeting (to make a quorate meeting) (***MA 11)***

A director may not count in the quorum or vote if a proposed decision of the board is concerned with an actual or proposed transaction or arrangement with the company in which the director is interested (***MA 14)***

- *Can be disapplied by Company's articles*
- Can count in the vote when the company (by ordinary resolution) disapplies the provision of the articles ***(MA 14(2) and 3(a))***

Declaring Interest:

Where a director has a personal interest in a proposed transaction or arrangement with the company, they must declare the nature and extent of this interest at the board (***s 177 CA 2006***)

Unless (s 177(6)):

a) It can't reasonably be regarded as likely to give rise to a conflict of interest
b) If the other directors are already aware of it
c) It concerns terms of a service contract that have or are to be considered by a meeting of the directors

Written Resolutions?

Possible to pass a board resolution in the form of a resolution in writing / another method which shows that all eligible directors have indicated to each other that they share a common view on a matter (***MA 8***)

- Must vote unanimously in favour of a resolution

Voting:

- Board resolutions are passed by a simple majority (***MA 7***)
- Directors with an interest can't vote (***MA 14***)

Admin:

- Directors must ensure that the company keeps a record, in writing, for at least 10 years of every unanimous or majority decision taken by the directors

As Agents:

Directors are agents of the company (company is the principal)

- They have both actual and apparent authority to bind the company into contracts with third parties (***s 40(1) CA***)
    - Each partner is an agent of the firm and an agent of each of the other partners (***s 5 Partnerships Act***) → the contract made by one partner binds both the firm and that partner
    - Actions done in the usual course of business by a partner with authority will bind the firm and all other partners (***s 6 Partnerships Act***)

To decide whether the firm is bound, look at:

1) Whether the partner has authority to enter into the transaction
2) Is the transaction done in the usual course of business?

Authority:

- **Actual authority** = director has consent from the other directors to act in a certain way
- **Apparent authority** = director acts without the company's prior consent (express or implied), but still binds the company to the contract
    - The company is estopped from denying the director's authority

Requirements (s 5 Partnerships Act):

The transaction is one which relates to the type of business in which the firm is apparently engaged (objective test); and

The transaction is one for which a partner in such a firm would usually be expected to have authority to act (objective test); and

The other party to the transaction did not know that the partner did not actually have authority to act (subjective test); and

The other party deals with a person whom he knows or believes to be a partner (subjective test)

- If the director acts without actual or apparent authority, they will be personally liable to the third party

Directors Duties

Directors are subject to a number of duties owed to the company

- Both *de jure* and *de facto* directors are subject to these duties
- For shadow directors, → general duties apply where the common law rules / equitable principles apply
    - Seems that will owe duties in relation to the directions / instructions given to *de jure* directors

Owed to:

- Directors owe a duty to the company only → means the only person who can sue for breach of duty is the company itself

Performance Duties

Duty to act within powers - s 171 CA:

A director of a company must:

a) Act in accordance with the company's constitution (articles of association) ***(s 171(a))***
b) Only exercise powers for the purposes for which they are conferred ***(s 171(b))*** **→ i.e duty to exercise powers for the proper purpose**

4 part test established in *Howard Smith Ltd v Ampol Petroleum:*

1) What power is being exercised
2) What is the proper purpose of this power
3) What is the substantial purpose for which it was in fact exercised
4) Was that a purpose proper

- Director can't be found in breach 'unless he knows that it is an improper purpose or of the facts which makes the purpose improper'
- Where a director acts for an improper purpose, they may be required to account for any gains made / compensate the company for any loss sustained (unless ratification occurs)
- An agreement entered into by a director in breach is voidable by company (unless ratified)
- BUT: a third party to such an agreement can enforce it against the company if the director had authority to enter into it

Duty to promote the success of the company - s 172 CA:

A director must act in the way he considers would be most likely to promote the success of the company for the benefit of its members as a whole (in good faith)

Typically success = an increase in share value

Must have regard to (s 172(1)(a-f):

a) The likely consequences of any decision in the long term,
b) The interests of the company's employees,
c) The need to foster the company's business relationships with suppliers, customers and others,
d) The impact of the company's operations on the community and the environment,
e) The desirability of the company maintaining a reputation for high standards of business conduct, and
f) The need to act fairly as between members of the company.

Court will apply a **subjective test** to ascertain whether a director has breached this duty (***Re Smith v Fawcett***) → means it is hard to establish if this section has been breached

- To create better transparency → quoted companies must provide a 's 172 statement' in their annual reports describing how the company has complied with the factors (unquoted companies on their website)
- Enlightened shareholder value → focus on the long-term sustainable growth and profit
  Requires directors to manage the relationship between the company and shareholders → aim to generate shareholder value whilst having regard to wider external impacts

Duty to exercise independent judgement - s 173 CA:

Directors must exercise independent judgement. This is not infringed by the directors acting:

a) In accordance with an agreement duly entered into by the company that restricts the future exercise of discretion by its directors, or
b) In a way authorised by the company's constitution.

Duty to exercise reasonable care, skill and diligence - s 174 CA:

Directors must exercise reasonable care, skill and diligence

Will consider:

a) The general knowledge, skill and experience that may reasonably be expected of a person carrying out the functions carried out by the director in relation to the company, and
b) The general knowledge, skill and experience that the director has.

The court does not distinguish between the standard expected of executives or non-executive directors (***Dorchester Finance Co Ltd v Stebbing***)

Conflict of Interests

Duty to avoid conflict of interest - s 175 CA:

Directors must avoid situations in which they have (or can have), a **direct or indirect interest that conflicts** with the interests of the company

- Must relate to a contract in which the company is not involved
  - E.g. applies in particular to the exploitation of any property, information or opportunity → it is immaterial whether the company could have taken advantage of the opportunity but decided not to do so (***Industrial Development Consultants v Cooley***)
- Any resulting contract is voidable at the company's instance (if the third party involved has notice of the director's breach)
  - Company can also require the director to account for any profit made as a result of the conflict
- No breach if the situation cannot reasonably be regarded as likely to give rise to a conflict of interest
  - E.g. where a director exploits an opportunity that falls outside the scope of their company's business
  - A director resigning to set up their own competing business is not a breach
- Only duty which can be authorised before by the directors in advance (***s 175(4) and (5)***)
  - The director in conflict cannot count in the quorum / vote on the authorisation
  - Can only be authorised by Directors if the articles allow it (if the articles don't → member approval is required)

A director is free to sit on the board of multiple companies (even if for a rival company)

Duty not to accept benefits from third parties - s 176 CA:

A director of a company must not accept a benefit from a third party conferred by reason of them either by a director or doing anything as a director

- Benefit = includes non-financial
- Company can rescind any contract and the benefit can be recovered
  - Can also claim damages in fraud from either the director in breach or the third party
  - Company can also summarily terminate the director's service contract and dismiss them
- There is no breach if the acceptance of the benefit cannot reasonably be regarded as likely to give rise to a conflict of interest

Duty to declare interest in a proposed transaction - s 177 CA:

If a director is directly or indirectly, interested in a **proposed transaction** or arrangement with the company, they **must declare the nature and extent of that interest to the other directors**

The declaration must be made *before* the company enters into the transaction
Must be a transaction with the company for the duty to be breached
Even if the company has disapplied ***MA 14***, the obligation to declare an interest under ***s 177 remains***

Exceptions:

a) If the director is not aware of the interest, or of the transaction or arrangement in question
b) If the interest cannot reasonably be regarded as likely to give rise to a conflict of interest
c) If, or to the extent that, the other directors are already aware of it (or ought reasonably to be aware of it)
d) If it concerns the terms of the director's service contract.

Declaration of interest in existing transaction - s 182 CA:

Where a director of a company is directly or indirectly, interested in a transaction or arrangement that **has been entered into** by the company, he must **declare the nature and extent of the interest to the other directors**

- Must be done as soon as reasonably practicable
- Declaration must be made at a meeting of the directors, or by notice in writing sent to all of the other directors, or by general notice of the interest given at a board meeting ***(ss 184 and 185 CA 2006).***
- This section *does not* apply if the director has already declared the interest under ***s 177***
    - But can be liable under both 177 and 182 if they do not disclose their interest in the proposed transaction and then again once it has been entered into
- Failure to comply with the requirement is a criminal offence punishable by a fine ***(s 183 CA 2006)***

Exceptions:

If the director is not aware of the interest, or of the transaction or arrangement in question
If the interest cannot reasonably be regarded as likely to give rise to a conflict of interest;
If, or to the extent that, the other directors are already aware of it
If it concerns the terms of the director's service contract.

Consequence of Breach

Potential remedies:

a) An account of profits
b) Equitable compensation for the loss suffered by the company
c) Rescission of any contract entered into as a direct or indirect result of the breach

d) An injunction, to prevent further breaches
e) Restoration of property transferred as a result of the breach of duty

Authorization?
Section 180(4)(a) provides that the general duties have effect, subject to any rule of law enabling the company to give authority for anything to be done by the directors that would otherwise be a breach of duty

Ratification of breach?
The shareholders can ratify a breach of a director's duty by ordinary resolution ***(s 239 CA)*** 1. Allows the director to escape liability to the company for breach of duty 2. Directors vote will *not count* at a general meeting / written resolution

Indemnity?
A director cannot avoid liability for negligence, default, breach of duty via a provision in the company's articles / their service contracts - ***Section 232(1)*** → such provision is void Provision for an indemnity is also void - Unless the company purchases and maintains insurance for a director - For proceedings brought by third parties

Relief from the Court?
• A court that has find an officer or auditor of the company liable, can grant them relief on such terms as it sees fit (***section 1157(1)***) • Can only be granted if the person seeking relief acted honestly and reasonably • Not for directors found liable for wrongful trading or where a third party is claiming

Directors Liabilities

1. **Failure to maintain company records** is an offence punishable by a fine (***s 1135 CA 2006).***
    - If the records in question are accounting records, the director(s) in default can be imprisoned for up to two years (***s 389***).
2. Specific offences relating to the **failure to file certain documents at Companies House**

- Failure to file a special resolution or a memorandum setting out its terms at Companies House within 15 days of it being passed is an offence punishable by fine (***s 30 CA 2006***).

3. Liability for **financial records** (***s 463 CA 2006***)
4. Liability for breach of **health and safety legislation**, namely the Health and Safety at Work Act 1974
   Directors can be imprisoned for up to two years and fined up to £20,000 for breaches of this legislation.
5. **Bribery** (***Bribery Act 2010***)
6. Making **political donations without shareholder approval**
7. Civil and criminal liability under **environmental legislation** (Environmental Protection Act 1990)

Ending Directorship

By Resignation:

- When a director resigns, they must complete form ***TM01*** (if an individual) or form ***TM 02*** (if a company) within 14 days
- Must also notify Companies House

Company's Articles / Shareholder Agreement:

- May contain a ***Bushell v Faith*** clause → gives someone who is both a shareholder and a director greater voting rights as a shareholder if the resolution in question is a resolution to remove that person as a director
- Where some or all of the company's shareholders are also directors, the shareholders may also include a provision in a shareholders' agreement obliging them to vote against the removal of their fellow shareholders from their office of director
  - If they then voted in favour of the removal of another shareholder as a director, the dismissed director/shareholder would have a claim for breach of the shareholders' agreement.

Removal:

Shareholders can remove a director by **ordinary resolution passed at a general meeting** (***s 168 CA***)

- Special notice is required for a resolution to remove a director (***s 168(2)***)
- Notice of the intention to pass the ordinary resolution must be given to the company at least 28 days before the general meeting
  - Company must inform the director and shareholders (if practicable)

- If not practicable, the company must give its shareholders notice at least 14 days before the general meeting, by advertisement in a newspaper or any other manner allowed by articles
- The director can speak at the general meeting, and can require the company to send copies of any written representations they want to make to the shareholders (***s 169 CA***)

Disqualification

Under the ***Company Directors Disqualification Act 1986*** ('CDDA 1986'), the court may disqualify a person from being a director for between two and fifteen years

- Length of disqualification depends on the director's behaviour in relation to the current offence and previous behaviour

Grounds for disqualification:

1. Conviction for an indictable offence
2. Persistent breaches of companies legislation
3. Fraud on a winding up
4. Summary conviction for failure to file a required notice or document
5. Being an unfit director of an insolvent company
6. Following an investigation and a finding of unfitness
7. Fraudulent or wrongful trading
8. Breach of competition law

Factors against Directors:

- Using money meant for paying VAT, PAYE or national insurance contributions as the company's working capital (known as trading on Crown monies);
- Paying excessive directors' remuneration; and
- Recklessly trading while insolvent.

Factors for Directors:

- Employing qualified financial staff;
- Taking professional advice; and
- A personal financial investment in the company.

Effects of disqualification:

A director subject to a disqualification order **cannot without the leave of the court** be a **director** or in any way **concerned in the promotion, formation or management of a company.**

Contravention of the disqualification order is a criminal offence and the director could be fined or sentenced to up to two years in prison

A director who is disqualified is personally responsible for the debts of the company if they are involved in the management of the company while disqualified ***(s 15 CDDA 1986)***

Shareholders

Shareholders have invested in the company in return for shares → they are the 'owners' of the company as they own a share of the assets

Becoming a Shareholder

First shareholders of the company = the 2 people who sign the memorandum of association as subscribers (automatic) (***s 112 CA 2006***)

Two ways for new shareholders to be added:

1) **The new shareholder could obtain shares from an existing shareholder by:**
   a) Buying some of the shares of an existing shareholder
   b) Receiving some of the shares of an existing shareholder as a gift
   c) Receiving the shares by way of transmission when a shareholder dies or becomes bankrupt, and electing to become a shareholder rather than transferring the shares to a third party
2) **A company can allot new shares**

Types of Shareholders:

Group of Companies

A shareholder can be a company

- Often several companies will be linked together because they form a network of companies where some of the companies own shares in the other companies

When a company owns shares in another company, it may be that one of the companies is classed as a subsidiary of the other.

- Under ***s 1159(1) of the CA 2006***, a company is a 'subsidiary' of another company, its 'holding company', if:
    a) That other company holds a majority of the voting rights in it; or
    b) That other company is a member of it and has the right to appoint or remove a majority of its board of directors; or
    c) That other company is a member of it and controls alone, pursuant to an agreement with other members, a majority of the voting rights in it; or
    d) It is a subsidiary of a company that is itself a subsidiary of that other company.

- A company is a 'wholly-owned subsidiary' of another company if it has no members except that other and that other's wholly owned subsidiaries or persons acting on behalf of that other or its wholly owned subsidiaries (***s 1159(2) CA 2006)***

Single-member companies

- Typically, when a company has one shareholder the individual is both the sole director and the sole shareholder
- If the company is a single-member company, there must be a statement to this effect on the register of members (***s 123 CA2006***)
- If the number of shareholders increases from one, there must be a statement stating that the company has ceased to have only one member, and the date on which that event occurred

Joint shareholders:

- Sometimes shares will be held by two or more individuals jointly
- The register of members needs to record both names but only one address (***s 113(5) CA 2006***)

Admin

Shareholders' agreements

- A shareholders' agreement will bind all of the parties and provide a remedy if one of its terms are breached
    - Only binds those shareholders who have entered into the shareholders' agreement
    - Whereas the company's articles of association bind every shareholder, present and future

Typically include:

- Restrictions on transferring shares;
- ***Bushell v Faith clauses*** → gives shareholders weighted voting rights when the resolution is one to remove that shareholder from their office as director; and
- A non-compete clause, preventing the shareholder from involvement in a business which competes with the company.

Can't:
- Restrict shareholders from voting a particular way in board meetings if they are also a director

PSC Register

All private and non-traded public companies must keep a register of persons with significant control

Allows third parties to understand who holds power in the company

Any shareholder who owns more than 25% of shares or controls more than 25% of voting rights need to be on the PSC register

- Can choose to keep at Companies House instead (***s 790 CA***)
- Must be done 14 days from the date the company made the change in its PSC register (***s 790VA CA***)

Companies House forms which must be completed when the information on the PSC register changes:

a) ***Form PSC01*** → by an individual who is to appear on the PSC register for the first time
b) ***Form PSC02*** → by any relevant legal entity who is to appear on the PSC register for first time
c) ***Form PSC04*** → any shareholder who already appears on the PSC register but whose details change
d) ***Form PSC05*** → any relevant legal entity who already appears on the PSC register but whose details change
e) ***Form PSC07*** → anyone ceasing to be a person with significant control

Internal Admin

Must keep up to date:
- Board minutes for every board meeting which takes place (***s 248 CA 2006***)
  - For 10 years
- Minutes of every general meeting (***s 355 CA 2006***)
  For 10 years
- The register of members
- The register of directors

The registers (known as statutory books) can be kept at the company's registered office or a Single Alternative Inspection Location (SAIL)
- A SAIL address is notified to Companies House on form ***AD02***, while movement of company records to the SAIL address is notified on form ***AD03***

- A form ***AD04*** is used to notify Companies House of company records moving from the SAIL address back to the registered office.
- Can also elect to keep these records on the central register at Companies House instead.

Individual Rights

General Meetings

General meetings = shareholders' meetings

- Occurs when the board want the shareholders to pass a shareholders' resolution
- Public companies must hold a general meeting once a year (***s 336 CA***)

Calling:

Called by the board of directors by passing a board resolution (***s 302 CA***)

By shareholders if:

- Shareholders (representing at least 5% of such paid-up capital of the company as carries the right of voting at general meetings can require the directors to call a general meeting (***s 303 CA***)
  - Request must state the general nature of the business to be dealt with (***s 303(4)(a)***)
  - Directors must call the meeting within 21 days of the request (***s 304(1)(a))***
  - The meeting must be held no later than 28 days from the date of the notice of general meeting (***s 304(1)(b)***)

By court:

Right to apply to the court to call a general meeting, if for some reason it is not possible for one to be held otherwise (***s 306 CA 2006)***

Notice:

The **notice requirements** under CA must be complied with (***s 301 CA***):

Directors must give notice to every shareholder & director (***s 310***)

Must give notice to the auditor (***s 502***)

Notice must be given in hard copy, in electric form, or by means of a website (***s 308***)

Notice must set out:

The time, date and place of the meeting (*__s 311(1)__*)
The general nature of the business to be dealt with at the meeting (*__s 311(2)__*)
The exact wording of the special resolution (*__s 283(6) (a)__*)
Each shareholder's right to appoint a proxy to attend on their behalf (*__s 325__*)

The **minimum notice required is 14 clear days** (*__s 307 & s 360 CA__*)

- The day the notice is received and the day of the general meeting are *not counted* in 14
- Where a general meeting notice is sent by post or email, it is deemed received 48 hours after postage (48 hours must be added to the 14 clear days) (*__s 1147(2) CA__*)

It is possible to hold a general meeting on short notice (*__s 307(4))__*:

a) Must be consent from a majority in number of the company's shareholders;
b) Who between them hold 90% or more of the company's shares (95% for public companies)

Quorum:

Must be a quorum of at least 2 (*__s 318 CA__*)

- Where a company only has one shareholder → quorum is one

Voting:

- Voting will be on a share of hands (*__MA 42__*)
- Each shareholder has one vote
- Right to send a proxy to a general meeting on their behalf

Option for a poll vote:

- Vote on the basis of one vote for each share that they own. Can be demanded by (*__MA 44(2))__*:
    a) The chair of the meeting
    b) The directors
    c) Two or more persons having the right to vote on the resolution
    d) A person representing not less than one tenths of the total voting rights of all the shareholders having the right to vote on the resolution

Declaration of Interest?

Shareholders are generally not prevented from counting in the quorum or voting if they have a personal interest in the matter (as they own the company, their interests are deemed the same as the company's).

Except:

a) A resolution to buy back some or all of a shareholder's shares

b) An ordinary resolution to ratify a director's breach of duty, where the director in question is also a shareholder

→ In these situations, can vote, but won't count if it is their vote which makes the difference

Admin:

- The right to inspect minutes of general meetings ***(s 358 CA)***

Written Resolution:

Written resolutions are permitted under ***s 288 CA*** for private companies (not public)

- Board will hand out / post / email a written resolution or place it on a website
  - Must include how to signify the agreement and deadline for signing (***s 291(4)***)
    - Unless articles state otherwise, lapse date is 28 days from circulation of the written resolution (***s 297 CA***) → doesn't matter when the shareholders acc received the written resolution
- The shareholders will then sign and return the written resolution if they want to vote in favour of it
- Must be circulated to every eligible member (***s 291(2) CA***)

  The shareholders who are entitled to vote on the resolution as at the circulation date (***s 289***)
- Passed when the majority of eligible members have signified agreement (***s 296 CA***)
- Each shareholder has one vote for each share they own (***ss 282(2) and 283(2) CA***)

A shareholder(s) who has 5% or more of the voting rights in the company are entitled to require the company to circulate a written resolution (***s 292 CA***)

- Includes up to 1,000 words on the subject matter of the resolution (***s 292(3)***)
- Company must then circulate a copy of the resolution and any accompanying statement to all eligible shareholders within 21 days of the request

Dividends

A dividend is a payment from the profits of the company to the shareholders **(income payment)**

Shareholders have a right to a dividend, if declared (***Model Article 30***)

Shareholders receive a percentage of the company's profits, based on the number of shares they hold and whether or not the shares are fully paid

Types of dividends:

There are two types of dividends:

Interim dividends → paid out during the financial year before the annual accounts have been prepared

Final dividends → paid out at the end of the financial year after the accounts have been prepared

Process:

Not automatically entitled:

a. As long as there are profits available for the purpose (sufficient distributable profit) (***s 830 CA 2006***) and
b. As long as the directors have made a recommendation as to its amount (***MA 30(2)***) and
c. This has been approved by the shareholders.

Process (MA 30):

1) Directors must hold a board meeting to recommend the payment of a dividend
2) Shareholders, in a general meeting, will then approve or declare the final dividend by ordinary resolution (allowed to reduce, but not increase the amount)
3) At this point, the dividend becomes a debt of the company owed to the shareholder

Exceptions:

- Directors can pay interim dividends without the need for shareholder approval (not considered a debt of the company)

Breach:

- Directors of a company who authorise payment of a dividend when there is insufficient distributable profit may be personally liable
- Shareholders who receive a dividend when they know or have reasonable grounds to believe that the payment is unauthorised may be liable to repay the dividend

Other Individual Rights

Shares:

- The right to transfer shares ***(s 544 CA)***

- All shareholders have the right to receive a share certificate (***s 769(1)(a)*** and ***s 776(1)(a) CA***)
    - Must issue this within 2 months of the allotment of shares (***s 769***)
    - Or within 2 months of a transfer of shares (***s 776***)
- A certificate is prima facie evidence of the holder's title to the shares (***s 768 CA***)

Register of Members:

Shareholders have a right to be entered on the register of members (***s 771 CA 2006 / Model Article 26)***

- Every company must keep a register of members (***s 113 CA 2006***) or they can elect to keep the information on the central register at Companies House (***s 128B***)
- A person cannot become a member of the company unless their name has been registered on the register of members
- Done as soon as practicable (or within 2 months of an allotment of transfer) (***s 771 CA***)
    - When a company allots new shares, it must enter the new shareholder or reflect an existing shareholder's increased number of shares (***s 554 CA***)
- Directors may refuse to register a transfer, but shareholder will then be entitled to be given a reason within 2 months of the transfer
- If the company has only one member, there must be a statement to that effect on the register of members (***s 123 CA***)

→ **It is a criminal offence if the register of members is incomplete or incorrect** (***s 113***)

Where the company keeps its register at its registered office, it must be available for inspection to shareholders (free of charge) and to anyone else for a fee (***s 116 CA***)

Directing Directors:

Shareholders may, by special resolution, direct the directors to take, or refrain from taking, specified action (***Model Article 4***) (rarely used)

- No such special resolution invalidates anything which the directors have done before the passing of the resolution

Right to inspect

Right to inspect, without charge:

a) The company's minutes of general meetings and all shareholders' resolutions passed otherwise than at general meetings;
b) All of the company's statutory registers
c) Directors' service contracts and any directors' indemnities
d) Any contracts relating to the company's purchase of its own shares.

Breach of Contract?

S 33(1) of the CA: the company's constitution is a statutory contract between each shareholder and the company, and between each shareholder and every other shareholder

- ***S 33(1)*** allows shareholders to take action against other shareholders of the company where that shareholder's membership rights have been infringed
- Right to seek an injunction under ***s 40(4) of the CA 2006*** to restrain the company from doing something prohibited by its constitution

Collective Rights

There are different ways in which members exercise their powers, depending on:

a) Whether the decision is a fundamental decision, relating to the constitution of the company (**special resolution**) or
b) To a decision which regulates the behaviour of the directors (**ordinary resolution**)

Changing the Constitution:

Requires a special resolutions → 75% or more of votes cast must be in favour (***s 283 CA***)

If a company does decide to change its articles, this must be done 'bona fide' for the benefit of the company as a whole (***Allen v Gold Reefs of Africa Ltd***)

Was originally a subjective test → if the shareholders honestly believe that the alteration is in the interests of the company

Subsequent case law has introduced an objective element → held that an amendment will not be for the benefit of the company if no reasonable person could consider it to be so (***Re Charterhouse Capital Ltd***)

Must be filed at Companies House within 15 days

Regulating Directors' Behaviour:

S 168 of the Companies Act 2006 gives the shareholders the right to remove directors (can't be taken away from them by the articles)

- Only an ordinary resolution is required → requires over half of the votes case to be in favour (***s 282 CA***)

BUT there are procedural rules which help to protect the directors

a) Want to prevent employment claims for wrongful dismissal
b) Articles may contain a weighted voting clause which give a director who is also a shareholder increased, or weighted, voting rights if a resolution to dismiss him is put forward at a general meeting

c) Directors who are also shareholders may be party to an agreement with other shareholders who have agreed not to vote for a resolution to dismiss them

Shareholder Approval

Certain acts by directors which require shareholder approval

- Require approval by an ordinary resolution of the company's shareholders
- If the director involved in the transaction is also a shareholder, they can vote on the shareholder resolution (even though they have a personal interest)

Substantial Property Transactions

SPT = where a director, in their personal capacity, or someone connected with a director:

a) Buys from or sells to the company
b) A non-cash asset
c) Of substantial value

→ Must be approved by the shareholders by ordinary resolution

Requirements:

Connected Person?

Either a member of a director's family or a company in which the director or a person / persons connected with a director *(ss 252-254 CA)*

Owns at least 20% of the body corporate's shares; or

Are entitled to exercise or control the exercise of more than 20% of the voting power at any general meeting of the company.

Members of family:

a) Director's spouse or civil partner;
b) Director's child or stepchild;
c) Director's parents;
d) Any person who lives in an enduring relationship with the director as their partner; and
e) Any children of a person who lives in an enduring relationship with the director as their partner.

Non-Cash Asset?

Any property or interest in property, other than cash (***s 1163 CA***)

Substantial?

An asset can be classed as substantial if (***s 191 CA***):

a) Its value is over £100,000
b) If it's worth more than £5,000 and more than 10% of the company's net asset value
   - To see net asset value look at the company's balance sheet

Exceptions:

An ordinary resolution is not needed to approve:

a) An SPT when the company in question is a wholly owned subsidiary of any other company
b) A transaction between a company and a person in his character as a member of the company
c) A transaction between a holding company and its wholly owned subsidiary
d) A transaction between two wholly owned subsidiaries of the same holding company.

Effects of Breach:

If the directors **fail to get shareholder approval for an SPT**, the **transaction is voidable** by the company (***s 195 CA***)

The following persons may be ordered to account to the company for any gain they have made and to indemnify the company for any loss or damage resulting from the transaction:

Any director of the company (or of its holding company) with whom the company entered into the arrangement

Any person with whom the company entered into the arrangement who is connected with a director of the company or of its holding company, and the director with whom any such person is connected; and

Any other director of the company who authorised the arrangement or any transaction entered into in pursuance of such an arrangement.

Loan to Directors

A company may not make a **loan to a director of the company** or its holding company, unless the transaction has been approved by the company's shareholders by ordinary resolution (***s 197 CA***).

Including:

a) A guarantee for a loan which a director has entered into with a third party
b) Providing security for a loan which a director has entered into with a third party

- If the director receiving the loan is also a director of the company's holding company, the holding company must also pass an ordinary resolution

- A memorandum setting out the terms of the loan and the company's liability must be made available for inspection at the company's office for 15 days prior to the general meeting and at the general meeting itself (***s 197(3) CA***)
- If by written resolution, a copy of the memorandum must instead be sent out with the written resolution

Exceptions:

- Expenditure on company business
    - This covers expenditure for the purposes of the company or for the purposes of enabling the director to properly perform their duties
    - Only available for loans up to a maximum of £50,000
- Expenditure on defending civil or criminal proceedings in relation to the company or an associated company
- Expenditure on defending regulatory proceedings or defending himself or herself in an investigation by a regulatory authority
- Minor and business transactions, as long as the transactions and any other relevant transaction or arrangement does not exceed £10,000

Effects of Breach:

- If money is loaned without an ordinary resolution, the transaction is voidable
    Can be affirmed within a reasonable time through an ordinary resolution

- The director who loaned the money and any director who authorised the transaction are:
    Liable to account to the company for any gain they have made and
    Are jointly and severally liable to indemnify the company for any loss or damage resulting from the transaction or arrangement

Guaranteed Service Contracts

General Rule = the board of directors can decide on the terms of a director's service contract → general powers to run the company (***MA 3***) and their specific power to decide on directors' remuneration (***MA 19***)

Exception = where the board is proposing to enter into a service contract with a guaranteed term of more than two years (long term service contracts)

- It is the guaranteed term element of the contract that requires authorisation, not the overall length of the contract.
- A ten-year service contract with a notice period of one year doesn't need authorisation by ordinary resolution

→ Must be approved by the shareholders by ordinary resolution (***s 188 CA***)

Process:

When the board proposes an ordinary resolution under ***s 188***, it must keep a copy of the memorandum setting out the terms of the proposed service contract at the registered office for 15 days prior to the general meeting, and at the general meeting itself ***(s 188(5))***

If the ordinary resolution is proposed by written resolution, a copy of the memorandum must be circulated to the shareholders along with the written resolution.

Directors' service contracts must be available for inspection by the shareholders at the company's registered office during their term and until a year after termination of the service contract ***(s 228 CA 2006)***

- Shareholders have the right to inspect them without charge and within seven days of requesting to see them (***s 229 CA 2006)***

No approval?

If the company didn't get approval from the shareholders, the guaranteed term element of the service contract would be void → there is an implied term that contract is terminable by the company at any time on reasonable notice (***s 189***)

Loss of Office (Payment)

Any payments for loss of office can only be paid with the prior agreement of shareholders by ordinary resolution (***s 217 CA***)

Also applies to:

a) Payments to past directors;
b) Payments to a person connected with a director;
c) Payments to any person at the direction of, or for the benefit of, a director or a person connected with a director.

Exceptions:
Provisions don't apply where a director has a legal entitlement to the payment (e.g. under their employment contract). Small payments up to £200 Damages for breach of an existing legal obligation Damages to settle or compromise claims linked with the termination of the office / employment

Effect of Breach:
The money is held by the recipient on trust for the company Any director who authorises the payment is jointly and severally liable to indemnify the company that made the payment for any loss resulting from it (***s 222 CA 2006***).

Protecting Minority Shareholders

Unfair Prejudice Petitions
Shareholders can apply to the court for an order for a remedy, where they feel that they have been **unfairly prejudiced as a shareholder** (***s 994 CA***): **Grounds:** a) The company's affairs have been conducted in a manner that is unfairly prejudicial to the interests of the members generally, or some part of its members; or b) An actual or proposed act or omission of the company is or would be so prejudicial → Must **cause harm** to a shareholder and it must **be unfair.** The court will apply an *objective test* → would a hypothetical bystander believe the act or omission to be unfair → **Remedy:**

a) The court may order the other shareholders, or the company, to buy the shares of the unfairly prejudiced shareholder (may want to cut all ties)
b) May impose a restriction on the company altering its articles of association, without the leave of the court
c) An order that the unfairly prejudiced shareholder has permission to bring a derivative action

Derivative Claims

A claim instigated by a shareholder for a wrong done to a company, which has arisen from an act or omission of a director (***ss 260-64 CA***)

- Allows shareholders to instigate legal action (rather than the board) because the board is neglecting to bring a claim or is refusing to do so
- Only arises because of an actual or proposed act or omission involving negligence, default, breach of duty or breach of trust by a director (***s 260(3)***)

Court Proceedings:

Claim must be issued & shareholder must apply to court for permission to continue the claim
Court will consider the application and the evidence in support of it (without a hearing)
The court will only allow the claim to continue if the application and evidence disclose a prima facie case for continuing.

The court then may:

a) Give directions as to the evidence to be provided by the company; or
b) Adjourn the proceedings to enable evidence to be obtained.

The court will then list a full hearing to determine the shareholder's application for permission to continue the claim. The court must refuse permission when: (***s 263(2***)

a) The court is satisfied that a person acting in accordance with ***s 172 CA 2006*** would not seek to continue the claim

   The court will not allow an individual who is not promoting the success of the company to continue the claim

b) The cause of action arises from an act or omission that has not yet occurred, but which has already been authorised by the company
c) The act or omission has already occurred and was authorised before it occurred or has been ratified by the company since it occurred

The court must also take into account (***s 263(3))***:

a) Whether the shareholder is acting in good faith in seeking to continue the claim;
b) The importance that someone acting in accordance with ***s 172*** (somebody who is acting in good faith to promote the company's success) would attach to continuing
c) Whether any past or future action or omission was authorised, or if not, would be likely to be ratified

d) Whether the company has decided not to pursue the claim; and
e) Whether the act or omission gives rise to a cause of action that a member could pursue in their own right.

Following the hearing, the court may grant permission to the shareholder to continue the claim on terms the court thinks fit, or adjourn the proceedings

Equity Finance

Share Capital = the amount raised by the issue of shares

Share = share in the company's share capital (***s 540***) → each share represents a fractional entitlement to the assets which form the capital of the company

Each share in a company must have a specified nominal value (***s 542 CA***)

- **Nominal value** = original value of the shares (even if increased in market value)

Types of Shares

Ordinary Shares

Companies are usually formed with ordinary shares

- Give shareholders the right to attend and vote at general meetings
- Entitled to receive dividends if they are declared (if directors recommend the payment and shareholders approve it)
- The rights attaching to the shares will be set out in the company's articles of association.
  - If they aren't, all shares rank equally

Preference Shares

Preference shareholders **receive enhanced rights** of some sort over and above ordinary shareholders

E.g. a guaranteed right to a dividend

Set out in the company's articles of association

Usually people who want to invest in a company → willing to forego voting rights in return for greater financial returns

Cumulative / non-cumulative:

- **Cumulative** = the preference shareholder has to be paid any missed dividends from previous financial years & the current financial year's dividend (as long as there are profits available to pay)
  - Ranks before payment of dividends to ordinary shareholders in current financial year

- **Non-cumulative** = if a dividend is not paid in a particular year, the shareholder loses the right to that year's dividend and does not have the right to receive it in the future

Participating:

- Participating shareholders have the further right to receive profits or assets, in addition to their other preference share rights

Allotting, Transferring and Buying Back Shares:

There are 3 ways shares can change hands:

a) Allotment
b) Buyback
c) Transfer (transmission)

Allotting Shares

Allotment = when a company decides to create shares and give them to an existing shareholder, or a new shareholder in return for payment (usually cash but can be property) (***National Westminster Bank v Inland Revenue Commissioners)***

- *The number of shares in the company increases*
- The existing shareholders' percentage shareholding decreases (unless they receive some of the new shares)
- Company will then issue a share certificate and enter / amend that person on register of members

Any constitutional restrictions on allotment?

- For companies incorporated before 1 Oct 2009, if they have not updated their articles → shareholders may have to pass an ordinary resolution to remove the Authorised Share Capital (the upper limit of how many shares a company could have)
- For other companies, the company articles may have a limit on the number of shares the company can have
    - If there is a limit, will have to be changed by special resolution

Directors authority to allot shares:

- Directors of a private company which has one class of shares have authority to allot shares without the permission of the shareholders (***s 550 CA***)

- As long as the company was incorporated under the CA 2006
- All that is needed is a board resolution
- If the company was incorporated before CA 2006, shareholders must pass an ordinary resolution to activate ***s 550***

- Directors of public / private companies with more than one class of shares must obtain the permission of the company's shareholders (ordinary resolution) ***(s 551 CA)***
  - Ordinary resolution must state the maximum number of shares the directors may allot and the date on which the authority will expire (no more than 5 years from OR)
  - The OR must also be filed at Companies House

Pre-emption rights?

Pre-emption rights = rights of first refusal over shares which are being allotted

A company must not allow 'equity securities' to a person, unless it has first offered them to existing holders of ordinary shares in the same company on the same / more favourable terms ***(s 561 CA)***

- Must offer existing shareholders the number of shares which will enable them to preserve their percentage shareholding in the company
- The proportion of the new shares they are offered must equal (as nearly as practicable) the proportion of shares they already hold in the company.
- The period for acceptance of the offer can't be less than 14 days

Can be excluded by the company's articles

For a private company with one class of shares, can also be disapplied by special resolution

For a public company / private with more than one class of shares, depends on company's initial authority to allot shares:

- If the ordinary resolution gave a general authority to allot (rather than authority in relation to a specific allotment) then s 570 allows the company to remove the pre-emption rights just by passing a special resolution
- If the authority to allot by ordinary resolution was in relation to a specific allotment → special resolution must be recommended by the directors of the company with a written statement setting out the reasoning / the amount and the director's justification of the amount

Doesn't apply to:

a) Allotment of bonus shares
b) If the consideration for the allotment is wholly or partly non-cash
c) If the shares are to be held under, allotted or transferred pursuant to an employee share scheme

Admin:

Copies of resolutions to be sent to Companies House within 15 days	All special resolutions Any ordinary resolution removing the authorised share capital in a pre-CA 2006 company Any ordinary resolution to activate s 550 in a pre-CA 2006 company Any s 551 ordinary resolution granting directors authority to allot
Company forms to be sent to Companies House	Return of allotment and statement of capital (Form SH01) within one month of the allotment Possibly form(s) PSC01, PSC02, PSC04 and PSC07, for new persons with significant control/ a change of which percentage band a person is in/ a person ceasing to be a person with significant control
Entries in company's own registers	Amend register of members within two months Amend PSC register if necessary
Preparation and allocation of share certificates	Prepare share certificates within two months of allotment

Transferring Shares

Transfer = where the shareholder **sells / gives shares to another shareholder or to a new shareholder**

- The total number of shares in the company does not change
    - The transferor's percentage shareholding decreases
    - The transferee's percentage shareholding increases
    - The total number of shares in the company does not change
- The company's articles may contain restrictions on transfer of shares
- BUT articles can't restrict a shareholder from selling the shares and can't stop a purchaser from buying them
    - Although a person doesn't become a shareholder until entered on the register of members
        - ***MA 26*** gives board discretion to refuse to register the transfer (won't become the legal owner of the shares)
        - Although at general meetings, the legal owners must vote in accordance with the wishes of the beneficial owner & must pay them dividends

Process:

1) The transferor must complete and sign a stock transfer form and give it to the transferee along with the share certificate relating to the shares (***ss 770–772 CA 2006***)
2) If the sale price of the shares is over £1,000, the buyer must pay stamp duty (currently charged at 0.5% rounded up to the nearest £5) on the stock transfer form
    - No stamp duty is payable if the shares are a gift
3) The transferee must then send the share certificate and stock transfer form to the company.
4) The company should then:
    a) Send the new shareholder a new share certificate in their name within two months (***s 776 CA 2006***)
    b) Enter their name on the register of members within two months (***s 771 CA 2006);*** and
    c) Notify the Registrar of Companies of the change in ownership of the shares when the company files its annual confirmation statement (***CS01***).

Transmission:

Transmission is an **automatic process** whereby:

a) If a shareholder dies, their shares automatically pass to their personal representatives (PRs); or
b) If a shareholder is made bankrupt, their shares automatically vest in their trustee in bankruptcy.

→ The trustee / PRs don't become shareholders, but are entitled to dividends declared (***MA 27***)

Buyback

Buyback = where the company **buys back some of its own shares from one or more shareholders** (reasorbs some of its shares so that total number in the company decreases)

- The shares in question are cancelled and the company has to pay the outgoing shareholder for the shares
- The remaining shareholders' percentage shareholding increases

Requirements:

The company's articles can't forbid it
The shares must be fully paid
The company must pay for the shares at the time of purchase
The shares must usually be paid for out of distributable profits or the proceeds of a fresh issue of shares made for the purpose of financing the purchase

Distributed profits = the company's accumulated, realised profits less its accumulated, realised losses

The shareholders must pass an ordinary resolution authorising the buyback contract

- A shareholder who holds shares which are being bought back can't vote in a written resolution procedure and at a general meeting, can vote but he resolution will not be effective if that shareholder's votes made the difference

A copy / summary of the buyback contract must be available for inspection for at least 15 days before the general meeting and at the general meeting itself

A copy of the buyback contract must be available for inspection at the company's registered office or SAIL as soon the contract has been concluded, for a period of ten years starting with the date of the buyback.

Buy Back out of Capital

Where a private company doesn't have enough distributable profits to fund a buyback, may buy back out of capital. Following requirements must also be met:

1) The company's directors must make a statement of solvency, no sooner than one week before the general meeting, stating that the company is solvent and that it will remain solvent during the year following the buyback.
2) Must have an auditor's report annexed to the statement of solvency
3) The payment out of capital must be approved by special resolution (in addition to the OR to approve the buyback contract)
4) A copy of the directors' statement of solvency and auditors' report must be available to members
    - Written resolution = must be sent along with it
    - General meeting = must be available for inspection at the meeting
5) Within 7 days of the special resolution, the company must put a notice in the London Gazette, stating that the shareholders have approved payment out of capital in order that the company can buy back its own shares
    - Must specify the amount of capital to be used, the date of the special resolution and where the directors' statement and auditors' reports are available for inspection.
    - Must also state that any creditors of the company may, within 5 weeks of the special resolution, apply for an order to prevent the buyback out of capital
    - Must also publish an equivalent notice in an appropriate national newspaper (one circulating throughout the part of the UK which the company is registered) or give notice to each of its creditors
6) The company must also file a copy of the directors' statement and auditors' report at Companies House
7) The directors' statement and auditors' report must be kept available for inspection at the company's registered office until 5 weeks after the passing of the special resolution
8) The payment out of capital must be made no earlier than 5 weeks after the date of the special resolution to approve the buyback out of capital, and no later than seven weeks after the date of the special resolution (so a 2 week window)

Debt Finance

Debt Finance

Debt finance = when businesses **obtain finance by borrowing money**

Two main types of debt finance:

Loans → where a business borrows money from a bank / other lender

Debt securities → IOUs which are issued by the company to the investor in return for a cash payment (have to be repaid by the company at an agreed future date)

Considerations:

Before a company borrows money, must check it is allowed to do so under its constitution

- Model Articles for private companies *don't* place any restrictions on borrowing
    - Under the general power conferred by Model Article 3, directors have an implied power to borrow money / charge company assets as security
    - If there are restrictions in company's articles / memorandum, the shareholders will need to pass a special resolution under ***s 21 CA*** to change the article to remove the restrictions
- Before a partnership borrows money, partners should check there are no restrictions in the Partnership Agreement (if there is, will probably need unanimous consent)

Types of Loans:

- **Secured loans** = business giving security to the lender over some or all of its property so that the bank can recover what it is owed more easily if the business defaults on the loan
- **Unsecured loans** = where the lender doesn't take security over the borrower's assets
    - Businesses will have to pay higher rates of interest for unsecured loans

Overdraft:

An overdraft facility is a contract between the business and its bank which **allows the business to go overdrawn on its current account**

- Type of temporary loan used to cover everyday business expenses when there is no other source of money available
- Known as an uncommitted facility → usually payable on demand (bank unlikely to demand repayment unless business is in financial difficulties)
- Businesses will have to pay a fee for the overdraft facility
- Bank will charge interest → generally on a compound basis (any unpaid interest is added to the amount borrowed and interest charged on the whole amount)

- As it is an unsecured loan, interest generally higher

Term Loans:

Term loan = business borrows a fixed amount of money for a specified period of time (must be repaid at the end of the term)

- Borrower will have to pay interest at regular intervals
- Usually used to buy a capital asset
- Can either be borrowed in one lump sum (fixed loan) or drawn down as and when needed (a loan facility)
- **Bilateral loan** = between 2 parties (typically business and bank)
- **Syndicated loan** = between the business and a number of different lenders, who jointly provide the money the business wants to borrow

Revolving credit facilities:

Revolving credit facility = the bank agrees to make available a maximum amount of money to the business throughout the agreed period of the revolving credit facility

- During the lifetime of the facility, the business can borrow and repay money
- Interest payable at regular intervals
- Business able to borrow amounts it has already repaid (as long as it doesn't exceed the overall maximum figure)
- Contract for a revolving credit facility is usually called a facility agreement

Debentures

Generally used to describe a loan agreement in writing between a borrower and a lender that is registered at Companies House

- Gives the lender security over the borrower's assets
- *Only* companies and LLP's can enter into debentures

Contractual terms of Loans:

Both a term loan and a revolving credit facility are 'committed' facilities → once the loan agreement has been signed, the bank must provide the business with the loan monies

Important clauses found in loans:

Payment of money to the borrower:

The initial clause of the facility agreement will set out:

The amount of the loan
The currency
The type of loan
The availability of periods during which the loan can be taken

Repayment and pre-payment

The bank can only **demand repayment of a term loan / revolving credit facility in accordance** with the **terms of the facility agreement. Can be:**

a) **A bullet payment** → repayment of the whole loan in one go at the end of the term
b) **Amortisation** → repayment in equal instalments over the term of the loan
c) **Balloon repayment** → repayment in unequal instalments, with the final instalment being the largest

Interest rates

The interest rate payable for the loan is a matter of agreement between the parties

- Will be expressly stated in the facility agreement
- Lenders will often want to impose default interest if scheduled payments are missed

Express covenants

Serious of covenants given by the business to the bank

Aims to ensure that the business conducts its business within agreed limits so that the lender has every chance of being repaid in full
Restrictions on the financial performance of the business to ensure the business stays solvent

Typical covenants:

a) Limitation of dividends → companies must ensure that dividends and other distributions to shareholders don't exceed a specified percentage of net profits
b) Minimum capital requirements → businesses must ensure that current assets exceed current liabilities by a specified amount of money / percentage
c) No disposal of assets / change of business → business must not dispose of assets without the lender's consent / change the scope or nature of the business
d) No further security over the assets → business must not create any further security over the whole, or any part, of the undertaking without the lender's consent
e) Provision of information on the business → e.g. annual accounts

Implied covenants
Terms may be implied into the facility agreement • By trade usage / courts (although limited)

Events of default
The facility agreement will contain 'events of default' → if the business breaches any of these terms, the lender may terminate the agreement if it wishes • E.g. failure to pay any sum due or commencement of an insolvency procedure

Equity Finance v Debt Finance:

Most companies use a mixture of equity and debt capital → the ratio of debt to equity capital is known as 'gearing'

- Companies with a high percentage of borrowing are referred to as being 'highly geared' (greater risk of insolvency)

	Equity Finance	**Debt Finance**
Risk of the investment:	✗ Buying shares in a company is a more risky investment than lending money • May not receive a good dividend / shareholder will lose capital value of their shares if the company goes insolvent	☑ Interest payments are a contractual liability so will be paid before dividends • Loan likely to be secured →
Involvement in the company	☑ Shareholders have certain rights to influence the direction of the company	✗ Lender is merely a creditor of the company, without any ownership rights
Repayment of capital	✗ Generally, a company doesn't repay a shareholders' capital, unless the company is wound up	☑ Loan capital must be repaid at some date in the future
Restriction on sale	✗ In a private company, shareholders are usually restricted in their freedom to sell their shares	☑ A lender can realise its capital earlier than the repayment date agreed by selling its debenture to a third party
Capital value of the investment	☑ Many shareholders invest in shares hoping they will increase in value	✗ Capital value of a facility agreement generally remains

		constant
Degree of statutory control	☑ Equity finance tightly controlled by the CA 2006	✗ Debt finance a matter of contract law → more flexible
Payment of income	✗ A company is able to pay a dividend to its members only if there are sufficient available profits	☑ Debt interest must be paid in accordance with the terms of the facility agreement, whether or not the company has profits available
Tax treatment of income payments	✗ The payment of a dividend is not a deductible expense for the company	☑ Payment of debenture interest is a normal trading expense of the company → deductible
Cost	✗ Cost of equity = likely returns to the new shareholder - For existing shareholders, an extra shareholder is a cost → their share of future dividends / capital growth decreases	✗ Cost of debt is the interest rate charged by the lender to the borrowing company - Can be favourable due to tax system as interest is tax deductible
Existing capital structure	☑ If the company already has a lot of debt, it may be able to obtain more finance only in the form of equity finance	
Equity restrictions	✗ Articles may restrict the company's ability to borrow	✗ The terms of existing facility agreements may restrict the taking of new loans / debt

Security

Often a lender will require security over the borrower's assets in return for loaning money

- If the business fails to repay the loan as agreed, the lender can seize the secured assets, sell them and pay itself out of the proceeds of sale
- Benefits lender = lowers risk of its not being repaid
- Benefits borrower = usually able to borrow at a lower rate
    - Downside = must accept restrictions on the use of the asset given as security

Charge = umbrella term for most types of security in CA 2006

Mortgage = umbrella term for security in LPA 1925

Initial considerations:

For the company

- The directors must make sure that the company has the power to grant security over its assets before entering into any security contracts on the company's behalf
- A company formed under CA 2006 has unrestricted objects (unless restricted by articles ***(s 30(1))***
  - Company has an implied power to grant security for any borrowing
- If there are restrictions, the company's shareholders must pass a special resolution to amend the company's articles ***(s 21 CA)***

For the lender

- The lender should make sure there are no restrictions on the company granting security and that the directors have the authority to act on behalf of the company in the transaction
  - Do this by inspecting the articles of the company, searching company records at Companies House and requesting copies of relevant board resolutions
- Look on Companies House to see if there is sufficient value in the property to provide adequate security for the proposed loan
- If over land, should also search Land Registry
- Should also conduct a winding-up search at Companies Court to check no insolvency proceedings have been commenced

Types of Security

Mortgages

Highest form of security

Lender may seek to take a mortgage over high-quality assets owned by the borrower

A mortgage (except over land) involves the transfer of legal ownership from the mortgagor to the mortgagee

- The title will be transferred back to the borrower when money has been repaid

A mortgage taken over land is a charge by deed, expressed to be by way of legal mortgage

Charges

Form of security which does *not* transfer legal ownership and *doesn't* give right to immediate possession of the property

Fixed charges

Chargor must create a separate fixed charge over each asset so that the lender has control of the asset

- If the chargor gets into financial difficulties, the fixed charge holder will have the right to sell the asset and be paid out of the proceeds of sale before other claimants → right of first claim over the proceeds
- Can have more than one fixed charge over the same asset

Floating charges

A floating charge secures a group of assets which is constantly changing (e.g. stock)

3 basic features:

a) They consist of an equitable charge over the whole or a class of the company's assets
b) The assets subject to the charge are constantly changing
c) The company retains the freedom to deal with the assets in the ordinary course of business until the charge 'crystallises'.
    - Crystallisation = chargor can no longer deal with the assets covered by the charge → turns into a fixed charge Occurs automatically when:
        - The chargor goes into receivership
        - The chargor goes into liquidation
        - The chargor ceases to trade
        - Any other event occurs which is specified in the charge document

☑ Allows the chargor to deal with the secured assets on a day-to-day basis

☑ Allows chargor to maximise the amount it is able to borrow (can be taken over the whole of a company)

✗ A fixed charge will take priority over a floating charge over the same assets

✗ Disadvantage for the lender is that the chargor is allowed to deal with the assets

✗ Certain other creditors have the right to claim money from the proceeds of sale of the assets covered by the floating charge if the company becomes insolvent before the charge holder gets the money

Book debts

Book debts are money owed to the company by its debtors

- Can be charged by a floating charge or fixed charge (where the charge holder had control over both the debts and the proceeds once they were paid)

Other types of security

- Personal guarantees
- A pledge (where an asset is physically delivered by the debtor to the creditor to serve as security until the debtor has paid their debt)
- A lien (gives the creditor the right to physical possession of the debtor's goods or assets until the debt is paid)
- Retention of title (on a sale of goods, the buyer doesn't get full title to the goods until they pay the full price to the seller)

Key terms in a charging document:

Security

- Will state that the borrower charges the property to the lender and what the type of security is (e.g. fixed or floating charge)
- The specific assets subject to each charge will also be listed

Representations and warranties

- The borrower will have to make a series of contractual statements relating to the assets which it's charging (intention of getting the borrower to reveal all relevant information about the assets)
- If there is another charge over the asset, borrower must disclose this

Covenants

- Borrower will have to make a series of covenants relating to the assets it is charging
- Enures the value of the assets is maintained by the borrower

Enforcement and powers

- The agreement will set out the circumstances in which the security becomes enforceable
- Will set out the lender's powers

Procedural matters for companies issuing debentures

- Likely to be the directors that negotiate with the lender the terms on which the loan is to be made and any security provided (usually just requires a board resolution)
- May be necessary to call a general meeting / written resolution to allow directors to count in quorum / change articles by special resolution

Priority of Creditors

Order of priority of creditors over the same asset is fixed by law ***(s 859A CA)***:

a) A fixed charge or mortgage will always take priority over a floating charge over the same asset ***(Re Castell v Brown)***

b) If there is more than one registered fixed charge or mortgage over the same asset, they have priority in order of their date of creation, not their date of registration. ***(Re Benjamin Cope & Sons Ltd)***

c) If there is more than one registered floating charge over the same asset, they have priority in order of their date of creation, not their date of registration.

It is possible for creditors to enter into an agreement between themselves to alter the order of priority → subordination (by a deed of priority)

A **negative pledge clause** can prohibit the company from creating later charges with priority to the floating charge, without their permission

- If a subsequent lender takes a charge over the same asset and has actual knowledge of the negative pledge clause → their fixed charge will be subordinate to the original floating charge.

Registration:

A new registration scheme was introduced for charges created by a company after 6 April 2013 → new voluntary system of registration

But, if company fail to register a charge in the requisite time period, may be void

Registration Process:

1) Within 21 days of creation of the charge, the company / person interested in the charge must file at Companies House a statement of particulars, a certified copy of the instrument creating the charge (*s 859A CA*) and the fee
    - Begins with the day after the day the charge was created

2) Once the docs have been delivered, the Registrar of Companies must register the charge ***(s 859A(2) CA)*** and include the certified copy of the charge on the register ***(s 859I(2) CA)***
3) The Registrar must give the person who delivered the documents a certificate of registration ***(s 859I CA)***
4) Form MR01 and certified copy of the charging doc will be put on the company's file
5) Charge will be fully valid against another creditor of the company / administrator
6) A copy of the charging document and Form MR01 should be kept available for inspection ***(s 859P CA)*** at its registered office or SAIL ***(s 859Q CA)***
7) If a fixed charge is taken over land, must also be registered at the Land Registry

Failure to register?

Failure to register the charge renders the charge void against a liquidator or an administration and against the company's other creditors ***(s 859H(3) CA)***

The company is still obliged to repay the debt, but the lender cannot enforce the security ***(s 859H(4))***

The original charge holder would lose its priority over the proceeds of sale

Late / inaccurate delivery

If the 21 day period for delivery of the required docs to Companies House is missed or the details are inaccurate → charge is void as against a third party

Limited power for the court to extend the period ***(s 859F CA)***

- Charge will have a priority only from date of actual registration → lose priority if other charges have been registered in meantime

Court has power to allow rectification of any statement or notice delivered to the Registrar for any inaccurate details ***(s 859M),*** and to order the replacement of a document on the register (***s 859N)***

Redemption of the loan

When the loan secured by a registered charge is repaid, a person with an interest in the registration of the charge may complete, sign and send Form MR04 to the Registrar of Companies at Companies House

Release of charge

If the lender decides to release the borrower's property from the charge / sell the asset covered by the charge, a person with an interest in the registration of the charge must complete, sign and send Form MR04 to the Registrar of Companies at Companies House.

Corporate Insolvency

A company is insolvent when (***section 122 and 123 of the Insolvency Act 1986***):

A creditor has served a statutory demand for an outstanding sum of £750 or more, and the company does not pay *or* come to an arrangement with the creditor within 21 days of service of the statutory demand;

A creditor has obtained judgement against the company, and has tried to enforce that judgement, but the debt *still* has not been paid in full or at all;

It can be proved to the court that the company is unable to pay its debts as they fall due (the '**cash flow test'**) ***(s 123(1)(e) IA)***

It can be proved to the court that the company's liabilities exceed its assets (the **'balance sheet test'**) ***(s 123(2) IA)***

Liquidation

Liquidation / winding up is the process whereby:

The **business stops tradings;**

Its assets are sold; and

The company ceases to exist

→ The directors' powers cease and the liquidator runs the company

- The liquidator will distribute the assets of the company to the creditors according to statute

Types of Liquidation

Three types of liquidation:

a) Compulsory liquidation
b) Creditors' voluntary liquidation
c) Members' voluntary liquidation

Compulsory Liquidation:

Compulsory liquidation is **commenced by a third party** (the petitioner) presenting a **winding up petition at court**

Usually because the company is unable to pay its debts ***(s 122 IA)***

How:

Creditors will usually prove a debtor's insolvency by issuing a statutory demand and, if the statutory demand remains unpaid after 3 weeks, issuing a winding up petition against the company

May alternatively obtain a judgement against the company

Effect:

If the company indicates that it will be able to pay the debt within a reasonable time, the court may adjourn the hearing to a later date

If the court orders the company to be wound up, the Official Receiver will automatically become the company's liquidator

Creditors' Voluntary Liquidation:

Initiated by the company, through discussion and agreement between the company's directors and shareholders

Usually because directors have been pressured by the creditor (don't want a personal claim)

Members' Voluntary Liquidation:

Commenced **by a solvent company because it wishes to cease trading** or because it is dormant and wishes to bring its affairs to an end in an orderly manner

- The directors must first swear a statutory declaration that the company is solvent

Powers of the Liquidator

The liquidators powers include:

a) Carrying on the company's business
b) Commencing and defending litigation on the company's behalf;
c) Investigating the company's past transactions;
d) Investigating the directors' conduct;
e) Collecting and distributing the company's assets;
f) Doing all that is necessary to facilitate the winding up of the company

Preserving and increasing assets:

Liquidators and administrators are under a **duty to maximise the assets available to creditors**

- Have the power to investigate the company's affairs generally, and to investigate the directors' actions prior to liquidation or administration
- May bring a number of claims (claimant is the company)

Key potential claims to increase assets:

a) Avoidance of certain floating charges ***(s 245 IA 1986)***;
b) Preferences ***(s 239 IA 1986)***;
c) Transactions at an undervalue ***(s 238 IA 1986)***;
d) Transactions defrauding creditors ***(s 423 IA 1986)***;
e) Extortionate credit transactions ***(s 244 IA 1986)***.

Avoidance of certain floating charges

Where 'at the relevant time' before the onset of the company's insolvency, **a charge was granted *without* the company receiving fresh consideration** in **exchange for granting security**

- **Relevant time** =
    - If the charge was created in favour of a person who is connected with the company, during the 2 years ending with the onset of insolvency
    - If the charge was created in favour of any other person, during the 12 months prior to the onset of insolvency
- **Onset of insolvency** =
    - **Compulsory liquidation** = the date of presentation of the winding up petition
    - **CVL** = the date the company formally enters into liquidation
    - **Administration** = when the company files a notice of intention to appoint an administrator (or date of administration if earlier)
- **Floating charge** =
    - If given to someone unconnected with the company, company must have been insolvent at that time / or insolvent as a result
    - If given to someone connected with the company, not necessary to show
    - **Connected** = a director of insolvent company / close relative / business associate of a director / an associate of the company (a company in the same group)

Invalid floating charges are automatically void under ***s 245 IA***

Preferences

A liquidator or administrator **can challenge a transaction** where the company, at the relevant time, has **given a preference to someone else**

- **Relevant time** =
    - If the preference was given to a person who is connected with the company, during the 2 years ending with the onset of insolvency; or
    - If the preference was given to any other person, during the 6 months ending with the onset of insolvency

- Company must have been insolvent at the time of the preference, or have become insolvent as a result of giving the preference
- Must be a desire to prefer the other party, not just an intention to prefer (i.e. through no other option - ***Re MC Bacon Limited***)
  - Where a preference is given to a person connected to the company, the desire to prefer is presumed

If the preference is proven, the court may:

a) Order the release of any security given by the company
b) Order the return of any property transferred as part of the transaction
c) Or the payment of the proceeds of sale of property forming part of the transaction to the company

Transactions at undervalue:

A liquidator or administrator **can challenge any transaction which the company has entered into at an undervalue** at the relevant time

- **Undervalue** = where the company makes a gift to the other person, or enters into a transaction and receives consideration which is significantly lower in value than consideration provided by the company
- **Relevant time** = during the 2 years ending with the onset of insolvency

Company must have been insolvent at the time of the transaction, or have become insolvent as a result of the company entering into the transaction

Defence = if the transaction was entered into in good faith for the purpose of carrying on the business and where there was reasonable grounds for believing that it would benefit the company

Extortionate credit transactions

A liquidator / administrator has the power to **challenge an extortionate credit transaction** made in the 3 years ending with the day on which the company went into administration / liquidation

Extortionate = requires grossly exorbitant payments / grossly contravene ordinary principles of fair dealing (rare)

Transactions defrauding creditors

A **transaction defrauding creditors** is a transaction at an undervalue which the company entered into in order to put assets beyond the reach of someone making a claim against it / to prejudice the interests of that person in relation to any claim they might make

Brought at the discretion of the court (either by company or creditors)

Other party may be ordered to return any property / discharge any security
No time limits

Distribution of Assets

There is a **distinct order of payment of different creditors** in an insolvency process:

1) Fixed charge holders will receive amount they are owed when the assets is sold
    - If there is a shortfall, the fixed charge holder will join the pool of unsecured creditors
2) Any surplus is paid to the liquidator
3) Liquidator will send a standard form to unsecured creditors (must fill in with details of the debt owed to them) → proving the debt
    - Liquidator will then approve or reject the creditors' claims
4) Then will make payments in the following order:
    i) The expenses of the winding up
    ii) Preferential debts, which rank and abate equally (share available money between them in a % according to what they are owed)
        - Salaries of employees for work carried out in the 4 months preceding date of wind up (max of £800 per employee)
        - HMRC for taxes which companies collect on HMRC's behalf (PAYE / VAT)
    iii) Money which is the subject of floating charges:
        - Subject to ring fencing → set aside a portion of the available money for unsecured creditors (up to a limit of £800,000 / £600,000 for charges created before 6 April 2020)
            - 50% of the first £10,000 of money received from the property which is subject to floating charges
            - 20% of the remaining money
    iv) Unsecured creditor, who rank and abate equally
    v) Shareholders entitled to anything left

Alternatives to Liquidation

Companies who wish to avoid liquidation could:

a) Administration (***Sch B1 IA 1986)***
b) Company voluntary arrangements (***Part I IA 1986***)
c) Schemes of arrangement (***ss 895-901 CA***)
d) Restructuring plans (***Part 26A CA***)
e) Free standing moratorium (***Part A1 IA 1986***)

f) Informal agreements with creditors

Administration:

Process where an **administrator** (an independent insolvency practitioner) is **appointed to run the company** and make changes **to improve its financial performance** / get it into a position where it can be sold

During this process there is a statutory moratorium → not possible for anyone to commence / continue with legal action against the company / enforce a judgement / issue a winding up petition without administrator's consent

Commencing Administration:

Either by:

a) **Court order**

If it is satisfied that the company is likely to become unable to pay its debts & the administration order is reasonably likely to achieve one of the 3 purposes

b) The **company**, its **directors** / the **holder of a qualifying floating charge** / an **unsecured creditor** filing certain documents at court

- By company / director
  - Must serve notice of intention of administration on: the court, any QFCH and any lender who is entitled to appoint an administrative receiver
  - Must file at court a statutory declaration that company is unable to pay its debts but is not in liquidation (can't use if a wind up petition has already been initiated)

- By QFCH
  - Floating charge must be enforceable
  - Only if the charge documents empowers the holder to appoint an administrator / an administrative receiver and it relates to the whole / substantially the whole of the company's property
  - If there is another QFCH with priority, must notify them in advance
  - Lender must file the notice at court with statutory declaration

Process of Administration:

- Once administration has started a moratorium comes into effect
- The administrator will put forward the proposals for the company to the creditors (can be amended by them)

- Administrator's proposals will be approved if a majority in value of the creditors vote in favour of them (provided that those who vote against the proposals do not constitute more than 50% in value of the creditors who are unconnected to the company)
- Pre-pack administration → administrator sells its assets and business straight away (sale is agreed before the company appoints an administrator)

Effect of Administration:

- The company is managed by the administrator → in control of the company's assets (although don't own them)
- Carries out the proposals approved by the creditors

End of Administration:

- Administration ends automatically one year from the date the administration took effect (but can be extended)
- Can be ended earlier (through application to the court by the administrator / creditor)

Duties of Administrator:

The administrator must perform their duties **in the interests of all of the company's creditors as a whole**

- Must have as a primary objective the wish to rescue the company as a going concern
- Or must try to achieve a better result for company's creditors that would be likely if the company was wound up
- If not possible, sell the company

Powers include:

a) Removing and appointing directors
b) Paying creditors (only with the court's permission if the payment is to an unsecured creditor)
c) Calling a meeting of creditors or shareholders
d) Dealing with property that is subject to a floating charge
e) Dealing with property that is subject to a fixed charge (with the permission of the court)
f) Investigating and applying to have the company's past transactions set aside or challenged
g) Commencing fraudulent or wrongful trading proceedings against directors.

→ Also have the power to do anything necessary or expedient for the management of the affairs, business and property of the company

Company Voluntary Arrangement:

A **CVA is a written agreement** (statutory contract) which **binds all of the parties to it**

- Allows a company to reach an agreement with its unsecured creditors so that the creditors will give the company time to trade out of trouble
- Generally used when the company's business is fundamentally sound, but is undergoing a temporary cash flower difficulty
- The proposals put forward for payment of creditors must be approved by:
    a) 75% or more in value of the company's creditors; **and**
    b) 50% or more of non-connected creditors
        Secured creditors are not allowed to vote
- CVA does not affect the rights of secured and preferential creditors, unless they agree to it

Restructuring under CIGA 2020:

The restructuring plan is **court-supervised** and is an **'arrangement' between the company and all of its secured and unsecured creditors and shareholders**

- Company must be likely to encounter financial difficulties
- Directors will prepare a restructuring plan and apply to court for approval to call meetings of the company's creditors and shareholders
- Implementation of the plan → 2 court hearings
    - In between, creditors and shareholders are divided into 2 classes → each class will be deemed to have approved the plan if 75% by value of that class vote for it
- Cross-class cram down provision → enables a dissenting class of creditors to be 'crammed down' so they can't block otherwise viable plans (sanctioned by the court)

Moratorium under CIGA 2020:

Corporate Insolvency and Governance Act 2020 allows directors of a company to implement a 20 day moratorium on creditor actions against the company → gives the company a payment holiday

The company is protected from actions by creditors relating to pre-moratorium debts

- Must pay the debts incurred during the moratorium in full
- Company must be unable to pay its debts / likely to become unable to pay its debts
- Can't enter one if entered one during last 12 months
- Only available for English companies with no outstanding winding up petitions against them
- The moratorium lasts 20 business days (beginning day after it comes into force) → can be extended by a further 20 business days
    - Can also be extended by the directors for a period of up to one year if the creditors who aren't going to get paid consent to this

- During the moratorium, the company's directors remain in control, but a qualified insolvency practitioner acts as an independent monitor (can terminate under certain circumstances)

Options for secured creditors:

Secured creditors may be able to appoint a receiver to take possession of the property which is the subject of the charge and deal with it for the benefit of the charge holder (as opposed to creditors generally)

- Will usually involve selling the property
- Charge document will usually state when a receiver can be appointed

Law of Property Act receivers

- LPA Receiver is appointed by a fixed charge holder → usually in the charge document
- Aim is to sell the charged property so that the creditor can be repaid

Administrative receivers

- Administrative receivers are appointed by floating charge holders, when the floating charge is over the company's whole undertaking
- Usually only for charges created before 15 Sept 2003 (after this date = administration route)

Claims against Directors

For wrongful trading

In a claim against a director for wrongful trading under ***s 214 IA***, the **court may order a director to contribute to the company's assets if:**

a) The company has gone into insolvent liquidation or insolvent administration;
b) Before commencement of the winding up, the director knew or ought to have concluded there was no reasonable prospect that the company would avoid insolvent liquidation; **and**
c) That person was a director of the company at the time.

→ Bought by a liquidator or administrator

The court may order a director who has been found guilty of wrongful trading to make a contribution to the assets of the company (assessed on a compensatory basis)

Defence:

- A director will not be liable for wrongful trading if they took every step with a view to minimising the potential loss to the company's creditors as they ought to have taken
- **Two stage test:**
  a) The general knowledge, skill and experience that may reasonably be expected of a person carrying out the same functions as are carried out by that director in relation to the company (**objective**), and
  b) The general knowledge, skill and experience that that director has (**subjective**)

For fraudulent trading

If, in the course of the company being wound up, it appears that the company's business has been **carried out with intent to defraud creditors of the company** / creditors of any other person / fraudulent purposes

- The persons who were knowingly parties to the carrying on of the business are liable to make such contributions as court thinks proper (on a compensatory basis)

→ Bought by liquidator / administrator

For misfeasance

Misfeasance is breach of any fiduciary / other duty by directors

Not just directors who are liable → covers company officers, liquidators or administrations or anyone else who has taken part in the 'promotion, formation or management of a company'

During the course of the winding up, directors may be ordered to contribute to the company's assets through compensation for misfeasance (***s 212 IA***)

May be ordered to repay / restore / account for money or property that has been misapplied in breach of duty

Land

Introduction

Fixtures v Chattels

When you attach an object to land (e.g. shelves / cupboards), it **converts from a chattel to a fixture**

- A fixture is treated as though it is part of the land to which it is attached → forms part of the purchase price of the property
- A chattel is separate from the land (can be removed at any time)

The Test:

If the contract is silent on whether an object is a chattel / fixture:

Two tests for identifying a fixture: (***Berkley v Poulett [1977]***):

1) Method and Degree of Annexation

- Whatever is attached to the soil becomes part of it (presumption that chattel has become a fixture)
- **Rebuttable** → if the object is easily removable could argue it is chattel

2) Object and Purpose of Annexation

- An object resting on the ground by its own weight alone can be a fixture if the purpose of placing it there was to enhance the reality
- An object which is only lightly affixed and can be removed easily may be a fixture, if it was placed in a room to make it more beautiful
- Where an object may be enjoyed better as a chattel (even if fixed)

Case Law Examples:

- ***D'Eyncourt v Gregory***: number of freestanding items were fixtures as part of the architectural design of the property
    - Tapestries fixed to the panelling in the walls
    - Portrait hung

- Carved kneeling figures & sculpted marble vases

- ***Leigh v Taylor***: tapestries never lost their character as chattels → had been stretched over canvas and then tacked to a framework of wood nailed to the wall
  - Hung merely for display = chattels
- ***Elitestone Ltd v Morris and another***: a bungalow rested on concrete foundation blocks set into the ground → tenants claimed it was a house, freehold owner claimed it was chattel
  - HoL: a house that is constructed so as to be removable may remain chattel
  - A house which is constructed so that it can't be removed at all is a fixture (part and parcel of the realty)
- ***Botham v TSB Bank plc***: fitted carpets, curtains, light fittings, gas fires (connected by a gas pipe) were all chattel. Fitted kitchen units were fixtures
  - Where 'the bath had been fitted built into the bathroom, the bath would become a fixture and its taps would, prima facie, follow suit'

Conveyancing of Land

Conveyancing = describes the procedure followed **to transfer title to land** (i.e the ownership of land)

There are 2 stages to the conveyancing transaction:

a) **Exchange of Contracts** (where the buyer obtains an equitable interest in the land)
b) **Completion** (where the parties execute a deed to transfer legal ownership of the land)
   - This deed is called a conveyance

The Contract:

- During the pre-contract stage, the buyer will investigate the property fully (find out all the rights and interests that exist over the property)
- The contract must be in writing and contain all the express terms agreed between the parties (***s 2 Law of Property (Miscellaneous Provisions) Act 1989***)
- Must be signed by or on behalf of each party
- On exchange, the contract becomes fully effective
  - Until exchange, either party may withdraw from the transaction without penalty
  - Once exchanged, will face penalties if withdraw (contractually bound)
- After exchange, the seller still has the legal title to the land
  - May remain in the property until completion (where the buyer pays the balance of the purchase price)
  - Between contract and completion, the buyer has an equitable interest in the property (estate contract)

Completion:

- To transfer the title to a legal estate or interest in land, the parties must execute a deed (***s 52 Law of Property Act 1925***)
- On completion, the legal title to the property is transferred to the purchaser using a conveyance of transfer

Defining Land

- **Property** = rights that confer upon a person **a degree of control over a resource** (e.g. leases, easements and covenants)
  - Doesn't need to be land (e.g. a car or shares in a company)

Typical definition = land 'extends upwards to infinity and downwards to the centre of the earth'

Airspace has been limited to such height as is necessary for them to enjoy in an ordinary way the land that they own and the structures that are placed upon it (***Bernstein of Leigh (Baron) v Skyviews & General Ltd [1977]***)

Legal Estates

Estate = a period of time

Where a person owns land, they own a period of time

Where a person owns an estate, it can create a lesser estate (or shorter period of time) → confer the benefit of such lesser estate on others

→ Possible to have 2 legal estates in the same piece of land at the same time (landlord with a freehold estate and tenant with the leasehold estate)

When you own an estate in land, you have the right to enjoy or possess that land and receive any rents or profits produced

When referring to ownership, don't refer to ownership of land, but to the concept of an estate or period of time in land

☑ **Freehold Estate (*s 1(1)(a) of the Law of Property Act 1925)***

☑ **Leasehold Estate (*s 1(1)(b) of the Law of Property Act 1925)***

Legal Third Party Rights and Interests

There are **2 legal third party rights and interests** recognised in ***s 1(2) of the Law of Property Act 1925*:**

☑ **Easement (*s 1(2)(a) LPA)***

☑ **Legal Mortgage (s 1(2)(b) LPA)**

Equitable Third Party Rights and Interests

An interest *not* within ***s 1(2)*** is an equitable interest

☑ **Equitable Interest under a Trust**

☑ **Restrictive Covenants**

☑ **Estate Contract**

☑ **Non-Legal Easements**

Licences

Licences → situations where **landowners**, whilst **allowing persons to use their land** in some way, **do not intend to create any kind of proprietary interest** in it (permanent interest)

- The person using the land will instead have a licence of some kind
- A licence is capable of authorising anything → ranges from rights of access to temporary accommodation (e.g. lodger) (***Thomas v Sorrell***)
- It is no more than a permission that rescues you from being regarded as a trespasser on someone's land (can be revoked at any time)

Bare licence
A licence **granted for no consideration** (***The Calgarth [1927]***)

Contractual licence
A licence **supported by consideration**

- Revocation of a contractual licence may give rise to damages for breach of contract
- In equity, it may be possible to restrain wrongful revocation by an injunction

Statute

Certain third party rights can arise by virtue of statute

Home Rights → a right of occupation as against the other spouse (for the non-owning spouse) (**s 30 of the Family Law Act 1996)**

Registration of Land

Prior to the passage of the ***LPA 1925*** and the ***Land Registration Act 1925***, estates and interests were treated in the unregistered system of land law

- As such, more than 40% of England and Wales (by area) remains unregistered
- 10% of all titles to land remain unregistered

Unregistered

Proof of Ownership of Title

Where the title to the property is **not registered at Land Registry**, sellers prove that they have the right to possession of the land by producing documents that show they and their predecessors in title have been entitled to possession of the land

- Typically show a bundle of conveyances to prove there's an unbroken chain of title
- ***LPA 1925*** → unless the contract provides to the contrary, the seller need only produce title deeds proving ownership of the land for the last 15 years (***s 44 LPA***)

Land Charges Register:

The Land Charges Register is a **public register of third party rights that affect unregistered land**

1) Details of the third party interests should be registered by the person with the interest *against* the name of the estate owner who has created the interest and whose land is to be burdened by it (***s 3, Land Charges Act 1972***)
    - Should be done at the time the interest is created

2) Such registration is deemed to constitute actual notice of the incumbrance and of the fact of the registration to all persons connected with the land affected, as from the date of registration (***s 198, Law of Property Act 1925***)
    - Anyone who buys the land is deemed to buy with actual knowledge of the land charge and will be bound by it
    - The land charge must be registered by the date of completion of the sale (date of conveyance)

- Where the land charge *hasn't* been registered, the purchasers of the land can take free of the unregistered land charge (***s 4 Land Charges Act 1972***)
    - Purchaser includes a mortgagee and a lessee
    - A person who receives a property as a gift takes subject all third party rights (whether registered or not)

Third Party Rights **that *are capable* of being registered as land charges:**

☑ **Estate Contract** = Class C Land

☑ **Restrictive Covenant** = Class D Land

☑ **Equitable Easement** = Class D Land

☑ **Family Law Act 1996** = Class F Land

Pre-1926 Rules:

Where an third party right / interest falls outside of the Land Charges Act rules, you must apply the rules which operated before the Act (**pre-1926 rules**)

☑ **Equitable interests under a trust** = enforceable **against anyone, except equity's darling**

☑ **Most legal interests** (legal leases / easements / mortgages) = **bind the world**

☑ **Pre 1926 equitable interests**

Removal of Interest:

A purchaser who discovers a third party interest before they buy the property may be able to take action to ensure that it is removed from the property before they complete the purchase

- **Can negotiate to get them to release their interest**
- Separate rules for equitable interests under a trust → done by overreaching

Registered

After the parties execute a deed to transfer ownership of the land from one to the other.
Where the title to land is **registered**, the deed takes the form of a **transfer**.

On the sale of a registered title, completion of the transfer doesn't transfer the legal estate from the seller to buyer (*s 27 **Land Registration Act***)

- Legal estate remains with the seller
- Will only pass to the buyer when their name is put on the register as the new owner of the land

The register will reveal the current owner and what other interests exist over the property:

a) **Property Register**
   - Contains a description of the land by reference to a title plan and address of the property
   - Reveals the legal estate which has been registered under the title number
   - Contains details of any rights that benefit the land (e.g. benefit of an easement)

b) **Proprietorship Register:**
   - Reveals the name and address of the legal owners of the land (the registered proprietors)
   - Records the price paid for the land by the current owners (if sold since 1 April 2000)
   - Records any limitations on the registered proprietors' ability to deal freely with the land

c) **Charges Register:**
   - Records rights which burden the land (e.g. a restrictive covenant)

Compulsory First Registration:

When landowners deal with their land in particular ways, the transaction can trigger an obligation to register the title (**compulsory first registration**)

- Application must be made within 2 months of completion (otherwise the transaction will be void with regard to the passing of the legal estate to the buyer)

Under ***s 4(1)(a) of the Land Registration Act 2002***, any transfer of a qualifying estate for valuable consideration will trigger compulsory first registration

☑ **Freehold** (***s 4(2)(a)***)

☑ **Legal mortgage** (***s 4(1)(g)***)

☑ Grant of a **lease** for a term of **more than 7 years** (*s 4(1)(c)*)

- Affects the leasehold estate (tenant must register the lease), the freehold estate can remain unregistered
- Unless the lease was granted before 2003 (then only had to be registered if term exceed 21 years ***(Land Registration Act 1925)***)

☑ Transfers of a **freehold by way of a gift** (*s 4(1)(a)*)

- Even if the estate transferred has a negative value (***s 4(6)***)

✗ Grant of an **easement** doesn't trigger first resignation

✗ **Gift in a will** doesn't trigger first registration

- BUT when the owner dies, the transfer of the freehold estate by an assent will trigger compulsory first registration (***s 4(1)(a)(ii)***)

Freehold Estates

An estate in fee simple absolute in possession → *s 1(1)(a) of the Law of Property Act 1925*

- 'Fee' = capable of being inherited
- 'Simple' = may pass to any class of heir
- 'Absolute' = it is not determinable or condition on any event (not limited)
- 'In possession' = entitlement to possession of the land now

The only time where a freehold comes to an end is when the owner dies, leaving no will or heirs (reverts to the Crown / Treasury Department)

Formalities (Legal)

Conveyances to be by deed (s 52 LPA 1925)
S 52(1) LPA 1925: A deed is required to *create* legal estates and interests in land. **If no deed = void**

What is a deed? (s 1(2) Law of Property (Miscellaneous Provisions) Act 1989)
S 1(2) Law of Property (Miscellaneous Provisions) Act 1989: **2. An instrument shall not be a deed unless** a) It makes it clear on its face that it is intended to be a deed by the person making it or, as the case may be, by the parties to it, and

b) It is validly executed as a deed
   i) By that person or a person authorised to execute it in the name or on behalf of that person, or
   ii) By one or more of those parties or a person authorised to execute it in the name or on behalf of one or more of those parties

Correct execution of a deed?
(s 1(3) Law of Property (Miscellaneous Provisions) Act 1989)

S 1(3) Law of Property (Miscellaneous Provisions) Act 1989:

3) An instrument is validly executed as a deed by an individual if, and only if
   a) It is signed
      i) By him in the presence of a witness who attests the signature or
      ii) At his direction and in his presence and the presence of two witnesses who each attest the signature, and
   b) It is delivered as a deed

- If the title is unregistered, the deed transferring ownership is called a 'conveyance'
- If the title is registered, the deed is called a 'transfer'

Registration (Unregistered)

Where the title to land is **unregistered,** the buyer **becomes the legal owner of the land** at the date of the conveyance

Proof of Ownership of Title

Where the title to the property is **not registered at Land Registry**, sellers **prove** that they have the right to possession of the land by:

Producing documents that show;
They and their predecessors in title have been;
Entitled to possession of the land

Typically show a bundle of conveyances to prove there's an unbroken chain of title
LPA 1925 → unless the contract provides to the contrary, the seller need only produce title deeds proving ownership of the land for the last 15 years (***s 44 LPA***)

Registration (Registered)

On the sale of a registered title, completion of the transfer doesn't transfer the legal estate from the seller to buyer (***s 27 Land Registration Act***)

- Legal estate remains with the seller
- Will only pass to the buyer when their name is put on the register as the new owner of the land
- From 1 December 1990, the whole of England and Wales became **an area of compulsory registration**
- Application must be made within 2 months of completion (otherwise the transaction will be void with regard to the passing of the legal estate to the buyer)

Under ***s 4(1)(a) of the Land Registration Act 2002***, any transfer of a qualifying estate for valuable consideration will trigger compulsory first registration

In registered conveyancing, the seller proves ownership by showing the buyer an 'official copy' of the entries on the register at ***Land Registry***

- **Property Register** = reveals the legal estate which has been registered under the title number
- **Proprietorship Register** = reveals the name and address of the legal owners of the land

Leasehold Estates

Terminology

1) **Tenancy** = short term lettings (e.g. on a weekly or monthly basis)
2) **Lease** = fixed term letting
3) **Grant** = the original creation of the lease or sublease
4) **Lessor / Landlord / Reversioner** = the original grantor of the lease
    - Retains the freehold estate, but has created a leasehold estate out of it → retains the freehold reversion
    - **Head lease and head landlord** = original lease agreement
5) **Lessee / Tenant =** the original grantee of the lease
6) **A sublease / underlease / subtenancy**

    The transfer of part of a leasehold interest from a tenant to a third party, in which the tenant keeps a remainder interest in the leasehold estate so that the property will go back to the tenant before eventually reverting to the landlord

    Must be for a period of at least one day shorter than the lease out of which it's granted

    The person who has sublet their property is called a sublessor or sublandlord

    - Will still have a leasehold reversion (interest) in the property

    The person who sublets is called a sublessee / underlessee / subtenant

7) **Assignment of the freehold reversion** = the act of transfer when you sell the freehold reversion in a property
8) **Assignment** = the transfer of an entire leasehold interest from a tenant to a third party
    - The assignor would assign the lease to an assignee

Diagrams

A ↓ 99 B	**Creation of a new estate (lease) out of an existing estate:** • A (the freeholder / owner of the fee simple) has granted a lease to B for 99 years • A is the lessor / landlord • B is the lessee / tenant. • A's interest after granting of the lease is a freehold reversion
A ⟶ D	**Transfer of an existing estate:** A has transferred their estate to D
A ↓ 99 B ↓ 50 C	• A has granted B a lease for 99 years. • B has granted an underlease / sublease / subtenancy to C for a term of 50 years. • B, after granting the sublease, has a leasehold reversion. • The lease between A and B is a head lease
A ⟶ D ↓ B ⟶ E ↓ C	A has assigned the freehold reversion to D (by deed). • D now becomes the head landlord or head lessor. B has *assigned* the head leasehold interest (a leasehold reversion) to E. E now replaces B as the substantial landlord (they are D's tenant and C's landlord)

Lease or Licence?

Classic definition of a lease = **a term of years absolute** (***s 1(1)(b) of the Law of Property Act 1925)***

- The tenant must have *exclusive possession* of the property for a <u>fixed</u> and <u>certain</u> duration

Characteristics of a Lease

1) Certainty of Duration

A term of years absolute = a term of years certain *or* liable to be determined by notice (***S 205(1)(xxvii) LPA)***

- **Fixed-term lease** = a lease granted for a <u>fixed</u> period of time
- **A periodic lease** = a lease granted for a <u>basic period of time</u>, either:

Express or

Implied by a regular payment of rent

Either party must be able to end a periodic tenancy by notice (***Prudential Assurance Co Ltd v London Residuary Body***)

- **Tenancy for life** = converts into a 90 year lease, determinable either on the death of the tenant or as provided by the agreement (***Berrisford v Mexfield Housing Co-operative)***

To be certain, the **date of commencement** of the lease **must be known to both parties at the start**

- Where there is no date specified on a lease, it's determined to start immediately
- A lease granted for an uncertain period of time *won't* be an estate in land (***Lace v Chantler***)

Exclusive Possession

Tenant must have the right to exclude anyone from the property

Necessary to look at **the effect of the agreement**, rather than any labels given

- E.g. where the landlord provides attendance / services which requires them to have unrestricted access to the premises, *there isn't* exclusive possession

There **will *not* be a tenancy**, even if the occupier has exclusive possession: (***Street v Mountford***)

Where the parties clearly don't intend to enter into legal relationships at all

Where occupation is required in connection with services provided or duties owed by the tenant to the landlord (e.g. contract of employment)

If the relationship between the parties is that of vendor and purchaser and occupancy takes place under a contract for the sale of land

If the owner has no power to grant a tenancy

Shared Occupation?

- ***Antoniades v Villiers***:

  Should take into account:

  a) The surrounding circumstances
  b) Relationships between the prospective occupiers
  c) Course of negotiations
  d) The nature and extent of the accommodation
  e) Intended and actual mode of occupation of the accommodation

- ***AG Securities v Vaughan***: 4 parties, each signed on different years. Each agreement was in the same form, except for the amount of rent. Whenever one agreement terminated, another party took over the vacant room. Each was responsible for their own rent.

- The agreements were independent of each other and did not confer a right of exclusive possession on any one party
- Occupants only had licence agreements

Need for Rent?

A tenancy can still arise, *even* where no rent was payable (***Ashburn v Arnold***)

Although, where rent is paid, it supports the view that the parties intended a formal relationship of landlord and tenant to arise

Lack of rent doesn't prevent a tenancy from existing, but it may have a bearing when determining whether it was the intention of the parties to grant a tenancy

Fixed Term Lease

Fixed term lease = a contract which gives the tenant the right to occupy the premises for a certain fixed period of time

Characteristics:

a. **Must be created expressly** → an express grant of the lease is needed to identify the length of the term
b. **Terminates automatically** at the end of the period of the lease → the tenant loses their right to remain on the premises and the landlord can take possession of them.
    - Termination by 'effluxion of time' = automatically, without either party having to sever notice
    - **Forfeiture** = a provision which allows the landlord to end it prematurely if the tenant fails to meet their obligations (e.g. failing to pay rent)
    - **Break Clause** = a clause in the express grant of the lease providing for either party to sever a notice on the other to end the lease prematurely

7 + years

Formalities (Legal)

Deed requirements (*s 52 LPA & S 1(2) and (3) of the Law of Property (Miscellaneous Provisions) Act 1989*)

Registration (Unregistered)

Pre-1926 Rules

Falls outside of the Land Charges Act rules → must apply the rules which operated before the Act (**pre-1926 rules**)

Under the pre-1926 rules, legal leases bind the whole world

A legal lease will bind the purchaser of the legal estate, even if the purchaser has no knowledge of the existence of the interest when they buy the property

Registration (Registered)

Registrable Disposition:

A legal lease for a term of more than 7 years **is classed as a registrable disposition (*s 27(2)(b)(i) Land Registration Act*).**

It will *not* bind a purchaser *unless* it is completed by registration → must be entered on the charges register of the mortgagor's title (***s 27, Land Registration Act 2002***)

This must be done by the date of registration of the transfer to the purchaser (***s 29 LRA***)

It will also not be considered to be legal until it is registered

- Also includes the disposition of a (currently unregistered lease) with 7 + years to run

Actual Occupation?

If a legal lease has *not* been registered, ***may* count as an unregistered interests which override,** if the person is in **actual occupation of the land (*sch 3, para 2, LRA*)** =

Is not required to be entered onto the register but are binding on the purchaser of the property

☑ Is **proprietary in nature**

'Actual occupation' depends on context:

- ***Williams & Glyn's Bank v Boland [1981]***: a wife (who had an equitable interest in land under trust) had actual occupation as there was 'physical presence on the land by the claimant'
- ***Abbey National Building Society v Cann [1991]***: a mother, who had an equitable interest in the property, was not in actual occupation when she sent her son to move in her furniture and put up curtains → held to be preparatory
- ***Lloyds Bank plc v Rosset [1989]***: the claimant was in actual occupation by visiting the property regularly while it was being renovated (she was occupying, so far as it was possible)
- ***Link Lending Ltd v Bustard [2010]***: still held to be in actual occupation, even though she had been absent for over a year in residential psychiatric care (possessions there, made regular visits, bills paid & intended to return)
- ***Thompson v Foy [2010]:*** similar to Bustard, but she did not want to return to live there (not in actual occupation)
- ***Kling v Keston Properties Ltd (1983)***: a car was parked regularly in a garage → this was the normal use of the property → could amount to actual occupation

The overriding status to a person in actual occupation occurs 'at the time of the disposition' (date of completion)

&

The *occupation* (not the interest) would have been obvious on a reasonably careful inspection of the land at the time of the sale, **or**

The purchaser had actual knowledge of the *interest* at the time of the sale

If enquiries were made of the person holding the interest before the sale, that person must have disclosed if they could reasonably have been expected to do so

3 - 7 years

Formalities (Legal)

Deed requirements (*s 52 LPA & S 1(2) and (3) of the Law of Property (Miscellaneous Provisions) Act 1989*)

Registration (Unregistered)

Pre-1926 Rules

Falls outside of the Land Charges Act rules → must apply the rules which operated before the Act (**pre-1926 rules**)

Under the pre-1926 rules, legal leases bind the whole world

A legal lease will bind the purchaser of the legal estate, even if the purchaser has no knowledge of the existence of the interest when they buy the property

Registration (Registered)

Overriding Interest - *Sch 3, Para 1, LRA*

A legal lease for a term of 7 years or less counts as an unregistered interest which overrides (***sch 3, para 1, LRA***).

- This lease is not required to be entered onto the register, but are binding on the purchaser of property
- **Relevant date** = date of completion of the purchaser
- Under the 1925 act, it was a term not exceeding 21 years. Leases already protected before the 2003 act will continue to be overriding (***sch 12, para 12, LRA***)

3 years

Formalities (Legal)

Parol Lease Exception

→ **Parol Lease Exception** (transactions that involve the grant of a lease for a term not exceeding 3 years)

S 52(2)(d) LPA 1925 → leases or tenancies or other assurances *not* required by law to be made in writing (parol lease exception)

S 54(2) LPA 1925: transactions that involve the **grant of a lease for a term not exceeding 3 years** can be granted without a deed and orally.

☑ The tenant must be entitled to take possession as soon as the lease is granted ***and***

☑ The lease must have been granted at the best rent which can be reasonably obtained, *without taking a fine*

Fine = tenant paying a lump sum at the beginning of the lease, in return for paying a lower rent during the term of the lease

Applies only to the creation of a lease

Registration (Unregistered)

Pre-1926 Rules

Falls outside of the Land Charges Act rules → must apply the rules which operated before the Act (**pre-1926 rules**)

Under the pre-1926 rules, legal leases bind the whole world

A legal lease will bind the purchaser of the legal estate, even if the purchaser has no knowledge of the existence of the interest when they buy the property

Registration (Registered)

Overriding Interest - *Sch 3, Para 1, LRA*

A legal lease for a term of 7 years or less counts as an unregistered interest which overrides (***sch 3, para 1, LRA***).

- This lease is not required to be entered onto the register, but are binding on the purchaser of property
- **Relevant date** = date of completion of the purchaser
- Under the 1925 act, it was a term not exceeding 21 years. Leases already protected before the 2003 act will continue to be overriding (***sch 12, para 12, LRA***)

Periodic Tenancies

Where the parties have not agreed a fixed term for the tenancy at the outset, **the regular payment of rent will give rise to a periodic tenancy**

- Works on a rolling basis
- The landlord and tenant agree the basic period of the lease and that the lease will continue to run from one period to another, *until determined by either party*
- Renews itself automatically at the end of each period

- The period depends on when the rent is paid by the tenant (e.g. a monthly period tenancy / weekly)

- Certain to continue until either party decided to end it by serving a notice to quit

Characteristics of a Periodic Tenancy

Creation:

Can either be created expressly, or implied (e.g. where a tenant goes into occupation with the landlord's consent and pays rent, measured by reference to a period)

Termination:

The length of notice required **depends upon the periodic term of the tenancy**

- General rule at least one full period's notice is required to terminate the tenancy
- This notice should expire at the end of a clear period (e.g. a weekly tenancy beginning on a Saturday can only be terminated by a week's notice that expires on a Friday)

Exception:

- Where premises have been **let as a dwelling** a notice served by either a landlord or tenant will not be valid unless: (***s 5 of the Protection from Eviction act 1977***)
    a) It is given in writing
    b) Contains certain prescribed information and
    c) Is given at least 4 weeks before its due to take effect
- Where it has been let as a dwelling & the occupier continues to reside there → the landlord must also obtain a court order to recover possession of premises
  (***s 3 of the Protection from Eviction Act 1977***)

Formalities (legal)

→ **Parol Lease Exception**

1) ***S 52(2)(d) LPA 1925*** → leases or tenancies or other assurances *not* required by law to be made in writing (parol lease exception)

2) ***S 54(2) LPA 1925:*** transactions that involve the **grant of a lease for a term not exceeding 3 years** can be granted without a deed and orally.

☑ The tenant must be entitled to take possession as soon as the lease is granted ***and***

☑ The lease must have been granted at the best rent which can be reasonably obtained, *without taking a fine*

Fine = tenant paying a lump sum at the beginning of the lease, in return for paying a lower rent during the term of the lease

Registration (Unregistered)

Pre-1926 Rules:

Falls outside of the Land Charges Act rules → must apply the rules which operated before the Act (**pre-1926 rules**)

Under the pre-1926 rules, legal leases bind the whole world

A legal lease will bind the purchaser of the legal estate, even if the purchaser has no knowledge of the existence of the interest when they buy the property

Registration (Registered)

Overriding Interest - *Sch 3, Para 1, LRA*

A period tenancy counts as an unregistered interest which overrides (***sch 3, para 1, LRA***).

- This lease is not required to be entered onto the register, but are binding on the purchaser of property
- **Relevant date** = date of completion of the purchaser
- Under the 1925 act, it was a term not exceeding 21 years. Leases already protected before the 2003 act will continue to be overriding (***sch 12, para 12, LRA***)

Equitable Leases

Where the formalities for the creation of a lease have not been complied with → equitable lease (estate contract) (***Walsh v Lonsdale***) → *see estate contract section for formalities etc….*

- An attempt to end this lease before the term expires will amount to a breach of contract (***Walsh v Lonsdale***)

Estate Contract

Is a contract to create or convey a legal estate in the land

- The buyer under the contract has an immediate equitable interest in the land

<u>*Example*</u>:

Period between exchange of contracts and completion of purchase, the buyer has an equitable interest in the property

Option to buy a freehold estate

Where a lease or an easement has not been granted using the correct formalities for law, an equitable lease / easement may be established (***Walsh v Lonsdale)***

Formalities (Equitable)

An Estate Contract is *not* capable of being legal *(s 1(2) LPA)*

It is capable of being <u>equitable</u> *(s 1(3) LPA)*

S 2 of the Law of Property (Miscellaneous Provisions) Act 1989:

A contract for the sale of an interest in land can **only be made in writing**

The terms may be incorporated in a document either by being set out in it or by reference to some other document

The documents incorporating the terms must be signed by, or on behalf, of each party to the contract

And the tenant has clean hands (***Walsh v Lonsdale***)

Exceptions:

Exceptions to above provisions (i.e. don't have to be in writing):

- ***5(a)***: short leases (***s 54(2) of the Law of Property Act 1925***)
- ***5(b)***: a contract made in the course of a public action

Registration (Unregistered)

Class C Land (LCA)

Under ***s 3, Land Charges Act 1972,*** the estate contract must be registered by the person with the interest, against the name of the estate owner who has created the estate contract and whose land is burdened by it (at the time the estate contract is created)

Must be registered on the Land Charges Register as:

- **A Class C(iv) Land Charge**

☑ Such registration is deemed to constitute actual notice of the incumbrance and of the fact of the registration to all persons connected with the land affected, as from the date of registration (***s 198, Law of Property Act 1925***)

Anyone who buys the land is deemed to buy with actual knowledge of the land charge and will be bound by it

✗ Where the estate contract *hasn't* been registered, the purchasers of the land can take free of the unregistered land charge (***s 4 Land Charges Act 1972***)

Registration (Registered)

IARE

An Estate Contract is classed as an interest affecting a registered estate.

It will *not* bind a purchaser *unless* it is subject to a notice on the Charges Register (***s 32, Land Registration Act 2002***)

- The notice may be agreed (entered with the consent of the registered proprietor) or unilateral (entered without the consent)

This must be done by the date of registration of the transfer to the purchaser (***s 29 LRA***)

Actual Occupation

An estate contract *may* count as an unregistered interests which override, if the person is in actual occupation of the land (sch 3, para 2, LRA) =

- Is not required to be entered onto the register but are binding on the purchaser of the property

An interest belonging to a person in actual occupation of the land (*sch 3, para 2, LRA)*

☑ Is **proprietary in nature**

'Actual occupation' depends on context:

- ***Williams & Glyn's Bank v Boland [1981]***: a wife (who had an equitable interest in land under trust) had actual occupation as there was 'physical presence on the land by the claimant'

- *Abbey National Building Society v Cann [1991]*: a mother, who had an equitable interest in the property, was not in actual occupation when she sent her son to move in her furniture and put up curtains → held to be preparatory
- *Lloyds Bank plc v Rosset [1989]*: the claimant was in actual occupation by visiting the property regularly while it was being renovated (she was occupying, so far as it was possible)
- *Link Lending Ltd v Bustard [2010]*: still held to be in actual occupation, even though she had been absent for over a year in residential psychiatric care (possessions there, made regular visits, bills paid & intended to return)
- *Thompson v Foy [2010]:* similar to Bustard, but she did not want to return to live there (not in actual occupation)
- *Kling v Keston Properties Ltd (1983)*: a car was parked regularly in a garage → this was the normal use of the property → could amount to actual occupation

The overriding status to a person in actual occupation occurs 'at the time of the disposition' (date of completion)

&

The interest will only override if

- The *occupation* (not the interest) would have been obvious on a reasonably careful inspection of the land at the time of the sale, **or**
- The purchaser had actual knowledge of the *interest* at the time of the sale
- If enquiries were made of the person holding the interest before the sale, that person must have disclosed if they could reasonably have been expected to do so

Leasehold Covenants

Types of Covenants

An expressly created lease or tenancy is likely to contain **promises made by the parties** to each other → these promises are known as covenants

- **Positive covenant** = requires a person to carry out work / spend money
- **Negative covenant** = places restrictions on what a person may do

A covenant **is *not* capable of being legal *(s 1(2) LPA)***

It is capable of being equitable *(s 1(3) LPA)*

Landlord's Implied Covenants

Quiet Enjoyment:

The implied covenant for quiet enjoyment is a <u>qualified</u> covenant

- It protects the tenant against interference with the tenant's quiet and peaceful possession enjoyment of the premises by the landlord or persons claiming, through or under the landlord (***Kenny v Preen***)
- The landlord, by letting the premises, confers on the tenant the right of possession during the term and impliedly promises *not* to interfere with the tenant's exercise and use of the right of possession during the term

S 1(2) and (3) of the Protection from Eviction Act 1977:

If any person unlawfully deprives (or attempts to deprive) the residential occupier of any premises of his occupation, he shall be guilty of an offence *unless* he proves that he believed, and had reasonable cause to believe, that the residential occupier had ceased to reside in the premises

If any person *with intent* to cause the residential occupier:

a) To give up the occupation of the premises, or
b) To refrain from exercising any right of pursuing any remedy in respect of the premises

Does acts likely to interfere with the peace or comfort of the residential occupier or members of his household, or persistently withdraws or withholds services reasonably required for the occupation of the premises as a residence, shall be guilty of an offence

Doesn't include things done before the grant of the tenancy:

'It would be inconsistent if the covenant for quiet enjoyment were interpreted to create liability for disturbances or inconvenience or any other damage attributable to the condition of the premises' (***Southwark LBC v Mills***)

- Inadequate soundproofing would not be a breach of the landlord's covenant for quiet enjoyment

Repair:

Obligations implied under ***s 11 of the Landlord and Tenant Act 1985***:

☑ To keep in repair the structure and exterior of the dwelling house

☑ To keep in repair and proper working order the installations for the supply of water, gas, electricity and for sanitation and

☑ To keep in repair and proper working order the installations for space heating and heating water

May have to remedy an inherent defect in construction if necessary to carry out repairs under ***s 11*** (***Ravenseft Properties Ltd v Davstone (Holdings) Ltd***)

✗ A landlord *isn't* liable to carry out a repair until he has been notified (***O'Brien v Robinson***)

✗ If there is no disrepair, a landlord *can't* be made liable under this implied covenant (***Quick v Taff Ely Borough Council***)

✗ Not required to rebuild or reinstate the premises in the case of destruction or damage by fire, tempest, floor or other inevitable accident (***2(b) LTA)***

✗ Not required to repair or maintain anything which the tenant is entitled to remove (***2(c) LTA)***

✗ Not required to carry out work or repairs that the tenant is liable for, by virtue of their duty to use premises in a tenant-like manner ((***2(a) LTA)***

- Tenant may have 'little jobs about the place which a reasonable tenant would do' (***Warren v Keen***)

Tenant's Express Covenants

Rent

There will be an **implied covenant by the tenant to pay the rent agreed** (in arrears)

Most landlords will thus include an express covenant in a lease for the tenant to pay the rent in advance

User

Will usually be a **restriction on the use to which the property can be put** (e.g. for residential or business purposes)

Not to sublet

If the landlord wants to restrict the tenant's right to deal with the lease, they will have to **impose an alienation covenant on the tenant**

Can be an 'absolute covenant' against assignments or sublets

More common is a 'qualified covenant' where assignments or sublets are prohibited, unless the landlord's licence or consent is obtained first

❌ A landlord may not unreasonably withhold consent (***s 19(1)(a) of the LTA 1927)***

☑ The landlord must either consent *or* give the tenant reasonable grounds for refusing consent within a reasonable period of the tenant's request (***S 1, LTA 1988)***

Qualifying Leases:

A qualifying lease = for a new tenancy of property that is ***not*** used wholly or mainly as a single private residence (so mostly for commercial properties)

- A landlord is allowed to reach an agreement with the tenant whereby the landlord may withhold consent to an assignment in specified circumstances and state conditions subject to which consent to assignment will be given (***s 22 of the Landlord and Tenant (Covenants) Act 1955***)

Enforceability of Covenants

The Landlord and Tenant (Covenants) Act 1995 applies to most tenancies **granted on or after 1 Jan 1996** (new tenancies)

- Old Tenancies = before 1 Jan 1996
- New Tenancies = after 1 Jan 1996

Old Leases (Enforceability):

Privity of Contract

Privity of contract lasts for the duration of the lease

Original Tenant's liability:

A
↓
B ⟶ C

Where an original tenant assigns a lease, it *doesn't* end privity of contract between them and the original landlord

- If C breaches any of the covenants in the lease, B remains liable to the landlord

- B will remain liable, even if the lease has been assigned many times

Original Landlord's liability:

A → C
↓
B

Where the original landlord assigns the reversion, they remain liable for breaches of covenant by the assignee of the reversion

Privity of Estate

Subsequent Assignee:

A
↓
B → C

Spencer's Case / City of London Corporation v Fell:

After an assignment, the **benefit of a covenant** by the original landlord, *which touches and concerns the land*, **runs with the term** granted by the lease

- C will have the benefit of any covenant originally granted by the landlord, which touches and concerns the land

The **burden of a covenant by the original tenant** which touches and concerns the land also **runs with the term**

- C will also have the burden of any covenant originally agreed by the tenant, which touches and concerns the land

Subsequent Assignee of the Reversion

A → C
↓

S 141 LPA 1925:

B	• Entitlement to the rent and the benefit of all the tenant's covenants in the lease that have 'reference to the subject matter of the lease' are annexed to the reversionary estate The benefit of the tenant's covenants pass to C (and any subsequent owners of the reversion) → allows them to sue the tenant ***S 142 LPA 1925:*** • Obligations under any covenant entered into by the landlord 'with reference to the subject matter of the lease' are also annexed to the reversionary estate - Binding on any subsequent owners of the reversion - Privity of Estate between assignee of the reversion and tenant

Real Covenants?

Working guide for determining if a covenant is 'real' (*P&A Swift Investments v Combined English Stores Group plc*):

The covenant benefits only the reversioner for the time being, and if separated from the reversion ceases to be of benefit to the covenantee

The covenant affects the nature, quality, mode of user or value of the land of the reversioner

The covenant is *not* expressed to be personal

The fact that a covenant is to pay a sum of money will not prevent it from touching and concerning the land, so long as the three other conditions are satisfied and the covenant is connected with something to be done on to or in relation to the land

Escaping Liability?

- Whilst the original parties to the lease will remain liable throughout their term, their successors in title are *only* liable for breaches committed while the lease or reversion is vested in them
- Under ***Moule v Garrett***, where one person discharges the liability of another (e.g. an OG tenant pays the missed rent of an assignee), they may seek to recover the amount they have paid from the person whose liability they have discharged → common law right
- Under ***s 77 LPA*** (unregistered) or ***Sch 12 para 20, LRA 2002*** (registered) → there is an implied covenant to indemnify a person who has covered a liability (only for immediate successor)

Summary:

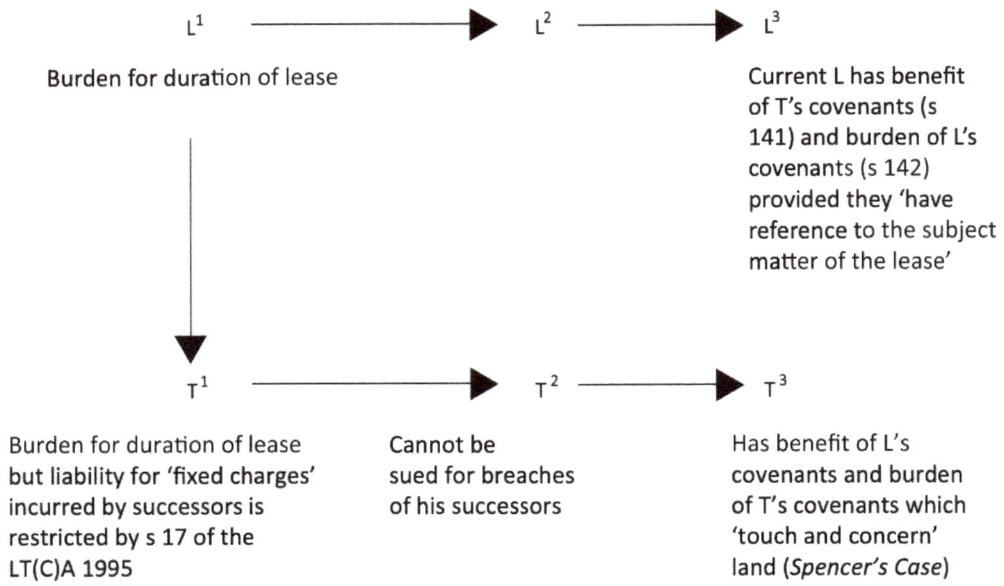

New Leases (Enforceability):

OG Tenant:

Where the lease is a new lease and the tenant assigns the lease, they are **released from the tenant covenants** (***s 5(2)(a) of the 1995 Act***)

- *Not* liable for any breaches by assignee
- Ceases to benefit from the landlord covenants (***s 5(2)(b)***), unless the covenants were expressed to be personal (***s 3(6)(a)***)

Exception - AGA

UNLESS: the lease contains an absolute or qualified covenant against assignment

- Landlord may (before giving consent) impose an authorised guarantee agreement (**AGA**) if reasonable

AGA = a condition that the tenant must agree to guarantee the performance of the tenant covenants by the assignee

Only made to guarantee the liability of their immediate successor

May be able to recover from the assignee under ***Moule v Garrett*** or through an express indemnity obtained from the assignee

OG Landlord:

Where a landlord assigns the reversion to a new head landlord there *isn't* an automatic release

- The landlord must apply to the tenant for release (***s 6(2)(a)***)
- If the landlord is released, they lose the benefit of the tenant covenants (***s 6(2)(b)***)

Subsequent Tenant:

From the date of the assignment, the assignee:

Takes the burden of the tenant covenants ***(s 3(2)(a))***

Acquires the benefit of the landlord covenants ***(s 3(2)(b))***

→ As long as the covenants are not expressed to be personal ***(s 3(6)(a))***

Subsequent Landlord:

From the date of the reversion, the assignee of the reversion:

a) Takes the burden of the landlord covenants ***(s 3(3)(a))***
b) Acquires the benefit of the tenant covenants ***(s 3(3)(b))***

→ As long as the covenants are not expressed to be personal ***(s 3(6)(a))***

- Also acquires the benefit of the right of re-entry (***s 4***)

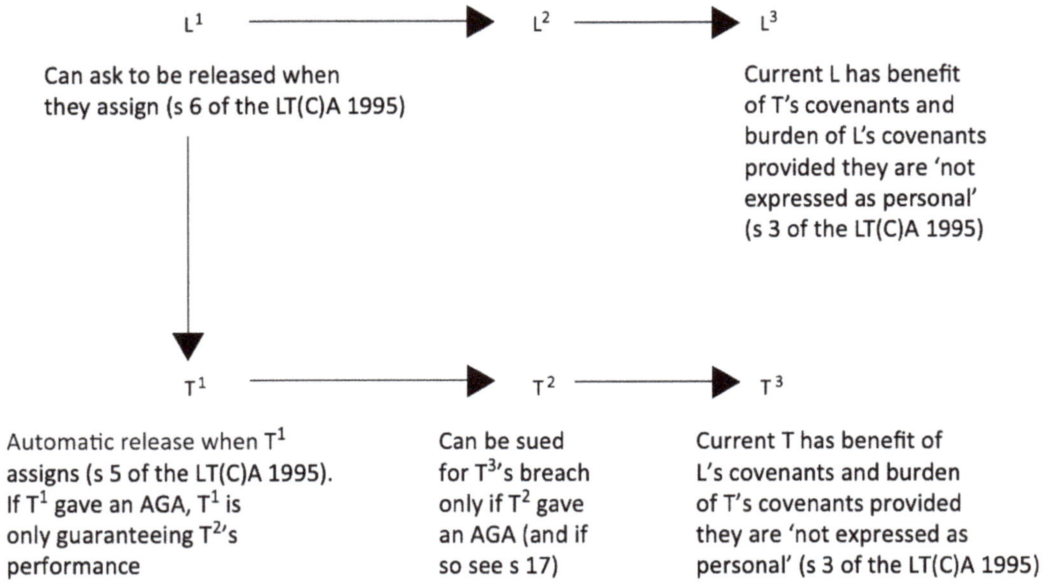

Remedies - Breach of Contract

Failure to pay rent:

Action for debt

Landlord can **choose to sue the tenant for debt**

✗ **BUT**: limited from bringing such a claim after the expiration of 6 years from the date on which the arrears became due (***s 19 of the Limitation Act 1980***)

☑ Where a landlord is suing a **former tenant** under a AGA or privity of contract (old leases) **for arrears of rent** → must serve a default notice in accordance with ***s 17 of the 1995 Act***

- Must be served within 6 months of the rent becoming due

Commercial rent arrears recovery (CRAR)

Sch 12 to the Tribunals, Court and Enforcement Act 2007 → introduced a procedure for **recovery of rent for commercial property**

- Used to recover rent payable in advance or arrears

☑ Rent has to become due and payable, and at least 7 days' notice of enforcement has to be served

- Is subject to a minimum amount of arrears (currently 7 days' rent)

☑ An enforcement agent is instructed to serve an enforcement notice on the tenant → binds the property in the tenant's goods from the time it's served

- Goods remain bound until the arrears are paid or the goods are sold

Forfeiture

- Means the lease will come to a premature end (discussed below)

Other Covenants:

Damages

If a party fails to fulfil an obligation, the other party may bring a claim seeking damages

- ***Hadley v Baxendale***: damages are limited to:
    a) Such as may fairly and reasonably be considered either arising naturally from such breach of contract itself; or
    b) Such as may reasonably be supposed to have been in the contemplation of both parties at the time they made the contract, as the probable result of the breach of it.

Specific Performance

Where damages are seen to be an inadequate remedy for compensation (exceptional cases)

Injunction

For **restrictive covenants**, claimant can get an **injunction to order the defendant not to contravene the covenant** (discretionary remedy)

Withholding Rent

There is a possibility of a set-off against rent (***Taylor v Beal***)

☑ The tenant must notify the landlord of the issue and that unless they carry out the necessary covenant, they will arrange for it to be done themselves

☑ Can then deduct the costs from future payments of rent until reimbursed in full (amount seeking to recover must be liquidated / a fixed sum)

Alternatively, if the tenant chooses to withhold payment of rent and is then sued by the landlord:

- Equity may allow the unliquidated claim to be set off against the liability for rent
- Only occurs where the connection between the 2 claims is sufficiently direct (manifestly unjust to not allow the set off)
    - Tenant's claim must be one that arises directly from the relationship of landlord and tenant created by the lease

Forfeiture

Enables the landlord to **terminate a fixed-term lease *before* it expires.**

Will have a right to forfeit where:

a) The lease contains a provision for the landlord to re-enter the property for a breach of covenant by the tenant (**a forfeiture clause**); **or**
    - Does not end automatically → landlord must decide whether to forfeit the lease or to treat it as continuing (waive the breach)

b) The lease is granted, subject to a condition that the landlord may forfeit it on the happening of some event

A landlord signifies an intention to forfeit either by:

Peaceable re-entry (re-taking possession)

Can't if it's a dwelling house and the person is lawfully residing at the premises (***s 2 Protection from Eviction Act 1977***)

Can't by violence (commit a criminal offence under ***s 6 Criminal Law Act 1977***)

Service of proceedings

Forfeiture for no rent:

☑ Must first show that the tenant had been given the opportunity to pay rent (a formal demand)

- Requires the landlord to attend the premises on the last day for payment at a convenient hour and demand payment of the exact amount (***Duppa v Mayo***)
- Most will include a provision in the lease dispensing with the need for a formal demand
    - Forfeiture clause will say the landlord has a right to re-enter when payment of rent is overdue (whether formally demanded or not)

☑ Tenant may seek relief from forfeiture → will usually be granted if the tenant acts reasonably swiftly and pays the arrears of rent and costs

Forfeiture for other breaches:

- Once its been established the the lease contains a right to forfeit, the landlord will serve on the tenant a notice under ***s 146 of the LPA 1925***
- Unless the tenant complies with the notice and remedies the breach, the landlord may choose to forfeit (tenant may be entitled to relief)

Freehold Covenants

Creating the Covenant

Covenant = promise contained in a deed

Amounts to a contract (although consideration is not always essential)

Most covenants are created when a landowner **wants to sell part of their property**

- E.g. sale of individual houses on a housing estate
- Individual office blocks etc…

Terminology

Covenantor = the person who makes the promise (the land has the burden of the covenant)

Covenantee = the person to whom the promise is made (the land has the benefit of the covenant)

Annexation = denotes that the benefit of a covenant is attached to the land of the covenantee so that it passes automatically to successors

- Annexation of the benefit of a covenant occurs at the time of creation of the covenant

Assignment = refers to the express transfer of the benefit of a covenant to a successor

Formalities (Equitable)

A Freehold Covenant is *not* capable of being legal *(s 1(2) LPA)*

It is capable of being equitable *(s 1(3) LPA)*

Where no trust is involved, the minimum formality requirement for the creation of equitable interests is that the **interest be created by signed writing** (*s 53(1)(a) of the Law of Property Act 1925*)

For restrictive covenants, will usually be contained in a deed as part of the sale transaction, so a valid deed will automatically comply with the requirements of signed writing

Registration (Unregistered)

Class D Land (LCA)

Under ***s 3, Land Charges Act 1972,*** the restrictive covenant must be registered by the person with the interest, against the name of the estate owner who has created the restrictive covenant and whose land is burdened by it (at the time the restrictive covenant is created)

Must be registered on the Land Charges Register as:

- A **Class D Land** (sub-section *ii*)

☑ Such registration is deemed to constitute actual notice of the incumbrance and of the fact of the registration to all persons connected with the land affected, as from the date of registration (***s 198, Law of Property Act 1925***)

Anyone who buys the land is deemed to buy with actual knowledge of the land charge and will be bound by it

✗ Where the restrictive covenant *hasn't* been registered, the purchasers of the land can take free of the unregistered land charge (***s 4 Land Charges Act 1972***)

Registration (Registered)

Freehold Covenants (IARE)

A covenant over freehold land is classed as an interest affecting a registered estate.

It will *not* bind a purchaser *unless* it is subject to a notice on the Charges Register (***s 32, Land Registration Act 2002***)

- The notice may be agreed (entered with the consent of the registered proprietor) or unilateral (entered without the consent)

This must be done by the date of registration of the transfer to the purchaser (***s 29 LRA***)

Enforcement of Covenants

Where the original covenantor breaches a covenantor to the original covenantee → fairly simple procedure

- The original covenantor and original covenantee are linked by privity of contract (so can sue)

Where there are successors in title, it gets more complicated

Benefit (Common Law)

The original covenantee

- The original covenantee will get the benefit of all the express covenants, positive and restrictive, real and personal, in the contract
- Possible for the original covenantee to enforce any express covenant against anyone who has the burden of the covenant (including successors)
  - Unless the covenantee has parted with all the land for the benefit of which the covenant was taken

Running of the benefit at common law (successors):

The **benefit** of **both positive and restrictive covenants** will **pass to successors of the covenantee at common law in 2 ways:**

By express assignment; or

Automatically (if certain conditions are met)

Express Assignment

It's possible for the benefit of a covenant to pass to a successor by express assignment

The assignment must (*s 136 LPA*):

a) Occur at the same time as the transfer of the land
b) Be in writing signed by the assignor
c) Written notice of the assignment must be given to the person with the burden of the covenant

Automatically

If there is no express assignment, the benefit of a covenant passes automatically at common law if: ***(Smith and Snipes Hall Farm Ltd v River Douglas Catchment Board):***

The covenant 'touches and concerns' the land of the covenantee

Must affect the mode of occupation of the land
Must, by itself, affect the value of the land

Both the original covenantee and the person now seeking to enforce the covenant must have a legal estate in the land

- Doesn't have to be the same legal estate (e.g. could be a freehold or lease, but has to be legal) (***S 78 LPA***)

The original parties must intend that the benefit of the covenant is to run with the land

- At common law, intention must be shown by express annexation of the benefit of the covenant to the land of the covenantee in the deed in which the covenant is created
- Can also rely on statutory annexation under ***s 78 LPA*** if created after 1925 →
  Provided the covenants touch and concern the land, benefit is deemed to be annexed

Burden (Common Law)

The original covenantor

- Typically the buyer of the land is the covenantor
- The original covenantor will continue to be liable for covenants they have entered into, even if they sell the land to someone else (***Tophams v Earl of Sefton***, applying ***s 79 LPA***)
  - ***S 79:*** 'the covenants relating to the land of the covenantor shall be deemed to have been made by the covenantor on behalf of their successors in title and persons deriving title under them, as well as on behalf of themselves (unless the deed contains a statement to the contrary)'

Keep in mind → the original covenantor can only be sued for damages at common law

- The successor covenantor can be ordered to remedy the breach in equity (so preferable)

Removing Liability:

If the original covenantor wishes to sell their land, they should:

Enter into a covenant with the new purchaser to perform the existing covenants

Require an indemnity for any future breaches

→ Can build up a chain of indemnities if the property is sold on again

- The covenants to which the indemnity applies will be noted in the Charges Register of the title affected
- ISSUE:
    - Only possible to rely on the chain of indemnity covenants if each person obtains one when they sell on the property → failure to do so breaks the chain
    - Also if the buyer who next obtains the covenant no longer exists, OG buyer liable
    - Or where the present owner is unable to pay the indemnity, previous owner may be out-of-pocket

Running of the burden at common law (successors)

General Rule:

✗ At common law, the burden of the covenant *does not* run with the land (***Austerberry v Oldham Corpn***)

- Follows basic common law rule that a person cannot be made liable upon a contract unless they were a party to it

?! **Unless:**

There has been a chain of indemnity

- Whilst it doesn't pass the burden of the covenants on to the successors in title. It does pass financial liability indirectly back to the party which is in breach

The principle of mutual benefit and burden

Mutual Benefit and Burden

A successor in title who takes the benefit of rights contained in a deed (e.g. easements) must accept the burden of covenants contained in the same deed (***Halsall v Brizell)***

Held that the burden must in some way be related to the exercise of the easement (***Rhone v Stephens)***

- Will be so where the covenantor can make a choice between accepting the benefit and burden together, or rejecting the benefit and thereby being released from the burden

Benefit (Equity)

Running of the benefit in equity (successors):

Equity will recognise that **the benefit of a covenant will pass to successors of the covenantee, where:**

a) The covenant 'touches and concerns' the land of the covenantee; **and**
b) The benefit of the covenant has passed to the successor of the covenantee either by express assignment or by annexation (***s 78 LPA***)

Express Assignment

Same rules as common law

Annexation

Usually the deed will contain an express annexation of the benefit of the covenants to the land

Where it doesn't, ***s 78 LPA*** may apply:

- Provided the covenants touch and concern the land, benefit is deemed to be annexed

Burden (Equity)

Running of the burden in equity (successors)

☑ In ***Tulk v Moxhay***, equity was prepared to enforce a covenant against a successor in title to the original covenantor where that successor had notice of the covenant

Over time, principle has been refined →

☑ **Recognisable conditions must be satisfied if the burden of a covenant is to run in equity:**

Restrictive only
The covenant must be restrictive in nature **Positive covenants do not run**

Touch and concern
The covenantee owned the land for the benefit of which the covenant was taken The covenant must touch and concern the land of the covenantee (doesn't have to be purely economic)

Intended to run
The parties must have intended the burden to run with the covenantor's land (e.g. expressly in a deed) In the absence of express wording, can be implied under ***s 79*** of the LPA Unless a contrary intention is expressed in the deed, it will be implied by statute that the parties intended the burden to pass to successors (after 1925)

Registration (Notice)
The covenant must be registered in the appropriate register → signifies notice • Unregistered land = entry of a Class D(ii) land charge against the name of the original covenantor on the Land Charges Register before date of completion - Unless pre-1926 → enforceable against everyone (except equity's darling) • Registered land = interest affecting a registered estate → enter a notice on the Charges Register before registration of the successor as the new proprietor

Remedies for Breach of Covenants

Original Covenantor

When they have an interest in the land:

The covenantee may obtain:

a) Damages
b) An injunction to restrain a breach of restrictive covenant
c) An order for specific performance for a positive covenant

Once the land has been sold:

- Where there is a breach of covenant by a successor, the only remedy available is damages

Successor to the Original Covenantor

- Appropriate remedy would be an injunction restraining the breach of covenant
- Open to the court to award damages in lieu of the equitable remedy where it is considered that, in the particular circumstances, an injunction is not appropriate

Discharge of Freehold Covenants

Express Release

The covenantee of the restrictive covenant can agree to the **modification or release of the covenant**

- Must enter into a deed with the owner of the burdened land
- The covenantee will seek a payment for release of the covenant

Common ownership

Where the burdened and benefited land **come into the same ownership**, the covenant will be extinguished

Section 84 LPA

Allows for an **application to be made to the Lands Chamber of the Upper Tribunal** → they have the power to release or modify restrictive covenants

Breach Insurance
Payment of breach insurance would ensure that, should a restrictive covenant be breached, the covenantor will be able to recover insurance for any loss incurred by the enforcement of that breach

Easements

Easement = a right that is attached to one piece of land, and imposes a corresponding burden on another piece of land

- **Positive Easement** = one that allows the owner of the land to use the land of another in a particular way (e.g right of way)
- **Negative Easement** = one that restricts the use of another person's land in some way → limited in practice
    - E.g. if a neighbour's property has an easement to receive light which flows over your property, this may prevent you from building on your land in a way which would block this right to light

Characteristics of an Easement

If the rights claimed don't have the essential characteristics, they can't be easements

- Instead will be classed as licences (permissions which can be withdrawn at any time)

4 characteristics necessary for a valid easement (*Re Ellenborough Park*):

☑ There must be a dominant and a servient tenement.

☑ An easement must 'accommodate' the dominant tenement.

☑ The dominant and servient tenements must *not* be owned and occupied by the same person

☑ A right over land *cannot* amount to an easement *unless* it is capable of forming the subject matter of a grant.

Dominant and Servient Tenement:
Dominant Tenement = the land which has the **benefit of an easement** **Servient tenement** = the land which is **subject to an easement** • Must own land to be a tenement → you cannot have an easement in gross (***Rangeley v Midland Railway Co)***

Right must Accommodate the Dominant Tenement:

The right enjoyed by the dominant tenement has to be one which not only enhances the owner's enjoyment of their land, but is also sufficiently connected with that land (***Re Ellenborough Park)***

Sufficient connection:

The two plots of land must be close enough to each other that one plot can *actually* benefit from the right over the other plot

'A right of way over land in Northumberland cannot accommodate land in Kent' (***Bailey v Stephens)***

Normal enjoyment:

- Right must be connected with the normal enjoyment of the property
- The right *can't* be one that is personal to the dominant tenement → i.e. can't be one that no successors would be able to gain from:
    - E.g. a right to walk your dog on your neighbour's land is personal → not everyone would own a dog and so would not be able to make use of this easement (licence instead)
    - Right to cross your neighbour's land to access local shops = valid easement → everyone can benefit from a right to local shops

Can't be Owned and Occupied by the Same Person:

'Dominant and servient tenements must *not* be owned and occupied by the same person' (***Re Ellenborough Park)***

- Owned *and* occupied → a landlord who owns a block of flats and lets one to a tenant can grant an easement to them → they don't *own and occupy* the flats

Right Capable of Forming the Subject Matter of a Grant:

The right must be one capable of being granted by deed

Factors:

1. There must be a capable grantor and a capable grantee
    - (There must be someone capable of giving and receiving an easement)
    - The person who grants the right must have the power to do so
    - The person to whom the right is granted must be capable of receiving it
2. Rights *can't* be expressed in language which is too wide and vague
    - A right to a 'view' is too vague and wide (***Dalton v Angus***)
    - A right to 'light' is fine → access of light to a window can be defined with some precision
        - But must be through a specific aperture (e.g. a window) ***(Colls v Home & Colonial Stores Ltd)***

- Not entitled to an easement of television reception (***Hunter v Canary Wharf Ltd***)

3. Question of extent to which the owner of the land is excluded from using the land themselves
    - ***Copeland v Greenhalf*** → raised doubts as to whether it's possible to have an easement that has the effect of excluding the owner of the servient land
    - The right is *not* an easement if the effect of it was to leave the servient owner without any reasonable use of his land ***(London & Blenheim Estates Ltd v Ladbroke Retail Parks Ltd)***
        - The exclusive right to park 6 cars for 9 and a half hours every day was so extensive a right as to leave the appellants without any reasonable use of their land → not an easement ***(Bachelor v Marlow)***
    - **New Test** = whether the servient owner retains possession and, subject to the reasonable exercise of the right in question, control of the servient land ***(Moncrieff v Jamieson)***
        - E.g. can have an easement to park on your neighbour's land only if they can still freely use the land to park on it themselves

4. The rights *can't* constitute mere rights of recreation:
    - BUT an easement can exist to use a golf course, swimming pool or a tennis court ***(Regency Villas Title Ltd v Diamond Resorts (Europe) Ltd)***
        - Considered a beneficial part of modern life → shouldn't be considered devoid of practical utility or benefit

Express Grant (Legal)

Where the owners of two neighbouring pieces of land agree that one of them is to have an easement over the land of the other → it has been expressly granted

- Where a person wants to retain rights over the land they are selling → reservation of an easement

Formalities (Legal)

An easement can be a legal third party right and interest under ***s 1(2)(a) LPA 1925***

For a specified time:

Must be for an interest **equivalent to an estate fee simple absolute in possession** or a **term of years absolute**

- I.e. Must be for a specified period (freehold or leasehold)
- Where the deed is silent as to duration, it is assumed that it is of unlimited duration (freehold)

Done by Deed:

Above deed requirements (*s 52 LPA & S 1(2) and (3) of the Law of Property (Miscellaneous Provisions) Act 1989)*

Binding?

Where the **dominant tenement** is **sold** after the creation of an easement, the benefit of the easement will **pass automatically** to the new owner ***(s 62 LPA).***

Where the **servient land has been sold** since the date of the creation of the easement, the easement ***may* be enforceable** against the new owner

Registration (Unregistered):

Pre-1926:

Falls outside of the Land Charges Act rules → must apply the rules which operated before the Act (**pre-1926 rules**)

Under the pre-1926 rules, legal easements bind the whole world

- A legal easement will bind the purchaser of the legal estate, even if the purchaser has no knowledge of the existence of the interest when they buy the property

Registration (Registered):

Registrable Disposition:

A legal Express Grant Easement is classed as a registrable disposition (*s 27(2)(a) Land Registration Act).*

It will *not* bind a purchaser *unless* it is completed by registration → must be entered on the charges register of the mortgagor's title (***s 27, Land Registration Act 2002***)

- This must be done by the date of registration of the transfer to the purchaser (***s 29 LRA***)

Will not be considered legal until it has been registered

Express Grant (Equitable)

3 possible equitable easements:

a. Equity recognises an express easement where ***s 1(2)(a) LPA*** (duration) has not been satisfied *but* it has been made in writing and signed by the grantor in accordance with ***s 53(1)(a) LPA***

b. Where an expressly created easement satisfies the duration requirements in ***s 1(2)(a) LPA*** but has not been made by a valid deed

   - → Equity recognises the easement so long as it satisfies the formalities for a valid estate contract ***(s 2 Law of Prop (Miscal Prov) Act)***

c. Where an easement should have been registered at the Land Registry as a registrable disposition but has not been done

→ Must then be done in writing (***s 53(1)(a) of the Law of Property Act 1925***)

Binding?

Registration (Unregistered):

Land Charges:

Under ***s 3, Land Charges Act 1972,*** the equitable easement must be registered by the person with the interest, against the name of the estate owner who has created the equitable easement and whose land is burdened by it (at the time the equitable easement is created)

Must be registered on the Land Charges Register as:

A **Class D Land** (sub-section *iii*)

☑ Such registration is deemed to constitute actual notice of the incumbrance and of the fact of the registration to all persons connected with the land affected, as from the date of registration (***s 198, Law of Property Act 1925***)

- Anyone who buys the land is deemed to buy with actual knowledge of the land charge and will be bound by it

✗ Where the equitable easement *hasn't* been registered, the purchasers of the land can take free of the unregistered land charge (***s 4 Land Charges Act 1972***)

Registration (Registered):

IARE:

An equitable easement is classed as an interest affecting a registered estate.

It will *not* bind a purchaser *unless* it is subject to a notice on the Charges Register (***s 32, Land Registration Act 2002***)

- The notice may be agreed (entered with the consent of the registered proprietor) or unilateral (entered without the consent)

This must be done by the date of registration of the transfer to the purchaser (***s 29 LRA***)

Implied Grant (Legal)

A legal easement can be **implied into the purchase deed where there is a sale of part of land**

Formalities

For the Seller:

There are certain easements which are available to sellers of land

- These easements will be impliedly reserved (held back) out of the land being sold, for the benefit of the land the seller is retaining

After a sale of part of their land, **a seller will have the right to exercise**, over the land sold to the buyer:

a) Easements of **strict necessity**; and
b) Easements **implied due to the common intention** of the buyer and seller at the time of the sale

Easements of Strict Necessity:

An easement of strict necessity arises where, without it, no use can be made of the land ***(Wong v Beaumont Property Trust Ltd)***

- Usually quite extreme situation → e.g. the land would otherwise be landlocked
- Where a right of way is required to access drains / sewers → may not be classed as one of strict necessity → alternative methods of drainage and sewerage are available (such as cesspits/soak-aways) and so the land could be used without the easement.

Easements of Common Intention:

An easement of common intention arises where the parties intend that the land is to be used in a particular way and there are easements required to enable it to be used in that way ***(Wong v Beaumont Property Trust Ltd)***

For the Buyer:

The **buyer** will have the right to exercise, over the land retained by the seller:

Easements of strict necessity

Easements implied due to the common intention of the buyer and seller at the time of the sale

Easements created under the rule in ***Wheeldon v Burrows***

Easements created under ***s 62 of the LPA 1925***

Easements of Strict Necessity:

An easement of strict necessity arises where, without it, no use can be made of the land ***(Wong v Beaumont Property Trust Ltd)***

- Where a right of way is required to access drains / sewers → may not be classed as one of strict necessity → alternative methods of drainage and sewerage are available (such as cesspits/soak-aways) and so the land could be used without the easement.

Easements of Common Intention:

An easement of common intention arises where the parties intend that the land is to be used in a particular way and there are easements required to enable it to be used in that way ***(Wong v Beaumont Property Trust Ltd)***

Wheeldon v Burrows:

It is implied into the sale of part transfer that the **seller grants the buyer** all the rights **previously used by the seller as quasi-easements**, as long as the right is:

Continuous;

Apparent;

- Continuous and apparent = requires some feature to be present on the servient tenement which would be apparent on inspection and must have a degree of permanence ***(Ward v Kirkland)***
    - E.g. a right of way may be apparent from the existence of a path

Necessary for the **reasonable enjoyment** of the land; and

- The right claimed should facilitate the reasonable enjoyment of the property (not as strict as necessity test)

Being used as a **'quasi easement'** by the seller prior to the sale of port

- **Quasi-easement** = a right being used over part of a person's land, for the benefit of another part of that person's land, that would be an easement if the two parts of the land were in separate ownership
    - Was the seller making use of the right before they sold the property?
- Requires unity of occupation → the seller must have owned both parts of land beforehand and used the land in such a way that would have created an easement (if owned by different people)

S 62 LPA:

Section 62 implies general words into a conveyance of land

3 requirements:

a) There must be a conveyance of part (freehold or lease)

b) *Prior* to the conveyance of part, the 'dominant' land must have enjoyed the benefit of a licence or permission capable of being an easement
    - A right to use a road to a farm that had been used up until 11 months before the conveyance still fell within s 62 ***(Costagliola v English)***

c) There was diversity of occupation at the time of the conveyance of part ***(Payne v Inwood)***

The land enjoying the relevant right will usually be tenanted initially, and then either the lease is renewed or the tenant acquires the freehold estate of that part of land
    - Required to convert a licence into an easement
- In ***Wood v Waddington***: diversity of occupation was not essential
    - Conveyance on sale may convert a quasi-easement into an easement, where it was continuous and apparent and was 'enjoyed with the land' (naturally attaches to the land)

→ Where there was diversity of occupation prior to the sale of part, then *only* ***s 62 LPA*** will work to create an easement. **BUT**: if there was unity of occupation prior to the sale → *either* the rule in ***Wheeldon v Burrows*** or ***s 62*** will work to create an easement

Effects:

- Enables existing rights of a permanent nature to be passed on automatically in a conveyance of land
- Means a person who merely has permission to use land in some way may acquire, after a conveyance is them made, an easement ***(Wright v Macadam)***
    - Wright, a tenant of property, had a licence to use a coal shed. When she was granted a new tenancy this amounted to a conveyance of land and the general words were implied into it.
        - The right to use the shed was capable of being an easement → its implied inclusion in a deed affected the grant → transformed it from being a licence into a legal easement

Binding?

Where the **dominant tenement** is **sold** after the creation of an easement, the benefit of the easement will **pass automatically** to the new owner ***(s 62 LPA)***

Where the **servient land has been sold** since the date of the creation of the easement, the easement ***may* be enforceable** against the new owner

Registration (Unregistered):

Pre-1926:

Falls outside of the Land Charges Act rules → must apply the rules which operated before the Act (**pre-1926 rules**)

Under the pre-1926 rules, legal easements bind the whole world

A legal easement will bind the purchaser of the legal estate, even if the purchaser has no knowledge of the existence of the interest when they buy the property

Registration (Registered):

Overriding (*Sch 3, Para 3, LRA*):

Implied legal easements may be an unregistered interest which override (***Sch 3, Para 3, LRA***)

- Aren't required to be entered onto the register but are binding on the purchaser of the property
- Relevant date = date of completion of the purchaser

ONLY IF (from 13 Oct 2006):

The purchaser actually knew of the easement before the purchase of the property, **or**
The easement would have been obvious on a reasonably careful inspection of the land, **or**
The dominant tenement can prove that they exercised the right in the year prior to the sale

Easements already protected before the 2002 act will continue to be overriding (***sch 12, para 9, LRA***)

→ Although Land Registry now has powers to require disclosure of the easement on a disposition of land (aim to reduce number of implied/prescriptive easements which exist 'off the register)

Prescription (Legal)

3 ways for an easement (by prescription) can be acquired:

a) Common law rules
b) Doctrine of lost modern grant (also common law)
c) Prescription Act 1832

Formalities:

Common Law:

Common law conditions:

User must be 'as of right'

Essential that the **user is 'as of right':**

Unchallenged by them (**without force**)

Exercised openly (**without secrecy**)

Without permission

- There is a difference between consent of an easement (which would block it from being by prescription) and tolerance of an easement (***Mills v Silver***)

Freehold v Freehold

The user must be a **fee simple owner against a fee simple owner** (freehold v freehold)

BUT:

☑ If the dominant land is occupied by a tenant → can still acquire an easement (any use of the right by a tenant is deemed to be use by their landlord (the freeholder))

✗ The servient land must *always* be occupied by the freehold owner

Continuous for a requisite period of time:

If the person exercised a right over the land and the owner fails to take any steps to stop them, they will, after a period of time, become entitled to the right

- **Common law rules** = where a user has been 'as of right' for **20 years**, the use is a continuous one
  - **Continuous** = the degree of use must be enough 'to carry to the mind of a reasonable person who is in possession of the burdened land the fact that a continuous right to enjoyment is being asserted, and ought to be registered if such a right is not recognised' (***Hollins v Verney***)
  - 20 years from the date at which the easement has first been in use (i.e. count from when there has been a dominant and servient tenement)
- **Raises a rebuttable presumption** that the right has been granted and exercised since '**time immemorial**' (1189)
- It cannot become an easement until there is a separate dominant and servient owner
- This means it can be easily defeated as the owner of the burdened land can show that the right has **not been in existence since 1189**

Lost Modern Grant:

Brought about to counter the easy rebuttable presumption that could be raised about easements granted 'since time immemorial'

- Court adopts a legal fiction → presumes that the right was created by an express grant of an easement when the use was first stated and that the document had been lost (***Mills v Silver***)

To claim an easement under the Lost Modern Grant, must prove that:

1) The easement complied with the common law rules
   - Incl freeholder v freeholder (***Simmons v Dobson***)
2) The right had been used for a long period, minimum of 20 years

Prescription Act 1832:

Under common law, easy to defeat prescription as just had to prove that the enjoyment began at some time after 1189

- Only the courts can grant an easement under the Prescription Act
- Prescription Act easements can only come into existence on the date the courts grant them

The claim for non-light easements can be based on (Section 2):

a) A period of **20 years' use** (immediately before the application to the court → i.e working backwards from when the court date is)
b) A period of **40 years' use** immediately before the application to the court

20 Years:

The claimant must show that the Common Law Rules are complied with

- E.g. showing there has been consent would defeat the claim

40 Years:

If 40 + years, this claim becomes 'absolute and indefeasible'

Claim can only be defeated by proof of:

a) Written consent at the start of the use; or
b) Oral consent given during the period of use

Removes need for freeholder v freeholder → can still acquire an easement this way if the servient land had been occupied by a tenant at some point during the 40 years

&

Without Interruption:

***Section 4, Prescription Act*:**

1) Requires the 20 and 40 year periods to be 'next before some suit or action':

   No right to an easement arises until a court action is brought to claim it; **and**

   - Must have first gone to court to claim the easement

   The 20/40 years' use must be continuous right up to the date of that court action

2) To constitute an interruption, the claimant's use of the right must have been prevented for a period lasting at least one year.
   - After becoming aware of the interruption (and the person responsible for it), they must have let it continue for a year.
   - Must be prevented from using their right → not just that they choose not to use it (***Mills v Silver***)

Right to Light (Prescription):

In the case of an easement of light, if the access and use of light has been enjoyed for:

a) A period of 20 years (***Dance v Triplow***); without
   i) **Interruption** and;
   ii) **without written consent**

→ **It becomes absolute and indefeasible**

Take into account:

- Can only be acquired in respect of buildings
- But must be through a specific aperture (e.g. a window) ***(Colls v Home & Colonial Stores Ltd)***
- Claimant must show that there is access of light and that there is use being made of it
- Statute gives no guidance as the amount of light to which the dominant tenement is entitled → for the courts to decide
  - Entitlement is to 'sufficient light according to the ordinary notions of mankind for the comfortable use and enjoyment … or for the beneficial use and occupation of the building' (***Colls v Home & Colonial Stores Ltd***)

Binding?

Where the **dominant tenement** is **sold** after the creation of an easement, the benefit of the easement will **pass automatically** to the new owner ***(s 62 LPA)***

Where the **servient land has been sold** since the date of the creation of the easement, the easement ***may* be enforceable** against the new owner

Registration (Unregistered):

Pre-1926:

Falls outside of the Land Charges Act rules → must apply the rules which operated before the Act (**pre-1926 rules**)

Under the pre-1926 rules, legal easements bind the whole world

A legal easement will bind the purchaser of the legal estate, even if the purchaser has no knowledge of the existence of the interest when they buy the property

Registration (Registered):

Overriding (*Sch 3, Para 3, LRA*):

Implied legal easements may be an unregistered interest which override (***Sch 3, Para 3, LRA***)

- Aren't required to be entered onto the register but are binding on the purchaser of the property
- Relevant date = date of completion of the purchaser

ONLY IF (from 13 Oct 2006):

The purchaser actually knew of the easement before the purchase of the property, **or**
The easement would have been obvious on a reasonably careful inspection of the land, **or**
The dominant tenement can prove that they exercised the right in the year prior to the sale

Easements already protected before the 2002 act will continue to be overriding (***sch 12, para 9, LRA***)

→ Although Land Registry now has powers to require disclosure of the easement on a disposition of land (aim to reduce number of implied/prescriptive easements which exist 'off the register)

Remedies

- Easements will be enforced by the courts if the owner of the servient land tries to prevent them from being used
- Court will grant damages if the owner of the easement has suffered loss by being deprived of the easement

- Injunctions may be obtained to ensure that the easement is exercisable by the dominant owner

Extinguishment

3 ways for an easement to be extinguished:

a) Where someone has the benefit of an easement, they can **expressly release it by deed**
b) Where someone has the benefit of an easement they can also **abandon the easement** ***(Moore v Rawson)***
c) Where someone owns the dominant tenement and then purchases the servient tenement, the easement will cease

Legal Mortgage

Terminology:

- **Mortgagor** = the owner of the estate in land who is borrowing a sum of money on security of the mortgage over the property
- **Mortgagee** = the lender who is taking security over the borrower's land

Creation

A **mortgage** ***is*** capable of existing as **a legal interest in land (*s 1(2)(b) LPA*)**

Freehold Mortgage:

Requirements for a legal mortgage (freehold):

Created by Deed:
Mortgage to be created by deed (***s 52(1) LPA 1925***) What is a deed ***(s 1(2) Law of Property (Miscellaneous Provisions) Act 1989)*** Correct execution of a deed (***s 1(3) Law of Property (Miscellaneous Provisions) Act 1989)***

Under *s 85 LPA*:

Demise: :
i) Mortgage takes the **form of a demise** (lease) for a **term of years absolute**, subject to a provision for the **lease to end on redemption of the mortgage** (rare)

Legal Charge:
ii) Borrower executing a charge by deed (**a legal charge**), expressed to be by way of legal mortgage • Doesn't convey any estate in land to the lenders (done through a deed) • Since 13 Oct 2003 mortgages over land with registered title can only be created in this way

Leasehold Mortgage:

A mortgage can be created over a leasehold estate either by a charge or by the creation of a sub-lease for a term of one day less than the term of the lease being mortgaged ***(s 86(1) LPA)***

Registration (Unregistered)

Pre-1926 Rules:

Falls outside of the Land Charges Act rules → must apply the rules which operated before the Act (**pre-1926 rules**)

Under the pre-1926 rules, legal mortgages bind the whole world

- A legal mortgage will bind the purchaser of the legal estate, even if the purchaser has no knowledge of the existence of the interest when they buy the property

Registration (Registered)

Registrable Disposition:

A legal mortgage is classed as a registrable disposition (*s 27(2)(f) Land Registration Act).*

It will *not* bind a purchaser *unless* it is completed by registration → must be entered on the charges register of the mortgagor's title (***s 27, Land Registration Act 2002***)

Remedies for Mortgagee

Continuing the Mortgage:

Debt Action:

If the **borrower has failed to make the agreed payments**, the mortgagee can commence an **action for the recovery of the debt**

- Only if the legal date for redemption has passed
  - Legal redemption date is usually set at one month from the date of the mortgage
- The mortgagee *cannot* recover arrears of the capital repayments if more than 12 years has passed since the payments first became due (***Limitation Act 1980***)
  - The lender cannot recover arrears of interest payments if they have been outstanding for more than 6 years

Take into account ⟶ remedy is generally of limited assistance

- If the borrower has failed to make the repayments of the mortgage, unlikely that they will have the money to satisfy any court order for repayment that may be made against them

Possession:

The right to take possession of land can mean 2 things:

a) If the mortgaged land is *not* subject to a lease, the lenders have a right to oust the borrowers from the property and take physical possession of the land

b) If the mortgaged land *is* subject to a lease, the lenders take possession of the land by directing that the tenants pay their rent to the lenders instead of the borrowers (no court proceedings)

Procedure:

Lenders can take possession of the mortgaged property 'before the ink is dry on the mortgage' (as soon as the mortgage has been completed) ***(Four Maids Ltd v Dudley Marshall (Properties) Ltd)***

- But terms of mortgage deed will often postpone this right until the borrower is in default
- Usually have to obtain a court order when exercising their right to take possession (can't use or threaten violence to get possession, ***s 6(2) Criminal Law Act 1977***)

For a dwelling house:

Where the property is a **dwelling house**, must also take into account ***s 36 of the administration of Justice Act 1970*** and ***s 8 of the Administration of Justice Act 1973***

a) ***S 36***: the court can adjourn the possession proceedings if the court is of the opinion that the mortgagor will be able to repay the 'sums due' or remedy the breach of mortgage within a reasonable time

Reasonable time = the outstanding term of the mortgage

Borrowers typically ask the court to postpone the sale so that they can set up a repayment schedule / sell the land and pay back the amount owed

b) ***S 8***: where the mortgage deed provides for the sum to be repaid by instalments, sum due means only the instalments which are in arrears at the date of the possession proceedings, *not* the full amount outstanding on the mortgage

- Court can exercise these powers only if it thinks the mortgagor will, within a reasonable time, be able to repay the arrears due and the arrears which have become due since the commencement of the proceedings

Effects:

The mortgagee will **take possession in order to sell the property or to intercept the income** from it

- Where the property is producing income, the mortgagee is entitled to use it to pay the debt owed to them
- They are *not* entitled to take any sum beyond that which is due to them
- The mortgagee does owe the mortgagor a duty to manage the property with due diligence

If they fail to do so → must account to the mortgagor for the income they did receive and also for any income they would have received had they managed the property correctly (***White v City of London Brewery***)

Appointment of a Receiver:

A mortgagee can **appoint a receiver to collect and redirect the income** from the property

The mortgagee does not incur the personal responsibility when taking possession but can use the income collected to repay the debt owed to them

The receiver takes control of the mortgaged land and either sells it or manages it (using income to repay the loan)

Must be appointed in writing (unless mortgage deed provides elsewise), (***s 109 LPA***)

The duties and powers of the receiver are governed by the mortgage document under which they are appointed and by the law of agency

Requirements:

Can only be appointed if:

a) The original mortgage was created by deed (implied right, ***s 101 LPA***); and
b) The power has arisen (legal date of redemption has passed) and has become exercisable
   - Happens under ***s 103 LPA*** if:
     i) The lenders have served notice on the borrowers requiring repayment of the loan and the borrowers have failed to comply with that notice for 3 months after service; or
     ii) Interest due under the mortgage is 2 months or more in arrears; or
     iii) The borrowers have breached a term under the mortgage deed

Application of Income:

The receiver must apply in the income in the order set out in *s 109 LPA*:

a) Outgoings on the property
b) Interest on any prior mortgages
c) Insurance premiums on the property and their own costs
d) Interest on the current mortgage
e) Capital on the current mortgage if directed to do so in writing by the mortgagee
f) The balance to the mortgagor

Ending the Mortgage:

Power of Sale:

When the lenders want to **secure repayment of the entire sum loaned** (capital and interest), they can **end the mortgage** (either through power of sale or foreclosure)

- When lenders exercise their power of sale, they sell the mortgaged property and use the proceeds of sale to pay themselves back the sum that they are owed under the mortgage
- The statutory power of sale is implied into every mortgage created by deed (***s 101 LPA***) and is usually expressly included in the mortgage deed itself

Under ***s 104(1) LPA***, the sale by the mortgagee passes to the purchaser the whole estate of the mortgagor:

a) Free from any estate or interests which the selling mortgagee took priority over
b) But are subject to any estates and interests which took priority over the selling mortgagee

Requirements:

The power of sale must have arisen and become exercisable

a) Arises on the legal date for redemption (***s 101 (1)(i) LPA***)
b) Becomes exercisable when one of the conditions in ***s 103 LPA*** have been complied with (can be varied by the mortgage deed)

The buyer must check that the mortgagee has a power of sale which has arisen, but does not have to check if this is exercisable (***s 104(2) LPA***)

Duties owed to borrowers:

Lenders owe 2 duties to borrowers when exercising their power to sell the mortgaged land (*Cuckmere Brick Co v Ltd v Mutual Finance Ltd*):

a) Lenders must act in good faith and not cheat the borrowers
b) Lenders must take reasonable care to obtain the true market value of the property at the date of the sale

Order of distribution:

The order of distribution is set out in s 105 LPA:

a) To repay the costs of redeeming prior mortgages (mortgages with priority over the selling mortgagee's mortgage)
b) To pay off the mortgagee's expenses of sale
c) To pay off the mortgagee's own mortgage
d) To pay any balance to the person entitled to the mortgaged property

Once the lenders have paid themselves back what they are owed, any balance goes to the borrowers.

Foreclosure:

The **right to foreclosure** arises either when:

a) The legal **date of redemption has passed**; or
b) When the mortgagor has **breached one of the terms** of the mortgage

Foreclosure = vests ownership of the property in the lender

- Able to take possession, sell and then retain all of the proceeds of sale (even if mortgage deed was less in value)

Process:

Lenders must obtain an interim court order (fixes a date by which the borrowers should pay the outstanding money)

→ Moves to next stage if they don't pay

Final order or order of foreclosure absolute → borrowers can then not redeem unless the court exercises its discretion

Take account of ***S 91(2) LPA***:

- Allows 'any person interested either in the mortgage money or in the right of redemption' to request that the court makes an order for sale instead of foreclosure
- Once this request has been made, the court can order that the property should be sold 'on such terms as it thinks fit'

Defence?

In practice, foreclosure is rarely used as equity gives the court discretion to allow the borrower to redeem the mortgage, even after an order for foreclosure has been made

- Will take into account the value of the property compared to the amount outstanding under the mortgage

Priority Rules

Generally, any rights **created after the date of the mortgage will *not* bind the lender** if the mortgage has been correctly protected

Between legal mortgages (Registered Land):

Where land is **subject to more than one mortgage,** the seller sells:

a) Subject to the prior encumbrances; and
b) Free from those which don't have priority

The lender who ranks first in the order of priority is entitled to be paid back in full first (before the other lenders get any money)

The order of priority depends on the order in which they are entered as registered charges in the charges register of the title to land (***s 48 Land Registration Act 2002***)

The mortgage that appears first ranks first

Between legal mortgages & other interests (registered):

To determine whether particular **third party interests** created by the mortgagor are binding on the mortgagee:

First determine whether the interest was created before or after the date of registration of the mortgage

Interest exists before the mortgage:

Registrable Dispositions & IARE

☑ All registrable dispositions and interests affecting a registered estate must be protected by a notice on the register by the date of registration of the mortgage to take priority over it (***s 29 Land Registration Act 2002***)

Overriding Interests:

☑ All interests which override must exist by the date of completion of the mortgage to take priority over it

- Where the mortgage finances the acquisition of a property, it is highly unlikely that an equitable trust interest will bind the mortgagee (unlikely to be living in the property) (***Lloyds Bank Plc v Rosset, Abbey National Building Society v Cann)***
- Where a property is mortgaged after its acquisition, then the mortgagee may be bound by any trust interest that already exists (***Williams & Glyn's Bank Ltd v Boland)*** → unless the mortgagee has overreached it

Interest created after the mortgage:

If the interest was created *after* the mortgage, the lender is *not* bound

EXCEPTION:

If the lender has given written consent to the interest

Home Rights

Home Rights → a right of occupation as against the other spouse (for the non-owning spouse) **(s 30 of the Family Law Act 1996)**

Formalities:

Requirements:

a) The parties are legally married
b) The home is, has been, or is intended to be the matrimonial home

Home Rights will typically end on death or divorce

The right is independent of and in addition to any equitable interest arising under a trust which the non-legal owning spouse or civil partner may have

Registration (Unregistered)

Class F Land (LCA):

Under ***s 3, Land Charges Act 1972,*** the home right must be registered by the person with the interest.

Must be registered on the Land Charges Register as:

- A **Class F Land** (a charge affecting any land by virtue of the Family Law Act 1996)

☑ Such registration is deemed to constitute actual notice of the incumbrance and of the fact of the registration to all persons connected with the land affected, as from the date of registration (***s 198, Law of Property Act 1925***)

Anyone who buys the land is deemed to buy with actual knowledge of the land charge and will be bound by it

✗ Where the home right *hasn't* been registered, the purchasers of the land can take free of the unregistered land charge (***s 4 Land Charges Act 1972***)

Registration (Registered)

IARE:

A Family Law Act right is classed as an interest affecting a registered estate.

It will *not* bind a purchaser *unless* it is subject to a notice on the Charges Register (***s 32, Land Registration Act 2002***)

- The notice may be agreed (entered with the consent of the registered proprietor) or unilateral (entered without the consent)

This must be done by the date of registration of the transfer to the purchaser (*s* ***29 LRA***)

✗ Will not count as an overriding interest (interest belonging to a person in actual oppocation of the land → ***sch 3, para 2 LRA***) as these rights are not **proprietary in nature**:

- ***S 30 of the Family Law Act 1996*** has been excluded (***s 31(10)(b), FLA)***

Trusts / Co-Ownership

Trusts of Land

The Trusts of Land and Appointment of Trustees Act 1996:

- Any new trust created over land after 1 Jan 1997 takes the form of a trust of land

Section 36 → whenever you have a co-ownership of land, you have a trust of land

- The legal owners = the trustees

Trustees powers:

S 6 of the 1996 Act **sets out in general terms the powers enjoyed by the trustees:**

- ***S 6(1)***: 'for the purpose of exercising the functions as trustees, the trustees of land have in relation to the land subject to the trust all of the powers of an absolute owner'
- ***S 6(2):*** gives trustees the authority to exercise the power to dispose of the legal estate in a specified way (can end the trust even if the beneficiaries have not requested it)
- ***S 6(3)***: gives the trustees power to buy land in England and Wales for the wide purposes set out in ***S 8 Trustee Act 2000***

    S 8 Trustee Act 2000: sets out the circumstances in which trustees can acquire land:

        S 8(1): When the land is to be bought for *occupation* by a beneficiary
        S 8(2): Can *only* buy a *legal estate* (not an equitable interest in land)

- ***S 6(5)***: requires the trustees to 'have regard to the rights of the beneficiaries' when exercising their powers
- ***S 6(6)***: requires the trustees to exercise their powers under ***s 6*** in line with the general rules of equity and law

Restrictions:

When selling trust land, the trustees must (*s 11 of the 1996 Act*):

a) **Consult** with the beneficiaries who are of full age, who have an interest in possession; and
b) **Comply** with the wishes of the majority in value (as far as consistent with the general interests of the trust)
   E.g. if there are unequal shares, comply with beneficiary who has more shares of value
   Ultimately down to trustees to make the decision

Rights of Beneficiaries:

For beneficiaries to have the right to occupy the land (*s 12, 1996 Act*):

a) Beneficiaries must be entitled to an interest in possession under the trust
b) The purpose of the trust must include making the land available for the beneficiaries to occupy, or
c) The trustees must hold the land so that it's available for them to occupy

Where the trustees do allow the beneficiary to occupy the land, they **can attach conditions to that occupation** (*s 13, 1996 Act*)
   E.g. imposing a condition that the beneficiary pays the outgoings on the property

Resolving disputes:

Where a dispute cannot be resolved amicably, the parties must **apply to the court for an order resolving the dispute** (*s 14, 1996 Act*)

- Under ***s 14***, 'any person who is a trustee of land or has an interest in property, subject to a trust of land, may make an application to the court'
- The court then has the power to make such order as it thinks fit, relating to the 'exercise by the trustees of any of their functions' or to 'declaring the nature or extent of a person's interest'

Section 15 sets out a **range of factors the court must consider** when making an order under ***s 14***:

a. Looking at the purpose of the trust
b. The intention of the settlor when creating the trust
c. The welfare of any minor who occupies or may occupy the trust land
d. The interests of any secured creditor of a beneficiary

Rights of Purchasers:

- Where a trust deed requires the trustees to obtain consents *before* exercising any function and the purchaser has knowledge of that requirement, they must only check that the 2 consents have been obtained (***S 10(1), 1996 Act***)
  - Where one of the persons whose consent is needed is not of full age, purchasers *don't* have to ensure that the consent is obtained (***s 10(3)***)

Registration (Unregistered)

It is *not* capable of being legal *(s 1(2) LPA)*

It is capable of being equitable *(s 1(3) LPA)*

Pre-1926 Rules:

Falls outside of the Land Charges Act rules → must apply the rules which operated before the Act (**pre-1926 rules**)

Under the pre-1926 rules, **equitable interests under trusts are enforceable against anyone**

Exception - Equity's Darling

Will not bind Equity's Darling → the bona fide purchaser of the legal estate for value without notice

Requirements:

1) Must be bona fide

The buyer must be **acting in good faith**

2) Be a purchaser

The buyer must **come within the definition of a purchaser**:

- A person who receives property other than by operation of law (operation of law = intestacy rules or bankruptcy)

- Includes a mortgagee or a lessee

3) Bought the property for value

The buyer must have given consideration for the purchase of the estate

- If no value given, referred to as a 'volunteer'

4) Taken the legal estate

The buyer must have **taken the legal estate in the property**

- They must have purchased a fee simple absolute in possession or a term of years absolute (***s 1(1) LPA***)

5) Bought without notice of the interest

The buyer must have bought the property ***without*** **notice that the equitable interest exists:**

a) Actual Notice:

- A person has actual notice of all facts of which they have (or have had) actual knowledge

b) Constructive Notice:

- A buyer is deemed to have constructive notice of any matter or fact which 'would have come to his knowledge if such inquiries and inspections had been made as ought reasonably to have been made by him (***s 199(1) LPA***)

c) Imputed Notice:

- A purchaser is deemed to have imputed notice of any matter of which their solicitor (or other agent) had actual or constructive notice

<u>*Case Law Example:*</u>

Kingsnorth Finance Co Ltd v Tizard [1986]: the purchaser, or their agent, must make all inquiries and inspections that, in the circumstances, ought reasonably to have been made

- Otherwise, the purchaser will not be equity's darling (deemed to have constructive notice)

Registration (Registered)

Restriction in Proprietorship Register:

The interests of beneficiaries under trusts of land must be **recorded by a restriction** in the proprietorship register of the owner's title (***s 40, LRA***)

- These interests can't be protected by a notice (***s 33, LRA***)
- A restriction will alert a buyer to the need to overreach
- If the buyer fails to overreach, the restriction will prevent the buyer being registered as the new owner
  - The buyer would have to get their money back / try to negotiate with the beneficiary to remove the restriction

Actual Occupation:

A trust interest ***may*** **count as an unregistered interests which override, if the person is in actual occupation of the land (sch 3, para 2, LRA)** =

- Is not required to be entered onto the register but are binding on the purchaser of the property
- The relevant date for assessing actual occupation is the date of completion of the purchase.

☑ Is **proprietary in nature**

'Actual occupation' depends on context:

- ***Williams & Glyn's Bank v Boland [1981]***: a wife (who had an equitable interest in land under trust) had actual occupation as there was 'physical presence on the land by the claimant'
- ***Abbey National Building Society v Cann [1991]***: a mother, who had an equitable interest in the property, was not in actual occupation when she sent her son to move in her furniture and put up curtains → held to be preparatory
- ***Lloyds Bank plc v Rosset [1989]***: the claimant was in actual occupation by visiting the property regularly while it was being renovated (she was occupying, so far as it was possible)
- ***Link Lending Ltd v Bustard [2010]***: still held to be in actual occupation, even though she had been absent for over a year in residential psychiatric care (possessions there, made regular visits, bills paid & intended to return)
- ***Thompson v Foy [2010]:*** similar to Bustard, but she did not want to return to live there (not in actual occupation)
- ***Kling v Keston Properties Ltd (1983)***: a car was parked regularly in a garage → this was the normal use of the property → could amount to actual occupation

The overriding status to a person in actual occupation occurs 'at the time of the disposition' (date of completion)

&

The *occupation* (not the interest) would have been obvious on a reasonably careful inspection of the land at the time of the sale, **or** The purchaser had actual knowledge of the *interest* at the time of the sale If enquiries were made of the person holding the interest before the sale, that person must have disclosed if they could reasonably have been expected to do so

Overreaching?

Where overreaching occurs, the **buyer will take the land free from equitable interests** that arise **under a trust**

- The interests of the beneficiaries cease to be attached to the land
- Attach instead to the sale proceeds

To overreach a beneficial interest:

a) The buyer must be acquiring the legal estate in the property
b) The buyer must pay the purchase money to all the trustees
c) There must be at least 2 trustees (or a trust corporation)

Express Co-Ownership

Co-ownership = when **2 or more people** have **concurrent interests** in the **same estate in one piece of land**

- Any land subject to co-ownership is held on trust (***ss 34 & 36, Law of Property Act 1925***)

There are 2 ways in which the co-owners can own the land:

a) Joint Tenancy
b) Tenancy in Common

Joint Tenants:

Where 2 people own the land as joint tenants, they are **treated by the world as being a single person**

- If either person dies, the survivor becomes the sole owner of the land
- If a joint tenant makes a gift in their will of their interest to a third party, the gift *isn't* effective
- If land held as joint tenants is sold, the joint tenants share the proceeds of sale equally

Tenants in Common:

If 2 people own the land as tenants in common, the law treats them as **owning distinct shares that may be equal or unequal in size**

- Hold the land in 'undivided shares'
- Where one dies, their share of the land falls to their estate and passes under terms of their will
- The tenants in common receive a share of the proceeds of sale, equivalent to the size of their distinct shares

The Legal Interest:

☑ Co-owners **legal** interests can *only* be held as joint tenants ***(S 1(6) of the Law of Property Act 1925)***

✗ You can't sever a joint tenancy of the legal estate into a tenancy in common ***(S 36(2) LPA)***

- A legal owner cannot act individually to 'sell' or 'give away' their interest in the legal estate and cannot separate out a share

✗ There can *only* be a max of 4 trustees who can own the legal estate in the land ***(S 34(2) LPA)***

- The first 4 people who are named will own the legal estate as joint tenants (***s 36(1)***)

✗ A legal owner must be 18 + (***s 1(6) LPA***) and of sound mind (***s 22 LPA***)

✗ Where one of the legal owners dies, the other becomes the sole legal owner (does not pass to estate)

The Equitable Interest:

Co-owners can hold the **equitable (beneficial) interest** as either:

a) **Joint tenants;** or
b) **Tenants in common**

- Where the title is registered and the beneficiaries hold as tenants in common, a restriction is automatically entered on the proprietorship register by Land Registry
- No restriction on the number of beneficiaries under the trust of land

How is the Equitable Interest held?

If you buy a property as co-owners, must decided **whether to hold the beneficial interest** as

a) **Joint Tenants** or
b) **Tenants in Common**

☑ There *may* be documentary evidence which clearly outlines intentions

✗ Where there is *no* evidence or it is inadequate, must use the **'Four Tests' rule** to determine how the beneficial interest is held

2 ways to prove that the equitable interest is held as joint tenants:

☑ **Meets all the four unities** *and* there is **express declaration in the deed**

☑ There is ***no* express declaration** in the deed **BUT** meets all the **4 unities** and **fails words of severance** test and **presumption** test.

4 Unities Test:

For an **equitable joint tenancy** to be formed, ***all* 4 unities** must be met:

Unity of interest

Requires that all co-owners have exactly the same interest in the property (same nature and same duration)

Unity of title:

- All of the co-owners must receive their interest in the land under the same document

Unity of time:

- Each co-owner's interest must vest at the same time

Unity of possession:

- Each must be entitled to possession of the whole of the land and can't exclude the other co-owner

→ If the co-ownership is to take the form of an equitable tenancy in common, the *only* essential unity is possession

&

Deed must contain an express declaration:

The deed transferring the land to the co-owners must contain an express declaration of how the co-owners should hold the equitable interest in the land (***Goodman v Gallant [1986]***)

- If unregistered, look at the conveyance to the co-owners
- If registered, the express declaration would be included in the transfer

→ Where there *is* an express declaration in the document saying how the beneficial interest is held → conclusive (don't need to look at the other 2 tests)

↓

If no express declaration, apply 3rd test

Does the deed contain words of severance:

Words of severance = words indicating that the co-owners intend to own separate and distinct shares in the property

- Where the deed transferring the land to the co-owners contains words of severance, the co-owners take the equitable interest in the land as tenants in common in equity

↓

If no words of severance, apply 4th test

Does equity presume a tenancy in common:

Must look at the circumstances of the purchase to see if they are such that *equity presumes* a tenancy in common:

a) Where co-owners buy the land as partnership property
   - Where business partners buy the land as a partnership asset, equity presumes that they buy the land as tenants in common in equity

b) Where co-owners lend money on mortgage
   - Where more than one person lends money to a borrower, the relationship between the lenders is that of tenants in common (rare)

c) Where co-owners make unequal contributions towards the purchase price
   Equity presumes that they buy as tenants in common in equity
   The size of each tenant in common's share is in proportion to his or her contribution

Severance of an Equitable Joint Tenancy:

Severance = the process of **converting** an equitable interest as joint tenants into a tenancy in common

If there are more than 2 joint tenants, and only one wishes to sever:

a) *Only* the severing party's share will be held under a tenancy in common
b) The other joint tenants will continue to hold the remaining 'share' of the property between them as joint tenants

Severance is only possible when a joint tenant is alive (can't sever a will)

Can be done by:

Severance by Notice:

3 requirements: (*s 36(2) of the Law of Property Act 1925*)

☑ The notice must be given in writing (but *doesn't* have to be signed)

☑ The notice must show the correct intention

☑ The notice must be correctly served (***s 196, LPA 1925***)

- Validly served if the sender can prove that, however it was delivered, the notice was actually left at the last known abode or place of business of the joint tenants (***s 196(3)***) (***Kinch v Bullard***)
- Notice will be deemed to have been served if it has *not been returned* by the Post Office as undelivered (even if it never arrived) (***s 196(4)***) (***Re 88 Berkeley Road NW9***)

✗ Must be for **immediate** severance → A notice in writing which expresses a desire for some time in the future *doesn't* count (***Harris v Goddard***)

Severance by alienation:

Severance by alienation = 'an act of a joint tenant operating on his own share'

- E.g. where the joint tenant sells, gives or mortgages their **equitable interest** to a third party
- To be effective it must be signed in writing (***s 53(1)(c) LPA***)
- Would remain a trustee (can't transfer their interest in the legal estate)

Bankruptcy of a co-owner results in an automatic severing of their equitable joint tenancy

- Their trustee in bankruptcy becomes the new tenant in common
- If they are then discharged from their bankruptcy, can again have an equitable interest (but remains as one in common)

Severance by mutual agreement:

For severance by mutual agreement, the co-owners must either (*Burgess v Rawnsley*):

a) Expressly agree to sever the joint tenancy in equity, or
b) The parties agree to deal with the land in a certain way (which would have the effect of severing)

→ Common intention will suffice (doesn't have to be a binding agreement)

Severance by a consistent course of dealings:

Any **course of dealing** by the joint tenants showing that **their interests should be treated as a tenancy in common** (rather than a joint tenancy)

- *Doesn't* have to amount to an express or implied agreement to sever
- Both parties must just act in such a way that it is clear that they both intend that their shares should from now on be held as tenants in common ***(Burgess v Rawnsley*)**

Severance by homicide:

Severance that occurs when one co-owner kills another

Where one of two joint tenants murders the other → severes the joint tenancy in equity
The victim's equitable interest in the land passes to the beneficiaries under their will
The murderer takes the legal estate in the land

Effects of Severance:

When equitable joint tenants sever the joint tenancy in equity → **the severing joint tenant takes a share in the property as a tenant in common**

- *Not* possible to sever a legal joint tenancy
- Where a tenant dies, their legal and equitable interests (if held as a joint tenant) pass to the remaining tenants automatically by survivorship (severance cannot be achieved through a will)
- Where a tenant dies and they are an equitable tenant in common, that can pass through the will
- You cannot 'add together' different equitable interests → each held in a diff manner

This should then be recorded on the title to the property:

- **Unregistered titles** → a memorandum of severance should be placed on the conveyance to the co-owners (to warn purchasers that the co-owners are now tenants in common in equity)

- **Registered titles** → a restriction should be placed on the register to indicate that the land is no longer held by the co-owners as joint tenants

Implied Co-Ownership

Resulting Trust:

The law **presumes that a resulting trust has arisen when:**

a) Two people buy land together, *both* contributing to the purchase price, **but**
b) The legal estate in the land is transferred into the sole name of one of them

In the *absence of evidence* that the contribution was means to be a gift or loan → **a resulting trust will arise in proportion to the size of the direct contribution to the purchase** of the property

The legal owner will hold the legal estate on a trust of land for them both, as tenants in common of the equitable interest (***Bull v Bull***)

How much to contribute:

Curley v Parkes [2004]:

☑ A contribution of all or part of the purchase money would suffice

✗ Payment of legal fees or other ancillary expenses would *not*

✗ Financial contributions to a joint account from which mortgage payments were made would *not* be sufficient

Constructive Trust:

There are **2 situations where a court would impose a constructive trust**:

Express (*but informal*) agreement
Implied by conduct

Express intention

→ If **both** are present, the **non-legal owners** will acquire an **equitable interest in the land under a constructive trust:**

Agreement to share equitable interest:
There **must be an agreement**, arrangement or understanding between the legal owners and the non-legal owners **to share the equitable interest** • All that is required is that a specific statement about ownership is made • Doesn't matter if the statement is deceitful, a trick or not fully intended (***Eves v Eves***) / (***Grant v Edwards***)

Non-legal owners acted to detriment / altered position:
The **non-legal owners,** relying on that agreement, arrangement or understanding**, acted to their detriment or altered their position** • The acts to the detriment must be strongly linked to, and dependent on, the common intention (***Grant v Edwards***)

Infer intention through conduct

Where there is **no evidence of an agreement** between the legal and non-legal owners to share the equitable interest, **but**:

Conduct infers common intention:
The court considers the **conduct of the parties** and can use the conduct **to infer a common intention** to share the equitable interest • Must establish that the non-legal owners have made direct contributions towards the purchase price (either initial purchase or mortgage instalments) (***Lloyds Bank v Rosset***)

Non-legal owners acted to detriment / altered position:
The non-legal owners must have **acted to their detriment or altered their position**

Effect:

Once the courts have established a constructive trust, they have discretion about the size of share they can award the non-legal owner.

Broad approach, taking into account (*Drake v Whipp*):

a) The parties' conduct
b) The direct and non-direct financial contributions (incl council tax / utilities etc)
c) Any non-financial contributions (such as housework)

www.ingramcontent.com/pod-product-compliance
Lightning Source LLC
Chambersburg PA
CBHW041747220926
51847CB00013B/130

* 9 7 8 9 6 9 4 9 9 2 8 9 1 *